For Ann Kerr-

Warmest wishes,

Bill Aberlt
12/6/300

Asia, America, and the Transformation of Geopolitics

American security and prosperity now depend on Asia. William H. Overholt offers an iconoclastic analysis of developments in each major Asian country, Asian international relations, and U.S. foreign policy. Drawing on decades of political and business experience, he argues that obsolete Cold War structures tie the U.S. increasingly to an otherwise isolated Japan and obscure the reality that a U.S.-Chinese bicondominium now manages most Asian issues. Military priorities risk polarizing the region unnecessarily, weaken the economic relationships that engendered American preeminence, and ironically enhance Chinese influence. As a result, despite its Cold War victory, U.S. influence in Asia is declining. Overholt disputes that democracy promotion will lead to superior development and peace, and forecasts a new era in which Asian geopolitics could take a drastically different shape. Covering Japan, China, Russia, Central Asia, India, Pakistan, Korea, and Southeast Asia, Overholt offers invaluable insights for scholars, policymakers, business people, and general readers.

William H. Overholt is Director of RAND's Center for Asia Pacific Policy and holds the Asia Policy Research Chair at the Center. Previously Dr. Overholt was Joint Senior Fellow at Harvard's Kennedy School and Asia Center. After eight years at a think tank consulting on national security issues, he ran investment bank research teams, mainly in Asia, from 1980 to 2001, and served as a consultant to several major political figures in Asia. He is the author of six books, including *The Rise of China* (1993), which won the Mainichi News/Asian Affairs Research Center Special Book Prize.

Asia, America, and the Transformation of Geopolitics

William H. Overholt

The RAND Corporation

CAMBRIDGE UNIVERSITY PRESS
Cambridge, New York, Melbourne, Madrid, Cape Town, Singapore, São Paolo, Delhi

Cambridge University Press
32 Avenue of the Americas, New York, NY 10013-2473, USA

www.cambridge.org
Information on this title: www.cambridge.org/9780521895873

First published 2008

Printed in the United States of America.

A catalog record for this publication is available from the British Library.

Library of Congress Cataloging-in-Publication Data

Overholt, William H.
Asia, America and the transformation of geopolitics / William H. Overholt.
    p.   cm.
Includes bibliographical references.
ISBN 978-0-521-89587-3 (hardback)
1. United States – Foreign relations – East Asia.   2. East Asia – Foreign relations – United States.
3. East Asia – Politics and government – 21st century.   4. Geopolitics – East Asia.   I. Title.
DS518.8.O84   2007
327.7305 – dc22   2007023917

ISBN 978-0-521-89587-3 hardback
ISBN 978-0-521-72023-6 paperback

To William Alvin Overholt (1917–1996)

In 1980, when I departed from scholarship and became a banker, my father, a Methodist minister and university dean, summoned me and urged me not to waste my life in search of money. This book, and some of the experiences noted here, reflects my committed, albeit inadequate, response to his principles.

About RAND

The study presented in this book was performed as part of the RAND Corporation's continuing program of self-sponsored independent research. Support for such research is provided, in part, by donors and by the independent research and development provisions of RAND's contracts for the operation of its U.S. Department of Defense federally funded research and development centers (FFRDCs).

This research was conducted within the Center for Asia Pacific Policy of the RAND National Security Research Division (NSRD). NSRD conducts research and analysis for the Office of the Secretary of Defense, the Joint Staff, the Unified Combatant Commands, the Department of the Navy, the Marine Corps, the defense agencies, the U.S. Intelligence Community, allied foreign governments, and foundations.

The RAND Corporation is a nonprofit research organization providing objective analysis and effective solutions that address the challenges facing the public and private sectors around the world. This study does not necessarily reflect the opinions of its research clients and sponsors.

Contents

Figures

Tables

Preface

This study examines how the structures and attitudes left over from the Cold War fit the current pattern of international relations in Asia and whether the post–Cold War adaptations of those structures and attitudes are serving the interests of the United States and the world. Then, to stimulate thought, it considers some alternatives that might evolve.

The structure of this volume reflects some crucial tradeoffs. Analysis of all the forces—political, economic, cultural, geopolitical, military—that affect Asia's strategic future could easily require the equivalent of a multivolume encyclopedia. The literature available for citation would fill a small library. Any attempt at such comprehensiveness would lose the main threads. Therefore I have chosen a relatively tight, provocative essay format. I have resisted the urge to elaborate many points at length and to put another three footnotes on every page.

Each section deliberately raises controversies that would require dissertations to resolve—and probably wouldn't be resolved even then. A key task for anyone trying to probe the range of future possibilities is to question reigning assumptions, to provoke and widen our imagination. If some proposition is already generally accepted, I have usually either ignored it or challenged it. There is something in the pages that follow that will upset virtually everyone—Chinese, Japanese, American, conservative, liberal, scholar, government official, private-sector executive. I hope to hear from anyone whose favorite preconceptions are not offended by what I have written so that I can attempt to correct the omission. It is my hope that disagreements will be mainly about interpretations rather than facts.

The intended audience is those who are sufficiently familiar with the conventional wisdom to be either interested in moving beyond it or sufficiently upset by the challenge of doing so to defend it in a way that moves our understanding forward.[1]

In contrast to academic research that relies almost exclusively on published literature, this book relies heavily on personal experience in addition to the published literature. I lived in the Philippines for one year, in Hong Kong for 16 years, and in Singapore for a short period. I have had political involvements of various kinds in the Philippines, Thailand, Burma, Korea, and Hong Kong. Since 1972, I have had the good fortune to know many key Asian leaders, starting with Singapore's Lee Kuan Yew, and much of the regional foreign-policy and economic-policy establishment. In the 1970s, Robert Scalapino and I gave more U.S. foreign-policy presentations for the U.S. Information Service to carefully selected Asian foreign-policy elites than any other Americans; these introductions provided the basis for friendships and conversations with Asian thinkers and decisionmakers that have persisted for decades. My responsibilities during the 1970s, at the Hudson Institute and as editor of a Columbia University publication, *Global Political Assessment*, which Zbigniew Brzezinski and I founded, included analyzing the implications of the Nixon Doctrine for future U.S. security policy in Asia, recommending future military deployments in Asia, consulting on Ferdinand Marcos's land reforms in the Philippines, analyzing China's trustworthiness for a potential Taiwan deal prior to Richard Nixon's trip to China, preparing a book on nuclear proliferation and nuclear strategies in Asia following the 1974 Indian nuclear test, and many other assignments.

---

[1] Excellent examples of the genre directed at such audiences include Morton Abramowitz and Stephen Bosworth, *Chasing the Sun: Rethinking East Asian Policy*, New York: Century Foundation Press, 2006; Thomas P. M. Barnett, *The Pentagon's New Map: War and Peace in the Twenty-First Century*, New York: G. P. Putnam's Sons, 2004; and David Shambaugh, *Power Shift: China and Asia's New Dynamics*, Berkeley, CA: University of California Press, 2005.

For three decades, I have benefited from a network of conferences with many sponsors but fairly predictable core attendance, where the principal thinkers about foreign policy in Asian countries come together.

In the 1980s and 1990s, I ran research teams for several investment banks, mostly from a base in Hong Kong. My research responsibilities required me to be in constant touch with policymakers and economic- and foreign-policy advisors in the principal Northeast and Southeast Asian countries, and I occasionally reversed roles and became an advisor myself. To take just one example, during the Asian crisis of 1997–1998, I was responsible for regional research for Bankers Trust, which was intensively involved in the crisis; for instance, it had the largest exposure of any bank to the Malaysian *ringgit*. Subsequently, I became head of economics and strategy for the Asian operations equity and fixed income of Nomura, Japan's largest investment bank, and advised some of the world's largest investors on how to handle the aftermath of the crisis. I followed developments in each country closely, sometimes writing far more detailed analyses than are available in the academic literature, sometimes supervising such research by others, always keeping in touch with people from the International Monetary Fund (IMF), the World Bank, and the appropriate finance ministries.

In short, I've spent three and a half decades working on Asian politics, Asian macroeconomic development, Asian financial issues, business strategies in Asia, and military issues in Asia.

This process was sufficiently intensive that I logged several million miles of air travel in the process of keeping in touch. That experience has provided the basis for some generalizations about views that are widely shared in Asia. Of course, personal experience is only useful to the extent that it is consistent with other kinds of evidence, but it can be crucial, because much of the real thinking behind policies never reaches print, and much of the passion is drained away by muted diplomatic language and spin doctors. Having spent much of my career in Asia, it constantly amazes me how different the assumptions in Japan or China about Washington are from the reality of American practice, and how different the assumptions in Washington about Asia so often are from the reality of what the Japanese or Chinese or Thais are thinking.

Personal experience is often very different from academic research, in several ways. First, facts. If one reads published documents, one comes away with negligible evidence of the powerful opinions on the Japanese right that a permanently divided Korea is a vital Japanese national-security interest; talking to people, one becomes aware of not only the intensity of the opinion on the right, but also the increasing breadth with which that opinion is held.

Second, judgment. Former British Hong Kong Governor Chris Patten was convinced that the way to ensure democratic reform of Hong Kong's legislature and other institutions was to confront China publicly and refuse to consult Chinese leaders. The result was that he created a nationalistic backlash and made early reform of the legislature politically impossible. The second most important institution for Hong Kong's freedoms was the Court of Final Appeal. In April 1995, I was spokesman for a deputation of Hong Kong executives (most of them Hong Kong Chinese) trying to get Chinese Premier Li Peng to reverse a critical decision about Hong Kong's future Court of Final Appeal; we had a very difficult and in some ways unpleasant conversation, but we succeeded because we understood how to deal with China's leadership. (You can't be the least bit soft, but you can't expect to make progress by publicly humiliating them, as Patten did.) At Nomura, where my senior Japanese colleagues were among the most impressive people I've ever met, three-quarters of my pay depended on their subjective interpretation of whether I'd understood and met their expectations. In the Philippine revolution and in Burma, many lives depended on my reading people and situations according to the way local people saw them. As a member of Corazon Aquino's executive committee in the Philippine revolution of 1985–1986, I continually warned against starting her stump speech with a blanket denunciation of the military; I dug out historical examples of Mao Zedong denouncing a few bad apples or a small minority of bad officers. She responded, through American political advisors who agreed with her, that she wasn't going to be a Jimmy Carter and change her views under pressure. When, a few weeks before the election, three of the kinds of threats I had warned about actually arose, her brothers summoned me to Manila and asked me to take responsibility for keeping her alive. Based on connections and experience, I assembled a team that included a retired British Special Air Service (SAS) officer who had done a superb job setting up Saddam Hussein's personal security, the retired head of the Australian Secret Intelligence Organization, and others. Needing to rally opposition in the army, I reviewed the country's top retired generals and made the call, over the opposition of many other advisors but ultimately on behalf of SCRAM,[2] to General Rafael Ileto, who had been exiled as Ambassador to Thailand and had had several heart attacks. Aquino survived. The retired general who authorized me to use his name in making the call to Ileto became Aquino's chief of intelligence. A firm I was associated with then took responsibility for her security for the first six months of her presidency.

It was experience in South Korea, Taiwan, and the Philippines as much as analysis that led me to argue that Deng Xiaoping's strategy would succeed and Mikhail Gorbachev's would fail[3] and to make those arguments during the years when the conventional wisdom held exactly the opposite. Today, academics and young military officers may debate whether China sees itself as on the same side as the United States on the issue of stopping North Korean nuclear proliferation, but I have been discussing that issue with Chinese generals and officials for more than three decades, and their contempt for North Korean management and their fear that North Korea would create damaging instability have been constant and deeply felt themes throughout that time. When Kim Il Sung died, some Chinese officials celebrated and took

---

[2] SCRAM was the Senior Cavaliers' Reform Army Movement, a group of retired generals who received less publicity than the Reform Army Movement (RAM), which comprised mostly active colonels and majors. The principal alternative to Ileto was General Manuel Yan, a superb officer, healthier than Ileto, a good ambassador to Indonesia, and an in-law of mine whom I greatly admired but who had defended Marcos too many times over the family dinner table to be an appropriate choice. The epitome of professionalism, he went on to serve presidents Aquino, Fidel Ramos, and Joseph Estrada well.

[3] I have made these arguments in many places over many years, including many times in a publication I edited, *Global Political Assessment*, published semi-annually by Columbia University's Research Institute on International Change from 1976–1988; they are summarized in William H. Overholt, *The Rise of China*, New York: W. W. Norton, 1993.

credit for a great victory; Kim Il Sung had just walked out of a confrontation with Chinese negotiators over his nuclear ambitions when he had a heart attack and fell dead. Those sentiments have resulted in China's taking far stronger measures than the United States has to try to bring Pyongyang into line; Washington and Beijing have important differences over tactics, but nobody who knows China's leaders can doubt that they and the United States are on the same side on the nuclear issue. Unfortunately, in some political and media circles, ideology and lack of experience overwhelm what every U.S. negotiator knows to be the facts about China's interests.

These concrete situations create very severe empirical tests; if one is wrong, millions of dollars may be lost, lives may be lost, or one's reputation as an analyst may be damaged in such a high-profile way as to be irreparable.

This book describes the situation the United States faced in the early Cold War, the strategies that were employed to achieve U.S. goals, and the institutions the United States created to win the Cold War. It then traces how the situation has changed, how key institutions have perpetuated themselves in an environment for which they were not designed, how the roles of those institutions have evolved in ways that in some cases would have surprised their creators, and how the strategies the United States is pursuing have changed in ways that often are not entirely conscious. Throughout, I have attempted to weave back into our understanding of geopolitics the central role of economic strategies and economic change. Economic development and economic rejuvenation constituted the core of the successful U.S. global strategy in the Cold War, but that central fact too often gets lost in the narratives of political historians and neglected, to a degree that has fundamentally changed America's role in the world, in much of the work of contemporary strategists.

Chapter One describes how strategic doctrines and institutions tend to perpetuate themselves long after they have become obsolete. Chapter Two analyzes the way Cold War strategies and institutions related to a changing Asian environment. Chapters Three through

Eight elaborate changing regional and country trends. Chapter Nine provides some brief scenarios to stretch our imaginations about what the future might bring. Chapter Ten presents the conclusions drawn from the study.

Acknowledgments

This book is part of a RAND effort to understand the ways new international economic, political, and military trends might affect future strategic relationships in Asia. The study began with a conference at RAND headquarters in Santa Monica, where RAND's Asia specialists communicated their views of their countries to each other. Participants included Evan Medeiros (China), Rachel Swanger (Japan), Olga Oliker (Central Asia), Rollie Lal (India), Norman Levin and Somi Seong (Korea), Angel Rabasa (Southeast Asia), Ashley Tellis of the Carnegie Endowment (methodology), and Nina Hachigian (United States). In addition, Nina Hachigian and Rollie Lal wrote papers on the history of U.S. Asia policy and on strategic trends in South Asia, respectively. None of these specialists is responsible for the views I have expressed here, which in all cases go off in different directions, but I have learned a great deal from them, not just from this one set of briefings but from many other interactions as well. I have also benefited from work by other RAND colleagues, including Roger Cliff, Keith Crane, James Dobbins, Mike Lostumbo, David Shlapak, Charles Wolf, Ted Karasik, and Chris Fair. Comments from colleagues, including James Dobbins, Dalia Dassa Kaye, Susan Everingham, and Greg Treverton, have been very helpful. I am particularly indebted to Rachel Swanger, Eric Heginbotham, and Ezra Vogel, whose detailed comments and thoughtful critiques have led me to reconsider and reformulate many points—not always to their satisfaction, but always to the reader's benefit.

As noted elsewhere, I have benefited from years of attendance at many seminars sponsored by many institutions. Among all of these, I want to single out Harvard's Asia Center series of annual Asia Vision 21 seminars. The Asia Vision 21 strictures against quotation both facilitate uninhibited exchange and limit my ability to account fully for my intellectual debts.

The Korea Foundation provided a generous grant that supported work by Norman Levin and Somi Seong on the Korea-China relationship and thereby contributed substantially to our ability to explore one of the most important aspects of Asia's evolving architecture.

Above all, I am indebted to the support of the RAND Corporation and its top management. It is always difficult to speak truth to power, and it is exquisitely difficult to do so when one's budget depends heavily on power, as RAND's does. The integrity of RAND in seeking the truth, and in articulating it to power, and the willingness of the U.S. government to support RAND's sometimes disquieting efforts decade after decade are, so far as my admittedly limited knowledge can discover, unique in history. This book would have been difficult to write outside that unique environment.

None of these people or institutions is responsible, of course, for my habit of looking at things through a prism that is different from most.

Overview

America's relations with Asia continue to rely on institutions that are a legacy of the Cold War. Since the Cold War was resolved long ago, it is important to inquire whether the same institutions continue to be appropriate. Is the post–Cold War situation equally amenable to the same institutions? Have those institutions evolved in ways that fit the new situation? Or have some sought to survive the advent of the new situation by evolving in ways that hamper attainment of U.S. interests?

Historical experience shows that when a foreign-policy era ends, the institutions, mindset, and interest groups that characterized the old era tend to persist into the new era, with inertia that often endures far longer than the institutions' utility. This happened, for instance, with George Washington's doctrine of No Entangling Alliances, which attempted to keep the new American nation free of dangerous involvements in foreign conflicts. The mentality of that 18th-century wisdom persisted through the middle of the 20th century, greatly hampering the country's ability to confront in a timely fashion the challenges of fascism and communism that were emerging in Europe and Asia.

Given this historical pattern, it is appropriate to question whether the great institutions of the Truman Doctrine and the Cold War are likely to remain appropriate for coming decades. The great Cold War institutions proved remarkably adaptive and resilient to different conditions during the Cold War era—the period of Sino-Soviet alliance, the period of Sino-Soviet antagonism, the periods of peace, and the times of the Korean and Vietnam wars. From time to time, however, aspects of those institutions outran their utility—as occurred, for instance, when policies that had proved successful in Western Europe, Japan, South Korea, and many other places produced traumatic failure in Vietnam. That outcome is characteristic: Old doctrines that have become fully or partially obsolete generally continue rolling forward like bowling balls until they smash into a new reality, usually at great cost in lives and treasure. It is to be hoped that by examining changed conditions and comparing new conditions with the assumptions embedded in current doctrine and policies, we can reduce the costs of future collisions between doctrine and reality.

Any analysis of U.S. relations with Asia must be undertaken with historical consciousness of the caricatures that arise and suddenly collapse. For the first half of the 20th century, Americans perceived China as an angel and Japan as a devil. For the second half, these images were reversed in American consciousness. Anyone who had suggested prior to 1945 that we would end up allied with Japan against China would have suffered ridicule. Anyone who today suggests that old images contain obsolescing, dangerous caricatures likewise risks offending powerful convictions and interests. But this volume takes that risk. When I was writing the speeches and papers that led to the book *The Rise of China*, the conventional wisdom was that Deng Xiaoping's China would collapse and that Mikhail Gorbachev's reforms would bring the Soviet Union into the modern world. President George H. W. Bush was even advised that China was on the verge of collapse. Fortunately, that misreading of reality, based on such ideological assumptions as the need for successful political reform to precede and undergird economic reform, only led to minor humiliations for the U.S. president. It could easily have led to calamitous miscalculations. At the time, my view that Deng Xiaoping's strategy was a recipe for success and that Gorbachev's political priorities constituted a recipe for Soviet collapse was so unpopular that some reviewers charged that these opinions could be held only by someone who had been bought by his employer to write such nonsense.

The U.S. and Western victory in the Cold War emerged from a strategy of nation-building and reconstruction. The strategy sought to build bulwarks of freedom by creating strong polities and economies in

Western Europe, Japan, Southeast Asia, and elsewhere. To accomplish this, American leaders created the Marshall Plan for Europe; encouraged the economic revitalization of Japan; funded aid and institution-building programs through the Agency for International Development (AID), the peace corps, education programs, and many other efforts; and, with their European allies, created major global institutions—the World Bank, the IMF, the General Agreement on Tariffs and Trade (GATT) (later the World Trade Organization, WTO), the Asian Development Bank, and other development banks—to stabilize the free world. The military protected the allies and others while this nation-building strategy gradually proceeded.

Without the military, the strategy would never have had time to succeed. Without the nation-building strategy, military defense was unsustainable. One need only look at Korea, where from 1954 to at least 1975, the North appeared stable and powerful, the South weak, impoverished, and politically unstable. Or one could look at Indonesia in the early 1960s, then a politically and economically hapless home to the world's largest Muslim fundamentalist movement (indeed, probably larger than all the other Muslim fundamentalist movements combined) and the world's third largest Communist Party, to understand the bleak prospect for U.S. policy in the absence of the Asian economic miracle that followed. Today's travails in Iraq would be minor compared with what would have happened if Indonesia's 15,000 islands, with between 100 and 200 million people speaking more than 600 languages, had disintegrated instead of experiencing an economic miracle.

The Asian economic miracle, supported both by U.S. aid and institution-building programs and by the vast regional expenditures that accompanied the Korean and Vietnam wars, contributed to U.S. victory in the Cold War in two ways. First, the economic takeoff gave citizens of Asian countries a stake in the stability and success of their countries, while giving governments the resources to build national administration, national infrastructure, and effective national military and police forces. From Japan to Indonesia, this drained the motivation for ideological extremism while endowing governments with the administrative, police, and military capacity to suppress the residues of that extremism.

Second, the Asian economic miracle changed the international priorities of most Western-oriented Asian governments. For centuries, the only path to wealth and power had been territorial aggrandizement; wealth and power were obtained by grabbing neighbors' territory, seizing their golden temples, and taxing their peasants. This was the world that gave rise to John Mearsheimer's now-obsolete observation that the emergence of a new power was invariably accompanied by violent upheaval. In the new world of the Asian miracle, a focus on domestic economic reform could lead to wealth and power at a speed unimaginable in the old era. Britain incorporated half the world into its empire on the basis of 2 percent annual economic growth. Now, Pacific Asian countries are routinely growing at 6 to 10 percent annual rates. Meanwhile, modern military technology made the use of military violence for territorial aggrandizement self-destructive. Countries that followed the old strategy, such as the Soviet Union and North Korea, collapsed, while those that followed the new strategy, such as South Korea and Singapore, came to tower over their neighbors. China, and eventually Vietnam, avoided the Soviet outcome by changing sides and joining the U.S.-led Asian economic miracle. Japan became recognized as a great power in the 1980s while still militarily neutered. China became recognized as a great power in the wake of Deng Xiaoping's strategy that began by cutting military expenditures from 16 percent of gross domestic product (GDP) to less than 3 percent and long before the country had any significant capability to project military power overseas.

The process that resolved the Cold War transformed the conditions under which Cold War–era institutions had been founded. In 1954, Japan seemed doomed to languishing as an economic backwater with unstable politics and the persistent risk of communist revolution. By 1989, it seemed on the verge of leading an Asian century in which it would overshadow the United States. Then the resurgence of a more entrepreneurial U.S. economy coincided with a dozen years of Japanese economic stagnation and with Chinese implementation of the most far-reaching economic reforms of the modern world. Thus emerged an

Asia substantially governed by Sino-American decisions, notwithstanding the strengthening of the U.S.-Japan military alliance. During this period, the United States towered over all other countries in economic size, military power, and cultural influence, but, paradoxically, from the Asian crisis of 1997–1998 onward, U.S. influence in Asia steadily declined, with China the principal beneficiary of that decline.

The Cold War phase of the Asian economic miracle had been dominated by mobilization systems loosely adapted from the Japanese system, with heavy state guidance of the economy, reliance on state-guided bank loans to implement that guidance, considerable nationalism toward foreign investment, and emphasis on giant state-supported industrial firms at the expense of smaller entrepreneurial and service firms. From the time of the Japan-Taiwan financial crisis of 1990 and the Asian crisis of 1997–1998, the Japan–South Korea–Thailand mobilization model, which was perfectly adapted to postwar reconstruction and to initial economic takeoffs but ill-adapted to the post-reconstruction era, suffered, and the more entrepreneurial, foreign-investment-friendly model of Taiwan, Hong Kong, Singapore, the overseas Chinese communities of Southeast Asia, and, increasingly, China itself became more successful. This heavily shifted not only the economic balance but also the political balance of the region from Japan and its followers to the entrepreneurial overseas Chinese who increasingly influenced Chinese policies. As in the past, a sharp economic shift led immediately to a sharp political shift.

After the Cold War, Japan, China, Taiwan, and the two Koreas rapidly evolved increasingly assertive forms of nationalism. Japan and China, and Japan and the two Koreas, adopted increasingly antagonistic postures toward one another. In Taiwan, Lee Teng-hui systematically cultivated Taiwan nationalism and antagonism toward China; his successor, Chen Shui-bian, built on that foundation an unsuccessful attempt to move sharply in the direction of formal independence. As this book was being written, there were signs of possible self-correction in both the Taiwan-China and the Japan-China surges of nationalism, but it remained unclear whether the upsurge of national assertion or the corrections would dominate the future.

The late–Cold War regional trend toward emphasis on stability in the interest of economic development, and the corresponding deemphasis on territorial aggrandizement over land borders, consolidated and began to spread beyond East Asia. China, prior to 1979 an ideological subverter of most of its neighbors, became a leading promoter of regional stability and by 2006 had resolved all but two of its 14 border conflicts to the satisfaction of the other parties. Vietnam, once the region's most aggressive power, followed this change of behavior. Indian and Pakistani leaders started recognizing in their rhetoric the imperative of economic priorities and peace with neighbors; after going to the edge of nuclear conflict, the two principal South Asian powers engaged in mutual visits, opened some transport links, and negotiated over an oil pipeline from Iran through Pakistan to India. India also became warmer toward China. It seemed possible that South Asia would begin to follow East Asia's lead toward an emphasis on peaceful economic development, but how fully this trend will develop in South Asia remains to be seen. Some Indian policymakers argue that the narrow electoral margins on which continued power depends in a democracy preclude for India the kinds of territorial compromises that have stabilized China's land borders.

In Pacific Asia, widespread resolution of disputes over land borders was partially offset by the increasing salience of conflicts over sea borders and a competitive search for energy security through national control of sources of oil and gas. Such conflicts became increasingly severe in Northeast Asia, with Japan twice on the edge of confrontation with South Korea over Tokdo/Takeshima Island in 2006 and also in an increasingly tense competition with China. China began drilling in undisputed seabed, but into a potential pool of oil and gas that might overlap into territory disputed between Japan and China, and Japan responded with warnings and with plans to drill in a disputed seabed. In Southeast Asia, however, the risks of confrontation dissipated as China, after initially making moves seen as aggressive (such as building shelters on Mischief Reef, which is claimed by the Philippines), led the region into a widely accepted Code of Conduct for mutual development.

The rising expressions of nationalism and the rising salience of seabed and territorial-waters disputes notwithstanding, in the year 2000 there seemed little reason for the region not to continue on its path toward rapidly improving prosperity and declining international conflict. Disputes about water are no less solvable than disputes about land, and the weight of history is light; the problem is that the world hasn't cared enough until now to evolve clear principles and procedures and precedents for resolution.

When nationalism seemed in danger of becoming disruptive, partial corrective measures were taken. Beijing learned that its missile-throwing excesses toward Taiwan in 1996 created a global image of a militaristic, dangerous China and resolved not to repeat them. A few years later, in 2006, both Beijing and Taiwan acted to cool what had occasionally flared into risk of real conflict, and new Japanese Prime Minister Shinzo Abe's conciliatory visit to Beijing was disproportionately reciprocated by a China anxious to reduce tensions. The central tendency seemed to be the gradual consolidation of peace and prosperity in East Asia and indications of its possible spread to South Asia.

Thus, if one projected forward from the year 2000, the likely scenario seemed fairly clear. The United States had the world's preeminent economy, the world's overwhelmingly preeminent military, the world's preeminent ideology (free-market democracy), and the world's preeminent cultural influence. Its principal opponent, the Soviet Union, had collapsed. Its other Asian opponents of note, China and Vietnam, had responded positively to the incentives to join the U.S.-nurtured global economic system and likewise had responded to the disincentives against persisting with border disputes, ideological proselytization, and subversion of their neighbors. Japan, a strong ally that nonetheless saw itself as competing with the United States for geopolitical preeminence in Asia, had suffered a decade of troubles, leaving it a loyal ally but no longer a serious competitor. Clearly, it seemed, Asia was headed for an era of U.S. dominance, reduced polarization, and consolidation of a 50-year trend toward peaceful economic cooperation at the expense of old geopolitical conflicts.

But that is not what happened.

What did happen was a series of strategic changes that are shaping post-post–Cold War Asia. (Post–Cold War Asia is a relatively straight-forward continuation of the Cold War structure with the Soviet Union absent, a structure that has persisted for a decade and a half. The more interesting phase, post-post–Cold War Asia, is what comes next.)

First, China's emergence triggered a reaction in the United States and Japan. China joined all the major economic institutions nurtured by the West in the Cold War, opened its economy far more than Japan did, resolved most of its border disputes to the satisfaction of its neigh-bors, and engaged in a very successful campaign for good diplomatic relations with most of its neighbors. All these seemed to support U.S. and Japanese interests, particularly in comparison with an earlier era when China was systematically attempting to destabilize its neighbors and spread communism globally. But its success challenged Japanese aspirations for regional leadership. In the United States, it evoked vari-ous theories that rising powers are inherently destabilizing and that undemocratic regimes are inherently aggressive and, more broadly, that since China is the only power that could conceivably challenge the United States, American military planning should focus on China. Given a thrust toward Taiwanese independence by Presidents Lee Teng-hui and Chen Shui-bian and China's threatening reaction to their initiatives, along with U.S. policy of ensuring a peaceful reso-lution, tensions over Taiwan became a particular focus for the U.S. military, and the increasing difficulty of that assignment necessarily induced an obsession at the U.S. Department of Defense with the risk of Sino-American war. That obsession was greatly magnified by various interest groups that had much to gain from building new weaponry for war with China or from hampering trade with China.

While China rose, Japan slipped. Through 1989, Japan's leaders were anticipating that the 21st century would be the Asian century and that Japan would dominate Asia. Japan's economic superiority would achieve at the end of the second half of the 20th century what its military power had failed to achieve in the first half. It would eclipse American power, which Japanese strategists portrayed as in inevitable decline due to U.S. incompetence at economic management. But a dozen years of stagnation and financial crisis, together with U.S. eco-

nomic resurgence and China's superior economic growth and openness, ended that dream. Japanese leaders responded by abandoning the
vision of regional leadership through economic diplomacy. Instead of
articulating a new, forward-looking vision, ascendant leaders sought to
build renewed national pride around a rewriting of the history of the
1930s and 1940s and adopted a resentful, threatened, defensive posture toward China's new eminence. Pressed hard by the United States,
increasingly nationalistic Japanese leaders greatly broadened the scope
and influence of their military while still confining military expenditures within 1 percent of gross national product (GNP), integrated
their military more closely with the United States, formally designated
China as a potential enemy for the first time, created military liaison
with Taiwan, agreed with the United States to bring Taiwan under the
umbrella of the U.S.-Japan alliance, and expressed a desire to amend
Japan's Peace Constitution.

Major changes occurred in U.S. relations with the region. American policy, which for a half-century had protected China from Japan
by keeping Japan disarmed and protected Japan from China by allying with Japan, tilted toward an emphasis on consolidating the military alliance with Japan, pressing for a revival of Japan's military, and
overtly targeting China as the object of the alliance, even formally
bringing the Taiwan conflict under the purview of the alliance. This
led China, which had long tacitly supported U.S. bases and alliances
in the region because they facilitated the peace and stability necessary
to China's economic revival, to change its view of American bases and
alliances, increasingly perceiving them as hostile.

In this way, post–Cold War developments polarized big-power
relations in Asia rather than, as would have otherwise been expected,
reducing polarization.

These changes were driven in part by several major changes in
U.S. priorities. The role of the military and the emphasis on spreading
democracy (and allying with democracies) rose, and emphasis on economic development and building regional institutions declined.

The Association of Southeast Asian Nations (ASEAN), disillusioned with the U.S. response to the Asian crisis by the Clinton administration and with the abandonment of economic priorities under George

W. Bush, and South Korea, in revolt against U.S. policies toward North Korea and against increasing U.S. reliance on Japan, both distanced themselves from U.S. policy. They still emphatically wanted a U.S. military presence to balance North Korea, China, and Japan, but their relationship with the United States became more distant than it had been, and their relationship with China became much warmer than before. The war in Iraq increasingly drained U.S. resources, attention, and prestige. Controversies over Guantanamo Bay, Abu Ghraib, and the definition of torture diluted American moral authority. Deprived of previously strong U.S. support, regional institutions that included the United States, such as the Asia-Pacific Economic Cooperation (APEC), went into decline, creating a vacuum that was increasingly filled by institutions and initiatives such as the Shanghai Cooperation Organization (SCO), the East Asia Summit, ASEAN+3 (10 ASEAN countries plus China, Japan, and South Korea), ASEAN+3+3 (adding India, Australia, and New Zealand), the Chiangmai Initiative, and others that excluded the United States. Japan and China sought competitively to build regional institutions that they could lead, while collaborating to build regional institutions that excluded the United States, like the East Asia Summit. For most Asian countries, including strong traditional allies like South Korea and Singapore, the degree of U.S. hostility toward China seemed gratuitous. The U.S. view that democracies were invariably more peaceful and better at development was inconsistent with the Asian experience, and the smaller countries of Asia mostly saw the differences between China's post-socialist, post-Leninist regime and themselves as developmental, whereas the United States saw a Manichean divide. Given China's rising influence relative to Japan and the unpopular U.S. shift toward emphasis on military power and democratization at the expense of its earlier focus on economic development and regional institution-building, these trends severely weakened U.S. influence in Pacific Asia.

The U.S. role is also shaped by a widening divergence between its increasingly exclusive military reliance on the U.S.-Japan alliance and its increasing political and economic reliance on its relationship with China. As noted, the United States has moved from a relatively balanced policy that protected both Japan and China from each other to one that emphasizes building up Japan's military and combining with it to target China. On the other hand, the United States copes with the war on terror, North Korea, regional crime and drugs and human trafficking, and Southeast Asian stability primarily through a bicondominium with China. The principal economic issues are being treated likewise: Regional free trade and regional freedom-of-investment drives are led by the United States and China, with Japan and India reluctantly coming along part of the way. Genetically modified food, an increasingly important issue, effectively involves a U.S.-Chinese alliance against Japan, India, and Europe. Among major regional issues, only on Taiwan and Afghanistan are U.S.-Japan ties more important and more cooperative than U.S.-China ties. The tension between military-ideological alignments and political-economic interests is increasingly severe and probably presages profound geopolitical change in the near future.

Closely related, there is increasing tension between vastly improved U.S.-Chinese cooperation on regional political-economic issues, including Taiwan, where Presidents Bush and Hu Jintao have shared a closer understanding than any of their previous counterparts, and the dynamics of the arms race in the Taiwan Strait. Both sides' military commanders have difficult tasks, the Chinese generals to ensure that Taiwan can never break away to full independence, the Americans to ensure that aggression is impossible. As they focus on every conceivable possibility, they easily come to fear and believe their worst-case scenarios. As Chinese forces become more capable, U.S. forces have no alternative to integrating themselves more closely with the Taiwan military. Within a few years, a choice may have to be made between abandoning the mission and accepting a degree of integration with Taiwan's military that would effectively reinstate the pre-1979 U.S.-Taiwan alliance. That would provoke a political crisis with China. This military logic has a dynamic all its own, quite independent of the determination of Washington, Beijing, and the center of gravity of Taiwan's politics not to risk a crisis. If this dynamic becomes dominant, Asia's politics take a quite different form from the one they take if policymakers are focused on economic competition and cooperative resolution of problems like energy security, terrorism, North Korea, and regional crime.

A number of other trends will affect Asia's future. The collapse of the Soviet Union has opened up Central Asia to a new version of the Great Game competition among big powers for influence over vast, impoverished, thinly populated, politically volatile areas affected by ethnic strife, Islamic fundamentalism, and vast crime and drug trafficking, as well as by a greatly escalated regional concern over energy security. In many ways, the Central Asian situation today resembles that of Southeast Asia in the 1950s, but the shift of U.S. policy away from its traditional focus on economic development and institution-building to an overwhelming priority for military power and democracy virtually precludes the kind of success that the United States achieved in Southeast Asia.

The rise of India, and the acquisition by India for the first time of resources that can underwrite some of its big-power ambitions, will subordinate much of the subcontinent to India's will to a new degree. While Pakistan is improving its economic management and performance, it is falling further and further behind India in economic weight, political stability, and international support from big powers. The big powers need Pakistan's cooperation over Afghanistan but are increasingly concerned about its involvements with nuclear proliferation, Islamic extremism, and the Taliban. The judgment of this study is that India will likely achieve major economic successes and as a result will enhance its global geopolitical standing but will remain politically impaired in its ability to implement rapid economic reform. Therefore, unless China stumbles, India is likely for the foreseeable future to fall further and further behind China as an economic power and a global political influence.

Since the geopolitics of Asia's last half-century has been driven by the Asian economic miracle—the success of Japan, South Korea, Southeast Asia, and China; the failure of the Soviet Union, North Korea, Burma, and others to keep up; and the belated but immensely consequential participation of India—any risk to the process of globalization on which the Asian miracle depends has potentially momentous consequences. By 2005, globalization was encountering severe headwinds, as indicated by the (possibly temporary) failure of the Doha trade round, the French and Dutch rejection of the European

Constitution, the declining priority for international liberalization in the U.S. administration and Congress, a mood of reform fatigue in China, and the apparent lapse of Japanese enthusiasm for economic reform after Junichiro Koizumi's departure. Any sharp setback in the process of globalization would undermine domestic political stability in Indonesia, Thailand, China, and India; reverse the progress of international amity that has resulted from the ability to grow rapidly and gain prestige by giving priority to domestic economic reform rather than geopolitical ambitions; and greatly weaken the standing of the United States, whose position in the region has been built on being the father of multilateral development.

These transformative trends are so powerful and complex that one cannot forecast a single clear future for Asian geopolitics and the U.S. relationship with Asia. Instead, to illuminate the range of possible outcomes, I offer a spectrum of scenarios:

1. Business as usual, with Cold War institutions remaining in place and an uneasy balance between economic mutual progress and geopolitical competition. I judge this scenario to be unstable.
2. Renewed Cold War, with U.S.-China military and ideological tensions dominating leaders' attention and consolidating a U.S.-Japan-Indian alliance against China. An arms race over Taiwan is the foundation of this scenario.
3. Reversal of alliances, driven by the increasing divergence between American military reliance on Japan and political-economic reliance on China. In this scenario, gradually increasing Chinese domestic liberalization and international political-economic cooperation with the United States lead to a successful effort to resolve the North Korea and Taiwan problems, and this pushes a (hypothetically) increasingly right-wing, nationalistic Japanese government into a rupture of the alliance.
4. Partial withdrawal of the United States. A strong U.S. public reaction against a hypothetically negative outcome of the Iraq and Afghanistan wars, together with a reaction against ASEAN and South Korean ambivalence toward the United States and

concern about being too entangled in Japanese-Chinese tensions, could conceivably lead the United States to pull back from its strong forward position in East Asia. This would risk an increasingly dangerous cycle of Japanese-Chinese competition and could endanger peace in the region.

5. Collapse of globalization. The French and Dutch votes in 2005 against the European Constitution, the failure of the Doha trade round, the increasing dominance of a protectionist U.S. Congress, and the stagnation of reform initiatives in China, Japan, and India lead to a vicious circle of trade and investment protectionism. Global stock markets collapse and global economic growth weakens dramatically. As in the 1930s, the countries that had opened the most get hurt the worst. The virtuous circles of increasing prosperity and peace reverse.

6. An era of peaceful, competitive economic dynamism. This scenario is in many ways the logical extrapolation of the Cold War experience, when countries gradually learned that the way to respect and prosperity lies through domestic economic reform rather than through territorial aggrandizement and military threats. This presumes the success of moderate governments in Japan and China; the reestablishment of old U.S. balances between China and Japan and between military and economic priorities; continued strong U.S. engagement in the region; U.S.-Chinese cooperation to resolve the Korean and Taiwan problems peacefully; continued strong U.S. and Chinese diplomacy to push the region toward multilateral economic liberalization; and Japanese engagement in a vision of the future that does not involve reversion to World War II–era attitudes toward neighbors.

It would be convenient to make a clear forecast of one of these or to assign probabilities to each scenario. But reality is far more complex. Asia's future is not a future that will be determined by the ricocheting of Newtonian bowling balls. It will depend on the perceptions and decisions of leaders, most of whom have not yet come to power. The purpose of an analysis like the one presented here is to help the advisors of those leaders question the preconceptions they hold and reflect on where the decisions they make may lead their countries. Some U.S. politicians have repeatedly started down roads that lead to a global economic crisis—for instance, the 1980s economic phobia about Japan or the 1993 drive to take away China's trade status. Some national-security leaders have equally eagerly charged down the road toward a new Cold War, based largely on theoretical arguments that new powers inevitably cause violent disruption or that non-democracies are inevitably less peaceful than democracies. China had an attack of war fever in 2002–2003 on the basis of a fanciful image that Chen Shui-bian was an evil genius and that the United States might be supporting him. Japan under Koizumi alienated nearly all of its neighbors by espousing a belief that somehow it could improve Japanese self-esteem by rewriting history without provoking the objects of that history.

None of these images or arguments had any substantial roots in contemporary reality. Fortunately for the peace and prosperity of our world, despite numerous dangerous false starts, Republicans and Democrats, Chinese leaders and Japanese leaders, Indian leaders and Chinese leaders have so far consistently reflected on the consequences of their passions and corrected their courses. But the frequency with which exaggerated fears, obsolete theories, and ideological images bring the major countries of the Pacific to the brink of gratuitous conflict and impoverishment is truly frightening.

For the United States, the great institutions of the Cold War, pre-eminent among them the U.S.-Japanese alliance and the synergistic marriage of military defense with stimulation of an economic miracle, have served the country brilliantly. But the post–Cold War divorce of the U.S.-Japan alliance from the parallel reassurance of China, the divorce of military considerations from the economic priorities that led to strategic success, and the ideological triumph of the idea that democracy is, in all situations, invariably the best path to stability, peace, prosperity, and human dignity can threaten much of the success achieved during the Cold War. The pain the nation is enduring in Iraq reflects in part the divorce of military strategy from economic strategy and the illusion that democracy can conquer all other problems. So far, these same issues have deprived the United States of its unipolar position in Asia, but an underlying policy wisdom regarding Asia has averted major conflicts and maintained the foundations of mutual prosperity.

Likewise, Chinese leaders have undercut their nation's standing by excesses of repression, but their courageous domestic economic reforms and international restraint have greatly enhanced their global influence and greatly improved the dignity of their people. The Chinese people are noticeably taller, healthier, better clothed, better housed, better educated, and, despite the continuing repression of dissent, freer than they were a generation ago. Japanese leaders have antagonized their neighbors but gradually and democratically implemented the reforms necessary to preserve the prosperity and a diminished but decent proportion of the international stature that a generation of earlier leaders had heroically achieved. Indian leaders seem to be overcoming a legacy that for two generations diminished their nation's stature, impoverished its people, and left huge populations in a condition worse than that of people in sub-Saharan Africa; if they can now achieve rapid growth with democracy and freedom, they will add a new inspiration to human development.

All the major countries are achieving a good deal less than they could but a great deal more than seemed even imaginable a generation ago. All face the risk that provincial politicians will take for granted the achievements of the previous half-century and will plunge us back into the conflicts and poverty of an earlier era.

MR. WILLIAM H. OVERHOLT

Managing Director
Bankers Trust Company
Author
China: The Next Economic Superpower

Photo of author from Lord Litchfield's collection of portraits of leaders of the Hong Kong business community, "The Men Behind…"

The author with Senator Ninoy Aquino, exiled leader of the Philippine opposition to Ferdinand Marcos. Aquino spent three hours explaining why, when he returned to Manila, Marcos could not afford to shoot him. Shortly thereafter, he returned and was immediately assassinated. When his wife, Corazon Aquino, subsequently ran against Marcos, the author was given responsibility for protecting her against multiple threats of assassination and incarceration.

Overholt meeting Chinese Premier Li Peng in April 1995. Members of the Business & Professionals Association of Hong Kong, largely Hong Kong Chinese business tycoons, visited Li to lobby for a reversal of his decision that, since British Governor Patten had unilaterally changed the Hong Kong legislature, he would defer announcing the structure of the Court of Final Appeal, the pinnacle of the post-British legal system. Overholt served as spokesman for the group and, following a very tense discussion, Li acceded to the request.

Overholt presenting his earlier book, *The Rise of China*, to Chinese Premier Zhu Rongji. Zhu, a good politician, said, "Oh, I already have this book. I keep it on the shelf beside my desk. But I'll keep this one too; since it has your signature, it's more valuable."

Overholt with the leaders of the Provisional Revolutionary Government, formed in December 1989 by pro-democracy tribal groups in Manerplaw, in the jungles of Burma. Overholt served as an advisor to the leaders.

The author giving a lecture to leaders of the All Burmese Students' Democratic Front at their jungle headquarters on how a small force can disrupt and divide a large army. Beside the author is Adele Anderson, who for decades has been helping minority Thai and Burmese tribal peoples.

Introduction: The Inertia of Foreign Policies

The new in history always comes when people least believe it.
—*Paul Tillich*[1]

The Cold War ended at the beginning of the 1990s, but the Cold War security structures have largely persisted. Across the Atlantic, mutual U.S.–European Union interests have drastically declined since the collapse of the Soviet Union. European behavior, particularly that of France and Germany, toward the United States has drastically changed, but NATO remains the core security structure. This creates tensions between the expectations, interests, and institutions of the old order and the realities of behavior in the new era. As James Thomson has said about the U.S.-European strategic partnership, "Strategic partnerships, alliances and international security institutions have their roots in shared perceptions of both interests and the threats to them. . . . When the perceptions diverge, as they now have, the institutions themselves are undermined."[2] Specifically, he argues, the U.S.-European partnership was rooted in a half-century of mutual struggle against Germany and a half-century of mutual struggle against the Soviet Union, and those overriding common interests have vanished.

In Asia, one sees the same thing. A structure built to defend Asia against the Soviet Union, and for a while against the Sino-Soviet alli-

---

[1] Paul Tillich, *The Courage to Be*, New Haven, CT: Yale University Press, 1952, p. xxvi.

[2] James Thomson, "US Interests and the Fate of the Alliance," *Survival*, Vol. 54, No. 4, Winter 2003–04, pp. 207–208.

ance, still persists four and a half decades after the Sino-Soviet alliance collapsed and one and a half decades after the collapse of the Soviet Union. There is no obvious reason why a set of institutions created to defend the periphery of Asia against the predations of the Soviet Union should be optimal for the new era. Some strategists jump to the assumption that China now fills the old Soviet shoes, but that is a case to be argued, not a self-evident reality. Is the assumption realistic, or is it an excuse for Cold War institutions to avoid the consequences of obsolescence?

The history of great foreign-policy doctrines and their associated institutions shows that they tend to develop great inertia during the time when they fit the strategic environment, and this inertia carries them well into new eras when they may no longer be appropriate.[3] Thus, for instance, the No Entangling Alliances strategy presented in President Washington's farewell address[4] became deeply ingrained in the American consciousness in the 18th century and continued to affect U.S. thinking prior to World War I, leaving the nation insufficiently prepared for that conflict. It then encouraged excessive demobilization after both world wars, leaving the nation inadequately prepared for both World War II and the beginning of the Cold War. Many lives were lost because of the inertia of an archaic concept.

Likewise, the U.S. Open Door Policy in China served the nation's interests well at the beginning of the century, but eventually

---

[3] For a more systematic view of this phenomenon, see William H. Overholt and Marylin Chou, "Foreign Policy Doctrines," *Policy Studies Journal*, Vol. 3, No. 2, Winter 1974. That research arose out of a three-volume study I managed at Hudson Institute for the U.S. Department of Defense to ascertain the implications of the Nixon Doctrine for the U.S. posture in Asia many years later. The study, entitled "The Future of the Nixon Doctrine," was completed in 1972. Its core argument, widely ridiculed at the time, was that the political future of the region would be largely shaped by a great wave of economic development. A small part of that analysis was later approved for journal publication (see William H. Overholt, "The Rise of the Pacific Basin," *Pacific Community*, July 1974).

[4] "Why quit our own to stand upon foreign ground? Why, by interweaving our destiny with that of any part of Europe, entangle our peace and prosperity in the toils of European ambition, rivalship, interest, humor, or caprice? It is our true policy to steer clear of permanent alliances with any portion of the foreign world." (George Washington, farewell address, September 17, 1796.)

it simply lost touch with the reality of Chinese weakness and Japanese aggression.

These great doctrines comprise core ideas that become regarded as axiomatic (e.g., the United States is better off leaving the Europeans to fight their evil battles themselves) and great institutions that implement or affect those ideas. The institutions include alliances such as NATO or the U.S.-Japanese alliance, other consequential organizations such as the Association of Southeast Asian Nations (ASEAN), informal but institutionalized relationships such as the U.S. relationships of cooperation with various Southeast Asian countries or the pattern of hostility between China and Japan, and institutionalized relationships between interest groups and government organizations.[5]

With the onset of the Cold War, the United States organized itself around the Truman Doctrine: "It must be the policy of the United States to support free peoples who are resisting attempted subjugation by armed minorities or by outside pressures."[6] This was interpreted in the National Security Council's NSC 68, the great 1950 formulation of Cold War policy toward the Soviet Union, as requiring containment, defined as "a policy which seeks, by all means short of war, to . . . block the further expansion of Soviet power." In the aftermath of the Korean War, which began in June 1950, the doctrine came to be interpreted as using all means, including war, virtually everywhere in the world. This served the country well in most of the world, including all the most important places such as Western Europe and Japan. Eventually, however, the same doctrine and institutions were applied to Vietnam, where much of the population did not see itself as under attack by Soviet subjugators, many of the military techniques that worked elsewhere were inapplicable, and support in public opinion and among U.S. allies proved inadequate to the task.

The searing pain of the Vietnam War gave rise to a fundamental alteration of the Truman Doctrine, namely the Nixon Doctrine:

---

[5] I use the word "institution" in a very broad sense. Its ordinary usage is also quite broad—it refers to organizations such as banks as well as to stable, systematized relationships (e.g., the institution of marriage).

[6] President Harry Truman, addressing a joint session of Congress, March 12, 1947.

First, the United States will keep all of its treaty commitments.

Second, we shall provide a shield if a nuclear power threatens the freedom of a nation allied with us or of a nation whose survival we consider vital to our security.

Third, in cases involving other types of aggression, we shall furnish military and economic assistance when requested in accordance with our treaty commitments. *But we shall look to the nation directly threatened to assume the primary responsibility of providing the manpower for its defense.*[7] (Italics added.)

This effort to shift the defense burden to allies has centrally informed U.S. policy in Asia and (with some lapses such as the second Iraq war) elsewhere ever since. It provides the moving spirit behind the George W. Bush administration's vigorous efforts to get Japan to vastly extend the role and geographical scope of the Japanese military. The initial thrust of getting allies to pay for their own defense has, however, evolved into an effort to get allies such as Japan and Britain to shoulder military burdens that may be far from themselves (e.g., in Iraq) and offensive rather than defensive. That evolution, long after the evaporation of the threats that inspired the doctrine, may now be causing problems of its own.

To say that the institutions formed to support these great foreign policies, these foreign-policy doctrines, develop inertia is a bloodless statement that drains away the importance of the phenomenon. In support of these policies, we build great institutions such as NATO. We mold powerful institutions like the U.S. Army and think tanks in specific ways that support these policies. Great industries and politically influential unions arise to support the needs of these institutions by supplying everything from armament to propaganda. We indoctrinate our people to understand that good lies on one side and evil on another. Of necessity, we raise the perceptions of good and evil within certain institutions (the military, the diplomatic corps) to the point

---

[7] The Nixon Doctrine was first enunciated on July 25, 1969. This version is from a speech by President Richard Nixon on November 31, 1969.

where large numbers of people are prepared to risk death in order to support good against evil. The result is momentum that is anything but bloodless. Outside of certain rarefied circles, to call into doubt the continuing relevance of NATO or the U.S.-Korea or U.S.-Japan alliance is dangerous heresy.

Nonetheless, times change. For the first half of the 20th century, right-thinking Americans understood that China was good and Japan was evil. Today only historians and old folks remember the depth of that conviction, but in that era, even our most respected social scientists traced the roots of Japanese authoritarianism to deep, resilient cultural traits rooted in child-rearing. The most famous anthropologist of that era, Ruth Benedict, began her seminal book about Japan in this way: "The Japanese were the most alien enemy the United States had ever fought in an all-out struggle. In no other war with a major foe had it been necessary to take into account such different habits of acting and thinking . . . we were fighting a nation fully armed and trained which did not belong to the Western cultural tradition. Conventions of war which Western nations had come to accept as facts of human nature did not exist for the Japanese."[8] In other words, according to Benedict and to the conventional wisdom of the era, the Japanese were dangerous aliens, and their dangerous alienness was deeply rooted in their culture.

For the second half of the 20th century, good and evil in Asia reversed themselves. Now right-thinking Americans came to understand that Japan was inherently good and China inherently evil. Japan was inherently pacifist and democratic, with interests eternally aligned to the United States. For much of the Cold War, Americans perceived China as a nation of blue ants, of soldiers agreeable to human-wave attacks against overwhelming odds, of women who didn't mind dressing in dowdy clothes to serve the goal of equality, of Beijing citizens who voluntarily came out in winter and swept the snow in unison.[9]

---

[8] See, for instance, Ruth Benedict, *The Chrysanthemum and the Sword*, Boston, MA: Houghton Mifflin, 1989, p. 1.

[9] The civic-minded snow-sweeping was recounted with considerable admiration in the U.S. press at the time of Nixon's visit to China in February 1972. Contrary to the impression of

I still recall, not long after Richard Nixon's 1972 visit to China, one of my colleagues at Hudson Institute, Marylin Chou, recounting a trip to Beijing, where she observed more than once a young Chinese girl sneaking out with her boyfriend to a park in early morning, looking around to ensure that nobody was watching, and pulling off the top of the dowdy Mao suit briefly so that the boyfriend could take a picture of her in a pretty pink sweater. Then the Mao suit went quickly back on before the authorities could notice. For us, this was important, riveting information: Chinese girls were, after all, seemingly not microcosms of their autarkic, politically closed society; in crucial ways, they were a lot like American girls. It is now profoundly embarrassing that we regarded such an observation as a blinding insight, but at the time, reasonably intelligent people saw it as just that. Fifteen years after 1985, when the change in Chinese clothing really started for adults, there were a half-billion Chinese girls wearing colorful outfits, often with American logos. Not only do the Chinese women wear attractive sweaters, the educated urban ones talk about politics and sex, and they surf the Internet much as their American counterparts do. Nonetheless, as I lectured about China in 2005, I continued to unearth in many quarters residues of the Cold War assumptions that Chinese are inherently anti-American, that Chinese culture is inherently mysterious and difficult to penetrate, or that Japanese are inherently peaceful and inherently submissive to America's bidding for the indefinite future. Above all, there was an assumption of an unbridgeable gap between China's political system and the democracies—in particular, a gap that can be bridged only by some kind of collapse. This assumption is completely belied by the evolution of Taiwan and Singapore, among others, but nonetheless it is deeply held.

Institutional impositions lead everywhere to cultural caricatures. Maoist autarky and political repression led Americans to think that Chinese people are culturally xenophobic and difficult to connect with. The reality is the opposite; the cultures of coastal China are diverse, cosmopolitan, and welcoming to foreigners. Only in India, the

---

U.S. leading newspapers, the snow-sweeping was, of course, rigorously enforced, not voluntary civic-mindedness.

United States, and a few western parts of Europe does one find similar cosmopolitan cultures and such a lack of xenophobia. Similarly, the U.S.-imposed Peace Constitution of Japan led to a Western view of Japanese culture as inherently pacifist and unaggressive. As a description of the overwhelming majority of the Japanese people (and most other peoples), that is certainly accurate, but it disguises the fact that as the Cold War began, the United States reinstalled a Japanese national-security elite, previously removed by General Douglas MacArthur, that included some very tough characters whose successors remain influential. Likewise, as I write this, a well-known American professor has just posted a comment on the Internet attributing the behavior of Japanese during the bubble years to a cultural tendency toward speculation; he clearly didn't live in Thailand during the property boom or in Silicon Valley during the technology boom. It is difficult to strip away such cultural caricatures, but we must, because they affect the way congressmen and generals think about vital foreign-policy issues.

The inertia of old foreign-policy institutions and beliefs is a normal, universal phenomenon. Like billiard balls, old institutions and old ideas roll inexorably forward until they hit a wall. When they do hit a wall, they often reverse quite suddenly. This is what happened with American views of Germany after World War II: Nearly a half-century of views of Germany as that time's evil empire, with political authoritarianism bolstered by an authoritarian family structure, slammed into the desperate need for German support against Soviet expansion, and this led to a rapid updating of images and institutions to conform to the new reality.

The problem of obsolete and inaccurate caricatures affecting foreign policy is much more severe regarding Asia than it is regarding Europe, because Americans have less information about or contact with Japan and China than they do with Britain and Germany. We have already addressed the early perception of Japan as utterly alien. The history of U.S. perceptions of China offers even more examples.

During much of the period before 1949, we viewed Chiang Kaishek's Guomindang Party as the force of democracy, even though its organizational structure, authoritarian leadership, formative advisors

(Joseph Stalin's representatives in China), economic structure, and much else were quite similar to those of the Communist Party.

When Chiang Kai-shek's government lost to the communists, disappointed Americans attributed this for quite some time to an understanding that the corrupt Guomindang forces had stolen villagers' rice and raped their women, while the more virtuous communists had not. In reality, the historical record shows only limited differences of virtue. The Guomindang won in the cities and was defeating the Communist Party in the countryside (the Long March), much as the Thai and Malaysian governments drove their communists into the distant boondocks. But then the Japanese invaded, focusing on the cities, and inadvertently tilted the balance toward the communists.[10]

Subsequently, Chiang Kai-shek's government in Taiwan again became associated in American minds with democracy, even though until the late 1980s it continued to have a slightly modified Leninist political structure, a modified socialist economic structure, and widespread belief at very high levels that "an eighteenth century ideology like liberalism could never defeat a nineteenth century ideology like Marxism."[11] In accordance with that belief, Chiang Kai-shek's son Chiang Ching-kuo was educated in Moscow, where he joined the Soviet Communist Party prior to becoming a highly repressive chief of internal security in Taiwan. Subsequently, driven largely by internal social changes, he midwifed much of Taiwan's transition to democracy—a transition completed by his successors.[12]

---

[10] The most popular account of the corruption of Chiang Kai-shek's Guomindang, albeit a latecomer to this theme, is Sterling Seagraves, *The Soong Dynasty*, New York: Harper & Row, 1985. While the Guomindang certainly was corrupt, the problem with Seagraves' implicit thesis is that the communists' behavior, including alliances with some of the same gangs, was not so very different. The most searching argument that the outcome of the civil war was determined not by issues of social support but rather by the Japanese intervention is the China chapter in Barrington Moore, *The Social Origins of Dictatorship and Democracy: Lord and Peasant in the Making of the Modern World*, Boston, MA: Beacon Press, 1966, chap. IV.

[11] This assertion was common among senior Guomindang officials and scholars alike during my visits to Taiwan in the 1970s.

[12] Under Chiang Ching-kuo, Taiwan came to allow the opposition party to be legal and to compete openly in a free election. But the Guomindang still controlled the island's major

Thus, we had a half-century with one assumption (Japan inherently evil, China virtuous) and a half-century with the opposite assumption, sprinkled with radical misconceptions. How do we know whether the geopolitical architecture of Asia is evolving in ways that render obsolete some of the key assumptions and institutions of the Cold War era? Will Southeast Asia and Korea remain tied to an alliance of democracies, or will antipathy to Japan mean that they move away from a United States that ties itself ever more tightly to Japan? Will Japan remain a pliant ally, only a more useful one because we have persuaded it to rearm, or will a rearmed, more nationalistic, more self-confident Japan expel U.S. bases and set a potentially troublesome independent course for the first time since World War II? Will China's rise threaten us with an alien system, or is it conceivable that many of China's interests and policies and structures will one day align better with ours than those of some of our current allies?

One titillating incentive to address such questions is the increasing post–Cold War tendency for political and economic behavior to be inconsistent with Cold War presumptions. RAND's Charles Wolf ranked various countries on the degree to which they supported U.S. policies regarding seven major international issues. He found that "China, India, Pakistan and Russia are more closely aligned with U.S. policies and interests than France or Germany."[13] That result may well have been affected by temporary issues, so we should not generalize it, but it is a useful warning that we are in a new era where preconceptions and reality may often diverge.

---

corporations and, through the government, controlled all banks and television stations. Therefore, as long as the Guomindang was unified, the opposition had no serious chance of winning a technically free election. Subsequent President Lee Teng-hui became the first indigenous, directly elected president. But he still exercised Leninist power over his party and abused that power to designate an unpopular successor, Lien Chan, as the party's candidate for president over the more popular James Soong. That split the Guomindang Party and allowed the opposition Democratic Progressive Party (DPP) to win. Subsequent Guomindang mismanagement of its position dissipated its resources and popular support, thereby creating a situation in which subsequent elections would be not only free, but also fair.

[13] Charles Wolf, "A Test to Determine Who's an Ally," *International Herald Tribune*, July 7, 2004 (http://www.iht.com/articles/2004/07/08/edwolf_ed3__0.php).

Part of the answer to these questions is that they cannot be finally answered, so we will have to resort to scenarios based on whatever trends we can pin down. There is one certainty I can establish at the outset, however: A decade and a half after the end of the Cold War, this is definitely the time to ask such questions.

CHAPTER TWO

Cold War Assumptions and Changing Realities

America's core interests are eternal: security, prosperity, freedom/democracy—for ourselves and others. The U.S. strategy for the Cold War in Asia, like any strategy, was based on choices—choices among these high-priority interests, choices about the tools to be used in achieving these interests, choices about the level of resources to be deployed, choices about how much we emphasize these values for others rather than just ourselves. Under George Washington's No Entangling Alliances strategy, we focused on tending our own garden; if Europeans and Asians chose to slaughter or enslave each other, well, that was their problem. Based on the same interests but a different understanding of the world, the Truman Doctrine and containment made a quite different choice. When President George W. Bush set out to transform the Middle East into a collection of democracies, beginning with the invasion and reform of Iraq, he tilted the emphasis even further.

As we explore the changing strategic architecture of Asia, two perspectives will interact. I shall try to characterize that evolving architecture, including the U.S. position within it. Simultaneously, I shall characterize U.S. policy and U.S. policy choices. These perspectives are analytically separable, but in reality they interact, because since the end of World War II, the United States has had more ability than any other entity to shape Asia's strategic architecture. It would be equally valid to undertake the same analysis from a Chinese or Japanese or Indian perspective, but the motivating concern underlying this essay is for U.S. policy, U.S. choices, and U.S. values. What I have tried to avoid is forcing Asia into the procrustean bed of Cold War presuppositions or current U.S. policy predilections.

From the onset of the Cold War after World War II, the United States believed (correctly) that it faced a serious threat to its military security and its way of life from a Soviet Union that sought to dominate as much of the world as possible and to transform the ideological beliefs and political structures of the rest of the world, including the United States, to conform to Leninist doctrine. This led, on March 12, 1947, to the enunciation by President Harry Truman, addressing a joint session of Congress, of the Truman Doctrine, the overarching statement of U.S. Cold War policy. All subsequent U.S. Cold War policies functioned within the context of this doctrine.

Gradually, the Truman Doctrine became concrete in specific policies and priorities. The core of the U.S. strategy for implementing it was the Marshall Plan, enunciated by Secretary of State George C. Marshall at Harvard University on June 5, 1947, three months after the formulation of the Truman Doctrine. The Marshall Plan committed the United States to providing $20 billion, at the time a seemingly enormous sum, to fund the cooperative economic and social revitalization of Western Europe, on the premise that a prosperous, democratic, reasonably just, mutually cooperating group of European states would transform fragile societies, vulnerable to communist subversion, into stable states that would constitute a formidable block supporting democratic values and U.S. defensive policies. In return for its funds, the U.S. demanded clear plans for economic and social development, cooperation among the countries in achieving that development, and, with varying degrees of explicitness, resistance to Soviet pressures.

With wide variations in detail, the Marshall Plan in Europe became the template for U.S. policies throughout the rest of the world. Although the United States did not provide massive economic aid to Japan in the manner of the Marshall Plan, in 1947–1948 it moved from treating Japan as an enemy to cultivating economic recovery and political coherence. It sent leading American economic experts to foster a revival of Japanese economic growth. It welcomed and encouraged the Japanese rejuvenation that began with stimulus from the Korean War, and it kept U.S. markets open to Japan at considerable domestic political cost. In Southeast Asia, the United States supported one formula after another—MAPHILINDO (Malaya, Philippines, and Indonesia), the Asia Pacific Council (ASPAC), ASEAN—seeking an Asian counterpart of the Marshall Plan's developmental cooperation. In support of this policy, the Agency for International Development (AID) dispersed large amounts of funds and advice, and for decades AID officers played a powerful role in almost every U.S. embassy in Asia.

The scope and means of the Truman Doctrine strategy took shape only gradually. Western Europe and Japan came first. Without military defense, U.S. allies would be overwhelmed before the economic and social strategy could be implemented. But the key to eventual victory or defeat was whether U.S. allies achieved superior economic prosperity and social development. Where they did, as in Western Europe, Japan, and ASEAN countries such as Singapore and Thailand, the U.S. triumphed. Where they failed, as in Vietnam, Laos, Cambodia, and Burma, U.S. strategy failed. Had Indonesia failed to develop, no amount of military effort could have succeeded in saving Southeast Asia. Where the economic results were lackluster, as in the Philippines, the United States continued to face instability and persistent communist and Islamist guerilla movements, with or without a large U.S. military presence. Where economic development succeeded, the United States won, with or without democracy; and where economic development succeeded (South Korea, Taiwan, Singapore, Thailand, and, to some extent, Indonesia), democracy generally followed. Eventually, South Korea's economy simply dwarfed North Korea's, Western Europe's and Japan's economies simply dwarfed the Soviet Union's, and the Soviet Union's economy collapsed. This economic emphasis and contemporary movement away from it will provide one of the central themes of this study.

In 1950, NSC 68 spelled out what the Truman Doctrine meant for U.S. strategy toward an expansionist Soviet Union: "Containment is a policy which seeks, by all means short of war, to (1) block the further expansion of Soviet power." The qualifier, "by all means short of war," was central to this formulation, as was a sense that limited U.S. power implied severe limits, possibly excluding Korea, on the geographic scope of the containment policy. However, when a Soviet-armed North Korea invaded South Korea in June 1950, containment became universally applicable to the non-communist world and containment was to be implemented by all means, including war. The Truman Doctrine became almost universally applicable, and military tools were no longer excluded.

The limits of this wide-ranging policy were that it was largely defensive and largely non-nuclear. The U.S. refusal to back Hungarian revolutionaries in 1956 and its refusal to back Chiang Kai-shek's ambitions to invade and recover the Chinese mainland made clear that it would not attempt to "roll back" existing communist systems. Likewise, President Truman's refusal to employ nuclear weapons during the Korean War made it clear that the United States would use nuclear weapons only in response to others' first use or to situations like a Soviet invasion of Western Europe that threatened the continued viability of democratic society.

The Truman Doctrine in Asia

The core of the Truman Doctrine and of containment everywhere was economic and social revitalization. Understanding the relationship between the vital tools of the Truman Doctrine is essential to understanding everything that followed. Like a carpenter who needs both his hammer and his saw, the Truman Doctrine in Asia, as elsewhere, required both military protection and economic development. At the end of World War II, the United States possessed the overwhelmingly most powerful military establishment in world history. Moreover, nobody in the Western establishment doubted that without military protection, Japan, Western Europe, and virtually any other area would quickly fall to Soviet power. But even with the greatest military power in world history, the U.S. position seemed fragile. Communist parties in Italy, France, and Japan, not to mention southern Europe, much of Africa, the Philippines, Malaya, Thailand, Indonesia, and southern Korea, held threatening positions in unstable societies, and in the aftermath of the Great Depression and two world wars, Marxist ideas gripped much of the West's intelligentsia. From the Great Depression through the end of the 1940s, even the United States had deeply divided intellectual and labor elites that might eventually have made the country's global position vulnerable to Marxist enemies had the great economic resurgence of the 1950s and 1960s not overcome the legacy of the Depression. The core of the problem the United States faced was economic and social, at home and even more so abroad. Without progress on those fronts, no imaginable amount of military power could ensure successful containment.

The U.S. theory of victory, therefore, was founded on economic and social development, on the Marshall Plan in Europe, and parallel efforts in Asia. Where economic and social progress succeeded, as in Japan, South Korea, Thailand, Singapore, Malaysia, and (with qualifications) Indonesia, the military threat greatly diminished or even vanished. Again, where economic and social progress failed, as in most of Indochina, no amount of military effort could succeed.

Within this global strategy, the United States confronted specific architectural conditions in Asia, as noted in Figure 1.[1]

Notwithstanding U.S. military power, it was difficult to overstate the vulnerability of the Western position in Asia during the early Cold War years. Until 1966, Indonesia had the world's third largest Communist Party (PKI), and the PKI had deep roots in Indonesia's military, especially the air force. When I began my career at Hudson Institute in 1971, fairly late in the Cold War, controversy still existed within the U.S. government as to whether Japan's domestic situation had stabilized sufficiently that we no longer needed to fear a communist takeover of Japan—not by the Soviet Union but from within. There was virtually no dissent among U.S. and European experts from the view that South Korea was inherently unstable and eternally vulnerable to a seemingly very stable and powerful communist North Korea.

---

[1] A list like this necessarily gains conciseness at some cost in nuance. For instance, although U.S. and Japanese economic interests were fundamentally aligned, there were rivalries, trade conflicts, and differences over whether Japan should be able to access the China market. The list focuses exclusively on the central tendencies.

Figure 1
Key Elements of Asia's Early Cold War Architecture

- The Soviet Union sought military and ideological domination of regions vital to the United States, including subversion of the United States itself.
- China was closely aligned with the Soviet Union.
- Maoist China was a disruptive, ideological, subversive force, sponsoring insurgencies in all its non-communist neighbors and systematically undermining U.S.-sponsored global institutions.
- U.S. and Japanese military, economic, political, and ideological interests were all positively aligned.
- U.S. and Soviet/China military, economic, political, and ideological interests were all negatively aligned.
- Centuries-old Sino-Japanese rivalries were suppressed by U.S. policy, which disarmed Japan and allied with it, thereby protecting both countries.
- India was marginal. Democratic but largely Soviet-aligned, India shared power on the subcontinent with a relatively powerful Pakistan that was closely aligned with the United States.
- Non-communist Pacific Asia, including Japan, was extremely fragile, ideologically and politically divided, and vulnerable to subversion, with weak governments and weak economies dependent on U.S. largesse. Major communist insurgencies threatened Malaya, the Philippines, Indonesia, Thailand, and Burma, as did major radical leftist movements in Japan and South Korea.
- Pervasive territorial conflicts divided the non-communist countries of Asia; Indonesia claimed most of Southeast Asia.
- The United States was the principal sponsor of development through multilateral economic liberalization in Southeast Asia.
- North Vietnam was an aggressive, expansionist power, determined to subordinate Laos and Cambodia, along with South Vietnam.
- Bipolar world, bipolar Asia unified the United States with its allies.
- Central Asia was under firm Soviet control—no vacuum as in the old days of the Great Game.

The Asian Economic Miracle and Political Consolidation

In this situation, the United States doggedly pursued its Truman Doctrine goal of nation-building, economy-building, and institution-building. The first fruit was the Japanese economic miracle, a takeoff at a sustained pace of 10 percent of the annual gross domestic product (GDP), growth never before seen in a large economy. (I do not mean to suggest that the United States was responsible for the takeoff; the Japanese deserve almost all the credit. But a wise U.S. policy actively supported it. Under less-enlightened leadership, the United States could have remained indifferent, matched Japanese protectionism with U.S. protectionism, or even imposed the kinds of catastrophic reparations that were imposed on post–World War I Germany.) By the beginning of the 1970s, the economic takeoff had in fact given enough Japanese citizens a stake in the status quo that the country was beyond the reach of communist subversion. (This is clear in retrospect, even though at the time, U.S. analysts were still uncertain.) Gradually, over many years, the successful economic policies of the democratic conservatives led to atrophy of the socialist and communist opposition. With this, Japanese democracy stabilized, and so did the Japanese-American alliance.

As this happened, Japan's international stature and influence rose, due to a combination of the prestige that comes from extraordinary economic success and the more tangible influence Japan gained from increasing domination of Asia's banking, manufacturing, trade, investment, and aid. The fact that Japan had reached the stature of a big power while adhering to its Peace Constitution became noted throughout the world as a new model of international behavior, and it became influential in other Asian countries' thinking.

During this period, U.S. ambassadors in Asia became expert advisors on land reform, economic competition, capital-market development, industrial policy, government institution-building, interest-rate liberalization, currency and inflation stabilization, and all the intricacies of development economics. In many countries (though not Japan, South Korea, or the Philippines), AID missions were more important than military missions. In all the emerging economies, they played a vital role, even when big military missions were also present.

The fruits of these efforts became apparent after a generation. By the mid-1960s, South Korea, Taiwan, Hong Kong, and Singapore were experiencing Japan-like takeoffs, and these were soon followed by similar takeoffs in Thailand, Malaysia, and Indonesia. Where these takeoffs occurred, citizens became supportive of the government, radical ideologies gradually deflated, and the military and police obtained sufficient resources to do their jobs effectively. In short, domestic politics stabilized throughout the region. This process was particularly dramatic in Indonesia, a fractious collection of 15,000 islands that originally contained not only the world's third largest Communist Party, but also the world's most powerful fundamentalist Islamic movement. With development after 1967, the social base for such movements largely evaporated. Because the social base evaporated, government repression of the PKI became permanent, the moderate Islamic groups (Nahdatul Ulama and Muhammadiyah) triumphed over the more radical ones, and the secular government gradually negotiated an understanding with them. (When economic development suffered a setback in 1998, the Islamic fundamentalist movement revived, although not to the level it achieved in the 1950s, despite the fact that democratization coincided with the crisis. This striking correlation contains a vital lesson that U.S. Middle East policy in the early 21st century has failed to heed: A high priority for democratization combined with a low priority for economic development is a recipe for failure, even when huge military forces are deployed to prop up the democracy.)

Moreover, international politics among these countries also became more peaceful. During the first generation after World War II, Southeast Asian politics was dominated by a horrific latticework of territorial claims, even among countries that were allies and quasi-allies of the United States or neutral in the Cold War: Thailand vs. Burma, Thailand vs. Malaysia, Malaysia vs. the Philippines, Malaysia vs. Indonesia, Philippines vs. Indonesia. As late as the early 1960s, Indonesia was seeking to claim most of Southeast Asia. But as the key countries learned the algorithm of rapid economic development, these territorial rivalries gradually faded in favor of a focus on domestic economic development. The regional economic association, ASEAN, the counterpart of European regional cooperation for the Marshall Plan, flourished even though its military counterpart, the Southeast Asia Treaty Organization (SEATO), faded quickly into irrelevance.

The reasons for this dramatic transformation of regional politics are straightforward. For centuries, the principal route to wealth and power had been conquest of neighboring territory. Wealth came from seizing neighbors' golden temples and taxing their peasants. The dawn of the Asian miracle transformed this ancient reality. Now wealth and power accrued to whoever grew the fastest by reforming the domestic economy. Conversely, the arrival of modern military technology put the quest for power through war at risk of achieving Pyrrhic victories.[2]

When Deng Xiaoping began China's great economic reform program, he followed the same path his successful neighbors had followed. He demanded that the people be given a rest after the Cultural Revolution and that the country focus on raising its inner reserve. China's military budget underwent a startling decline, from about 16 percent of GDP in the mid-1970s to about 3 percent as Deng's reforms gathered pace, and later sank still further. To accomplish this, China gradually withdrew support from the many guerrilla and subversive movements that Mao Zedong had backed in order to destabilize China's neighbors (and many other nations). At the time of Mao's death in 1976, China had been backing subversive movements in virtually all of China's non-communist neighbors, in addition to much of Africa and Latin America. Within a few years of Deng Xiaoping's accession to power, China withdrew support from all of them and became an avid supporter of stability—even to the point of supporting Nepal's king against self-styled "Maoist" guerrillas. China also gradually settled most of its land boundaries in ways acceptable to its neighbors. By 2005, only the borders with India and Bhutan were in dispute, and even there, India and China engaged in an increasingly relaxed dialogue about settlement. China's settlement of its border with Russia in 2005 resolved territorial claims that over time had involved vast swaths of territory and had cost many lives. Notably, China settled on terms that were quite conservative and acceptable to Russia, even though the settlement occurred at

---

[2] I have explored this phenomenon in several publications, among them, William H. Overholt, "Progress and Politics in Pacific Asia," *International Security*, Spring 1983; and William H. Overholt, "The Pacific Basin Model: The Moderation of Politics," in James Morley (ed.), *The Pacific Basin*, Washington, DC: Academy of Political Science, 1986, pp. 35–45. Note that these observations concerned relations among Asian countries that were mostly friendly to the United States and that they predated Zheng Bijian's "peaceful rise theory" for China by two decades. This is important because anyone who makes note of this pattern today is likely to be accused of buying into Chinese propaganda.

a time when China's power was rising sharply, Russia's was declining sharply, and the Russian territory was rapidly depopulating.

Next to experience this shift of priorities was Vietnam. For decades, in some ways for centuries, Vietnam had bled itself by seeking expansion at the expense of its neighbors. It had followed victory in South Vietnam with predatory invasions of Laos and Cambodia. But as the century ended, it discovered the magic of rapid economic development through domestic reform. Suddenly Vietnam developed friendlier relations with its neighbors, including membership in ASEAN and a rapprochement with China that resembled China's gradual settlement with Russia.

Now, as I shall discuss in Chapter Six, the same shift of priorities shows preliminary signs of possibly spreading to India. The lesson of the Asian miracle had spread from Japan to Southeast Asia and then, somewhat surprisingly, to China and Vietnam, and perhaps it will spread on to India.

This gradually evolving shift of Asian countries' priorities was no different from what happened in Western Europe after World War II. Two of history's bloodiest wars finally convinced France and Germany that the road to wealth and power ran more smoothly through domestic economic development than through slaughtering each other with the power of modern weaponry. Likewise, development of the most destructive military technology, nuclear weapons, forced the United States and the Soviet Union to step back from direct military conflicts for half a century. Neither the outcome nor the logic of these reconsiderations was different in Europe or America from those of its Asian counterpart. In the European and American cases, the predominant consideration was the destructiveness of modern military technology; in the Asian cases, there was a more even balance between new economic development opportunities and new military destructiveness.

This alteration of priorities throughout the globe marked a new phase of history. The new era is not consistent with structural-realist theories, based on the economics and weaponry of a previous era, that any rising power will violently disrupt the system. Nor is it consistent with neoconservative notions, explicit or implicit, that any country professing communist or leftist ideologies must somehow be aggressive, like the old Soviet Union. Nor is it predominantly the outcome of interdependence, the liberal theorists' route to peace that failed so bitterly a century ago when an era of economic liberalization and attendant hopes for peace ended in world war. These varieties of theorists have missed one of the most important cusps of human history.

Crucially, this new era creates a shift in the balance of considerations, and therefore a shift in the balance of probabilities, not, of course, anything like an absolute guarantee of peace. The power of late 20th-century weaponry creates a watered-down version of the balance of terror that helped preserve the peace between the United States and the Soviet Union, and the power of new economic strategies creates extraordinary improvements in the standards of living of countries that are governed by leaders wise enough to recognize the new era and astute enough to follow successful economic policies. Those countries, like South Korea, that give priority to peaceful economic development, end up dwarfing those, like North Korea, that pursue traditional military priorities, so the balance of power shifts in favor of peaceful countries. Economic successes in turn wither the roots of fanaticism, and mutual gains ease many frictions among different ethnic and social groups—as one can see vividly when walking the streets of Singapore or Hong Kong. But of course, no structure of incentives provides absolute guarantees against demagoguery, stupidity, or ancient hatreds, particularly in regions like South Asia where the advent of nuclear weapons preceded the advent of Asian miracle–era geopolitics.

It is important to note that, somewhat ironically, this shift within Asia and Europe from a focus on territorial conquest to domestic economic development has depended upon a powerful U.S. military presence. The ability of Japan to achieve an economic miracle while keeping military expenditures below 1 percent of GDP, the ability of Park Chung Hee to cut South Korea's military budgets in the 1960s, the ability of Deng Xiaoping to cut China's military budgets in the 1980s despite conflict with the Soviet Union, and the ability of Southeast Asian states to limit their military expenditures have all depended on knowledge that the United States would weigh in to preclude the most extreme scenarios.

Just as had happened in Japan's post–World War II rise, China's rise to geopolitical eminence preceded its acquisition of any significant military power. The historic shift in the balance of geopolitical payoff between economic priorities and military priorities belies the arguments of those who claim that the rise of a new power necessarily leads to violent upheavals in the reigning system. Indonesia's rise in Southeast Asia was arguably faster and more dramatic than Germany's rise in Europe, but it led to regional stabilization rather than regional upheaval. China's and Vietnam's rises have so far followed the same pattern. That is the central experience of Asian geopolitics in the Cold War and in the immediate post–Cold War era.

Given the extreme cultural antagonism toward the West that has arisen in some parts of the Middle East and could possibly later arise in Central Asia and Africa, it is crucial to underscore how violent and destabilizing Islamic fundamentalism and anti-colonialism were in Indonesia in the late 1950s and early 1960s and, even more, how violent, destabilizing, and antagonistic to Western values the Chinese Cultural Revolution (1966–1976) was. Moreover, the extent to which Indonesian cultural rage and anti-colonialism and Chinese cultural rage against Western institutions and values resonated throughout the world was far greater than the influence of violent Islamist rage today. The speed with which both of these movements subsided as the citizenry was given a modicum of prosperity and education proved truly remarkable. In 1976, anyone who predicted the transformation of China into a nation of greedy capitalist shopkeepers would have encountered the same ridicule as anyone today who ventured to predict that economic progress could stabilize Central Asia.

Domestic stabilization and a regional shift of priorities away from territorial greed simplified the U.S. task of stabilizing a non-communist Asia with regimes that the United States found compatible. "Compatible" often did not mean that these countries were a microcosm of U.S. democracy. The U.S. Cold War strategy focused on economic development, protected by the military. Political democracy, while desirable, was never the top priority. The most successful societies, other than Japan—i.e., South Korea, Taiwan, Thailand, and Singapore—gradually moved toward democracy after a period of developmental authoritarianism. Democracy failed economically and lost popular support in the early post-colonial days of South Korea, Indonesia, and Thailand, and disillusionment with democracy lay behind popular support of Ferdinand Marcos's constitutional coup in the Philippines in 1972. The region's (and the world's) leading developing-country democracy at the outset, the Philippines, just never made it into the modern world. The region's only democracy that was successful from the beginning, Malaysia, was under continuous martial law and organized around a coalition of three communal parties that totally dominated throughout the Cold War era. Throughout the region, though, economic development created educated middle-class societies that both demanded more freedom and democracy and were more capable of making the collective choices that successful democracy required. More subtly, economic development created complex economies that were more difficult for narrow elites to manipulate in order to keep themselves in power. Thus, whereas South Korean democracy in 1960–1961 failed utterly to provide prosperity or domestic stability or national security, South Korean democracy after 1988 proved among the most successful in the third world. The U.S. strategy that slighted democracy in the short run therefore proved supportive of democracy in the long run.

The Philippine experience exemplifies the reasons why most Asian countries rejected democratization at an early stage of development, even though they found it the only workable option when they had achieved a higher level. From independence through the end of the 1960s, the Philippines was Asia's most democratic country, with courts and free press and electoral systems refined over many years of U.S. tutelage; with a legislature that, unlike Japan's, had full scrutiny of policy and budgets; and with two parties alternating in power, rather than the typical Asian pattern of an elite coalition that commanded such overwhelming resources as to preclude effective competition (Malaysia, Singapore, post-1955 Japan, Taiwan in 1988–2000). Likewise, at independence and for many years afterward, the Philippines led all developing countries on all measures of economic and social development, including literacy, newspaper readership, roads per unit of territory and population, and the like. Manila was the trade and investment hub of Asia. Before World War II, the better-governed

Philippines had attracted substantial immigration of poverty-stricken Japanese. So many Japanese served Filipino families as gardeners that the Filipinos' image of Japanese was of gardeners. Likewise, through the 1960s, large numbers of poverty-stricken Hong Kong residents migrated to the more-prosperous Philippines, where the Hong Kong women typically served as amahs, raising children and serving as maids. From there, the Philippines' relative position steadily declined, because electoral politics ensured total social dominance by a tiny elite minority that had the wherewithal to compete effectively, an adversary court system effectively excluded the vast majority of the population that could not afford a lawyer, complex judicial practices made it impossible for an impoverished government to afford justice, and a complacent elite had no incentive to make the investments necessary to spur economic development. In a startling reversal, by the 1980s, even Hong Kong secretaries typically had live-in Filipino maids.[3]

Other countries had roughly parallel experiences. In South Korea, the first attempt at democracy was repudiated when it became associated with disorder and national weakness. Indonesian democracy failed when it became, as in the Philippines, an elite game out of touch with popular needs.[4] U.S. policy succeeded because it acknowledged these realities.

The U.S. Cold War strategy treated economic development as the core strategy, used the military to protect that process, and relegated democratization to third place. The success of those strategic choices transformed Asia and changed world history.

In this regard, it is worth underlining the dramatic shift in U.S. strategic priorities in the 21st century. Martial law would have rendered the principal Asian miracles—South Korea, Taiwan, Malaysia, Indonesia, Thailand—that were crucial to consolidation of the U.S. position in Asia ineligible for the Millennium Challenge Account, which

---

[3] On the emergence of martial law in the Philippines, see William H. Overholt, "Martial Law, Revolution and Democracy in the Philippines," *Southeast Asia Quarterly*, Vol. 2, No. 2, 1973.

[4] On Korea, see Sejin Kim, *The Politics of Military Revolution in Korea*, Durham, NC: University of North Carolina Press, 1971. On Indonesia, see Herbert Feith, *The Decline of Constitutional Democracy in Indonesia*, Ithaca, NY: Cornell University Press, 1962.

is the counterpart for Africa of the Cold War aid programs for Asia. Deprived of aid based on such criteria, the principal Asian countries probably would have fallen to communism. The elevation of democracy to a primary criterion for aid, on the argument that democracy facilitates economic growth and ensures peace, is inconsistent with the Asian experience and may ironically inhibit replication of the Asian miracle elsewhere, particularly in Central Asia.

The Truman Doctrine strategy proved remarkably resilient in the face of substantial changes in the region. Because the Soviet threat remained prominent, the Sino-Soviet split of 1959 did not affect the strategy, nor did Sino-American rapprochement after 1972 and Sino-American alignment after the Soviet invasion of Afghanistan in 1979. The stabilization of Japan in the late 1960s and Japan's rise to near-dominance of Asia by the 1980s, together with the stabilization of Southeast Asia and Korea in the 1970s, validated the strategy rather than making it obsolete. China's reversal of both economic and geopolitical policies after 1979, moving toward a market economy and seeking to stabilize Asia rather than to destabilize it, provided a dividend that had been unimaginable from 1949 to 1979.

What did force a fundamental amendment of the Truman Doctrine strategy was the Vietnam War. In Vietnam, the post-1950 Truman Doctrine's mandate to defend any non-communist society by any means short of nuclear war ran into a wall. America was defending a country, South Vietnam, that had failed to join the Asian miracle and that saw Western colonialism as a far greater danger than Soviet subjugation. The United States was using military means that proved ineffective within established military limits and within the limits of public support at the time. Whether the war could have been successful had the Nixon presidency not collapsed remains a subject of legitimate debate. In any event, however, the failing war led, years before the collapse of the Nixon presidency, to the Nixon Doctrine (quoted in Chapter One), a fundamental revision of the Truman Doctrine that sought to reduce U.S. responsibility for defense of Asian allies by putting more of the burden onto them.

Of course, the United States had always sought assistance from others, beginning with extensive allied support for U.S. forces in the

Korean War. But the Nixon Doctrine elevated this to the core of U.S. policy, making it a consideration of the highest priority.

The burden-shifting failed in Vietnam, but Nixon's amendment of the Truman Doctrine has persisted and expanded in East Asia ever since. The United States withdrew its troops from Thailand, reduced them in South Korea, and acceded to a Philippine request to withdraw troops from the Subic Naval Bay and Clark Air Base. Most important, the new doctrine of burden-sharing has led the United States during the administrations of George H.W. Bush and George W. Bush to press for Japan to rearm and to support U.S. military activities in Iraq and Afghanistan, as well as in Asia. That decision has fundamentally altered the geopolitics of Asia, with consequences that remain unclear.

Events in the Middle East have taken a different direction. The Iranian revolution and the Soviet invasion of Afghanistan in 1979 led to the Carter Doctrine: "Any attempt by an outside force to gain control of the Persian Gulf region will be regarded as an assault on the vital interest of the United States of America, and such an assault will be repelled by any means necessary, including military force."[5] It remains to be seen whether the post-Vietnam humility of the Nixon Doctrine or the combination of post–Cold War military confidence and the Bush Doctrine of spreading democracy will dominate U.S. foreign policy in the future. Two developments are likely to be decisive: the outcome of the Iraq war and the evolution of the Taiwan issue. The result of these conflicting trends is that the post–Cold War United States has no consensus on the purpose or means of its foreign policy. This is characteristic of a transitional era.[6]

---

[5] President Jimmy Carter, State of the Union address, January 23, 1980. For an interesting commentary on the Carter Doctrine, see Lawrence E. Grinter, "Avoiding the Burden: The Carter Doctrine in Perspective," *Air University Review*, January–February 1983.

[6] To add to the confusion, the Reagan Doctrine emphasized, in the manner of the Nixon Doctrine, support for local freedom fighters, as in Afghanistan. There is also a Powell Doctrine, emphasizing that the United States should use the military only for clear purposes when overwhelmingly decisive force can be brought to bear. The confusion of all these doctrines is symptomatic of an era in which every situation evokes a new "doctrine" that, in sharp contrast with Washington's No Entangling Alliances or the Monroe Doctrine or the Truman Doctrine, generally lasts only as long as a single presidency or even a single situation

In the meantime, other developments have rapidly reshaped the post–Cold War architecture of Asian geopolitics.

Post–Cold War Developments and Architectural Changes

Since the end of the Cold War in the early 1990s, crucial new developments have changed the shape of Asia. The Soviet Union collapsed. In 1979, China stopped fighting the Asian miracle and instead joined it, thereby deepening and accelerating the miracle and its political consequences. That brought a historic rise of Chinese prestige and influence. Meanwhile, Japanese failure to reform a troubled economy led, just at the moment when Japan had seemed on its way to Asian dominance, to a dozen years of stagnation, 1990–2002, and the consequent collapse of Japanese prestige, financial dominance, and regional industrial hegemony. Japan, which had expected to completely overshadow the United States in Asia, instead became its handmaiden and, shedding its former policy of economic diplomacy, began expanding the role of its military without (or prior to) changing a constitution that clearly forbade many of its new activities. Southeast Asia and South Korea, while nervous about China's new power and prestige, found the new China more compatible than the old and discovered that they had the option to lean toward China when they disagreed with U.S. policies.

Chinese openness to foreign direct investment drew the United States and Europe back into Asia on a large scale; this created an economically multipolar Asia and completed the demolition of Japan's once-imminent regional dominance. Politically, the collapse of the Soviet Union seemed to imply a hegemonic position for the United States, but China's new dynamism created some diplomatic and economic, if not military, balance. Meanwhile, the U.S. failure to rescue Southeast Asia from the Asian crisis of 1997–1998 and ASEAN disagreement with the downgrading of economic priorities from 2001

---

during a single presidency. The historian has to decide which of the pieces called "doctrines" actually shape U.S. foreign policy and institutions for a sustained period of time. In practice, this is not difficult.

onward led that region to shift toward greater neutrality. A different set of disagreements led South Korea to cooperate less with the United States. The result was a net loss of U.S. leverage in the region despite increasing military dominance. All of these developments fundamentally altered Asian balances and alignments.

By 2005, the architecture of geopolitics in Asia looked quite different from that outlined in Figure 1. The predominant features of Asia's architecture in 2005 were those noted in Figure 2.

The contrast between the architectural elements noted in Figure 2 and those in Figure 1 is quite sharp. It would be remarkable if the institutions, especially the network of bases and alliances but also the military planning and technological investments, created to manage the conditions in Figure 1, were entirely appropriate to manage the very different conditions of today. Indeed, crucial signs of strain have begun to appear. In Asia, the reignition of Sino-Japanese hostility, after two decades of being suppressed by U.S. pressure to keep Japan disarmed and deter any Chinese threat to Japan, threatens to reverse one of the two principal achievements of U.S. policy during the last half-century (containment of the Soviet Union and preventing the reemergence of a Sino-Japanese rivalry).

Key stresses and strains in U.S. policy become explicable in the light of these new elements of Asia's architecture. U.S. presidents tend to come to office with a profoundly antagonistic Cold War view of China but then to mellow very quickly into a managerial view of the U.S.-China relationship. These shifts are not accidental but rather reflect the reality that on the current major Asian issues other than Taiwan—the war on terror, North Korea, Pakistan, regional crime, regional drug trafficking, regional human trafficking, freedom of trade, freedom of investment, genetically modified foods—the president finds himself dealing mainly with China and mainly in a cooperative mode. The alliance structures, attitudes, and interest groups of the Cold War era do not readily accommodate such new realities. Not surprisingly, each president finds himself quickly at odds on these issues with a Congress that largely reflects the momentum of old interest groups and Cold War ideas.

Stresses have also arisen in other institutions. At the turn of the decade, the Pentagon's new leaders put enormous, impressive, and suc-

Figure 2
Key Elements of Asia's Architecture in 2005

- No country is seeking to transform U.S. politics or assert hegemony over countries of vital interest to the United States.

- Threats to U.S. security are increasingly from terrorism, guerrilla warfare, and proliferation of weapons of mass destruction (WMD), not traditional security threats.

- China is joining the system rather than subverting it.

- Asia's architecture is determined by the United States, China, and Japan.

- India is rising, but the gap with China continues to widen

  –Vietnam is rising but is not yet a regional geopolitical force
  –Russia is a Central Asian power, not a Pacific or South Asian power.

- Sino-Japanese rivalries are reviving.

- Korea is torn between a consensus need for alliance with the United States and rising concern about excessive confrontation with the Democratic People's Republic of Korea (DPRK) or the U.S.-Japan alliance dragging it into a confrontation with China.

- China is the principal sponsor of development through multilateral economic liberalization in Southeast Asia; Southeast Asia is no longer dependent on U.S. largesse.

- Interest alignments are increasingly blurred

  –The U.S.-Japan military/ideological alliance continues to strengthen
  –U.S.-Chinese political-economic cooperation grows as well.

- Asia is increasingly multipolar.

- An economically dynamic, militarily weak (for now) China is replacing Japan as the regional leader.

- Pakistan's relative decline leaves India the hegemonic South Asian power.

- Vietnam is joining the Asian-miracle system and eschewing further geopolitical expansion.

- The Central Asian political vacuum has revived the Great Game.

- U.S. priorities have shifted from economy- and institution-building to more exclusive military- and democracy-building.

cessful effort into modernizing the U.S. military. They introduced new technology, stripped out unneeded personnel, introduced more-efficient decision processes, and generally brought the Cold War military into the 21st century. This modernization was one of the more formidable and more successful institutional transformations in American history, and it left other U.S. government institutions far behind. But the architects of this new military came to office denouncing the waste of U.S. military resources on peacekeeping and nation-building, only to discover that these were the core tasks of the new era, that their time in office would be largely preoccupied with those tasks, that they would be judged almost exclusively on the basis of their ability to perform those tasks, and that they had in fact created a very, very modern Cold War military when there was in fact no more Cold War. In Afghanistan and Iraq, that military performed the Cold War–like tasks of defeating the Taliban's and Saddam Hussein's conventional armies with amazing skill and speed, but as of this writing has been unable to completely achieve the decisive tasks of the new era, namely, defeating insurgencies and building viable states. To justify continued building of a Cold War–style military, some civilian leaders of the Pentagon resorted to characterizations of China that were difficult to square with reality. Such developments are characteristic of the end-of-era rationalizations that historically have been used to preserve old institutions despite new realities.

Similarly, in the diplomatic arena, the Armitage Report (discussed on p. 131) demanded a return to the Cold War's relatively exclusive emphasis on the U.S. relationship with Japan. It appeared in a context of intense criticism of President Bill Clinton for visiting China without visiting Japan at the same time to explain himself—notwithstanding the fact that Clinton had visited Japan twice without visiting China and had concretely strengthened the military alliance with Japan, while his visit to China was largely symbolic. The Armitage Report, and the spirit of it, were subsequently implemented by replacing China specialists in most top foreign-policy and national-security roles with Japan specialists. The new Armitage Report–inspired policy pressured Japan to explicitly target China as an object of its military policy and of the alliance and to expand the role of the Japanese military. The new policies swam against the tide of increasing U.S. reliance on cooperation with China to achieve its principal political and economic goals in Asia (a theme elaborated on pp. 233–235), and it inadvertently but powerfully contributed to the ascendancy of an increasingly right-wing government in Japan that alienated most of Japan's neighbors and damaged the United States by association. As with the reversals of presidential attitudes toward China, by 2007 the National Security Council Asia staff was once again headed by a China specialist, and the crowning achievement of the Assistant Secretary of State handling Asia was a North Korea nuclear deal midwifed by China and bitterly shunned by Japan.

Thus, in presidential campaigns, in Congress, in the military, and in diplomacy, the momentum of the Cold War era carried into a new and quite different era, hampering the United States in fighting the wars it actually needed to fight and impairing its ability to achieve its principal diplomatic and economic objectives in Asia.

The next chapter elaborates by country and subregion the trends that are creating this new structure. In the process, it will clarify some items in Figure 2 that might appear controversial. Chapter Nine will present scenarios to explore possible outcomes of these architectural changes.

CHAPTER THREE

Regional Trends

Today that instinctive belief that the West is in a sense almost definitely superior in every sense is disappearing. The global imagination is changing, and because the global imagination is changing,
as India or other Asian powers emerge today, the impulse to join
the West will be less. That indeed in some ways each will discover
their own identities even more. But what I find surprising is how
few people in the West have noticed that this is happening.

—*Kishore Mahbubani*[1]

Asia's most important regional political trend has been rising nationalism, and its most important economic trend has been the emergence
since the 1990s of a new phase of the Asian miracle. Both of these
trends are fundamentally reshaping Asian geopolitics.

Outbreaks of Nationalism

Across the region, a combination of nationalism, nationalist outbursts,
and assertions of national identity has been occurring in ways that
could potentially change the structure of Asian international politics.

---

[1] Kishore Mahbubani, "Will India Emerge as an Eastern or Western Power?" Annual Lecture, Center for the Advanced Study of India, University of Pennsylvania, Philadelphia,
PA, November 9, 2006, published as Occasional Paper Number 27, January 2007 (http://
casi.ssc.upenn.edu/research/papers/Mahbubani_2007.pdf). Mahbubani, now dean of the
School of Public Policy at National University of Singapore, was Singapore's Ambassador to
the United Nations and is that country's most prolific foreign-policy commentator.

China, Japan, Korea, Taiwan, India, and the United States have all become more nationalistic and assertive in the recent past. One could debate whether the overall level of nationalism is higher, but the overall level, by whatever measure, is less important than the potential transformation of Asian politics. The Taiwan government's deliberate fostering of local nationalism under Lee Teng-hui, through such measures as substituting nationalistic Taiwan history courses for Chinese history courses, and the overt thrust toward independence under Chen Shui-bian had the potential to create a regional maelstrom. The rise of Sino-Japanese tension in the Koizumi era carried the risk that the region would increasingly polarize around a revival of the Sino-Japanese conflict of the first half of the 20th century. North Korea's drive for nuclear weapons and international recognition, together with South Korea's revival of an active pan-Korean identity, raised the risk of military conflict on the peninsula that had been the stomping ground of the Sino-Japanese war, the Russo-Japanese war, and the Korean War. Indian assertiveness resulted not so much from a surge of nationalistic feeling as from a surge of resources, caused by faster economic growth, enabling it to do something about its old ambitions. Much of what changed was the context: U.S. nationalism, expressed in the triumphalism of being the world's leading economic, military, and cultural power, as well as by the ideological determination to transform the world starting with Iraq and the Middle East and to forcefully prevent the rise of any peer competitor, changed the context in which other countries expressed their identities.

Multiple causes are enhancing nationalistic expression. New generations are leading several of the Asian countries, most notably South Korea, and they possess neither the old Cold War fears of the Soviet Union nor old loyalties from the Korean War and other regional conflicts. Both the new and old leaderships of Korea disagreed strongly with U.S. policies toward North Korea under George W. Bush, and they no longer felt constrained by Cold War anxieties in expressing what they saw as overriding national interests. In the 1990s, the fierce sense of common Korean national identity that often threatened to destabilize Korean politics in the 1960s and 1970s had gone dormant. Prodded by the renewed crisis over North Korean nuclear weapons and encouraged by a new administration that was less willing to accept U.S. policies, pan-Korean nationalism in South Korea awoke with great vigor.

Japan's long financial crisis, in 1990–2002, created a sense that old policies had failed and old leaders were weak. The political right in Japan had the only strong policy response to the domestic financial crisis, the only leaders who were articulating a fundamentally new foreign policy (rearming and standing up to China), and the only leader (Koizumi) who combined personal courage, reformist policies, and political support. Koizumi's successor, Shinzo Abe, and his foreign minister, Taro Aso, both come from a right wing that believes Japan's post–World War II leadership and posture betrayed the national heritage, which must be restored by asserting a revisionist view of Japanese history, enforcing patriotism in the schools, and honoring patriotic symbols like the Yasukuni Shrine. Aso said that it is not necessary for the visits to the Yasukuni Shrine to stop because of foreign criticism; he called for the emperor to start visiting the Yasukuni Shrine; and he specifically praised the Yushukan museum of the Yasukuni Shrine, which portrays a heroic view of the Japanese invasion of China and of World War II as a liberation of Asia. The exhibits in the shrine state, among many other things, that Japan had to fight World War II because U.S. President Franklin D. Roosevelt had a grand scheme to destroy Japan, that it entered (not invaded) China to suppress anti-Japanese forces and to liberate China from Anglo-Saxon oppression, that Japan did China a great favor by driving Russian forces out of China, that the 14 first-class war criminals convicted in the Tokyo trials were "heroic Japanese leaders," and that Japan's conquest of Korea at the beginning of the 20th century occurred at the request of Korean patriots to liberate Korea from Chinese oppression.[2] It even states that Mahatma Gandhi's emergence was a response to the Japanese liberation of Asia. Abe, the succeeding prime minister, cast doubt on the validity of the Tokyo War Crimes Tribunal and wishes to recast Japan's wartime history in a posi-

---

[2] Although I have visited the Yasukuni Shrine, the visit was some time ago and I did not take notes. Therefore, this list is adapted, with permission, from the private communication of a summary prepared by a Brookings Institution scholar, Jing Huang, during a long visit to the Yushukan in 2006.

tive light.[3] Shortly before taking office, he let it be known that because he had such a strong nationalist record, including many visits to the Yasukuni Shrine, he could forgo such visits while prime minister, but this position was based on affirmation of the right-wing values embodied in visits to the shrine, not in repudiation of them.[4] Abe's administration followed through by enacting a law that requires teaching to be "patriotic," attempting to deny the Japanese government's World War II role in coercing thousands of local women to serve as "comfort women" for Japanese soldiers,[5] and beginning to suppress mention in history texts of the military order to civilians on Okinawa to commit suicide before the U.S. invasion.

It was no coincidence that the Yushukan museum was upgraded from a shabby collection to a first-class museum in 2002. The endorsement of such views by some of Japan's most powerful political leaders, and specifically by the foreign minister, is not a minor historical footnote; it is a major development, the resurfacing of an important but heretofore largely invisible (to foreigners) force in Japan's domestic and foreign politics. This is doubly important because the desire of U.S. national-security leaders to push Japan into rearmament and a much wider-ranging alliance security role has effectively allied the United States, wittingly or unwittingly, with this resurgent tendency in Japanese politics.

---

[3] See Yoshisuke Iinuma, "After Koizumi," *Oriental Economist*, Vol. 74, No. 1, January 2006, p. 11.

[4] In response to criticism, the Yasukuni Shrine's museum made minor modifications of its assertions, under the guidance of Hisahiko Okazaki, one of Japan's most distinguished right-wing diplomats. Okazaki changed the assertion that Roosevelt provoked Pearl Harbor in order to lift the United States out of recession to an assertion that he deliberately provoked Pearl Harbor for strategic and ideological reasons. Okazaki reinforced the assertion that full-scale Japan-China warfare was the consequence of Chinese provocation, and he decided to retain the shrine's original mischaracterization of the Nanjing massacre. Okazaki acted in an "unofficial" capacity, just as Prime Minister Koizumi visited the shrine only in an "unofficial" capacity. See Hisahiko Okazaki, "Telling the Truth at Yasukuni," *Japan Times*, February 24, 2007.

[5] Abe's efforts regarding the comfort women stirred a vigorous reaction in Washington. The best scholarly account is probably Mindy Kotler, "Protecting the Human Rights of Comfort Women," testimony before the Subcommittee on Asia, the Pacific and the Global Environment of the House International Relations Committee, February 15, 2007.

Unlike the Chinese public, the Japanese public has thus far leaned strongly against the trend to heavy-handed nationalism. The capture of Japan's leadership positions by a political leadership with strong right-wing views does not reflect a proportionate shift in public opinion. Public opinion does fear the rise of China, and it does react very negatively when the Chinese denounce Japanese actions or riot against them, but most of the public would not support confrontation with China and is unaware of Japanese actions (discussed in the next chapter) that much of the rest of Asia sees as confrontational. Japanese public opinion, which in the early postwar years was sharply polarized between a nationalist right and a socialist left, has become heavily centrist as a result of national prosperity and the collapse of international communism. The majority of the public thought Koizumi's visits to the Yasukuni Shrine were a bad idea. The most prominent Japanese business leaders, centered on the Keidanren business association, have also criticized the visits and the gratuitous hostility toward China.

But each time China reacts to a Yasukuni Shrine visit or a textbook revision, and particularly after anti-Japanese textbook riots in 2005, more of Japanese opinion shifts in the nationalistic, anti-Chinese direction. By 2005, the public was fairly evenly split about whether or not the anti-military clauses of Article 9 of the Japanese Constitution should be revised. Wittingly or not, rightist Japanese leaders have discovered a virtuous circle for themselves: Each time one of their actions provokes conflict with China and South Korea, they get more public support. Moreover, extreme views are beginning to penetrate popular culture; books portraying South Koreans and Chinese as cannibals and Chinese culture as based on a foundation of prostitution have recently been extraordinarily successful. So extreme are these highly popular publications that they would be considered intolerable in any other modern democracy.[6] Some observers would like to attribute such

---

[6] I am indebted to a not-yet-published article by my RAND colleague Eric Heginbotham for documentation of the extraordinary popular success of this hate literature in Japan. For an example, see the work of Bunyu Ko—a comic book, but representative of the literature—described as follows in the leading U.S. journal of education:

"Bunyu Ko's comic book Introduction to China is not for the fainthearted. In 300 graphic pages, it claims that the Chinese are incapable of democracy, prac-

developments in public opinion entirely to hostile Chinese actions, but the fact that the trends regarding Korea are exactly parallel belies such a view.

Taiwan's past two leaders, Presidents Lee Teng-hui and Chen Shui-bian, have been assertive nationalists pushing the island in the direction of independence. This push started with Lee's abolition of most teaching of Chinese history in favor of a nationalistic version of Taiwanese history and led to the point where Chen now repeatedly declares that Taiwan is already independent and sovereign. Those policies have evoked an enormous outpouring of nationalist emotion on China's mainland and have induced large increases in China's military budget. Combined with the steady strengthening of the U.S.-Japan alliance, some U.S. military leaders' emphasis on China as a target of that alliance, and the February 2005 "2+2" declaration of the alliance's interest in Taiwan, this has mobilized popular and leadership nationalism in China. Analyses that attribute Chinese nationalism primarily to leadership attempts to divert attention from domestic problems are wrong on two counts. First, hundreds of discussions convince me that there is more nationalism from below than from above. Chinese leaders fear the fervor of student nationalism, and young Chinese criticize their leaders for insufficient national assertiveness. Second, as one travels around China, the predominant opinion one hears is that China's leaders are doing their best, and doing well, under rather difficult circumstances. Even academics, usually hostile to the government in all developing countries, give the Chinese government far more credit than their South Korean counterparts have ever given their government. Certainly, Chinese leaders do promote nationalism, but not out of a need for diversion; the need for diversion is minimal, and the need to keep up with the nationalism of youth is great.

---

tice cannibalism, and have the world's leading sex economy. In one sequence, famous political figures say the country is the source of most of Asia's contagious diseases. In another, illustrated with naked, spread-eagled women, China is said to have exported 600,000 'AIDS-infested' prostitutes." (David McNeill, "Japan's History War," *The Chronicle of Higher Education*, April 27, 2007.)

India has always been nationalistic and assertive. India marched into Goa and seized it, refused to compromise with Pakistan over Kashmir, acted decisively to split Bangladesh from Pakistan, and both ignited civil war in Sri Lanka and later sent an expeditionary force (unsuccessfully) to quell that civil war. Gunfire occurs daily across the India-Bangladesh border. What has changed for India is that rapid economic growth has given it the resources and confidence to assert its nationalistic impulses in ways that were once beyond its means. Everywhere in India, one hears a sense of emergent national destiny, cocktail talk of dominating Asia, and leadership demands that other countries acknowledge India as a great power.

The epiphenomena of this rising nationalism are everywhere—Chinese naval intrusions into Japanese waters, Chinese drilling for gas on the edge of disputed seabed territory, Japanese leaders' visits to the Yasukuni Shrine, approval of chauvinist Japanese textbooks, Japanese-Korean naval mobilization over conflicting claims of sovereignty over an island (Tokdo/Takeshima), and wild, outraged South Korean and Chinese protests against Japanese actions. South Korean protests over approval of a revisionist Japanese history text in 2005 included demonstrators chopping off fingers in front of the Japanese embassy in Seoul. But they are just that—epiphenomena. These kinds of problems have festered for half a century, occasionally bubbling up but never cumulating into major international problems.

Above all, the United States has become more nationalistic, adopting a turn-of-the-century rhetoric of triumphalism, a national-security doctrine that explicitly rules out allowing the emergence of any peer competitor, a revolutionary posture in the Middle East, new national priorities focused less on economics and more on military strength, and greater pressures on Japan to become a militarily supportive Asian analogue of Britain. In its search for incremental military advantage against China, the U.S. posture has shifted from a half-century of reassuring both Japan and China, albeit in radically different ways, to one that has polarized them. Most of this was happening before 9/11. All of it was magnified by 9/11. U.S. Middle East policies, in turn, inspired nationalistic reactions in Indonesia and Malaysia.

In short, the U.S. push for a broader and more assertive Japanese military posture, Koizumi's anti-China thrust, Japanese-American inclusion of Taiwan as an object of alliance interest, Chen's assertions of Taiwanese sovereignty, and Chinese paranoia about Taiwan and Tokyo have all combined into what threatens to become a regional vicious circle of nationalism.

This circle contains many nuances, however. In Taiwan, the nationalistic administration of Chen Shui-bian had reached an advanced state of political disintegration by 2006, with Chen having become (in domestic polls) one of the world's most unpopular leaders; the centrist Taiwanese distaste for provoking China was reasserting itself. In parallel with this, the Bush administration, which in its early days had emphasized doing "whatever it takes" to defend Taiwan and appointed a key official who explicitly promoted Taiwanese independence, became exasperated at Chen's constant roiling of relations with China. With cross-strait relations in a war fever, the Bush administration changed key staff and President Bush even stood on the steps of the White House with Chinese Premier Wen Jiabao and warned Taipei against further efforts to change the status quo. On the mainland, more-nuanced policies, including economic carrots and invitations to opposition leaders to visit Beijing and address the Chinese people while excluding the missile-throwing excesses of 1996 and the rhetorical overkill of 2000, began to calm tensions.

In Japan, a reaction against Koizumi's antagonizing of most of Japan's neighbors led the nationalist Abe to make a successful visit to Beijing immediately after he became prime minister. The Chinese welcomed the relaxation of tensions despite Abe's continued pursuit of tough policies. (Wen Jiabao subsequently visited Tokyo and made an enormously conciliatory speech that had a very favorable impact on the Japanese public. A few days later, Abe made a gift of a plant to the Yasukuni Shrine. Nothing substantial changed in Japanese policy, but China decided to ignore the rightist symbolism and emphasize conciliation.) South Korea, on the other hand, reacted very strongly against Abe's visit, and Japan refused to participate in a preliminary U.S.-China-Russia deal with North Korea, reached in February 2007, to freeze some nuclear programs in return for economic concessions.

In Washington, the trends were more mixed; in the congressional elections of November 2006, the revolutionary nationalism of the right-wing Republicans suffered a massive loss of public support in the wake of increasing problems in Iraq and Afghanistan, but protectionist elements among the Democrats promoted an anti-China agenda that had the potential to create even more nationalistic tensions across the Pacific than had occurred under the Republicans.

Beyond individual nationalisms, Asia in the new century saw a new assertion, expressed in multifarious, often subtle, but determined ways, that the long era of European domination, and specifically U.S. domination, of world culture and economics and politics would be challenged and incrementally rolled back. This is the trend that Kishore Mahbubani refers to in the quotation that begins this chapter. Japanese leaders are seeking to rebuild a national identity based on a reinterpretation of World War II that is anathema to the United States. The current South Korean government has opposed American demands for the right to use U.S. forces in Korea for operations elsewhere in Asia and at one point formally requested that Japan be formally labeled a potential enemy of the U.S.–South Korean alliance—just when the United States is betting its whole regional posture on the relationship with Japan. Meanwhile, top officials of older Korean governments give speeches saying they are glad the era of U.S. hegemony is over.

Chinese, Southeast Asians, and Indians are forming balances that allow them to use the United States when it is convenient and ignore it when it is inconvenient. Throughout Asia, there is a strong rejection of the American ideological thrust, expressed in the Bush administration's effort to democratize the Middle East by force, beginning in Iraq, and to promote its ideas of government everywhere as expressed in President Bush's 2005 inaugural address. From South Korea to Australia, polls show that a majority of local people trust China more than they trust the United States. In 2001, the center of gravity of thought in the new administration in Washington was best expressed by the title of Francis Fukuyama's book *The End of History*[7] and the Pentagon's subsequent published determination never to allow a "peer competitor" to arise. By 2006, there was a consensus in Asia and among even lifelong advocates of U.S. policy, including Michael Armacost (quoted at the beginning of Chapter Eight), that U.S. influence was declining and, more strongly among Asians, that its dominance was waning permanently. In Japan, Korea, China, Southeast Asia, India, and Iran, there was more of a sense of the beginning of history, the beginning of an era when U.S. and European views will have to stand in line along with those of other great civilizations and compete on a more equal basis. Regional organizations such as the East Asia Summit and the Shanghai Cooperation Organization (SCO) arose to institutionalize such views. While Japan competed vigorously with China for leadership of new regional organizations such as the East Asia Summit, it cooperated enthusiastically in setting up organizations that excluded the United States.

The drain of the Iraq and Afghan wars on U.S. energies accelerated the emergence of these new attitudes and new regional structures. But that emergence was happening anyway, driven by the revival of other great civilizations (Confucian, Indian, Persian), the decline of the dependence on America previously necessitated by the common Soviet threat, and reaction against U.S. policies that shifted priorities away from economic development and regional institution-building to an overriding emphasis on military dominance and bilateral alliance with an increasingly isolated Japan.

---

[7] Francis Fukuyama, *The End of History and the Last Man*, New York: Free Press, 1992. Fukuyama's argument was that representative democracy and market capitalism have defeated alternative ideologies. Some part of that thesis may well stand the test of time; even Chinese leaders are inching closer to acceptance of large parts of it. Conservatives and many others in Washington in 2001–2002 also believed U.S. global dominance was likely to endure, and many believed that U.S. power was so great that it could downplay much of the global (e.g., United Nations) and regional (e.g., Asia-Pacific Economic Cooperation (APEC)) institution-building characteristic of previous postwar U.S. administrations and could rely primarily on unilateral decisions and coalitions of the willing. That view lost credibility within five years.

The New Phase of the Asian Economic Miracle

The first phase of the Asian economic miracle was based on a Japanese-model mobilization system. That system of governmental mobilization of resources for development had its roots in Japan's preparations for World War II, when the key to potential victory was effective government control of the financial and economic resources needed for prosecuting the war. The mobilization system the Japanese created at that time, labeled the 1940 System, emphasized highly centralized control of finance and heavy industry.[8] The system gave priority to bank loans rather than capital markets as a means of finance, because the government could exert more influence over banks than it could over capital markets. The Japanese government discouraged foreign equity investment, because such investment would get in the way of government management and anyway ran counter to the nationalistic impulses that underlay the whole mobilization system. Companies viewed as crucial to the war effort, or subsequently, to postwar reconstruction, received preferential access to finance. A "main bank" system, in turn, put each of the large conglomerates under the financial influence of a single main bank and saddled that bank with considerable obligation to support each principal business unit of the conglomerate. As part of a "convoy system," large conglomerates ensured that each company within the group would be protected by the others; the original virtue of that system was that no critical component of the war effort could ever face bankruptcy. The mobilization system curtailed shareholder rights in order to facilitate government guidance of the major firms. Through administrative guidance, the government could set direction for the large conglomerates. Through total control of half of postwar government finances, which were formally off-budget and therefore not subject to the scrutiny of elected officials, the bureaucracy played the dominant role in government economic decisions.

---

[8] On the 1940 System and its development, see Tetsuji Okazaki and Masahiro Okuno-Fujiwara (eds.), *The Japanese Economic System and Its Historical Origins*, translated by Susan Herbert, New York: Oxford University Press, 1993. On its later evolution into the Japanese crisis of 1990–2002, see William H. Overholt, "Japan's Economy: At War with Itself," *Foreign Affairs*, January–February 2002.

Most other Asian-miracle economies copied major features of the mobilization system. This having been said, there were also wide variations: For instance, Taiwan allowed more foreign direct investment than Japan did—indeed, encouraged it—but the government owned the banks, the ruling party owned many of the major companies, and the government control of the banks ensured that favored companies and sectors would be treated well.

This system worked quite well for wartime mobilization, and it worked quite well for the era of Japanese postwar reconstruction and South Korean/Thai/Indonesian initiation of rapid growth. This was a period of capital shortage, relatively simple growth issues, and political instability. In the mobilization model, governments funneled capital into companies and projects, and they were able to make reasonably efficient choices because the technologies and management problems were fairly simple. They avoided making wasteful political patronage choices because they were frightened—of the Soviet Union, of North Korea, of an ideologically predatory China, and of their own weakness. Moreover, in an age of regional political instability, Japan and South Korea, the most successful mobilization systems, had the advantage of being relatively homogeneous societies that were easier to govern.

However, by 1990, the policies that had facilitated the early miracle were becoming caricatures. Favored sectors developed elephantiasis, with, for example, more money being poured into construction in Japan than in the entire United States. Choices became complex, and political patronage almost completely displaced considerations of economic efficiency. Government programs like the fifth-generation computer (artificial intelligence) consistently failed. Japan's politics became organized around Liberal Democratic Party (LDP) "tribes" in the legislature that fed off the favored sectors and were, in effect, wholly owned subsidiaries of those sectors. Cheap capital flooding into the property and stock markets produced the largest financial bubbles in world history. Main banks and convoy systems and government aid propped up whole sections of the economy that were obsolete and bankrupt, and government propping up of both the banks and key companies (even retail firms such as Daiei) became a key reason why Japanese government debt became proportionately the largest in the developed world.

Stimulating a post-bubble economy to avoid collapse became an even bigger reason.

Japan and Taiwan suffered bubble collapses in 1990. The principal emulators of the Japanese system, most notably Thailand, South Korea, and Indonesia, suffered parallel bubble bursts in 1997–1998, and all the other open economies of the region suffered as well. Thailand, South Korea, and Indonesia appeared different, because in Japan and Taiwan, the borrowed, wasted money was in local currency, whereas the Thais, Koreans, and Indonesians borrowed and wasted foreign currencies and therefore had mislabeled "currency crises" when the bubbles collapsed. But the great crises of the 1990s occurred in economies with similar structural features. Eventually, political channeling of funds leads to bubbles, and eventually bubbles collapse. The great Thai stock- and property-market collapse of July 1997 resulted from the same kinds of policy-induced bubbles as the great Japanese and Taiwanese stock- and property-market collapses of 1990.

In addition to deriving from common structural features of the mobilization system, the Asian crises were somewhat exacerbated and moved closer together for a common reason. Under the Basel Accord, banks are prohibited from doing international business unless they maintain capital equal to 8 percent of their assets (loans). The cascading domestic crisis of the Japanese banks drastically depleted their capital. As a result, they had to drastically reduce their loans. Many of the less creditworthy and less strategically important outstanding loans were loans to Asian companies and governments. Thus the domestic crisis of the Japanese banks led them to withdraw substantial funds from neighboring countries in 1997–1998. Until key governments release statistics that are currently kept secret, we will not know the relative contributions of local vulnerabilities and Japanese banking withdrawals. We do know that Japanese banks dominated Asian lending in the 1980s and 1990s and they drastically decreased their Asian assets, which declined by $212 billion, from a peak of $367 billion in June 1995 to $155 billion by the end of 1998, then continued to decline rapidly in subsequent years. According to the annual reports of the Hong Kong Monetary Authority, Japanese capital evacuation from Hong Kong in 1997–1998 amounted to 150 percent of GDP. Even if half of this comprised loans to Japanese rather than local companies, the shock to the countries involved was severe. Asian countries have always experienced sporadic bubbles, and those bubbles eventually collapse, but the interaction between the local bubbles and the Japanese banking contraction made the collapses worse and made them coincide far more than usual.[9] In short, the scope and intensity of the Asian crisis were epiphenomena of Japan's domestic financial crisis, and the Asian crisis of 1997–1998 was just a continuation of the Japan-Taiwan crisis of 1990.

After the bubbles collapsed, the wartime mobilization and recovery model was obsolete. Japanese dominance of the regional banking system was over; according to the authoritative Bank for International Settlements, Japanese banks' Asian assets had declined to a low of $77 billion by June 2003. These cold numbers bespoke both a Japanese and a regional financial calamity. In the future, the winners would be economies that encouraged foreign investment, globalized their economic regulations, emphasized competition, and encouraged entrepreneurship. In this new era, the mobilization economies and relatively homogeneous, inward-looking societies of Japan and South Korea had relative disadvantages, while more-diverse, open, competitive, globalized, and entrepreneurial economies had a special advantage. Since geopolitical influence derives very heavily from relative economic performance, it is important to understand the competitive positions of the various actors in the new Asian economy.

Now the *social* advantages accrued to diverse economies with global diasporas, most notably China, India, the United States, and Indonesia. Indonesia remained somewhat hampered by its failure to completely solve the Phase One problem of political stability. Japan and South Korea are now disadvantaged by their homogeneity.

---

[9] Singapore's situation was similar, according to a speech made by a minister at that time, but the minister was reprimanded, and Singapore did not publish the numbers. The Singapore government and other governments have refused scholars' requests to make available the loan numbers. Thailand's financial collapse in July 1997 resulted from withdrawal of foreign bank loans, and the overwhelming bulk of Thailand's bank loans were from Japanese commercial banks; foreign investment in the stock market kept rising until October of that year.

The *policy* advantages accrued to highly open, entrepreneurial economies that emphasized competition. These included the smaller ethnic Chinese economies (Hong Kong, Taiwan, Singapore), the United States, and (after the turn of the century) China. With a lag, India began emulating China's economic opening and began to enjoy the fruits of an Asian miracle–style takeoff, although it was potentially hampered, as we shall see later, by failure to provide the kinds of education and infrastructure that sustained the successes of the United States and China.

It was startling how quickly the more-diverse, open societies associated with China gained competitiveness and displaced the old stars, Japan and South Korea. The following list showing the competitive ranking of the economies in Asia was derived from a systematic 2007 study by a Swiss firm, IMD,[10] which cannot be accused of bias on this issue:

- United States (1)
- Singapore (2)
- Hong Kong (3)
- China (15)
- Taiwan (18)
- Malaysia (23)
- Japan (24)
- India (27)
- Korea (29)
- Thailand (33)
- Philippines (45)
- Indonesia (54).

As many in Washington often forget in their fear of China, the United States remains the most competitive; but among the Asian actors, China and the ethnic Chinese communities cluster at the top. Notably, the Malaysian economy is also dominated by its large Chinese

---

[10] *IMD World Competitiveness Yearbook 2007* (http://www.imd.ch/research/publications/wcy/index.cfm).

minority. Through 1992, Japan was always ranked first. From 1993 onward, the United States has always been first. In 1994, IMD ranked Japan third and China 34th.

Hong Kong became the headquarters of a global manufacturing, services, and trading empire, while the more-managed economy of Singapore remained a much more limited island economy—albeit a spectacularly successful island economy. Shanghai, which moved more decisively toward competition and openness than Hong Kong, threatened to displace Hong Kong in many respects and rapidly became the regional headquarters of a range of Fortune 500 companies.[11]

The experiences of South Korea and Taiwan in the new phase of the Asian economic miracle were more complex. South Korea had followed Japan more closely than any other country and as a consequence was least ready for the new era. But it reformed more decisively than Japan, which, for instance, failed to create the kind of modern, internationally competitive banking system that one would expect of a first-world economy. But South Korea was severely disadvantaged relative to much of the rest of the region and retains a reputation for coolness toward foreign investors and for inward-looking policies. As in Japan, South Korea's most competitive firms (e.g., Samsung, Hyundai) have become even more competitive, but the overall economy has lost its "miracle" qualities.

Taiwan, on the other hand, had evolved by the 1980s into a far more diverse, open, market-oriented economy than either South Korea or its own economy of earlier decades. The old economy, dominated by large, Guomindang-connected enterprises much like the mainland's state enterprises and by state-contolled banks, had given way to an entrepreneurial economy based on numerous private, mostly indige-

---

[11] In brief, Shanghai introduced a competition policy, while Hong Kong determinedly defended its oligopolies; Shanghai encouraged a proliferation of foreign schools, while Hong Kong severely limited foreign schools; and Shanghai moved to much more market-oriented property and medical systems than Hong Kong did. On the competition between Hong Kong and Shanghai, see William H. Overholt, "Hong Kong or Shanghai?" *China Business Review*, Spring 2004. On Hong Kong's economic success, see William H. Overholt, "A Decade Later: Hong Kong's Economy Since 1997," *Hong Kong Journal*, Vol. 3, July 2007. As of July 27, 2007: http://www.hkjournal.org/archive/2007_fall/4.htm.

nous Taiwanese firms whose process engineering in several sectors had become superior to that of any other country[12] and whose extraordinary manufacturing prowess was disguised by the fact that their products were increasingly exported primarily from the mainland. Importantly, the Taiwan economy, like its sister economies in Hong Kong, Singapore, and the mainland, is extremely open to foreign investment. Despite these advantages, Taiwan's progress has been hindered by the policies of the major political parties. The governing DPP under President Chen Shui-bian and his predecessor limited investment in the mainland. The government pursued radically contradictory policies, advocating that Taipei should become a regional economic hub but limiting access to mainland China, which was the main supplier, export platform, and customer of the firms that Taipei wanted to build its hub role around. Meanwhile, the opposition Guomindang dragged its feet on much-needed economic reforms that would have reduced its ability as a political party to be a major economic actor. As a consequence, beginning in 2005, South Korea's per capita income exceeded Taiwan's.

Whereas the Asian economic miracle, from 1955–1990, arose as an offshoot of Japan's protected wartime mobilization model, the new era of the Asian economic miracle is one of globalized entrepreneurial dynamism in China, Hong Kong, Taiwan, Singapore, the overseas Chinese communities of Southeast Asia, and India.

Japan's effort to adapt to this new era was half-hearted. Its banks remained insular and globally uncompetitive. Many of its major firms continued to practice lifetime employment and to have salaries determined by seniority. Remarkably few global firms found Tokyo a satisfactory place in which to site a regional headquarters—in sharp contrast to New York and London. Prime Minister Koizumi, to his

---

[12] Taiwan's superior process engineering in a wide variety of electronics industries and a number of more-traditional industries is widely acknowledged. The United States and Europe, and even Japan's electronics giants, have largely ceded this area to superior Taiwanese management and engineering efficiency. In areas outside Taiwan's specialties, such as petrochemicals, Japanese process engineering remains the world leader. (I am indebted to the work of Lily Wu, an independent consultant who was once Asia's top-ranked investment bank electronics analyst, on these matters.)

credit, enacted the economic reforms necessary to save the economy from financial meltdown and depression in the wake of the crisis of the 1990s, and he began political reforms designed to shake up the corrupt LDP patronage system. With crisis averted, however, his successor, Abe, showed little interest in vigorous economic reform and quickly reversed Koizumi's historic decision to expel from the LDP numerous key figures who opposed his most vital economic reform, the privatization of the Postal Savings Bank.

China's position in the new era remains somewhat ambivalent. By opening its economy widely to foreign investment and foreign trade, in sharp contrast to Japan, it has led the new era and reaped the advantages. It avoided having an economic crisis like those of Japan and Taiwan through heroic reforms undertaken by Premier Zhu Rongji in the decade prior to 2002. Zhu reformed banks, drastically curtailed the state enterprises, bankrupted prestigious companies such as GITIC, slashed government employment and government regulations, and in general put the whole economy on much more of a market basis. In doing so, he preempted the crisis of the mobilization economy, whereas South Korea and Thailand did those things only after a crisis had occurred. Heroic as Zhu's reforms were, however, the Chinese economy could not be completely moved into the modern era in such a short time. For a decade, it has had the best of its modern, market-oriented side and has avoided the worst of its old mobilization-economy side. But by 2003, the Chinese people were stressed and tired of Zhu's reforms, which, among other things, cost 50,000,000 state enterprise jobs and 25,000,000 manufacturing jobs. The new leaders who took office in 2003 let the banks expand loans out of control and by 2007 were facing the risk of bubbles in the stock market and elsewhere that, if not addressed decisively, could threaten China with an eventual crisis. It is too soon to tell whether the new leaders will act as decisively as their predecessors.

Along with China, the other big winner in the new phase was the United States. From an economy that the Japanese, with substantial reason, treated with contempt in the 1980s, a polity where the Republicans cut taxes and the Democrats increased spending with seeming disregard for the vast deficits that ensued, and a social atmosphere of increasing paranoia that the country was about to be subordinated by ten-feet-tall Japanese, the United States rebounded and became the leader in technological progress, entrepreneurial innovation, productivity growth, and financial efficiency.

As with China, a question hangs over the future of the U.S. triumph. At the moment of its greatest success, it lay on the cusp of a return to financial profligacy, a determination to blame self-inflicted wounds like the huge current account deficits on the Chinese, a reaction against the globalization that was the fount of American success, and a shift in national-security policies that seemed to be draining resources without achieving proportionate victories. It is too early to tell whether the next administration will create a gratuitous crisis of globalization and China relations that would be far more consequential than the current administration's unnecessarily severe quandary in Iraq.

The Geopolitics of the New Geoeconomics

As had happened in Japan, China's rise to geopolitical eminence occurred as a result of economic prowess that long predated any military prowess. By 2000, even though China still had negligible ability to project military power abroad, it was already viewed by Europe, Japan, and the United States as one of the world's major players. Japan possessed formidable naval vessels that would be deployed to the Indian Ocean to help the United States in its war in Afghanistan. Russia, despite all its weaknesses, had a military that could threaten many of its neighbors and a nuclear arsenal on the same order of magnitude as that of the United States. Even India and South Korea had forces that could pack considerable punch away from their own shores. In contrast, China had formidable forces for defending its own territory, but it lacked power-projection capability. Like Japan in its era of miracle growth, though, China's burgeoning economy and decisive leaders commanded global geopolitical respect and influence. (Like Japan, it also stimulated a good bit of paranoid fear in the United States.)

Of course, within military establishments, a great deal of the respect for China derived from forecasts of the military power China might possibly attain in the future. But that was not the primary source of respect from, for instance, European or Japanese or Southeast Asian political leaders.

The other key political dynamic of the earlier Asian economic miracle was the changing focus from international territorial disputes and ideological divisions to domestic economic development. The trends here were mixed.

The post–Cold War era did see strong continuation of the trend toward de-emphasis of international territorial and geopolitical conflicts. In Southeast Asia, these remained muted among traditional U.S. allies, while the principal villain of earlier efforts at regional domination, Vietnam, got the message and began to focus on domestic economic development. Had it not learned this lesson and changed its focus after two generations of warfare, Vietnam would probably have ended up as the North Korea of Southeast Asia, dwarfed by Thailand. But it became one of the world's fastest-growing economies, following the path of the earlier Asian-miracle economies. In contrast, Indonesia and Thailand, formerly the undisputed leaders of Southeast Asia, continued to flounder in the wake of their 1997–1998 crisis. Southeast Asia may be poised for one of the great ironies of history. Vietnam's expansion triggered the urgent efforts of its neighbors to modernize their economies and the vast Vietnam-era U.S. expenditures that financed the infrastructure of the Asian miracle in the 1960s and 1970s, thereby consolidating the non-communist countries of Asia and limiting the spread of communism. But Vietnam's conversion to the tenets of the Asian miracle could end up making it the leader of Southeast Asia if its politics evolve along with its economy.

Likewise, China persisted in its policies of promoting stability rather than instability among its neighbors, thereby gaining influence. As part of this continuing process, China finished settling all of its main border disputes, except those with India and Bhutan, to the satisfaction of the other parties. Relations with India, in turn, achieved a tremendous improvement, and amicable border talks are under way. The resolution of China's land territorial disputes with Russia was particularly noteworthy. China's power was rising, Russia's was declining; the disputed area of Russia was depopulating, and China faced severe population pressures; but China simply renounced its claims.

The newest development was the emergence of signs that India might join this trend. Through the early part of the 21st century, South Asia's international relations have been like Southeast Asia's in the 1950s and 1960s. Unlike China, which has put a premium on stability and friendly relations with neighbors since shortly after reform began in 1979, India has been slow to moderate its interventions and border disputes with its neighbors or to tone down its avowed goal to become a great power. But the trends that earlier moderated Southeast Asian, Korean, and Chinese politics have now also begun to appear in some Indian foreign policies. Relations with Pakistan, on the verge of nuclear warfare as recently as 2002, have improved in tone, and the two sides have opened some formerly blocked transportation routes in Kashmir. India is no longer either fomenting civil war in Sri Lanka or intervening militarily to quell the war its agents once encouraged.[13] It remains unclear whether India will proceed to actual compromises or whether its great-power ambitions will overwhelm its incentives to focus on growth. More on this in Chapter Six.

Thus the geopolitical moderation encouraged by the Asian miracle has continued and expanded. Land boundaries, ideological differences, and aspirations to regional hegemony are far less important sources of conflict than they were 10 or 20 or 50 years ago. The rise of new Asian powers has reduced conflicts, not increased them.

It is worth reemphasizing the earlier point that the trend toward a priority for common economic progress rather than territorial conflict is not unique to Asia. The same realization of the destructive power of modern warfare and the benefits of cooperative, peaceful development has been the central dynamic of Franco-German relations and European development since World War II. France and Germany arrived at this conclusion, with U.S. encouragement, some years before the same

---

[13] I am indebted to an unpublished paper by RAND colleague Rollie Lal that underscores the change of mentality among India's leaders due to the new confidence in the benefits of economic development.

realization dawned in Asia, but it took two of history's bloodiest wars to convince the Europeans. This new dynamic creates a shift in world history that invalidates theories of international behavior that cite earlier German, Japanese, and U.S. experience as decisive evidence that emerging powers will always violently disrupt the existing international system. However, this auspicious progress is challenged by a number of new trends. First is the reemergence of Sino-Japanese rivalries after a half-century during which they were suppressed by the post–World War II U.S. policy of keeping Japan disarmed and protecting it against any Soviet or Chinese threats. This is particularly important because Japan was the principal example and principal advocate of a diplomacy based more on economic prowess and less on military might, so its change of course could conceivably affect the entire dynamic of the region.

Second, while land borders have become less disputatious, seabed and territorial-waters claims remain omnipresent and are becoming more salient because of rising concern about energy security. Five Southeast Asian countries and China have overlapping claims, many of which exceed what could reasonably be claimed under international law. Japan, Russia, Korea, China, and Taiwan have overlapping claims in Northeast Asia. There is no obvious division among good guys and bad guys regarding these claims. China's claims are, not surprisingly, the largest, because of China's size, but they are also based in part on contradictory use of the continental and archipelagic principles (under international law, claims should use one but not both) and in part on arguments of historical presence that have no force under international law. Taiwan matches China's huge claims. Japan bases its claims in part on the spoils of the war in which it colonized Korea and the war with China that led to its colonization of Taiwan. One Malaysian deputy prime minister was known for his nighttime helicopter flights to plant evidence of Malaysian occupation of key islands. Japan is piling concrete on bits of coral in order to buttress territorial claims, and the U.S. Armitage Report of 2000 urged Japan to be more assertive about such claims.

For years, such conflicts were managed in Southeast Asia primarily by a brilliant Indonesian team, which unfortunately was fired after

President Suharto fell. For decades, leaders did not address these conflicts with anything like the attention they devoted to land conflicts, because the importance of seabed and territorial-waters claims seemed much more theoretical. To take one example: In 1974, I requested an appointment with the U.S. Deputy Assistant Secretary of Defense handling Asian issues, Morton Abramowitz, presented him with a copy of a Chinese map showing territorial-waters claims stretching almost to the beaches of Malaysia, and requested research funds to analyze the implications of those claims. He replied, wryly, "Bill, there are a lot of interesting issues in Asia. Some of them are important. Come back when you've found an important one." With the emergence of new technologies, new maritime competitions, and new resource anxieties, my old issue has finally become important. However, at this time there is no concerted international effort to resolve the complex conflicting claims.

In connection with these claims and concerns over energy security, Japan, China, and India are all expanding their naval forces. All three are profoundly concerned about energy security, and all three have adopted a competitive view (not shared by the United States) that ownership of energy resources is crucial to energy security. That view has set off a competition over the location of pipelines and over acquisition of oil fields and oil companies. India's military plans explicitly include preparation for a possible naval war with China over resources. Since the disputed seabed is widely believed to contain substantial oil fields, the naval and energy competitions reinforce each other. Unlike the Southeast Asian countries and China, Japan has never been willing to compromise any of its territorial disputes (with Russia, South Korea, China, and Taiwan), and as naval/energy competition heats up, this becomes increasingly important.

Third, religious conflicts seem to be rising in key areas and interacting with the "war on terror." So far, these problems seem to be manageable in the countries that are experiencing rapid development, and the countries experiencing rapid development are the geopolitically consequential ones. Japan has no significant domestic religious or war-on-terror divisions. China has two that are emotive and consequential in human-rights terms—Tibet and the Uighur movement to create an East Turkestan state in Xinjiang Province—but these involve tiny populations and are unlikely to be ominous for China's future. In an era of fundamentalist Islamic violence and the emergence of a powerful, violent fundamentalist Hindu movement (RSS), India would seem to be at greater risk, but so far the occasional dangerous outbreak of communal rioting has been overshadowed by democratic engagement; Indian democracy has given all the major religious groups a sense of belonging, and now Indian economic development is increasing the stake of most major ethnic and religious groups in social stability.

Indonesia has more serious problems. It experienced an almost completely successful repression and remission of fundamentalist demands for an Islamic state during the years of rapid economic development under Suharto, then a partial relapse during the Asian crisis and its immediate aftermath, and it now seems to be heading back, albeit somewhat unsteadily, toward more economic growth and more-placid politics. Likewise, since the Asian crisis, Thailand has had an outbreak of Muslim separatism in its southern area near Malaysia, which the Thai government has mishandled, but it seems unlikely to endanger Thailand's economy or territorial integrity. Philippine democracy, unlike India's, has never given its Muslim population a sense that it has a vital stake in Philippine society; on the contrary, the Christian majority has consistently deprived much of the Muslim population of traditional lands and of needed infrastructure investment. The consequences are not revolutionary but are an incessant drain.

On the whole, the dominant trend in East, Southeast, and South Asia continues to be one where economic growth (and in India's case, democracy) increases religious groups' stakes in society and limits terrorism, rather than a trend toward ascendant religious and terrorist conflict. It would take catastrophic developments (which are quite possible) in Pakistan or Afghanistan or a developmental collapse in Indonesia (which is not likely) to engender a significant reversal of these trends.

Fourth, crucial changes in U.S. policies are affecting the prospects for continued progress toward placidity. In the Cold War era,

U.S. determination to never again allow Sino-Japanese competition to spiral out of control was the U.S. policy goal second only to defending the region against Soviet expansion.[14] The usual formulation for this was that the United States served as "the cork in the bottle," preventing any reemergence of Japanese aggression toward China, while promising absolute U.S. commitment to the defense of Japan against any threat from the Soviet Union or China. In other words, U.S. policy both protected China against Japan and protected Japan against China. The U.S. troop presence in Japan served to reassure the Japanese that the commitment to defend them was credible; it also reassured China that Japan would not be allowed to rearm and become aggressive again. The presence of U.S. troops in Japan attracted (privately stated) Chinese support for just that reason.

However, after the Cold War, beginning with U.S. criticism of Japan for offering only money, not troops, in support of the first Iraq war, the United States began to pressure Japan for actual military support. This pressure reached much higher levels during the later George W. Bush administration, and simultaneously, the United States increased emphasis on China as the target of the alliance and on the alliance's interest in Taiwan. The abandonment of the earlier goal was never explicit; it just seemed to be forgotten. Current U.S. policy ensures a gratuitous level of Sino-Japanese tension.

Another crucial change was equally important and equally implicit. Beginning in 2001, the U.S. strategy in the region shifted from economic development and institution-building protected by the military to a priority focus on military and geopolitical concerns. Regional institution-building was superseded by ad hoc coalitions of the willing that addressed each problem (North Korea, the tsunami, and so on) separately. This was in part a response to 9/11, but long before 9/11, it was the philosophy of the new foreign-policy team, in which even the secretary and deputy secretary of state were career-long

---

[14] This was seldom explicitly articulated, but a determination to ensure that the rivalries that led to World War II would never be allowed to recur was the core of U.S. policy after the war. That was the main purpose of disarming Japan. When I participated in policy-oriented meetings in Washington as a Hudson Institute analyst in the 1970s, the determination to avoid a recurrence of Sino-Japanese rivalry was always at the forefront of consciousness.

military figures. As James Mann, the premier chronicler of the George W. Bush foreign-policy team, which he called the Vulcans, put it:

> The Vulcans were the military generation. Their wellspring, the common institution in their careers, was the Pentagon. The top levels of the foreign policy team that took office in 2001 included two former secretaries of defense (Cheney and Rumsfeld), one former undersecretary of defense (Wolfowitz) and one former assistant secretary of defense (Armitage). Even Rice had started her career in Washington with a stint at the Pentagon, working for the Joint Chiefs of Staff.
>
> In the 1940s the Wise Men had concentrated on constructing institutions, both international and in Washington, that would help preserve democracy and capitalism in a threatened Europe. The Vulcans were different. They were focused above all on American military power.[15]

In sum, Asia's half-century-long trend toward focusing on extraordinary economic development rather than geopolitical and ideological conflict as the path to wealth and power began with Truman Doctrine priorities for economic and institutional development and had its greatest model in a disarmed Japan. That path now has considerable momentum created by its own success. China got onto the path by copying its neighbors, not through U.S. pressure. India has taken its first, albeit tentative, steps along that path by emulating China. Conceivably, therefore, the changes in Japanese and U.S. policies will be of little consequence for the model, whose success derives from the rapidity of reformist development and the destructiveness of modern

---

[15] James Mann, *The Rise of the Vulcans*, New York: Viking Penguin, 2004, pp. xiii–xiv. The rest of the volume provides thorough documentation of its central theme, the shift to military priorities. In a later chapter, Mann emphasizes that the Vulcans included not a single one "whose career had been devoted primarily to diplomacy or to building international institutions. There was no one with the background of, say, Dean Acheson or Averell Harriman. . . . Even some of the internal differences within the team . . . were ultimately debates about the application of military power" (p. 274).

military technology, not from geopolitical pressures. But the changes create risks, and we cannot yet know the scale of those risks.

This description of the principal trends differs sharply from the standard scripts of the national-security establishments in each of the major powers. But it fits the facts better than the nationalistic scripts. If one looks at the more nationalistic parts of the national-security establishments of each country, one finds the following views—not primarily official in documents but pervasive in thought, conversation, and the rhetoric of their media supporters.

The Chinese national-security establishment's script has been that Taiwan's recent drive toward independence, supported by the United States, and Japan's resurgent militarism create a great threat to Chinese national security. Japan's rearmament, its government's approval of textbooks that gloss over the realities of Japan's aggression in World War II, and top leaders' visits to the Yasukuni Shrine and praise for a museum that glorifies Japan's wartime aggression as a liberation of Asia provide evidence for this script. Harboring residual sentiments left over from World War II, powerful elements of the Japanese right wing are determined to support Taiwanese independence and prolong Korean division. Much of this is true. But the overall script is weak. The United States has focused on peace in the Taiwan Strait and, while preparing to defend Taiwan if necessary, has sharply rebuked provocative moves toward independence. Japan's rearmament has been limited to 1 percent of GDP for defense. Shrill Chinese rhetoric and anti-Japanese riots have certainly caused part of Japan's rightward shift. The visits to the Yasukuni Shrine have had limited public and elite support other than a widespread public sentiment that Japanese leaders should not be seen as caving in to Chinese pressures.

The textbook issue deserves particular scrutiny on both sides. The offensive Japanese textbooks are used by a tiny number of schools, none of which are public schools except for a few for handicapped students, and only 0.4 percent of Japanese students use them. Chinese publications have disingenuously used the figure of 10 percent, but that is the stated aspiration of the publisher, not the reality of the schools. Since Chinese textbooks that gloss over the truth of China's participation in the Korean War and of the suffering and death caused to his fellow Chinese by Mao's policies are used by virtually all Chinese students of the period, Chinese leaders have no standing to criticize Japan's textbooks. The real history-teaching problem in Japan is quite different. Throughout the postwar period, most Japanese teachers have had strong antiwar views, but those who have sought to teach about the history of the war have been intimidated by right-wing groups, so most schools simply do not teach the history of the modern period, particularly the war. The result is a society relatively naïve about that part of the country's history and potentially vulnerable to manipulation; it is not unusual for decent, educated, middle-of-the-road Japanese people to believe that what happened in World War II was perfectly normal for a time of war. This situation contrasts sharply with Germany, where most people have a clear idea of what happened in World War II and a clear attitude that it should not happen again. Scrutiny of the way this situation developed in Japan provides a sobering lesson in how effective the hard right can be and how far it can and will go in intimidating people to achieve its aims. Thus the Japanese history issue has a sobering real side, but again the situation is so much worse in China that the Chinese have no right to protest.

The right-wing Japanese national-security establishment's script has been that the rise of an unstable, expansionist, ideological China creates a threat to Japan's national security and its sea lanes and therefore must be countered by tighter alliance with the United States, an expanded military, and assurance that Japan is buffered from the Chinese danger by an independent Taiwan and a divided Korea. This story has some relation to reality. Chinese naval intrusions into Japanese waters do occur. China is drilling for gas adjacent to an area claimed by Japan. China has replaced Japan as the country with preeminent regional influence. But ultimately the Japanese nationalist script is as weak as its Chinese counterpart. A quarter-century has already elapsed since China stopped trying to impose or sell its ideological model to any other country. Except on the Taiwan issue, China has been much more willing to compromise its principal international disputes than Japan has been. China's anti-Japanese riots reflect not instability, but rather the constant up-sizing of the U.S.-Japan alliance and the explicit focusing of the alliance and Japanese rearmament on China and Taiwan, capped by the explicit inclusion in February 2005 of Taiwan as an object of interest for the alliance.

The American nationalists' script treats renewed Sino-Japanese tensions as completely independent of U.S. policy and often labels an aggressive China as the problem. Based on statistics from other times and other regions, it sees China as inherently more dangerous than other countries because China is not a democracy. In its most extreme version, it perceives Taiwan as an Asian Munich, defense of which is essential to deter China from proceeding onward to other potential conquests. The most outspoken "realists" argue that all rising powers challenge the status quo and present a threat to the dominant power of the day. Many neocons argue or assume that communist states are inherently aggressive, like the old Soviet Union. The problems with this script are as serious as those with the Chinese and Japanese scripts. Changing U.S. policies and changing Japanese politics are at the core of the reemergence of Sino-Japanese rivalries. China has much better relations with its neighbors than democratic India has, and it has been much more accommodating and successful in resolving territorial issues than Japan, which, behind an American shield, has been totally intransigent with all its neighbors. China's systematic settlement of land borders with weaker powers, to the satisfaction of those weaker powers, hardly betokens an Asian version of Hitler's or Stalin's expansion. The central trend of post–World War II Asian history has been that successive rising powers (Japan, Indonesia in Southeast Asia, China) have embraced the status quo rather than rejecting it.

The nationalist scripts in each of the principal powers have influenced national policies but have not dominated them. Koizumi visited the Yasukuni Shrine and Japanese ministers signed an alliance communiqué that mentioned Taiwan (gingerly), but Japanese military budgets remain small and Japanese troop deployments innocuous. Chinese military budgets rise and Chinese rhetoric on Taiwan is shrill, but the military budgets remain a much smaller fraction of GDP than they were three decades ago, some new policies reach out to Taiwan, and more than 5 percent of Taiwan's population now lives and works on the mainland, to some degree reestablishing old cultural ties. Some Pentagon generals talk of "China-focused strategy," but the U.S. president rebukes Taiwan for provoking China. The trend of economic development pacifying geopolitical tensions remains powerful but faces more countertrends than it did in the past. Thus the regional trends by themselves are indeterminate. We must look at what is happening in each of the principal countries in order to discern what might consolidate regional relationships along old lines or drive them into new geometries.

CHAPTER FOUR

Asia's Big Powers: Japan and China

We began with the observation that the images and relationships of one era often carry over into a quite different era and dominate the thought and actions of intelligent people long after they should. In the previous chapter, I began the process of painting a picture of new realities, but this chapter bears the primary burden of challenging stereotypes and digging beneath prevailing assumptions. I plan to aim a heavy cannon at the stereotypes and to show that many things look very different from Seoul or Bangkok than they do from Washington. But as I do this, there is a risk that I might deliver the wrong message. I learned something of that risk from a previous book, *The Rise of China*.[1] In the late 1980s and early 1990s, most Westerners thought that Gorbachev was a god who was going to do wonderful things for the Soviet Union. At the same time, particularly after the Tiananmen Square incident on June 4, 1989, most were convinced that China was on the verge of collapse. I was convinced, on the contrary, that, as bad as June 4 was, Deng Xiaoping's strategy would create another Asian miracle and Gorbachev's strategy would destroy the Soviet Union. I made the argument as strongly as I could, absorbed the resulting abuse from reviewers, then enjoyed having been right. But I also found that my arguments about China's looming success spawned a whole genre of gee-whiz articles and books with the theme that China was going to take over the world, ignoring all the risks and constraints on what

---

[1] William H. Overholt, *The Rise of China*, New York: W. W. Norton, 1993.

China might be able to accomplish. Thus I learned that making a forceful point can result in a loss of balance and perspective.

Americans like the good cowboys to wear white hats and the bad cowboys to wear black hats. I need to muddy things up a bit, but not to switch the black hats and the white ones. I ask the reader's indulgence and engagement as I struggle to get this balance right.

Japan

> The nationalists were not seeking to pick a fight with China. Their fight was with the post-1945 Japanese order—decadent and corrupt, spiritless and materialistic, corseted by a constitution written by a foreign conqueror, reduced to an existence of crippled sovereignty, living a life of self-deprecation, and not even knowing it. If their lament upset China, that could not be helped, for the nationalists were addressing their enfeebled countrymen and no one else. They spoke of reviving respect for culture, history, and tradition. And, because their fight was against the post-1945 order, their thoughts returned to the distinctly modern, pre-1945 world of statehood defined in terms of sovereignty and the right of belligerency.
>
> —*Masaru Tamamoto*[2]

Japan has held an important place in global and regional geopolitics twice. From the late 19th through the mid-20th century, with the partial exception of Thailand, it was the only substantial Asian power to retain its prowess in an era of political fragmentation and technological backwardness and to thereby avoid succumbing to Western colonialism.[3] The first Asian economic miracle was Japan's rise during the Meiji era, starting in the mid-19th century. Its prowess was based on

---

[2] Masaru Tamamoto, "How Japan Imagines China and Sees Itself," Japan Institute for International Affairs Commentary Number 3, May 31, 2006 (www.worldpolicy.org/journal/articles/wpj06-1/Tamamoto.pdf).

[3] Thailand did not succumb to Western colonialism, but its success was due to diplomatic finesse and to the mutual deterrence in Indochina of French and British colonialism, not to modernization. Through the early post–World War II era, Thailand remained one of Asia's

its own modernization but also, even more importantly, on the utter failures of its neighbors, China, Korea, and Southeast Asia, to modernize and stabilize themselves. Japan's subsequent economic failures in some of the decades before World War II left it a military power that could mobilize extraordinary resources for regional predation but sometimes could not feed its own people adequately. Waves of impoverished Japanese became farmers in Brazil and gardeners in the Philippines. Although it had enormously impressive military power, Japan lacked an economic foundation proportionate to its ambitions, and it lacked the cultural sophistication and sensitivity to convince its conquests to accept their fate. Japan's inward-looking homogeneity fatally hindered the task of organizing, incorporating, and persuading large foreign populations.

The Rise and Fall of Japan's Economic Supremacy in Asia

In contrast, Japan's postwar position as one of the world's most important powers has been economically rather than militarily based. Until the early 1970s, most of the world regarded Japan as a defeated power that produced cheap toys and low-quality cars and probably was doomed to being a backward, heavily agriculture-based economy. The central thesis of Herman Kahn's 1970 book *The Emerging Japanese Superstate*,[4] that Japan was on the way to becoming an important power again, drew ridicule from seemingly authoritative reviewers. But by the mid-1970s, foreign-policy elites began to acknowledge the importance of Japan's extraordinary economic growth, and from the late 1970s through 1989, there was fear abroad, and rising confidence at home, that Japan had a superior strategy of economic growth, based in part on confining military expenditure to less than 1 percent of GDP and in part on exceptional government ability to direct the nation's resources. Much of the industrialized world began studying, in admiration, Japanese quality circles, just-in-time inventory manage-

---

most backward countries, a status that changed only after its Asian-miracle growth from 1960–1996 finally brought it into the modern world.

[4] Herman Kahn, *The Emerging Japanese Superstate: Challenge and Response*, Englewood Cliffs, NJ: Prentice Hall, 1970.

ment, labor-management relations, and industrial policy. Ironically, the transformation from disdain to fear occurred simultaneously with the gradual post-1975 decline of Japan's economic growth rate and the gradual replacement during that period of focused, efficient economic management by patronage-dominated management.

During the 1980s, the United States experienced a panic that Japan was on the verge of dominating the American economy. After all, the Japanese made better cars and cheaper steel, and they bought the Pebble Beach golf course and Rockefeller Center, along with Los Angeles hotels and Hawaiian real estate and much else. Japan came to dominate Northeast and Southeast Asian financial markets, trade, and industrial development (except in China, which in that period was closed and therefore didn't count). That era, however, lasted only about a decade, from the late 1970s through 1989. In 1990, the Japanese stock and property markets experienced the greatest bubble collapses in world financial history, and the Japanese economy stagnated through 2002. During that period of stagnation, the focus of exaggerated Western admiration and paranoia shifted to China.

Japanese recovery began in 2003, when its economy was finally saved from financial collapse by growing exports to China and then gradually recovered some of its own momentum. But the heyday of the mobilization economy and its siblings around the region was over. Future growth is constrained by demographic decline and the drag from what remains of the old mobilization system: huge government debt (170 percent of GDP), weak banks, an array of uncompetitive firms, and a system generally poorly prepared for the entrepreneurial era of Silicon Valley.

During the 12 years of stagnation, most Japanese families maintained high standards of living, with per capita incomes still in the vicinity of $50,000, but they suffered in dignified desperation as their wealth diminished with a property-market decline of more than half and a stock-market decline from 38,915 on December 29, 1989, to 7,607 on April 28, 2003—a decline of more than 80 percent. A middle-class family with a $700,000 apartment in Tokyo might, for instance, have had 30 percent equity ($210,000) and 70 percent remaining on its mortgage. The value of such a house typically would have declined to about $300,000, leaving the family with negative equity of $190,000. Meanwhile, the family probably would have had much of the rest of its net worth invested in the stock market, where it would have suffered proportionately far more terrible losses. Since the family could still pay the mortgage, it could maintain its standard of living until retirement but would henceforth live in dread of its prospects after retirement.

Japan faces many years of social distress in its core manufacturing areas such as the Kansai around Osaka, in its rural areas, and among the coming generation of retirees whose pensions must either be cut or be inflated away, because the government is so indebted after the years of stagnation that there is no scenario under which it could ever pay the real value of promised pensions. This, combined with slow Japanese reform, means many years of slow growth unless Japan drastically changes many aspects of its society, including its attitudes toward women's work, the roles of the elderly, and practices that impede the rate of creative destruction in the economy.

Nonetheless, Japan still has Asia's biggest economy, more than twice as big as China's in nominal terms. (If one makes adjustments to reflect differences in the purchasing power of the two currencies, then China's is bigger.) The strong Japanese firms, such as Toyota, are getting stronger; a recent slogan among investors in the global car industry has been "Buy Toyota, Sell the Rest." In industries such as cars, consumer electronics, and computer gaming, which internationalized early and functioned outside the protected areas of the mobilization economy, Japanese companies lead the world. Japan's network of overseas manufacturing operations remains powerful and efficient; Honda's and Toyota's operations in the United States outperform their indigenous U.S. counterparts by virtually any measure (quality, reliability, market-share trend, profitability, etc.). Japanese companies still tower over American and European competitors in Southeast Asia. Relocation of long-protected lower-value-added manufacturing and software operations to China and India could yield rapid productivity gains.

In short, Japan remains an economy of formidable scale that will remain at the leading edge in key sectors. It will not go into decline in any absolute sense. It will provide a powerful mobilization base for whatever military capability the leaders decide to adopt. But it will not add rapidly to the (already high) prosperity of working Japanese families, it will not restore the lost prestige of Japanese economic management and political leadership, and, unless it opens decisively, it will not have anything like the regional influence of China's smaller but more open economy.

Post-Bust Politics

The end of the old era of Japanese economics entails the end of the old era in Japanese politics and foreign policy. The "1955 political system," which persisted until well into Prime Minister Koizumi's term of office, was a merger of conservative groups that endowed one party, the Liberal Democratic Party (LDP), with overwhelming resources: The country's financial institutions, its most powerful business organizations, the principal government bureaucracies, powerful agricultural lobbies, and nationalist groups banded together and created a political system that they could control. No opposition could muster the organization and money to compete effectively; the opposition has consistently been incoherent on policy and divided over politics. For most of the post-1955 period, the LDP inner circle rotated the job of prime minister, with little regard for popular appeal; in turn, the public has been apathetic about politics for much of the era, yielding a disconnect between citizenry and decisions unusual in a democracy. As in South Korea, Taiwan, and Singapore during their takeoff periods, and China now, this dominance by one party has provided the stability that nurtured economic growth and protected the ability of the conservative political elite to pursue tough-minded, long-term economic growth policies without fear of being displaced by a competing party. As in those other East Asian miracle economies, one of the prices paid for this stable relationship between the political elite and business needs was extraordinary corruption.

Within this system, the prime minister was traditionally a captive of party factions, and the party factions were captives of major interest groups. The legislature was divided into "tribes" (*zoku*) representing various interest groups. As much as half of government funds were off-budget, outside political scrutiny, giving the LDP leadership and the bureaucracy financial control exempt from democratic accountability to an extent unprecedented in other advanced democracies.

All this worked extremely well and had strong public support as long as the economy functioned well. But, as in other Asian mobilization economies, the interest groups got out of control, spending wildly on unnecessary infrastructure and overcapacity. Conflicts of interest wrecked the banks. Protection made much of Japan's industry go soft; when the crunch came in the 1990s and the economy had to be opened up somewhat, a vast swath of protected industries, from electrical appliances and electronics companies to a wide range of consumer- and intermediate-goods companies, suddenly found themselves uncompetitive. Industries such as simple electronics that should have moved to Taiwan and South Korea two decades earlier suddenly departed for China, leaving many families and some large areas, including Osaka and the Kansai, feeling despair. Financial mismanagement created world history's greatest stock, property, and construction bubbles, bringing the economy to the edge of financial meltdown and leading to a dozen years of stagnation, from 1990 to 2002. That discredited both the 1940 economic system and the 1955 political system.

Prime Minister Koizumi, who was Japan's top leader from 2001 to 2006, understood this and was able to benefit from electoral reforms that occurred during the LDP's brief absence from power during the years of stagnation. Politically, he ran against his party and derogated the factional structure that had dominated the 1955 system. His successful battle cry was a threat to "destroy the LDP"—his own party. Financially, he attacked the taproot of the old financial system, the Postal Savings Bank, the largest bank on earth and the principal source of patronage funding for the hitherto highly effective but extraordinarily corrupt 1955 political system. His victory on that issue in 2005 seemed to presage a new era in Japanese politics in which the taproot of the old system would indeed gradually—very gradually—die. Koizumi's successor, Abe, has seemed much less interested in either economic or political reform, and in fact, he reversed Koizumi's expulsion of anti-postal-reform politicians, but the withering of the Postal Savings system, if it persists, will permanently change Japanese politics.

Koizumi also strengthened the position of the prime minister and weakened the roles of interest groups and the government bureaucracies, shut down much of the Postal Savings system, reduced somewhat the country's wildly inflated infrastructure spending, and privatized some of the state enterprises. These reforms are gradually draining patronage resources away from the bureaucrats and the interest groups.

Following on an administrative reform initiated by former Prime Minister Ryutaro Hashimoto, Prime Minister Koizumi increasingly appointed his own advisors, rejecting the past system whereby the prime minister meekly accepted the advisors sent over by the bureaucracies. Increasingly, Koizumi refused to take the formerly near-mandatory advice of the LDP Policy Research Council, thereby shifting control of policy from the party to the government. He increasingly disregarded the factional politics that have constituted Japan's real political structure. Gradually, the policymaking process shifted from primarily bottom-up decisionmaking, in which the prime minister for the most part gave his blessing to decisions made by lower party and government organs, to a top-down process whereby the prime minister and the chief cabinet secretary decide what they want to do, get the support of needed coalition partners (notably the Komeito), and then go to the Diet for legislation or instruct the ministries to implement their wishes. The virtue of the new process is increased speed; for instance, the 2001 anti-terror legislation passed the Diet in only three weeks.[5] The cost of the new process in foreign policy is that a prime minister or chief cabinet secretary with little knowledge of, for instance, Korea or China may override Foreign Ministry experts at substantial cost to the country's standing with its neighbors. Under Koizumi, Japan reaped both the full benefits and full costs of the new structure.

Koizumi also advocated changing the constitution to provide for direct election of the prime minister—a change that did not happen during his term but has substantial support as a future amendment. Japan's politics evolved quickly, at least by Japanese standards, under

---

[5] For a full description of the new system, see Tomohito Shinoda, *Koizumi Diplomacy: Japan's Kantei Approach to Foreign and Defense Affairs*, Seattle, WA: University of Washington Press, 2006.

Koizumi. Japan's prime minister remains far weaker than most other heads of government in advanced countries, and it remains to be seen whether Koizumi's successors can consolidate and expand his gains, but he made vital changes and set the stage for further ones, including possible direct election of the prime minister.

This evolution of Japanese domestic politics is a leading example of successful adaptation to a new era. The old 1955 system was wary of strong leadership and after the early days of reconstruction, rarely tolerated it. Japanese democracy has not been like other democracies. To an extent that has rarely occurred elsewhere, power rested with the interest groups and power brokers operating behind the scenes. After Prime Minister Tanaka was cast out of office over the Lockheed scandal in 1972,[6] he nonetheless designated the next six prime ministers from behind the scenes—an outcome unimaginable in the United States or most Western European democracies. In more recent times, Chief Cabinet Secretary Hiromu Nonaka was more powerful than the overt leadership. The amounts of money changing hands behind the curtain transcended the imaginations of most Americans. The assembled power, mainly financial, was such that the opposition and the titular leadership could be kept firmly under control most of the time. Occasionally, a leader like Yasuhiro Nakasone was allowed to emerge, but only a leader who represented the toughest, most nationalistic, and most reliable public face that was politically acceptable and only for a short time.

This was what the Guomindang in Taiwan attempted to achieve after 1988—free elections, but with such overwhelming control of business, banking, and the media that the opposition's situation was hopeless. The Guomindang, however, made the mistake of choosing a leader, Lee Teng-hui, who split the party. (Lee retained Leninist powers from Taiwan's pre-democratic era to designate the Guomindang candidate to succeed him. He insisted on choosing Lien Chan, a relatively

---

[6] Lockheed paid a ¥500 million bribe to Prime Minister Tanaka to get him to pressure All Nippon Airways to order its large-capacity jet rather than competitors' jets. Investigations by a U.S. Senate subcommittee in 1976 turned this into a huge scandal that discredited Tanaka as a formal government official.

unpopular figure, over James Soong, who was far more popular. Soong left and formed his own party. Between them, the two Guomindang-origin candidates won a majority in the 2000 election, but because they split the vote, the opposition Democratic Progressive Party (DPP) won.) Otherwise, Guomindang rule might have persisted indefinitely. The LDP has been far more subtle and sophisticated in balancing factions and would never risk entrusting a leader with the Leninist powers that Lee Teng-hui used to split the Guomindang.

The ideal of most Pacific Asian leaderships is what Japan's LDP has so far achieved: free elections combined with such an overwhelming concentration of resources in the dominant party that there is little risk of defeat. The leadership of the Chinese Communist Party has spent years studying the Guomindang, the LDP, and other parties such as Mexico's PRI (Partido Revolucionario Institucional), trying to find a formula that will allow liberalization without much risk of losing power. It wants to achieve what the LDP and Malaysia's ruling Barisan Nasional achieved, without making the mistakes that the Guomindang and the PRI made. It is essential to understand the parallels between Japan's dominant party system and the dominant party systems of its neighbors; these party systems are a spectrum, not a Manichean split. China's leadership aspires to be part of that spectrum and to evolve as others did toward mechanisms of increased public accountability but, like the LDP, without much risk of losing power.

As it did with its economy, Japan evolved a sophisticated system of Conservative Party dominance much earlier than the neighbors did. As with its evolution into a fully market economy, it has in some ways fallen behind South Korea and Taiwan in the development of a full democracy in which the legislature oversees the entire budget, the opposition has a reasonable chance of attaining power, and the legal system functions according to modern industrial democratic norms. (Japanese judges are far more subject to the desires of the ruling party than judges in other industrial democracies. Japanese prosecutors are less fallible than those in other democracies: 95 percent of Japanese defendants confess—often after lengthy interrogation intensified by sleep deprivation, slapping, and extended confinement in rooms that are freezing cold—and 99.9 percent are convicted.[7]) Koizumi gave both the economy and the polity a strong shove in the direction of modernization.

By the eleventh year of stagnation, 2001, Japan's LDP system seemed doomed. National finances were teetering on the edge of national and global catastrophe, and both the public and the political leadership were desperate for new ideas, new policies, and new leadership. Koizumi rose to the occasion. He attacked the LDP, threatening to destroy it, while preserving it as a base for his own power. He chopped away at the taproot of the 1940 economic system and the 1955 political system, namely the Postal Savings Bank, and bet his career on that; after fighting during virtually his whole tenure as prime minister, in 2005 he won that battle, with a political campaign in which, for the first time in many years, popular votes were decisive on a great national political issue. While gradually chopping away at the financial base of the backroom politics, he made structural changes that could allow his successors to become real leaders.

That leaves in place a hybrid system. If other strong leaders eventually succeed Koizumi, they will have the new structural advantages of (real but still somewhat limited) leadership along with a structure where a large proportion of government revenues are beyond democratic accountability, the opposition remains emasculated, the public is relatively apathetic (something that began to change in Koizumi's last year but could revert back), judges' careers depend on fidelity to the

---

[7] Karel van Wolferen calculated an acquittal rate of 0.2 percent (van Wolferen, *The Enigma of Japanese Power: People and Politics in a Stateless Nation*, London: Papermac, 1990, p. 290). The entire section of his book on the legal system is quite revealing. In 2007, an article in *The Economist* calculated an acquittal rate of just 0.1 percent ("Confess and Be Done with It," *The Economist*, February 10, 2007, pp. 41–42). China's acquittal rate, still low, is six and a half times larger, at 0.66 percent. Taiwan has an acquittal rate of 12 percent, the United States, 17 to 25 percent (see Chinese Law Prof Blog, http://lawprofessors. typepad.com/china_law_prof_blog/2006/11/chinas_low_acqu.html). There is considerable disagreement as to exactly how such rates should be compared and interpreted. There is no disagreement, however, that the low acquittal rates in Japan and China result in part from large-scale mistreatment, by Western standards, of the accused. For a sympathetic overview of the Japanese legal system, see David T. Johnson, *The Japanese Way of Justice: Prosecuting Crime in Japan*, New York: Oxford University Press, 2002.

policies of a dominant party, and a large proportion of the old system of elite management remains in place. This could, in the unlikely extreme, lead over a long time toward executive dominance of a kind that would be most unusual for an industrial democracy. Alternatively, it could lead to a debilitating war of attrition between the forces of a new order and the forces of LDP reaction. Or it could lead Japan in the direction of normal democracy. The outcome is unpredictable.

The one thing that seems predictable is that the emerging regime will evolve, perhaps gradually, into something quite different from its predecessors. The Asian dominant-party systems rest on an economic structure that gives the leading party such powerful economic levers that it can discipline its own coalition within broad limits and emasculate the opposition. But Japan's economic revival depends upon rapid evolution toward a more entrepreneurial economy at home and a more open economy internationally. Each economic liberalization, each increase in transparency, and each international opening measure drains away a flow of financial resources from LDP coffers. In Japan, as in China, the leadership knows that economic success will entail political change.

To understand why this is so, it is crucial to understand how the system was constructed. Most major industries were highly protected, and they paid off LDP politicians to ensure that such protection would continue. When foreigners, often the United States, insisted that the industry be opened up to imports, that would create a new source of patronage. Take beef, for example. The government would work with certain groups to set up a Japanese-controlled beef-exporting industry in the United States, so that the business would remain as much as possible in Japanese hands. The grateful companies concerned would contribute generously to LDP coffers. To the extent that American companies were actually allowed to export beef, the imports would be channeled through vulnerable individuals or businesses that were required to turn over the bulk of their profits to LDP politicians. Many of these transactions were illegal. To some extent, of course, this is how politics works in all democracies, but in the Asian dominant-party systems, the scope and scale of such transactions are so different as to fundamentally alter the nature of the system. As competition and transparency increase, and as foreigners become more involved in the economy, the system itself is gradually changing.

These assertions about fundamental change would be disputed by some leading authorities on Japanese politics who argue that old ways are deeply entrenched and likely to reassert themselves. The case for enduring change depends on the gradual abolition of the Postal Savings system; the gradual control of bloated infrastructure budgets; the gradual opening of sectors such as construction, retail trade, and agriculture to competition; and gradual diminution of tariff and non-tariff trade barriers, because these things have funded single-party dominance. And it rests on the continuation of Koizumi's mobilization of interest in political participation, especially by youth. Those who believe that the old ways will reassert themselves have to believe that in Koizumi's absence, those trends will be reversed. In his first few months in office, Prime Minister Abe seemed to be reversing some of the trends, but his popularity fell rapidly, implying that this may no longer be an effective way to govern Japan. It would be foolish for any analyst to write dogmatically about the eventual outcome. Future readers can observe these indicators and decide for themselves which way the system is headed.

In this process of economic and political reform, the right-wing conservatives within the LDP have led, while the LDP traditionalists and the liberal opposition have bleated ineffectually. The Democratic Party of Japan, the principal liberal opposition, has continued to be typical of opposition parties in Asian countries where the dominant party controls overwhelming resources; it has been beset with poor, divided, and frequently changing leadership and incoherent policy platforms.

In these Asian systems, the disconnect between popular sentiment and national policy is much greater than it is in Western democracies, and that is particularly true of foreign policy. This fact gives a newly ascendant right wing the potential to take foreign policy rather far down a path that is neither deeply grounded in public opinion nor very well understood by it.

Post-Bust Foreign Policy

The acceleration of political change affects Japan's international future. So far, the changes have primarily benefited the political right. During and after Japan's 12 years of economic stagnation, the country's rightists seized the opportunity to argue that the nation had wasted two generations on a system that didn't work. The Japanese people, they argued, had lost their national pride, their national discipline, their international standing. It was time to restore them by, among other things, building a modern military, paying respect to the heroes of World War II and other wars at the Yasukuni Shrine, and standing up to China.

The leadership on economic reform has come primarily from the right. The leadership on political reform has also come primarily from the right. Prime Minister Koizumi and his successor, Prime Minister Abe, are leaders who have taken pride in visiting the Yasukuni Shrine and standing up to China. (In his early months, Abe refrained from visiting the shrine, telling confidantes that his past record in this regard was so well established that he did not need to do it anymore.) Symbolically, the leader of the forces demanding that Japan pay more attention to good relations with its Asian neighbors, Yasuo Fukuda, stepped aside before the September 2006 election because he was seen as too old and faced inexorable defeat by the younger, more dynamic nationalist leader, Abe.

While Koizumi visited the Yasukuni Shrine and alienated Japan's neighbors out of electoral opportunism (he needed the support of the hard right), Abe adopts his right-wing posture out of ideological conviction. He is so firmly part of the right that he has more tactical room for maneuver. He doesn't have to verify his right-wing credentials by visiting the shrine. Abe tried to dampen Asian anger over Japan's new posture and historical revisionism by visiting China and South Korea shortly after his election. The Chinese leaders accepted his gesture (the South Koreans vigorously rejected it), but they decided that the tensions had gotten out of hand and sent Premier Wen Jiabao to give an exceptionally conciliatory speech thanking Japan for its apologies and historical concern. That speech offset a somewhat boorish attack on the history issue by President Jiang Zemin during a state visit to

Japan in November 1998. When Abe nonetheless sent a gift of a tree to the Yasukuni Shrine almost immediately after Wen's visit, the Chinese decided not to react in any significant way.

The center of gravity of the Japanese public respects those who have led the country toward economic recovery, who have repudiated the conspicuously failed parts of the old political system, who have confronted North Korea over its kidnappings of Japanese citizens and its militaristic posturing (the issue that catapulted Abe to power), and who have stood up to a China that is increasingly seen as abusive and dangerous because of its protests over history-text revision and Yasukuni Shrine visits, its big anti-Japanese riots in 2005, and its naval intrusions into Japanese waters. This rightward move fundamentally conditions Japan's new foreign-policy choices.

Of necessity, Japan's foreign policy is changing even more than its domestic economics and politics. The old foreign policy that aspired to dominate Asia through peaceful economic diplomacy collapsed when the economy ceased to grow quickly. Building on the prestige of its superior economic performance, Japanese dominance of Asian financial markets, and its increasing dominance of industrial markets in the smaller countries of the Asian littoral, Tokyo foresaw a century when Asia would lead the world, with Japan as the unquestioned leader of Asia. By the end of the 1980s, numerous Japanese publications were denigrating the United States as economically incompetent and doomed to decline, leaving Japan as the unchallenged leader. In the new century, the economy is still big, but the 12 years of stagnation and the emergence of new competitors have destroyed any possibility that Japan would ever again have the degree of preeminence that would underwrite regional political dominance. Unlike in the 1980s, U.S. and European banks can now compete with Japanese banks. While Japan retains by far the largest share of the region's industry, South Korea now has more trade with China than with Japan and the United States combined. Japan's economy is still by far the biggest, but there is enough competition that the era when Japan could dominate its neighbors has ended just when it was beginning. Because China has a more open economy than Japan, every country in the region has more trade with China than with Japan. Despite all of China's economic problems, Japan's shining economic prestige of the 1980s has been ceded to China.

Japan's postwar diplomacy was audacious and successful. Japan's success, along with its adherence to the alliance with the United States, provided the foundation on which the U.S. victory in the Cold War in Asia was built. Japan's economic stimulus and policy example helped stabilize all the smaller countries of the East Asian littoral. Nonetheless, while the U.S.-Japan alliance has endured and has functioned loyally and successfully for 60 years, there are long-term stresses, particularly with the Japanese right wing. Unlike Germany and Britain, but more subtly than France, much of Japan's national-security elite has never accepted the shift to U.S. leadership as permanent. The United States reinstalled more of the wartime political and business leadership in Japan than it did in Germany, thereby stabilizing the country at the cost of entrenching an elite that retained a profound distaste for U.S. dominance and rejected many U.S. values. The U.S. decision to retain the emperor, celebrated at the time as a brilliant and magnanimous contribution to Japan's postwar stability, inhibited the kind of thorough moral repudiation of the war that occurred in Germany. Half a century later, the United States is beginning to experience blowback from those postwar decisions. Prime Minister Abe and many of his right-wing colleagues are lineal descendants of figures rescued from disgrace in the frantic effort to stabilize a conservative elite in time to counter Stalin's thrusts into Asia.

Much of the core of the national-security leadership in particular continues to reject the victors' history. Mitsubishi still files court briefs that deny the validity of the Tokyo War Crimes Trials, whereas Germany's Siemens would not think of legally denying the validity of the Nuremberg Trials. Japan still claims southern Sakhalin, now controlled by Russia, and Tokdo/Takeshima Island, now controlled by South Korea, as its territory, based on its victory in the Russo-Japanese War, whereas Germany has abandoned all its old revanchist claims. By the 1980s, it seemed to Japanese leaders, particularly those on the right, that U.S. dominance was very temporary indeed; with its faltering heavy industry and its twin deficits (budget and trade), U.S. economic management was clearly incompetent, and its global role was due for sharp decline. Moreover, China still appeared hapless, and Europe was far away and divided, so Japanese dominance was imminent. By 1988–1989, the mood of the financial and foreign-policy establishments resembled the later triumphalism of the early George W. Bush administration.

Japan has been one of America's most loyal military allies, surpassed in loyalty only by Britain and Australia. This is a partnership with deep roots and resilience tested by many crises and strains. But it has never had the full dimensions of the U.S.-British partnership. Whereas Britain has deliberately positioned itself as an economic and diplomatic bridge for the United States, Japan's instinct has been to edge the United States out of Asia economically and politically so that it would have to deal with an Asia organized under Japanese leadership. That was the implication of Japanese derogation of American economic competence in the 1980s, the proposal for an Asian Monetary Fund (blocked by the Clinton administration) during the 1997–1998 Asian economic crisis, the subsequent Japanese efforts to enlarge the Chiangmai Initiative for currency swaps, a Japanese proposal of an Asian Currency Unit, and enthusiastic support of the East Asia Summit process, which excludes the United States. The determination, sometimes subtle, sometimes not, behind this string of proposals comes through whenever Americans express concern about being excluded. I am writing these words as I return home from a conference where the leader of the Japanese side said, "Asian people will be very angry if the U.S. tries to push its way back into these programs," an assertion that would be completely true only for Japan, although partially true for Malaysia and China.

The Transformation of Military Posture

The bursting bubble of 1990, followed by a dozen years of stagnation, the rise of a dynamic China, and the extraordinary vitality of the U.S. economy, shattered the vision of Japan dominating Asia through economic preeminence with as much finality as World War II shattered Japan's effort at military leadership. The economic prestige was gone. The financial hegemony was gone. Preeminence in Asian industrial markets remained, but dominance was replaced by a status of first among equals. Ascendancy ended just when Japan's leaders intended it to begin. This left Japan floundering, in need of a new economic structure, a new political structure, and a new foreign-policy vision. As one Japanese scholar put it:

> Japan is in the midst of a grand social transformation. Political manners, economic rules, patterns of everyday life and international relations are all in flux. The last time Japan saw change of great magnitude was after the defeat in the Second World War by American design. This time, there is no blueprint, and the Japanese are groping for a vision.[8]

The collapse from imminent ascendancy coincided almost perfectly with the first Iraq war and U.S. denunciations of Japan for contributing only money to that effort rather than putting soldiers at risk. The search to replace a bankrupt foreign policy immediately encountered U.S. demands for a more active military involvement, the first of a long series of crises over North Korean missile tests and nuclear ambitions, shock that an ascendant China was replacing Japan's regional leadership, and a strengthening of the domestic position of the Japanese right. The result has been an acceleration of trends toward becoming a "normal" country with a "normal" military.

This greatly widens the range of foreign-policy and military options available to Japanese leaders.[9] In addition to facilitating an emergent consensus among the foreign-policy elite on becoming a "normal" military power, the collapse of the old policy, together with the U.S. military's strong pressure for tightening the alliance and focusing it on China, has facilitated the surfacing of Japan's hawkish nationalists; they are a numerically small but very well-organized and well-financed group that is distinguished by its overt hostility to Korea

---

[8] Hikari Agakimi, *"We the Japanese People"—A Reflection on Public Opinion,* Japan Institute of International Affairs Commentary No. 2, May 17, 2006 (http://yaleglobal.yale.edu/display.article?id=7444).

[9] For a view very different from my own, i.e., that this translates into a broad revitalization of Japan, see Kenneth B. Pyle, *Japan Rising: The Resurgence of Japanese Power and Purpose,* New York: Public Affairs, 2007.

(South and North alike) and China, its quiet but determined commitment to Taiwan's independence, its view that a permanently divided Korea is a vital Japanese national interest, its disdain for the American-imposed constitution, its determination to overcome what its members see as a soft and decadent Japanese society, and a broad inclination toward a pre–World War II view of world affairs.

The Japanese public generally does not have strong views or even strong awareness of foreign-policy and national-security issues. In this situation, Prime Minister Koizumi's appointment of hawkish nationalists to key positions, U.S. pressures for a stronger military and a more explicitly anti-China military posture, and China's nationalist excesses have permitted the nationalists to gain a disproportionate influence over Japan's national-security policies.

The extreme right, heavily overlapping with the hawkish nationalist group although not identical to it, has been particularly well-organized, well-financed, and tough-minded. Throughout Japan, virtually all teachers remain intimidated by the far right and therefore do not teach the history of the prewar and wartime period. One of Prime Minister Abe's first acts after taking office was to ensure the passage of a law that requires Japanese teaching to be "patriotic," a vague requirement that could be used to institutionalize the half-century of intimidation of Japan's teachers. When the head of one of Japan's most prestigious business associations, Taiyu Kobayashi of Toyo Keizai Doyukai (Japan Association of Corporate Executives), criticized Prime Minister Koizumi's visits to the Yasukuni Shrine, a firebomb was placed at his house; fortunately, it did not explode. When one of Japan's most reputable politicians, Koichi Kato, criticized the visits, his house was burned by a right-wing arsonist who tried to commit *seppuku* nearby.[10] Criticism of the arson by Japanese media and leading politicians was very muted, due to fear of the right. When a respected scholar wrote on the website of the Foreign Ministry's think tank, the Japan Institute of International Affairs (JIIA), what most foreign observers saw as a balanced commentary about the danger of Japan's becoming isolated,

---

[10] See "Kato Vows to Speak Out Despite Arson Linked to His Yasukuni Criticism," *Mainichi Daily News*, September 8, 2006.

a right-wing commentator attacked it, and the intimidated president of JIIA issued an abject apology and shut down the website.

It is important not to underestimate Japan's military potential. It can send an Aegis destroyer to the Indian Ocean to help the United States manage a war in Afghanistan, and it can land a spacecraft on a tiny asteroid hundreds of millions of miles from earth. Military-related functions are scattered widely through the budgets of civilian ministries. Japan's military structure provides a magnificent mobilization base—it has very high technology and is top-heavy with officers, so expansion could be fast. For decades, Japan buried functions such as research on missile guidance and high-energy lasers in places like the Ministry of Education, so the foundation for a high-tech military became much more solid than was once apparent. At the same time, its military budget remains at a low 1 percent of GDP, not counting military research functions that have been allocated to other ministries, and is not accelerating. The expansion of military influence and the military's sphere of responsibility is very real, but as a share of Japan's giant economy, the military budget remains proportionately among the world's smallest.

As one would expect at a major historical turning point, the trends are contradictory. On one hand, recent developments in moving Japan's military toward normality unequivocally infringe at least the English language version of Article 9 of its constitution. (See the text of Article 9 in Figure 3.) For decades, the government justified the very slow expansion of military organization and military functions by stretching the language of the constitution so as to argue that policies were consistent with it. In the Koizumi era, this lip service was largely abandoned because no stretching of the words could possibly accommodate actual policies. So far, public opposition to revision of Article 9 has been sufficient to deter political leaders from tabling such a revision. North Korean threats may eventually solve this problem for the revisionists, but they have not yet done so. Moving ahead without revising the constitution is a very big step for a supposedly rule-of-law-based country to take. This development has been pushed hard by U.S. demands for stronger Japanese military support, while the United States says that it is up to the Japanese to sort out the associated domestic

Figure 3
Japan's Long, Slow Road to a "Normal" Military

- 1946: Article 9 of Chapter II Constitution:

  "Aspiring sincerely to an international peace based on justice and order, the Japanese people forever renounce war as a sovereign right of the nation and the threat or use of force as means of settling international disputes. 2) In order to accomplish the aim of the preceding paragraph, land, sea, and air forces, as well as other war potential, will never be maintained. The right of belligerency of the state will not be recognized."

- 1950: National Police Reserve formed as a 75,000-man paramilitary force, then incorporated into the National Safety Force in 1952.

- 1954: National Safety Force turns into Self Defense Forces (SDF).

- 1992: U.S. criticism of purely financial contribution to the Iraq war.

- 1990s on: Nashi-kuzushi: whittling away at Article 9 through precedents.

- Post–Gulf War decision to patrol sea lanes extensively.

- Deployments with United Nations: Cambodia (1992–1993), Golan Heights, Rwanda, Mozambique, Timor (2002).

- 1996: SDF scope of operations expanded from Japan-Korea-Taiwan to all of China, Southeast Asia, Australasia.

- 2000: Koizumi pushing for revision of the constitution, including Article 9.

- 2001: Overt U.S. demand for active military support.

- 2001: Deployment of task force to Indian Ocean to support United States in Afghanistan.

- 2002: Japanese navy urges United States to strongly request Aegis cruiser as part of Afghanistan support mission.

- 2003: Decision to acquire ballistic missile defense.

- 2003: SDF scope of operations expanded to Middle East.

- 2003: Cabinet approves dispatch of ground force to Iraq in non-combat role.

- 2004: Deployment of small force to Iraq.

- 2004: Defense Policy Outline names China, DPRK as threats for the first time.

- 2005: Taiwan peace is explicitly included under U.S.-Japan alliance.

- 2005: Joint amphibious operations with United States near San Diego.

- 2006: Appointment of chief of staff of SDF.

- 2006: Plan to revise Peace Constitution.

- 2007: SDF upgraded to a ministry.

problems. In effect, the United States has allied with the hawkish nationalists in demanding that the Japanese government change or ignore the American-imposed constitution.

Under Koizumi, the national-security functions were upgraded in the bureaucracy, and the military leadership came to be treated for important purposes as a ministry, for instance, in the 2+2 meetings (of foreign-policy and defense leaders from both sides) with the United States. Under Abe, the defense function officially became a ministry. The role of uniformed officers within the national-security functions has been upgraded and that of civilians downgraded. The military now has much more direct access to the prime minister, who in turn has much broader freedom of action regarding national-security decisions.[11] The Ministry of Foreign Affairs, always weak, has become weaker, paralleling what happened in the United States during the same period. Within the Foreign Ministry, those dealing with the United States and with military issues have gained stature, while those dealing with China and traditional diplomacy have lost influence. Japan's military is very high-tech compared with those of its neighbors, having "intelligence satellites, missile defences, and command-and-control networks, as well as systems that hint, for the first time, at power-projection capabilities, including in-flight refueling, long-range air transports, precision-guided munitions (PGM), assault ships and flat-top helicopter transports."[12] It practices amphibious landings, as it did in San Diego in December 2005, an interesting function for a military constitutionally limited to a purely defensive stance. Its assigned role, once circumscribed to a small area from Korea to the northern Philippines sea boundary, now encompasses all of Asia, Australasia, and most of the Middle East.

It is important to underscore both the dramatic changes that are occurring and the paradoxical fact that the path toward military normalization has been very gradual. So far, in budget and equipment, it remains very much a normalization, not a militarization, even though

---

[11] See Christopher W. Hughes, *Japan's Reemergence as a "Normal" Military Power*, London: International Institute of Strategic Studies, Adelphi Paper 368-9, 2005, esp. pp. 60ff.

[12] Ibid., p. 14.

the tone with which the changes have been made has been that of the hawkish nationalists.

Japan has become ever more closely tied to U.S. policy and ever more integrated with the U.S. military, leading some in the Bush administration to characterize the likely outcome as Japan serving as America's Britain in Asia. But the hawkish nationalists who are among the most important political forces behind these moves are those who were quick to denigrate the United States in the 1980s, who characterize World War II as a valid struggle against U.S. and European colonialism, who express contempt for a U.S.-imposed constitution, and who desire a much more independent Japan in the future. At this point on the cusp of history, it would take a brave or foolish analyst to predict whether Japan will remain a pliant subordinate of the United States, a prickly Gaullist ally, or an independent force that often actively opposes the United States. None of these outcomes would constitute a bigger change than what has happened to Japanese policy since 1989.

Nationalism and Japan's Diplomatic Isolation

On its current political trajectory, with the rising influence of the hawkish nationalists, the least likely outcome would be the pliant "Britain in Asia" that has been a popular vision in Washington since the turn of the 21st century. Rising Japanese nationalism has been directed primarily at China, but it is a proud reaction against the smashing of one vision of preeminence in 1945 and another vision of preeminence in 1990. Nationalism cuts in all directions. The famous book, *The Japan That Can Say No*, which provided the first dramatic public notice abroad of rising Japanese nationalism, was about saying no to the United States.[13] During the Koizumi administration, both Koizumi's successor (Abe) and his successor's foreign minister (Aso) flaunted their visits to the (conspicuously anti-American) Yasukuni Shrine.

---

[13] Shintaro Ishihara, *The Japan That Can Say No: Why Japan Will Be First Among Equals*, New York: Simon & Schuster, 1991. The author is the current governor of Tokyo, and his son played a prominent role in Koizumi's cabinet and became acting LDP secretary general under Abe.

The current foci of right-wing nationalism are China and North Korea, but relations with South Korea were also very sour in 2005. The Japanese central government did not contradict a prefecture that reasserted a claim to Tokdo/Takeshima Island, a disputed but hitherto dormant claim on an island under South Korean control—a reminder that whereas Russia and China have both been compromising on numerous old territorial disputes, Japan has remained completely intransigent. Japan and South Korea twice mobilized naval forces over that dispute in 2006. For the United States, those near-confrontations posed the risk that two allies would engage in a military clash—an ironic blowback from Armitage Report pressures on Japan to be more assertive on territorial waters issues.

Some candidates for future top leadership roles emphasize the need to upgrade Japan's international image by subscribing to a revisionist view of World War II. Some leading figures supplement visits to the Yasukuni Shrine with praise of its shocking, anti-American museum, which is equally offensive to Koreans, Chinese, Americans, Singaporeans, Australians, and Europeans.

Americans reading media accounts of violent Chinese and South Korean reactions often feel that they are quaint overreactions, but Americans who have visited the museum express shock and horror at the portrayal of Japanese aggression in World War II as a heroic liberation of Asia from Europe and American colonization and at the minimization or denial of many important events that occurred. In the summer of 2006, Koizumi's last visit to the United States as leader prefigured what might happen in the future if the trend toward right-wing revisionism continues. The two countries talked about a great honor for Koizumi, an address to a joint session of Congress. But House International Relations Committee Chairman Henry Hyde, a World War II veteran, made clear that Koizumi's visits to the Yasukuni Shrine precluded that. In response, Koizumi said he wasn't interested in a congressional address anyway, and Bush escorted him to Elvis Presley's memorial at Graceland instead. Similarly, Prime Minister Abe's visit to Washington was marred by serious controversies over his efforts to back away from previous Japanese acknowledgments of responsibility for forced prostitution (comfort women) during World War II.

The Western generation of 9/11 is now very distant from the generation of Pearl Harbor, so it may be difficult for the new generation to understand intense Asian reactions to the increasing Japanese leadership portrayal of World War II and what preceded it as a heroic liberation of Asia. Since Japanese schools have for two generations mostly refrained from teaching modern Japanese history in order to avoid becoming embroiled in controversies with right-wing groups, contemporary Japanese have even less consciousness of what happened six and seven decades ago. Hence, in order to understand contemporary Asian reactions, one must, with some reluctance, indicate why the view of the Japanese as liberators elicits such antagonism in most of Eastern Asia.

For South Koreans, the memories of women being kidnapped and forced to serve for years as comfort women did not seem like liberation. In China, the senseless slaughter of the Rape of Nanjing and the large numbers of innocent people killed by the medical and chemical experiments of Unit 731 did not seem like liberation. When I lived in the Philippine city of Iloilo in 1964, attending Central Philippine University, the older teachers at the university made periodic pilgrimages to a place in the jungle where university leaders, all peaceful academics and Christian religious figures, were rounded up by Japanese troops and slaughtered. The professors' jungle prayer vigils, some of which I attended, kept wartime memories alive. My family's elderly maid, who came from the mountainous interior of the island, was proudest of one moment in her life: During the war, there were no men of military age in her village because the men either had been killed by the Japanese or had fled for their lives. But one day a Japanese fighter aircraft failed above the village, and the pilot parachuted out. The women of the village, including our maid, jumped on him and bit him to death. The women also took pride in having had parties for Japanese soldiers where they served camote, a sweet-potato-like tuber which is very nutritious after one has washed it thoroughly in the stream to remove the arsenic. When the Japanese soldiers came, they served camotes without washing them in the stream, and many Japanese soldiers died. Such was their appreciation for being "liberated."

Before the war, the Philippines had a large immigrant Japanese population, many of whom served as gardeners. After the war, that population essentially vanished. Japanese were simply not welcome after all the atrocities of the war. It was the returning U.S. general, Douglas MacArthur, not the Japanese, who was greeted as a liberating hero. When peace came, Americans were welcome, but Japanese largely were not. Some Japanese soldiers remained in jungle hiding places for many years after the war was over—one of them for about three decades—fearful of what the local people would do to them. As late as the 1980s, it was crucial for a Filipino running for election to have been on the U.S. side in the war; when people discovered in 1985 that Marcos's war medals from fighting the Japanese were fake, it was a huge blow to his standing. No other army in Asia elicited such powerful adverse reactions.

Today, Japanese youth are being told by many of their leaders that what happened in World War II was just part of the normal exigencies of war, and it is increasingly common among innocent, educated, middle-class people to believe that. Now the most important leaders are visiting a shrine and praising a museum dedicated to the proposition that the war was a valid liberation, so it is not surprising that the "liberated" peoples have a violent reaction. If Germany erected a shrine with a museum that praised Hitler's "liberation" of Poland and Russia and pretended that the Holocaust did not occur, the reaction in Washington would be similar to the reactions that Koreans, Chinese, Filipinos, and others have to the visits of Koizumi, Abe, Aso, and other key leaders to the Yasukuni Shrine and the praise some of them lavish on the Yushukan museum.

Fast-forward from 1964 to a quarter-century later. By 1989, Japan was admired as the exemplar of economic development throughout Asia. Its economic model attracted emulation throughout Northeast and Southeast Asia—and throughout much of the world. Its foreign-policy model of attaining regional and global leadership through disarmed economic dynamism was admired as an inspiration for other countries to prosper and become influential through peaceful means. Its investments were welcome, and trade with Japan was universally acknowledged to be the most important driver of the Asian economic miracle that by now had spread from Japan to its immediate neighbors and all the way to Indonesia. Economic admiration was reinforced by political appreciation; the Japanese economic miracle was the key to most of Asia's victory over communism.

At the same time, there was another side to this. One day I sat in the office of one of Thailand's leading businessmen and political leaders. I was there to interview him about Thai politics and economics for an investment-banking research paper. But he was agitated and wanted to talk about Japan. The Thai government, he said, had requested tenders for a new steel mill. Australia had proffered superior technology and the lowest price. (Japan leads the world in steel technology but does not transfer it lightly.) But when it became clear that the Australian firm would win, virtually all the potential Thai customers of the steel mill had gathered at the prime minister's office to say that they all were in joint ventures with Japanese companies and would not be allowed to buy steel from any non-Japanese firm. The government had to award the contract to the Japanese company. In one sector after another, the Thai leader I was interviewing said, the Japanese were using their financial dominance, industrial strength, and unique cooperation among companies, embassies, and aid agencies to take effective control of Thai domestic economic policy. That concern had resonance throughout Northeast and Southeast Asia.

Fast-forward another decade. Along with a group of senior Japanese executives, I am sitting in Shanghai at the China headquarters of one of the biggest Japanese companies. The Japanese general manager of the company is complaining about the difficulties of managing a Chinese staff. "The problem with these Chinese is that they are just like Americans. They want to be promoted to top management. They demand individual incentives and reject our group incentive programs." The Chinese welcomed Japanese money. They did not welcome Japanese companies' heavy emphasis on control. Unlike Americans and Europeans, the Japanese were not comfortable putting a local Chinese in control of their China business.

This experience of a half-century of Japanese efforts at regional military control, followed by a half-century of gradually tightening economic control, weighs heavily on the reactions of countries from Korea to Indonesia as the environment changes from one of Japanese dominance to one of multipolar economic competition after Japan's decade of stagnation and China's quarter-century of dynamism. Japan is disadvantaged by its history of seeking control. China is disadvantaged by its quarter-century of promoting chaos under Mao. In Korean and Southeast Asian eyes, Japan bears the heavier burden of history, and China seems to them to have repudiated its past misdeeds more decisively. U.S. national-security leaders often seem oblivious to this vital point as they seek to organize America's Asia policy ever more tightly around the U.S.-Japan alliance; such obliviousness threatens the alliance with South Korea and weakens relationships with key Southeast Asian countries.

In addition, two other, related aspects of Japan's posture have disadvantaged it in the regional power competition. First, as discussed earlier, although Japan's economy is much larger than China's, the Chinese economy is more open, so almost all Asian countries now have more trade with China than with Japan. The fact of greater Chinese openness surprises many whose image of the two economies is a hangover from the days when China was relatively autarkic and Japan was perceived as a fellow capitalist economy. But in 2005, China's total trade (exports plus imports) was 70 percent of the value of its GDP, whereas in Japan, an island economy that one would expect to have a greater exposure to trade, total trade was only 24 percent of GDP. Japan's economy is nominally several times as large as China's and has been experiencing a period of restructuring, so one would expect that it would provide one of history's greatest opportunities for foreign direct investment, but in 2005, Japan received only $38.8 billion of foreign direct investment, while China received $60.6 billion. One need only study the many ways in which the Japanese system has blocked attempts by foreigners to take over major listed companies to understand why Japan receives so much less.

The casual traveler doesn't need statistics to see China's greater openness. Drive on the roads of Japan and Korea and one rarely sees foreign-made cars; drive on China's roads, and Volkswagens, Buicks, and Hyundais are everywhere. Go through Japanese Customs and every incoming visitor has to present his or her passport to a Customs agent, with perhaps one out of every five visitors' bags being opened for inspection. In the past decade of visiting Beijing and Shanghai half a dozen times each year, I have never seen a Customs agent look at a passport or open a bag. (Immigration does, of course, check passports, as in other countries.)

China's superior openness results from the central experience of its development: Every major opening and liberalization has led to further economic success, and every wave of economic success has been associated with economic opening or liberalization. In contrast, Japan's era of greatest economic success, 1955–1975, was associated with a highly protectionist economic mobilization system. Such systems are very good at mobilizing resources for war, at mobilizing resources for recovery from war, and at initiating development in impoverished economies, but they are far less efficient, as the Japanese have painfully discovered, at creating sustained economic performance over the long term in normal times.

Chinese society is also more open. Although Taiwan has a long historical relationship with Japan—in fact, the first Taiwanese president of Taiwan, Lee Teng-hui, spoke Japanese as his first language—more than 5 percent of Taiwan's population has moved to mainland China to work or to accompany working family members, something that could never happen with Japan's proudly homogeneous society. There are many varieties of Chinese, speaking many dialects in addition to Mandarin, and China's vast global diaspora creates links to virtually every country in the world. As a result, more of the neighbors make money with China, more of them visit and live in China, and more of them absorb and appreciate Chinese culture.

Second, with the bloom off the Japanese economic miracle, the social legacy of the mobilization economy has proved unattractive. Japan's system empowers the government and enriches Japanese companies, but protectionism, cartels, and regulations raise prices and effectively transfer much of people's income to large corporations and interest groups. Japanese per capita incomes of around $50,000 are spectacularly high compared with those of their Asian neighbors, but the people have to live in tiny apartments and pay exorbitant prices for food and many other things. The middle-class Japanese family lives a lifestyle not a great deal better than that of the middle-class Filipino family. In 2000, on an investment trip to Kunshan, two hours outside

Shanghai, I noticed the farmers' homes, attractive two-story detached houses with nice furniture and all the accoutrements of modern living, including DVD machines that then cost about $35 there. I asked my Japanese colleagues, Who lived better, Shanghai farmers or mid-level Tokyo stockbrokers? They were unanimous in favor of the Shanghai farmers. (Elsewhere in China, farmers are frequently quite poor, and in a few areas they are desperately poor, but in a broad swath around Shanghai, they are full participants in the modern economy.) As a result, the once-worshipped Japanese mobilization model is in disrepair, and despite widespread residual poverty, the more market-oriented Chinese model now has the prestige.

All these things have, in the wake of Japan's great 1990 bubble-burst and a dozen years of stagnation, greatly reduced its standing relative to that of China. The rise of the hawkish nationalists under Koizumi has further reduced Japan's standing and worsened its isolation in Asia. As one respected Japanese commentator put it:

> If how the normalizers want to see themselves creates friction with neighboring countries, if what they say for domestic consumption is understood very differently abroad, they seem not to care. We may soon be hearing talk of Japan's diplomatic "lost decade." However, as Japan becomes more isolated and alienated from the rest of Northeast Asia, and as the cost of this isolation to the national interest becomes evident, calmer political forces should come to the fore. So long as Yasukuni remains a diplomatic sore spot, the acceptance of any Japanese political ideas abroad is unlikely.[14]

Cultural Uniqueness and Foreign Policy

As a major power in a globalizing world, Japan finds itself increasingly disadvantaged by its elites' determination to emphasize Japan's cultural homogeneity and uniqueness. Its principal competitors, the United States, India, China, and the European Union, are diverse societies with multiple ethnic groups, multiple cultural strains, and multiple languages or dialects (with the exception of parts of the United States).

---

[14] Tamamoto, op. cit.

Compared with Japan, they are relatively open to immigration and to having families move abroad for extended periods of time if work requires.

Japan, in contrast, has hung back from globalization. It prides itself on a (partially accurate) self-image of cultural and racial homogeneity, and its elites emphasize uniqueness. To preserve its homogeneity, the country allows only a trickle of immigration. As a rule, Japanese families do not like to venture abroad except for brief vacations. When I was a senior executive of the great Japanese investment bank, Nomura, based in Hong Kong, all my U.S., European, Chinese, Korean, and Southeast Asian colleagues brought their families to live with them in Hong Kong, but none of my numerous Japanese colleagues did. Some of them had served consecutive tours in places such as London, Zurich, and Hong Kong, and they left their families behind in Tokyo all that time, because many of the wives did not like the idea of living abroad and, above all, because the Japanese educational system would not accommodate children who moved overseas and then wanted to come back. Such children would be disadvantaged educationally and rejected socially. At one time, Japan tried to promote needed immigration while maintaining homogeneity by allowing, for instance, ethnic Japanese to migrate back from Brazil, but even the children of expatriate Japanese could not fit into the education system, so the government abandoned the experiment.

In some ways, this emphasis has conferred great advantages on the country. Japan can reasonably claim to be the world's most civilized society. It is difficult, at least for me, to imagine a higher compliment than this. Social life is pleasantly orderly. People are safe; the rate of violent crime is very low compared with that in the United States. Things just work better than they do in Europe, the United States, China, or India. Social and business relationships are ritualized in a way that reduces uncertainty and conflict. Social, political, and economic institutions evolve in a more dignified and socially conservative way than elsewhere, although the country's spectacular postwar rise and its equally spectacular bubble-burst in the 1990s have severely challenged that pattern. By comparison, Japan's principal competitors are boisterous, disorderly, unpredictable, unsafe, and generally less civilized. The Japanese people are right to put an exceptionally high value on their civilization. To me, after having traveled all over the world, the word "refined," with all its positive associations, automatically evokes thoughts of Japan.

While these advantages are so substantial that Japan is unwilling to abandon them, there are corresponding disadvantages. The emphasis on uniqueness encourages protectionism and provincialism. The country's economic policies resist imports and foreign ownership to a much greater extent than do Europe, the United States, and China. Soon India may be added to the list of countries that are much more economically open. Unwillingness to accept immigration and family emigration leaves Japanese companies with less of a global network of social connections than their Chinese, Indian, European, and American counterparts have. At a late 2006 conference in New York, a professor from the University of Michigan, Ann Arbor, said that when he had asked the provost for a list of all the university's ties with China, he expected a couple pages; instead he got more than 60 single-spaced pages. Despite the fact that Japan is an ally whose postwar ties to the United States go back twice as long as China's, a comparable Japanese list would be only a fraction as long. For a long time after World War II, the costs of such policies were not apparent, but now Japan's restrictions on imports create a striking shortfall of exports. Protectionism has led to an economy with a very narrow range of internationally competitive goods (notably cars, consumer electronics, and computer games), lack of foreign competition has left major institutions such as banks, far behind their peers in other advanced democracies, and lack of social ties has left Indians and Chinese with proportionately far more diverse social networks and deeper social ties around the world.

Along with protectionism, the emphasis on uniqueness and homogeneity has brought widespread provincialism. (Of course, provincialism is prevalent in all societies, and perhaps increasingly so in the United States, but there are important differences of degree.) In the 1970s, Japanese trade negotiators did not realize how they sounded when they argued that U.S. beef could not be allowed into Japan because Japanese intestines were a different length from American intestines, and European skis could not be allowed because Japanese snow was different. In 2006, at a conference I attended just before writing this, one very senior Japanese executive argued that imports in general must be restricted because Japanese housewives are unaccustomed to foreign things and won't buy them because they believe foreign things are unsafe; in response, a former U.S. trade negotiator asked why, if people won't buy them anyway, the imports need to be restricted. At the same conference, a senior Japanese government official bitterly denounced China for trying to push a certain Chinese standard for computers, only to hear his American audience ask why they couldn't use their Blackberrys in Japan and why Japan and Korea were the only countries in the world where foreigners couldn't use their cell phones.

These attitudes penetrate very deeply into even the most cosmopolitan institutions. Tokyo University aspires only to be just what it is, namely, Japan's most outstanding university. In contrast, Peking University, Qinghua, Jiaotong, and Fudan consciously benchmark themselves against the world's best; they have a long way to go, and they know that, but they continually put in place programs to move toward their goal.[15]

Such small exchanges are part of a larger syndrome. As noted elsewhere in this book, Japan has experienced a large domestic demand for books and magazines that caricature neighboring societies, notably Korea and China, in ways so insensitive and vicious that they would be intolerable in most other advanced societies. Japanese leaders and much of Japanese society have difficulty understanding why Koreans, Chinese, and Southeast Asians would be troubled by senior officials' endorsement of the revisionist views of World War II; after all, that was just a domestic effort to restore the nation's pride. Top officials have argued that the revisionist view of the war was necessary to raise Japan's standing in the world, apparently not realizing how it has in fact reduced Japan's standing. Prime Minister Abe says that by rewriting the past, he is creating a "beautiful Japan," but South Koreans, Chi-

---

[15] As part of this, a Jiaotong University index ranking the world's universities by objective indices of research influence has become the leading global standard. Notably, it does not overrate either Jiaotong or the other leading Chinese universities. See Institute of Higher Education, Shanghai Jiao Tong University, "Academic Ranking of Universities Worldwide—2005" (http://ed.sjtu.edu.cn/rank/2005/ARWU2005Main.htm).

nese, Singaporeans, Australians, and even those few Americans who are aware of the issue see the revisionist process as ugly, not beautiful.

The sense of uniqueness has pervasive inward-looking consequences. One sees this in language education. Japanese students are required to take six years of English in order to graduate from high school; Chinese are required to take seven. Given the far higher general quality of Japanese education, one would expect far more Japanese to speak basic English and to speak it at a much higher standard. However, the reality is the opposite, because the typical Chinese attitude is that success depends on globalization, while the typical Japanese attitude (although it is changing slowly) is that globalization is a bother. (Of course, an American author writing these words cannot do so without acknowledging shamefully that we Americans are behind most Asian countries, including both Japan and China, in learning foreign languages. American provincialism increasingly causes difficulties for a country that aspires to manage the world, but that is a subject for a different study.)

Similarly, notwithstanding Japan's extraordinary export successes in cars and consumer electronics, one sees the disadvantages of its attitude toward the outside world in commerce. In 2005, I visited a popular tourist town just outside Japan's great port city of Nagoya and found a large ceramic planter that struck me as a marvelous piece of art. I wanted to buy it and ship it to my home in California, but the owner of the shop insisted that there was no way to pack it for shipping and no shipping service that would send it to California for me. The only possibility was to carry it on the train to downtown Nagoya (actually a physical impossibility) and ship it from there. In contrast, during the same year, I found myself in Tibet wanting to buy and ship home a large, multipart, inlaid enamel screen. This was a much more difficult packing and shipping task, in one of the world's locations most distant from a major port. The Tibetan shopkeeper didn't think twice about packing the screen quite professionally and shipping it by DHL. There are two differences here. One is that both the Japanese shop owner and the great Japanese courier company, Yamato, are comfortable and complacent with a focus on the Japanese market; foreigners just aren't that important. The other is that, unlike the Chinese market, the Japanese market doesn't have pervasive DHL, FedEx, and UPS offices offering international service and forcing their local counterparts to compete.

The emphasis on homogeneity and uniqueness persists despite the fact that Japan's great successes have consistently come when it opened up and globalized. The first time was in the early Meiji era (mid-19th century), when the United States forcibly opened Japan, and Japan went on a spree of investigating and borrowing foreign technology and foreign institutions (a British-style navy, a German-style education system, and so forth). Globalization made Japan Asia's only great success story of the era, enabling it to maintain its independence at a time when neighbors fell to colonialism and to become a modern industrial economy while its neighbors remained miserably backward. The second era of great successes was the period from 1955 to 1975, when Japanese companies scoured the world for better ways of doing things, borrowing U.S. ideas of quality control and improving on them to the point where Japanese quality control was far better than that anywhere in the United States, and similarly borrowing and improving on U.S. ideas about things like employee recreation centers and innumerable other institutional arrangements. Both eras of Japanese globalizing success were the result of overwhelming foreign military pressure; this is a crucial contrast to China, which went through a period of fanatical xenophobia but then decided on its own that rapid and thorough globalization was the key to achieving its domestic and foreign aspirations.

In the same way, Japan's great corporate successes—Toyota, Honda, Sony, Panasonic, Nintendo—have been those that broke free of protectionist barriers and competed in the global marketplace. Honda's employment and markets are more American than Japanese, although its management and ownership remain strictly Japanese. The lesson of these great global Japanese firms is that the Japanese can compete successfully anywhere, but only when they break out of the protected domestic market.

Japanese society is, of course, globalizing. Educated younger Japanese are much more curious about foreign things than their elders are. Unlike my Nomura business colleagues in Hong Kong, my Japanese colleagues at Harvard's Kennedy School of Government in 2002 did bring their families with them. During the 1990–2002 era of crisis, the government allowed a flood of inexpensive foreign-made goods to enter the country and thereby improved the living standards of people whose incomes were stagnant. More Japanese are learning English now, and more are taking their mandatory English lessons seriously. Prime Minister Koizumi launched a campaign to encourage foreign direct investment. But Japan is moving much more slowly than its major competitors, and its failure to connect to other countries has played a major role in its increasing isolation from its neighbors during the Koizumi/Abe era. South Korea, Asia's only other relatively homogeneous society, has suffered from similar problems, so it is hardly surprising that these two intimately connected but proudly unique societies have clashed severely and repeatedly long after one would have expected colonial resentments to fade.

The emphasis on inward-looking uniqueness and homogeneity has tremendous foreign-policy consequences. Because Japan is more protected, its larger economy now has less trade with its neighbors than the smaller Chinese economy does—and correspondingly less economic influence. Because it is more protected, it receives less foreign direct investment than China does, and over time it will receive less technological stimulus from foreigners. Because Tokyo is so much more provincial than Hong Kong or Singapore, the tiny Chinese city states, particularly Hong Kong, will remain the international financial capitals of Asia, with Shanghai rather than Tokyo the long-term challenger, for the same reason.[16]

As noted, from Prime Minister Koizumi to the average Japanese, visits to the Yasukuni Shrine and the rewriting of history are seen in Japan largely as methods of rebuilding Japanese pride and confidence

---

[16] One of the best ways to understand the relations of Asian countries to the wider world is by assessing their efforts to turn their capital cities into regional Asian centers. On the basis of the numbers, Tokyo is the natural financial hub of Asia, and the government is trying to build an international financial center in Tokyo's Nihonbashi district, but it sees the problem primarily as a real-estate arrangement. South Korea wants to make Seoul/Inchon a great regional hub like Hong Kong, but like the Japanese, the Korean leaders don't understand how provincialism and protectionism hinder their efforts. Taipei has for years sought to challenge Hong Kong as a regional hub, but it does not want to face up to the reality that firms will not accept being divorced from their largest supplier and market, the mainland.

in the aftermath of a difficult century. Not surprisingly, people with such a view see the protests of Koreans, Chinese, Singaporeans, Australians, and the chairman of the U.S. House International Relations Committee as inappropriate intrusions on Japanese domestic affairs.

When all this led to Japanese isolation from its Asian neighbors, Tokyo's solution under Prime Minister Koizumi was to "handle it through the alliance." Similarly, as we shall see, Washington has used the military alliance with Japan to displace more-nuanced and non-military relations with other Asian countries. On both sides, in other words, the U.S.-Japan alliance has become a substitute for a nuanced policy toward other Asian countries. As an inevitable consequence, both Japan and the United States have experienced increasing difficulties with other Asian countries, including both allies (e.g., South Korea) and non-allies (e.g., China). Some of these difficulties would have arisen anyway, but Tokyo is paying a high price for using the alliance as a substitute for a foreign policy, and Washington is paying a high price for betting its whole position in Asia on an inward-looking and increasingly isolated Japan.

There are periodic, often wise, efforts within the Bush administration to build broader, more-nuanced relationships, symbolized by Deputy Secretary of State Robert Zoellick's concept of getting China to be a "stakeholder" in the global system, Treasury Secretary Henry Paulson's prestigious Strategic Economic Dialogues (SEDs), and Admiral William Fallon's insistent reopening of the military dialogue with China. But these have remained at the margin of U.S. relationships with Asia. Characteristically, Zoellick resigned after being refused promotion to higher office, Paulson's SEDs have been judged in Washington to have achieved little, and Fallon's exemplary effort at dialogue, although in my view it was the minimum any responsible power should do, initially attracted severe and public criticism at very senior levels. The so-called China-centered military strategy, the reorientation of Japan and the alliance to support that strategy through such means as the February 2005 2+2 announcement (detailed elsewhere in this book), along with other efforts to gain incremental military advantage, continue to dominate all other aspects of the U.S. relationship with Japan, China, Southeast Asia, and India.

What the Future Could Bring

Tokyo's response to post-1990 economic and foreign-policy disappointments has been to leverage its relationship with the United States even more than in the past and, since economic diplomacy has failed, to expand the reach of its military. Japan remains quite tightly tied to the United States for some years to come, but in historical terms, its relations with all major countries are in flux. The future choices Japan makes could depend on key events of varying probabilities. The orderly continuation of current trends would probably have Japan very tightly tied to the United States for another decade but gradually asserting itself on various issues, gradually strengthening its military to the point of considerable self-confidence, and then arranging the departure of U.S. troops from its soil while retaining some form of looser alliance with the United States. The Foreign Ministry emphasizes that Japan needs to remain tightly anchored to the United States for the indefinite future in order to avoid drifting into a dangerous situation the way the country did in the 20th century after it ended its alliance with Britain. But that is not currently the direction in which the country's right-wing politicians and national-security elites are headed, and the baseline scenario for Japan probably must be based on their views, not those of the Foreign Ministry.

There is an alternative scenario that would become particularly probable if Japan were to experience a period of unexpectedly rapid economic and social liberalization. The generation of people under 45 years of age is more socially liberal, more cosmopolitan, and more inclined to open the still heavily protected economy. If women were to enter the workforce in much larger numbers and at much higher levels, if domestic competition were given freer rein, if barriers to trade and investment were to come down the way they have in China, and if global best practices were embraced eagerly as they were in Meiji Japan and in contemporary China, Japanese growth could surprise on the upside, and a younger generation could assume power more quickly. The early emergence of such generational power could also reverse the rightward trend of recent Japanese domestic politics and result in a rapprochement with China, consistent with continued alliance and friendship with the United States, driven by cosmopolitan business leaders.

On the economic downside, a renewed outbreak of LDP political factionalism, combined with continued hapless opposition and public apathy, could conceivably lead to a period of political incoherence and economic malaise. This might well accelerate the drift toward more-assertive right-wing nationalism, because the leadership of that movement tends to operate behind the scenes and to be most effective in the absence of a strong, effective democratic leadership. If one were to extrapolate the narrow experience of 2007 into the indefinite future, this would be the outcome.

Looking further at alternatives, one can also see a scenario in which a sharp break with the United States occurs as a result of nationalistic trends developing more rapidly than current trends would suggest. Within the right, there is a powerful tendency to see dependence on the United States as debilitating, confrontation with China as inevitable, and Taiwanese independence and permanent division of Korea as vital Japanese national interests. This set of views, basically an echo of the colonial and World War II eras, is not the mainstream view today, but it is held by groups that under Koizumi and Abe, and under U.S. pressure for Japanese rearmament, have captured leadership roles in Japanese foreign and national-security policy.[17] For these groups, prominent visits to the Yasukuni Shrine, even if not by the prime minister, are a vital symbol. As one thoughtful Japanese official put it, such visits play the same role for right-wing senior officials as did the requirement centuries ago to step on a picture of Jesus Christ to demonstrate anti-Christian credentials. Because of the influence of this group, a U.S.–South Korean effort to engineer a peaceful unification of Korea or a peaceful settlement of the Taiwan issue consistent with the

---

[17] On a trip through China in September 2004 with RAND's president, James Thomson, I became uncomfortably aware that when we write scenarios, many in Asia and elsewhere take them as predictions. Scenarios such as the one drawn here are far from predictions. They are plausible stories, hopefully consistent with known facts, about what could imaginably occur in situations when we are incapable of predicting actual outcomes. We write scenarios when there are chains of events with substantial probabilities that we cannot predict. Even after writing scenarios, we often need to mention a few "surprises," which have very low probability but are not impossible, events that would have substantial consequences if they did occur.

"one-China" formula could trigger a major crisis in the U.S.-Japanese relationship.

Few countries have had as traumatic an era as Japan had in the 20th century. Its leaders spent the first half of the century in a catastrophic quest for domination of Asia through military means, the second half in a desperate effort at reconstruction followed by a failed bid for dominance of Asia by economic means. The depth of the Japanese elite's overreaction to recent Chinese successes has far more to do with despair over a century of failed efforts at domination than with any Chinese provocation.

The extent of the regime change under way—a transformation of the country's economy, its politics, and its national-security policy—is generally underestimated in the West and perhaps as little understood in Japan itself. The Japanese people are emerging from a great trauma burdened by a political system designed to inhibit change of direction, an economic system suffering from elephantiasis, a financial system burdened by the heaviest debt of any advanced economy, a national-security system torn between total dependence on the United States and rising nationalism, and a population structure that is graying and declining. But they also have one of the world's most educated populations, the world's most disciplined workforce, some of the world's most competitive businesses, some of the world's most innovative technologies, a rising generation that is more cosmopolitan and more balanced between work and family, strong support from the United States, some evolution of the political system toward one that will permit real leadership, and the energy of a rising nationalism. Fifteen years ago, nobody predicted that Japan would find itself at such a crossroads. The future 15 years hence is even more difficult to predict.

If they wished to, Japan's leaders could inspire their people and the world with a vision of social maturity; of increasingly wise employment of women and older people and of competition and globalization to achieve growth in an economy with a graying and declining population; of peace through increasing integration with and understanding of their neighbors; and of sustainable environmental practices in which Japan is poised to lead the world. Elements of all these are in place.

But so far, instead of inspiring their people with a grand vision of the future, the new era's leaders have preferred to prettify a difficult past.

As the 21st century began, the United States decided to bet its entire position in Asia on the alliance with Japan. In effect, it has bet not just on the Japanese nation but in particular on a newly assertive national-security elite that represents a rather narrow and unrepresentative slice of Japanese society. In all of American history, the United States has never before made such a bet anywhere in the world, with the arguable exception of the bet on Britain in World War II. The current bet is not on the Japan of 1945 or 1975 or 1989 (the year before the bubble burst) or 2000, but on a rearming Japan with an economy, a polity, a foreign policy, and a military evolving faster and more unpredictably than those of any other advanced country, under a new and increasingly right-wing leadership that wants to rebuild national morale by reengineering a failed vision of the first half of the 20th century rather than through an inspiring new vision of the future. Rarely in world history has such a power made such a consequential bet.

China

There is great disorder under heaven, and the situation is excellent.

—Mao Zedong

To understand China you just need to know multiplication and division. Anything multiplied by 1.3 billion makes your successes seem overwhelming. Any achievement divided by 1.3 billion seems insignificant.

—Zheng Bijian, China's leading foreign-policy spokesman, 2006

The weakness of Korea and (especially) China was the main driver of 20th-century Asia's horrible cycle of war, famine, and death. Had China and Korea been strong, coherent powers of the kind they had been for much of known history, the Sino-Japanese and Russo-Japanese wars would never have occurred, the Japanese invasion of Manchuria would have been deterred, the Japanese attack on Pearl

Harbor would never have occurred, and World War II would have been European War II, for better or worse possibly not even engaging the United States. Japanese aggression was, of course, the most immediate part of the problem, but Chinese and Korean weakness and division would have attracted—and did attract—predators from all the strong countries of the world even if Japan had been a placid, peace-loving, inward-looking country. Chinese and Korean power vacuums have been the bane of modern Asian and American history. Now that is changing, with benefits and risks yet to be determined. At the beginning of the 21st century, the U.S. national-security elite was obsessed with the risks and frequently unwilling to reflect on the benefits.

The horrors and humiliations China suffered during two centuries of weakness turned mid-20th–century China into a fearsome troublemaker. The second quarter of the century saw the rise of a nasty but unifying dictatorship under Chiang Kai-shek's socialist, Leninist, Soviet-advised Guomindang Party, which competed with a very similar socialist, Leninist, Soviet-advised Communist Party. Both intended to modernize China's technology, society, and economy. It was not an accident that both of the main contenders to rule China were socialist in their economics and Leninist in their politics. Leninism is about tough methods of political control, socialism centralizes control of the nation's resources under political leaders, and both were perfectly adapted to the overwhelming challenge of reuniting China after two centuries of internal disintegration and foreign depredation. Largely because it secured key urban areas first, the Guomindang drove the communists into the rural areas, and then into the most peripheral rural areas (the Long March), just as would later happen to communist parties in Thailand, Malaysia, and the Philippines. Like its counterparts in non-communist Southeast Asia, the Chinese Communist Party was headed for extinction.

Had this process continued uninterrupted, Chiang Kai-shek might well have become the modernizing Park Chung Hee of China. But the Japanese invasion interrupted it, shattering Chiang's urban-based rule, and inadvertently brought to power a peasant-based jacquerie of the kind that has arisen many times in history (for instance, in the French Revolution) but has rarely achieved power. Chiang was reduced to dependence on reactionary warlords and landlords on the mainland and, as a consequence, went on to lead what was unquestionably the world's most corrupt regime, but he later modernized Taiwan. The architect of Taiwan's great land reform, which became the basis of social stability and growth, later told me that he had simply unrolled the plans he had made for land reform on the mainland before the Japanese invasion.

The core views of the Maoist revolution were those of jacqueries everywhere: If you kill the landlords, everyone will be more prosperous; if you kill the bureaucrats, society will move forward unimpeded by corrupt obstacles; and if you eliminate the foreigners, local purity will lead to unity and dignity. Among peasant movements throughout the world, these ideas are as common as they are inconsistent with reality.

Although Mao's power was a product of peasant chiliasm and Japanese intervention rather than either Chinese culture or existing Leninist ideology, the historical moment gave Mao not only power, but also the ability, briefly, to remold China as a caricature of himself. For two centuries, China had been weakening, fragmenting, and suffering invasions. China's elites had tried empire. They had tried military dictatorship. They had tried warlords. They had tried some socialism and some capitalism, and even a bit of democracy. They tried broad strategies such as combining Western technology with Eastern culture— something that seemed to work in Japan. A big part of China had a brief go at achieving salvation through a Christian cult led by a putative brother of Jesus Christ (the Taiping Rebellion, 1850–1864). Like contemporary Iranians, the Chinese also tried going back to past verities—in this case, Confucian verities (the Tongzhi Restoration, mid-19th century). Nothing worked. The system, both at home and abroad, seemed stacked against their success.

For a decade after the communist victory in 1949, the new government tried to emulate the stolid Soviet bureaucratic socialism. Although to Western economic eyes the results of the five years preceding 1958 were fairly good, Mao didn't seem to think this worked either. He tried to break out of it in the Great Leap Forward of 1958–1961 and succeeded only in starving tens of millions of his countrymen.

It is common and convenient in many Western circles (particularly national-security circles) today to see contemporary China as a reincarnation of the Soviet system, but that is not the Chinese view. The common Chinese phrase for the era of the Soviet model is "Borrowed suit. Didn't fit. Threw it away."

It is only in this context of seemingly having tried everything and failed that the Cultural Revolution, 1966–1976, can be understood: It was an attempt to destroy every major manifestation of the old Chinese system of rule, from teachers to government bureaucracy to Communist Party bureaucracy, and to reject every aspect of the extant international system.

In this period, the Maoist movement became Samson trying to destroy the global temple. Mao promoted instability as a good thing, at home and abroad. He underwrote revolutionary insurgencies in every non-communist Asian neighbor, as well as throughout Africa and Latin America, and inspired violent outbreaks even in America's leading universities. To Mao, the great postwar institutions that the United States and its allies had created to bring order and prosperity to the postwar world—the General Agreement on Tariffs and Trade (GATT), the World Bank, the IMF, the U.S. alliance system—along with the integuments of Western life, namely, markets, material incentives, and universal suffrage elections, were all instruments of delusion and oppression that kept China and other third-world countries from achieving dignity and a decent life. This Maoist challenge had sufficient resonance in the world's rice paddies and barrios and, peculiarly, America's Ivy League universities that today's Islamism, which uses similar logic and similar cultural rage to challenge the same institutions, is diminutive by comparison.

The good news about the pinnacle of Mao's foolhardy jacquerie, the Cultural Revolution of 1966–1976, was that it was so destructive that it harmed and alienated every major group in Chinese society—farmers, workers, industrialists, intellectuals, government, Communist Party, and the army. The resulting near-universal revulsion caused a sharp technocratic reaction—China's Thermidor. It brought to power different top leaders, led importantly by Deng Xiaoping, a cosmopolitan with a French education as opposed to provincials like Mao who had never traveled, an organization man as opposed to anti-bureaucratic Mao, and an urban rather than rural sensibility. The new leadership looked to successful Hong Kong, Taiwan, South Korea, and Singapore as models of how a Confucian society could modernize.[18] What Deng did was pretty much what Chiang Kai-shek would probably have done three decades earlier had the Japanese not smashed the progressive part of his political base.

Within a few years, China had not only different top leaders but also quite different institutional structures (notwithstanding continued rule by the Chinese Communist Party, which was just as different from Mao's party as Chiang Kai-shek's Guomindang was in 1927, 1947, and 1967), different policies, and different social groups supporting the regime. In short, China had undergone a major regime change, despite continued Chinese Communist Party rule.[19] Failure to appreciate the full extent of the regime change, away from both Stalinism and Maoism, has led to a potentially catastrophic misreading of China in much of the West.

Faced with potential collapse, after long bureaucratic ossification in the Soviet Union and after the Cultural Revolution in China, the two countries took different paths. The Soviet system was institutionalized, and except for Gorbachev's feeble efforts at the end, Soviet leaders followed the logic of their system until it collapsed.[20] The Chinese system was not institutionalized; it was just emerging from a charismatic era typical of revolutions—e.g., the French Terror—and typical of the infancies of some Chinese dynasties. Therefore, taking advantage of the universal Chinese disillusionment with Maoism, Deng Xiaoping turned Mao's priorities on their head. At home, he sought to

---

[18] This emulation of the earlier Confucian economic miracles and the forecast that this strategy would succeed is the central theme of Overholt, 1993, op. cit.

[19] For some definitions of *regimes* and *regime change*, see T. J. Pempel, *Regime Shift: Comparative Dynamics of the Japanese Political Economy*, Ithaca, NY: Cornell University Press, 1998, pp. 20ff. The phrase *regime change* has been hijacked as a term for forcible overthrow, as in the U.S. overthrow of Saddam Hussein, but the original broader, deeper meaning remains the core definition in political science.

[20] For a summary of why Gorbachev's strategy was doomed to failure and Deng's likely to succeed, see Overholt, 1993, op. cit., chap. 1.

create stable organizations, and he insisted that leaders with radically different ideas such as Li Peng and Zhu Rongzhi work together rather than engaging in a destructive struggle. Instead of rejecting all things foreign, he sought the secrets of successful development from the cosmopolitan experiences of South Korea, Hong Kong, Taiwan, and Singapore. Instead of Mao's priorities ("Politics in command" and "All power flows from the barrel of a gun"), he learned from his neighbors the core lesson that power and prosperity would flow from a priority for economic development; following the example of South Korea's Park Chung Hee, he cut the military budget from 16 percent of GDP to 3 percent (it is probably now about 2.5 percent [see box], despite exaggerations from some quarters in the West), and he shifted from sponsorship of revolution in all of China's non-communist neighbors to sponsorship of stability in all of them. Deng characterized his national strategy as Four Modernizations (agriculture, industry, science and technology, defense), with defense consigned firmly to the lowest priority.[21] Instead of seeking to defeat or destroy the major U.S.-sponsored development institutions, China gradually joined all of them—the IMF, the World Bank, the World Trade Organization (WTO), the Asian Development bank (ADB), and others. Chinese officers and scholars privately praised U.S. alliances with Japan, South Korea, the Philippines, and others as sources of needed stability in Asia.[22]

---

[21] Zheng Bijian later created a "Peaceful Rise" theory around Deng's priorities and contrasted it to the view of U.S. "realists" who argue that any rising power will automatically be an assertive troublemaker. Zheng's work has been treated as pure propaganda by much of the U.S. national-security establishment, but it just codifies the shift of priorities from geopolitics to domestic economics that Deng implemented based on the experience of the other Asian-miracle economies. As noted elsewhere in this book, I had been writing about this phenomenon among the Asian-miracle economies, primarily focused on U.S. allies, for many years before it became a China controversy, indeed before China's rise was even an established trend. In Asia, the phenomenon started with Japan's example of power and prosperity for a disarmed country and with Park Chung Hee's slashing of South Korea's military budget after his 1961 coup. For one version of Zheng's argument, see "Peacefully Rising to Great Power Status," *Foreign Affairs*, September/October 2005, pp. 18–24.

[22] China's view of the U.S. alliances was often different in reality from the public rhetoric. From the mid-1970s until recent years, I have had conversations with a wide variety of Chinese military officers, government officials, and scholars who virtually all affirmed the value to regional stability of the U.S. alliance system and its associated bases. From Deng onward,

China then embarked on a search, largely in the Western industrial democracies, for global best practices on the premise that China must import whatever worked, regardless of ideology and regardless of origin. (Deng's most widely quoted aphorism became, "It doesn't matter whether a cat is black or white so long as it catches mice.") The resulting globalization opened China's economy to foreign trade and foreign investment to an extent that far exceeded that of Japan.

More important, China embarked on a wave of institutional globalization. It reorganized its central bank on the model of the U.S. Federal Reserve. It adopted securities regulations from New York, London, and Hong Kong and appointed dozens of regulators from those financial capitals to help reform its markets. It copied Taiwan's regulations on foreign portfolio investment. It copied Singapore's institutions for managing foreign-exchange reserves. It emulated France's military procurement system. It adopted international accounting standards for its listed companies—at a time when countries such as Indonesia were reluctant to do so. It welcomed the Western world's most powerful banks as strategic partners in its banks and appointed executives from Western banks to positions as high officers and directors of Chinese banks. More fundamentally, it adopted the ideal of the rule of law, a reversal of millennia of Chinese adherence to a Solomonic ideal of justice delivered by the individual judgment of (supposedly) virtuous officials. Likewise, after millennia of cultural emphasis on unity, it adopted the idea that efficiency was best achieved through competition. It adopted English as a second language, now requiring seven years of English study for a high school diploma. And it sent the

---

the U.S. and China shared the goal of regional stability and the value of institutions that supported it. Early on, residual ideology required, however, that Chinese public rhetoric affirm that all foreign bases should be removed from all countries. Likewise, specific Chinese relationships, for instance, that with North Korea, similarly required public rhetoric to demand removal of U.S. bases, while private conversation and actual belief often said the opposite. This view of the value of the U.S. alliance system came under fundamental challenge when Lee Teng-hui and Chen Shui-bian began their push toward an independent Taiwan and the United States moved to block China's reactions to that push. The opposite view became increasingly strong when the George W. Bush administration repeatedly tightened the U.S.-Japan alliance and both Japan and the United States appeared increasingly to identify China and Taiwan as particular objects of concern for the alliance.

The Chinese Military Budget

It is virtually impossible to reach consensus regarding the Chinese military budget. The Chinese omit key items, and their military budgets have been rising at a double-digit pace for a number of years. However, in the early reform years, the People's Liberation Army (PLA) was starved to the point where, by the mid-1990s, its technology, training, and capabilities were pathetic. Although the military budget has been catching up from those years of starvation, it nonetheless steadily declines as a share of the total government budget. Western hawks emphasize the former points and don't mention the latter. Doves do the opposite.

Popular accounts are extraordinary for the ways in which they inflate the numbers. In the days of high Chinese inflation, it was an accepted convention that economic growth rates were presented with the inflation taken out, while military budgets were presented with the inflation left in. This made a difference of as much as 20 percentage points. When the Chinese military was heavily engaged in civilian-style businesses, some national-security hawks liked to include the revenues from the PLA's bottling of Dr. Pepper and distribution of Baskin-Robbins ice cream as part of the military budget, even though most of the profits went to the generals personally, not to purchase weapons. Chinese leaders knew this, so in 1998–1999, the officers were forced to sell their businesses. The government then had to buy back most of them, which increased the military budget. Soldiers' pay, a few dollars a month, had to be raised to compensate for the lack of business revenues. All of these adjustments resulted in large increases in the military budget but not a lot of increase in actual military power.

There are many decisions an analyst has to make in estimating the Chinese military budget. One must decide whether or not to apply purchasing power parity (PPP) adjustments. Applying them multiplies Chinese budgets by a factor of four. Western national-security analysts with an interest in maximizing the estimates can apply PPP adjustments indiscriminately to the military budget even when the military's most sophisticated equipment was imported at international prices—making PPP adjustments inappropriate. One can treat a semi-literate Chinese corporal as if he were paid like—or had comparable military value to—a technologically sophisticated American corporal. One can include as military expenditure almost anything that has potential military value. For instance, one can include as military a tiny bit of the electronics industry or almost all of it. Dozens of such choices, many legitimately debatable, made primarily in classified documents, make it almost impossible for scholars without access to such documents to reach reasonable judgments about the conflicting estimates of the Chinese military budget.

Hence it is best to focus instead on capabilities. The Chinese military has good capability to defend its home territory, and it is acquiring greater capability to defend against Taiwan becoming independent. It has remarkably little capability to project power outside its borders. Japan, South Korea, and India have more.

Capabilities have increased enormously in response to Taiwan President Lee Teng-hui's efforts to move toward independence. A key controversy concerns whether the PLA remains primarily focused on Taiwan or has broader ambitions. When U.S. national-security hawks see the PLA acquiring capabilities to knock down satellites or to attack carriers far out at sea, they often conclude that China is reaching for great-power status. However, that is debatable. If there were a war over Taiwan, Beijing would face immediate defeat if it confined its efforts to the strait. Therefore, any competent Chinese general would try to blind the United States (kill its satellites) and go after the carriers before they reach the strait. Like the Vietnamese and the Iraqis, they would not play by rules that are convenient for the United States. There is much evidence, often ignored, that the PLA isn't seeking a broader range of exclusive power. In my conversations with Chinese officials, they plead for more U.S. military commitment to defend the Strait of Malacca—a request that is inconsistent with trying to push the United States out of the region. If their intentions are aggressive, why are they more willing to compromise their border issues to the satisfaction of the other parties than India and Japan are?

For the latest Washington assessment, see U.S. Department of Defense, *Military Power of the People's Republic of China 2007: A Report to Congress Pursuant to the National Defense Authorization Act*, Washington, DC: Office of the Secretary of Defense, 2007.

children of its elite abroad, to the industrial democracies, for their education, to an extent that probably has no parallel in a great civilization since the Romans entrusted their children to Greek educators. As discussed below, the search for best practices even extended—albeit more tentatively—into politics. Gingerly and fearfully, in a way that mimicked Taiwan's development, it started experimenting with elections in the villages, in the party, and in novel urban experiments.

All these forms of institutional globalization proceeded a step at a time, carefully evaluated before the next step was taken. Such gradualism is often disparaged in the West. For instance, many Western economists, led by Jeffrey Sachs and the World Bank, were initially inclined to denigrate China's gradualism in economics. That denigration has changed only gradually as the Asian gradualists have consistently outperformed countries in Eastern Europe and elsewhere that have followed more abrupt strategies ("shock therapy") informed by what was called the Washington Consensus. Similarly, Western lawyers and politicians frequently denigrate China's gradualism in law, accounting, and politics, implicitly treating it as shameful that China has advanced only a quarter of the way from King Solomon to Justice Marshall after a decade of trying to implement the rule of law. Political reform doesn't really count, in this estimation, until the nation's president is directly elected. But in historical terms, the change of practice and mentality in both economics and politics is astoundingly rapid for an impoverished country comprising one-sixth of humanity. As in early Meiji Japan, it is this institutional globalization that accounts for China's extraordinary economic growth.

U.S. and European disdain for Chinese economic and political gradualism is both profoundly sincere and profoundly hypocritical. Western politicians and pundits believe what they say, but they would never prescribe such a strategy for their own countries. No successful Western country has ever developed democratic institutions from scratch, privatized its state enterprises, or changed its legal tradition through shock therapy. Western countries have, in fact, done these things far more gradually than either China or Taiwan or South Korea.

While China's economic, institutional, and political changes have been step-by-step and seem agonizingly gradual to Westerners who implicitly wish China would turn into a modern industrial democracy overnight, as well as to many frustrated Chinese, they have not been slow in historical terms. Indeed, they have occurred very rapidly compared with the speed at which they developed in the West. Chinese redistribution of land rights from the communes to families occurred virtually overnight in historical terms. The adoption of a U.S. Federal Reserve–type structure for China's central bank was almost instant. The adoption of the rule of law will take decades, and Western critics will denounce the system's weaknesses for much of that period.

Looking at the slow progress of the rule of law or of international accounting standards, many Western scholars are quick to accuse China of insincerity. To judge what the appropriate standard is, it is useful to go through a little exercise: Estimate how many lawyers, judges, and accountants it would take to approach the standards that critics would find acceptable for a population greater than that of Africa, Latin America, and the Middle East combined. Then start from 1992, when China had perhaps 50 appropriately trained accountants, about the same number of appropriately trained lawyers, and probably no appropriately trained judges, and imagine the fastest conceivable path for training the needed people and legislating the needed standards. Put into the model such obstacles as the fact that judges are appointed by local officials, not by the central government, and that local officials would actively and perhaps violently resist rather than surrender such powers. I believe that after going though such an exercise, virtually any reader will conclude that China's progress has been more rapid than a reasonable person could have assumed possible at the beginning. (It was in 1992 that China decided that listed companies would have to meet international accounting standards. The decision to seek the rule of law was also made in the early 1990s.)

Western Political Images and Chinese Reality

The image of China as a successor state to the Soviet Union has a number of vitally important aspects in much of Western thought about China. For much of the national-security establishment, it justifies a view that since China is communist, it must be expansive like the old Soviet Union. The facts that China has been far more willing to compromise on its border disputes than any of its large neighbors and that it is on better terms with its immediate neighbors than either Japan or India are inadmissible in the face of the convenience of the successor-state image.

The other aspect of the successor-state image that has played a central role in Western national-security thought concerns domestic politics: the image of gerontocrats stubbornly defending an old socialist system until its inevitable collapse, of the Chinese counterparts of Leonid Brezhnev, Yuri Andropov, and Konstantin Chernenko slowly dying in their expensive chairs while their antique system withers away. No image is as pervasive in the Western media and U.S. congressional rhetoric about China as the Brezhnev fallacy. No image could be further from reality.

Originally, part of this image was applied to Chinese economic gradualism. When Eastern European and Soviet communism collapsed, Western advisors, led by Jeffrey Sachs, were quick to argue that only "shock therapy" or variations on it could bring successful development. Chinese incrementalism received short shrift, and its transitional formulations such as the "socialist market economy" (1994) attracted ridicule. (From the first day, leading Chinese professors said, "Ignore 'socialist'; that's political cover. 'Market economy' is the goal.") World Bank publications rejected with contempt papers suggesting that the Chinese model of economic development had its virtues. (I had some personal experience in that regard.) In fact, however, shock therapy imposed horrible traumas wherever it was tried, and its partial implementation in Russia was responsible for turning the economy over to a dozen billionaires and various groups of gangsters. No economy where that approach was tried has ever grown more than half as fast as the Chinese economy. Subsequently, there was a gradual segue during which those contemptuous of Chinese gradualism said, well, they really hadn't meant to criticize China's approach, but it was inapplicable for technical reasons in the countries they were advising, and anyway the peculiarities of the statistics of their countries exaggerated the depressions and hyperinflations that their policies seemed to have caused. In a sharp reversal, the World Bank, with greater candor than some of the scholars, became a great fan of China's successes.

Chinese incrementalism did not mean slow reform—an aspect of the mistaken image. One-sixth of the world's people were restored to family farms from dismantled communes in part of a decade. State enterprise employment declined by 60 million people in a decade. Manufacturing employment declined by 25 million in a decade. The top levels of government were cut by half in less than a decade. Incrementalism meant that the leaders thought about each step and generally field-tested each before acting, but they then acted very decisively.

The same erroneous image that incrementalism obfuscates reform is as central to Western concepts of Chinese politics today as it was to Western views of Chinese economic gradualism in 1995. The Brezhnev image is absolutely pervasive—and absolutely false.

After a lecture I gave at Peking University in 1998, a graduate student stood up and asked, "Dr. Overholt, we have been assigned your book, *The Rise of China*, and Gordon Chang's book, *The Coming Collapse of China*. Chang argues that China's economy is reforming, but its politics is stagnant and the tension between the two will cause collapse. What do you think?" I responded, "The fact that you were assigned those books in a leading university, and that you can stand up in front of 2,000 people and ask that question, is your answer. Twenty years ago you would have gone to jail either for having the books or for asking the question."

Today's Chinese leaders come from different backgrounds (urban, educated, unideological, focused on economic progress) and have different values from those of their predecessors. Chinese society is open rather than closed, and the Chinese economy is open rather than closed. Chinese intellectual life, once as stultified as anywhere on earth, is now as lively as anywhere on earth. Globalization has replaced xenophobia. Promotion is based overwhelmingly on expertise, not on ideological slogans. Leaders make decisions after wide consultation with interested parties (I have sat in on many such meetings), and the private economy has dispersed the resources for political influence very broadly throughout the society. Elections and other accountability mechanisms are appearing everywhere. Villages hold elections. Within the party, elections are held at all levels, with more candidates than openings. Villages are told to post their revenues and expenditures on a bulletin board for all to see, cities to post them on the Internet. Major policies are openly debated. Investigative reporters denounce corrupt officials—within limits that are frustrating to them—and their leeway to do so, even though limited, changes the tone of society. While China remains, on balance, unfree and undemocratic, the spread of freer speech and of consultation mechanisms is quite similar in scope and pace to what happened earlier in South Korea and Taiwan, which are now more democratic than Japan and more robust than virtually any other democracies in the developing world.

Political Experiments

In one political experiment, Nanjing's leadership designated an electorate of 10,000 well-educated citizens to vote periodically on the performance of government department heads. After each such election, the two department heads with the fewest votes have to step down. The designer of that experiment was promoted at a very young age to head one of the most dynamic provinces, Jiangsu, where he is designing more-advanced experiments. To the south, Shenzhen initiated the separation of judicial, executive, and legislative powers. Yunnan made having won an election at some point a prerequisite for senior provincial positions. At the national level, the National People's Congress became much more assertive in criticizing government policies and top officials, and it acquired a major role in vetting new laws and policies—while still stopping well short of voting down the most important government programs.

Most controls on speech have ended; calling for the end of Communist Party rule or for the overthrow of top officials remains unacceptable, but Phoenix TV has sponsored debates about what kind of democracy should evolve in China, with Western democracy one of the three alternatives. The Central Party School studied whether China should evolve along the lines of Japan or Taiwan or some other model. In 2003, the practice of Great Man (Mao, Deng, Jiang) rule ended, and the new leaders were expected to stick to legally defined roles. The military, police, ideologues, and close relatives of former leaders found themselves completely left out of the Politburo Standing Committee (the group that directly rules China). The official ideology was changed, through constitutional amendment, from one based on dictatorship of the lower classes (soldiers, peasants, workers) and class struggle to one that emphasized rule in favor of modern technology and modern social practices and the harmony of a middle-class society. This was a sharp repudiation of the core of Marxist-Leninist thought, and many Chinese scholars argued that it was as important a step toward acceptance of the ideas underlying social democracy as were the early steps toward acceptance of the ideas underlying the market economy.

Interest groups multiplied. Urbanites demonstrated against being moved out of their homes in the name of development. So did peasants whose farms were being transformed into shopping malls. Women rioted against forced birth control. The leadership publicized the drastic rise in the number of demonstrations and was fearful of the disorder, but in March 2007, the Public Security Bureau circulated a memo saying that the demonstrations and the proliferation of nongovernmental organizations (NGOs) were important ways for the people to vent their frustrations and must be treated as such. While religious persecution continued to occur, the number of new adherents of Buddhism and Christianity in China probably exceeded the number added by those religions at any other time in history. Through all of this, China remained a repressive dictatorship dominated by its Communist Party, but there have been few times in history when one-sixth of the world's population experienced such rapid political evolution. China's leaders were determined to stay in power, and they were fearful that change would get out of control, but they saw their politics, like their economy, as an underdeveloped work in progress. They did not try to freeze it, and they did not try to get other countries to adopt it; instead, they debated, privately and publicly, how it should evolve. By 2003, there were no Brezhnevs or Chernenkos among China's political leaders. Nonetheless, and this is crucial for international relations, many influential Americans continued to think of China as characterized by a dynamic economy and a stagnant polity.

In short, China is doing in politics what it did in economics. It is examining the lessons of its neighbors, testing various reforms, and putting reforms in place brick by brick. The above changes constitute a regime change compared to the pre-reform era, just as the economic changes amount to a system change. Moreover, the leadership expects further regime change in the future. On September 6, 2006, Premier Wen said, "We are confident that when the people are capable of running a village through direct election, they will later be able to run a township, then a county and a province."[23]

At the Central Party School, influential scholar-officials conduct studies of Taiwan's Guomindang, Japan's LDP, Indonesia's Golkar, Mexico's PRI, and Europe's social democratic parties. There is incessant debate about the next steps. Should they allow open, organized factions within the party, on the model of the LDP? Should they hold town elections as well as village elections, moving up-market, on the model of the Guomindang?

The point of this is not that China has become a free society. It has not. Nor has it become a democratic society or anything approaching

---

[23] "Democracy Will Come Slowly, Says Wen," *Agence France Press*, online, 1:01 p.m., September 6, 2006 (http://www.afp.com/home/).

one. Advocating displacement of the Communist Party is still largely forbidden. Many of the regime's human-rights practices are ruthless and brutal. The continuing suppression of much religious expression is inhumane and counterproductive. South Korea's Park Chung Hee had the right approach to strange religious sects: He ignored the Moonies (followers of Sun Myung Moon) and let them become rich. When South Korea evolved into an educated, middle-class society, mainstream religion became more attractive than odd cults. When the West criticizes the lack of human rights, it is correct. But most Western observers miss key points. China does not seek to export its current system of government. Chinese leaders do not see their current system as anything more than a transitional phase. Most see the Taiwan political system, like the Taiwan economic system, as more advanced than their own. They dislike aspects of it, but they want to study its successes and move up in that direction, not to drag it down to their level. They diagnose many of China's problems, such as the need for transparency and accountability, in the same terms as Western critics do. They do not accept Western democratic ideology, but they accept individual practices, such as village elections, because those practices have specific pragmatic value in reducing corruption. They want to discover and test these things themselves, step by step, rather than succumb to foreign ideological browbeating, but they are willing to consider nearly everything.

The ultimate goal is to create something like Japan's LDP that will leave the party in power but have enough of a connection to the people to maintain stability and enough accountability to raise efficiency and set limits on corruption. As noted above in the discussion of Japan, that goal is the common grail for all the most successful Asian systems in their early development: Japan, South Korea, Taiwan, Malaysia, Singapore, China, and now Vietnam. Of these, only South Korea, where the parties were always more entourages than institutions, and Taiwan, where the dominant party messed up and split itself, have achieved full democracy. Japan is the most successful at creating a coalition with such overwhelming economic and organizational power that it has been able to endure for generations with little risk of losing power. (The 18-month Murayama government of 1994–1995 was the sole post-1955 exception.) China got started a quarter-century later than the others, and Vietnam got started a decade later than China. There are great controversies among China experts about how successful China will be, but when considering these controversies, it is essential to put them in the context of what the other Asian-miracle economies sought and achieved. Most Western observers in 1965 thought Japan was condemned to be a marginal economy for the indefinite future. Most Western observers in 1975 thought that South Korea and Taiwan were unstable and hopeless; the Carter campaign of 1976 had as its moral center of gravity the demand that we stop tolerating these abusive regimes and withdraw our troops from South Korea. Such a triumph of ideological indignation over gradual nurturing would have cost the peace and deprived Asia of two vibrant future democracies.

That brings us to one more aspect of the Western images, namely, the Manichean view that there are Leninist systems on one side of a great political and moral chasm and democracies on the other, with no connection between the two sides other than a Soviet-style collapse into the chasm. That has not been the pattern in Asia. Taiwan, Singapore, and South Korea all began as socialist or quasi-socialist economies led by leaders with Leninist visions. Taiwan and Singapore had fully developed Leninist parties. Taiwan and South Korea under Chiang Kai-shek, the early Chiang Ching-kuo, and Park Chung Hee were considerably more abusive of human rights than China is today. But today these are the most robust democracies in the developing world.

It is not inevitable that China will continue to follow the path of those democracies. If China's leaders lose their reformist economic courage, both the economy and the polity could suffer some great discontinuity. Even if they remain on a reformist economic path, the emergence of reactionary leaders, possibly triggered by a conflict with the United States and Japan, could lead to political reform getting out of synch with economic reform.[24]

---

[24] For the opposite view, the most articulate, albeit implicit, exposition of the Soviet analogy is that of James Mann in *The China Fantasy: How Our Leaders Explain Away Chinese Repression*, New York: Penguin, 2007. His international views are succinctly laid out in "A Shining Model of Wealth Without Liberty," *The Washington Post*, May 20, 2007. Although I have cited Mann's views of U.S. priorities positively, he doesn't understand China's politi-

Having said that, I would like to emphasize three errors that the West must avoid. China is not politically stagnant; it is reforming the polity as it reforms the economy. Contrary to a growing Western literature, the experience of all the similar systems in Asia shows that it is not possible for a classic Leninist dictatorship to coexist indefinitely with a dynamic economy. And while discontinuity is always possible, those who confidently forecast that China will suffer discontinuity or that India will invariably outperform China's economy because of superior political stability are betting against the entire modern Asian experience. All the Asian-miracle economies have experienced relatively smooth transitions to more popularly accountable systems. Every Chinese leader I have spoken with is intensely conscious of that, and the advisors constantly debate the right path, on which there is no consensus. There is no guarantee that China will evolve into something matching the U.S. or British models. However, there is absolute Chinese consensus, as there was in Taiwan and South Korea and Singapore, that China will choose its own path and will reject ideological bludgeoning by foreigners.

---

cal dynamism, caricatures others' views, and impugns the moral integrity of those who do understand China's political dynamism by arguing that they have sold out to dark money. The rationale he gives that China's middle class has been bought off was equally applicable to South Korea and Taiwan at similar stages of development, but they didn't coalesce into eternal Leninism. If he really understood the money flows in American politics, he would know that Taiwan lobbying money exceeds China lobbying money by an order of magnitude and that weapon builders' lobbying money exceeds all other corporate lobbying money by a very large margin. When corporations turn to consultants, they usually want accurate facts; that is why they pay a great deal for Bloomberg News and little or nothing for Fox News or liberal newspapers. Mann thinks any U.S. loss is a Chinese gain. He portrays China, falsely, as trying to proselytize its political model around the world the way the old Soviet Union did. Chinese leaders don't think China's politics constitutes a "shining model," so it is strange that Mann does. What Chinese leaders do say is that economic progress usually precedes successful democratization and reduction of corruption and that Western efforts to reverse the order only cause strife and economic failure. Looking out from China at the relative performance of South Korea/Taiwan and the Philippines/India, it should be hard to dismiss the Chinese argument. Commentators like Mann ignore the substance of the argument in favor of ideological assertions based not on facts but on ideological caricatures and implicit Soviet analogies.

Economic Dynamism and Political Influence

Because China's economy grows much faster than Japan's, China now has the prestige among its neighbors that Japan's superior growth inspired in the 1970s and 1980s. Because China's economy is more open than Japan's, it has more economic influence on the region than Japan's much larger economy has. The smaller countries' trade growth is driven by dynamic China, not by slower-growing Japan, and increasingly, exports to China are overtaking exports to Japan and the United States in absolute terms. Mutual direct investments and intricate divisions of the value chain in manufactures with China far outstrip those with Japan. In key situations, China's economic dynamism has had a decisive influence on its neighbors. The technology bust at the beginning of the new century could have had a seriously depressing effect on key neighbors and a potentially disastrous effect on a few, such as the Philippines, but a takeoff of exports to China cushioned the impact of that bust on the most vulnerable.[25]

The two most important impacts of China's economic dynamism have, surprisingly, been on its two biggest neighbors, India and Japan. For India, China's economic dynamism provided a wake-up call that India was falling behind and also a model of how to increase growth by opening and liberalizing the economy. This has been an indispensable contributor to the doubling of India's economic growth rate. Moreover, India's trade surplus with China has given India confidence in its ability to compete, and that confidence has shifted India's domestic political balance a bit more in the direction of reform. At a June 2005 board meeting in Delhi of RAND's Center for Asia Pacific Policy, India's finance minister declared that "China's economic success has

---

[25] During the period when the extraordinary stimulus from China was saving Asian economies from the technology bust (2001 and thereafter), it became an accepted shibboleth in the West that China's success was draining the trade and investment away from its neighbors and debilitating them. I was invited to five conferences on this theme by different agencies of the U.S. government. My airplane ticket to return home from Hong Kong to the United States was paid by one such conference. The leading U.S. newspapers carried major stories to that effect. But the facts were the opposite. Exports and foreign direct investment into the Asian countries that were not (like Indonesia) suffering from severe domestic mismanagement rose along curves that look like astronauts' shuttles taking off. A large Chinese trade deficit opened up with these countries just when they needed the stimulus.

been the best thing that ever happened to India." The mutually beneficial economic interactions have contributed to the warming of political relations.

Likewise, the Japanese are quite conscious that accelerating exports to China provided the stimulus in 2003 that pulled Japan out of its dozen years of economic stagnation. This has made Japanese decisionmakers sensitive to any forces—such as, for instance, U.S. pressures for revaluation of the Chinese currency—that might slow Chinese growth. Moreover, leading Japanese business groups increasingly see the health of their companies as dependent on the relationship with China, so the leading elements of Japanese business oppose disruptive moves like Prime Minster Koizumi's visits to the Yasukuni Shrine. This example, however, shows the limited effect of economic attraction on politics, because these positive economic trends have coincided with a drastic downturn in Japanese-Chinese relations.

The resultant prestige and the mutually beneficial economic interactions convey influence—not coercive power, not hegemonic influence, but geopolitically important influence nonetheless.

China's economic takeoff has had an additional vital influence on regional geopolitics: the creation of an increasingly multipolar Asia.[26] China's rise itself creates a much more competitive Asia, both economically and politically. In addition, China's openness to trade and investment has drawn the United States and Europe back into competitive-scale trade and investment in the region. Compared with the previous trend toward overwhelming Japanese dominance of regional trade, investment, and banking, this is a development of system-changing scale.

---

[26] In 1980, total U.S. foreign direct investment in East and South Asia, on a historical cost basis, was $8.5 billion (State Department Bureau of Economic Statistics, http://bea.gov/bea/di/diapos77.htm). By 2005, it had grown spectacularly, to $376.8 billion (U.S. State Department, Bureau of Economic Statistics, http://bea.gov/bea/di/usdctry/longctry.xls)(websites accessed October 21, 2006).

China as a Regional Leader

Both Japan and China became politically influential when their economies entered long periods of sustained rapid growth. In neither case has leadership been a function of military power; it was so before World War II, and it could be so in the future, but the enormous influence of Japan in the 1980s and of China in the early 21st century has so far had nothing to do with military prowess. China has additional qualities that contribute to its leadership potential. It is one of the most attractive and influential civilizations in world history, with great literature, art, and philosophy; in these dimensions, it overshadows Russia and Japan, notwithstanding the impressive achievements of those civilizations.

China's qualities as a civilization are magnified by its geographic scale and its openness. Of the two, openness is the more important. Russia also possesses geographic scale, but it cannot compare with China's historic or current range of influence. Except during the brief period when Maoism closed China off from much of the world, Chinese society has been and is inherently diverse, cosmopolitan, and open. These qualities it shares with India, Indonesia, the European Union (EU), and the United States. The Chinese and the Indians speak many dialects, have very diverse racial characteristics, and have diasporas that connect their citizens with all parts of the world. Both present a sharp contrast to Japan and Korea, which have more homogeneous, more inward-looking societies. China is far ahead of India in taking advantage of its cosmopolitan qualities for economic and political advantage, but it is important to note the degree to which they share this advantage in contrast to Russia, Japan, and Korea. Among the cosmopolitan societies, China and the United States have achieved a high degree of national unity and central purpose in comparison with the EU, India, and Indonesia.

China's weakness as an international leader is, of course, its politics. Most Asian countries see this as a developmental issue—China as backward rather than China as politically alien. Many Westerners see Chinese communism as being separated by a great ideological divide from the Asian democracies. Singapore, Taiwan, and South Korea, along with their neighbors, see their own recent pasts as quite similar to China's. The founding leaders and institutions of contemporary Singapore, Taiwan, and South Korea were heavily Leninist in politics and predominantly socialist in economics, and they evolved gradually away from that over several decades of economic success.

These observations have two important geopolitical implications. First, most Asian countries see Chinese authoritarianism very differently from the way the United States sees it, namely, as a developmental backwardness that China is likely to grow out of if it continues on its successful economic path. This means that Asian leaders quickly grow weary when their U.S. counterparts ratchet up the rhetoric about democracy versus communism; they heard the same rhetoric directed at themselves by Jimmy Carter and others a generation ago when Taiwan was more Leninist than China is today and Singapore's People's Action Party (PAP) had just recently distanced itself from its heavily Leninist origins. Second, they nonetheless do regard Chinese politics as unquestionably backward and unpleasant and until recently dangerously volatile, and this limits China's attractiveness as a regional leader.

The baseline scenario for China over the next ten years is continued rapid economic growth, continued economic liberalization, continued economic globalization, continued social liberalization, continued political consolidation, continued but slow political liberalization, steadily rising regional and global political influence, and relatively limited military power except for the defense of the China mainland itself and the concentrated single issue of Taiwan. This scenario leads to an impressive continued rise in China's regional and global stature, but it is not a scenario that leads to China taking over the developing world. In the period 2015–2020, China will still be a very poor country with limited technological prowess and enormous problems. Toward the end of that period, China will become a graying society with a poor ratio of working to non-working population—the problem Japan has already encountered. It will still be facing horrific problems employing its people, revitalizing agriculture, rebuilding a collapsed medical system, paying the pensions of its vast numbers of retired people, revitalizing a severely damaged natural environment, and managing rural-urban migration on a scale the world has never before seen.

There are a number of alternative paths China could take, depending on the evolution of its leadership and the pressures that come from abroad. If Europe and the United States react strongly against the adjustments required by continued globalization and impose repeated, wide-ranging discriminatory barriers to Chinese trade and investment, a Chinese reaction against globalization could occur. All the benefits globalization has provided to all parties notwithstanding, one can never rule out completely the kind of reversal that happened in the 1920s and 1930s. At that time, Latin America was in the position China is in today and along with Europe and America was enjoying the fruits of globalization. Many world political and business leaders expected Argentina to become the world's most prosperous economy. However, the United States reacted sharply against globalization, and the Great Depression hurt the most open economies most, shocking them into generations of protectionism from which Latin America has never recovered.

China could also suffer a similar outcome from a domestic leadership crisis of courage. The tremendous growth China achieved in the years of Deng Xiaoping's and Zhu Rongji's leadership required stressful change on a level few societies could tolerate. Continued growth will require similar changes, and it is not inevitable that current or future leaders will have either the courage or the political support to implement them. If they do not, China's economy will slow and will lack the resources to handle the unemployment, the medical problems, the pension problems, the environmental degradation, and the urbanization that will squeeze China's coffers with or without strong leadership.

Alternatively, Europe and the United States might go protectionist, and China might remain open, leading an Asian renaissance based on the lessons learned between 1979 and 2000. The West would then gradually decline, and China would gradually regain its traditional position as the pinnacle of world technology and culture. This would be the modern equivalent of what happened to the old Islamic world. When Middle Eastern Islam was open and globalized, it was the pinnacle of world civilization, while Europe was provincial, closed-minded, poor, and technologically backward. As Europe opened and Islamic civilization turned inward, the two exchanged positions. A contemporary version of this would be the logical outcome of, for instance, current popular attitudes toward globalization in France and among protectionist elements in the U.S. Congress.

International political developments could also alter China's path. Serious clashes over Taiwan or over seabed and territorial-waters disputes could drain China's resources and end its economic miracle. Even without clashes, overinvestment in the military would reverse Deng Xiaoping's wise concentration of the nation's resources on economic development and slow China's growth while the economy still needs every resource available.

One can also imagine these issues taking an optimistic rather than a pessimistic turn. If China resolves or freezes the Taiwan issue, initiates a regional program of cooperative seabed development, and works with the United States to unify Korea on mutually acceptable terms, the results would not be limited to (very substantial) economic dividends. The whole foundation of the Cold War system would then have dissolved, and old alignments might become so obviously obsolete that entirely new arrangements would arise. This would certainly happen if, at the time, Japan had a right-wing government that objected to a unified Korea and a one-China resolution of the Taiwan conflict.

The Rise of China and the Rise of Japan

The economic takeoffs of China and Japan have turned both into major regional and global political players. There have been considerable similarities in the economics of both countries. Both, for instance, started from economic mobilization systems, gradually created more market-oriented economies, and worked their way up from agriculture and basic textiles to modern industry by serving the global market. However, the economic and political consequences of their rises have been quite different, and U.S. strategic thinking has been slow to appreciate the implications of these differences.

Until 1990, Japan was becoming a regional economic hegemon. It dominated Asia's banking, foreign investment in Asia, and trade in East and Southeast Asia. Japanese banks could control any international deal they wanted to. Cars in Southeast Asia largely meant Japanese cars. Japanese foreign direct investment overshadowed once-vigorous U.S. and European investment. China and Russia were minor players in the regional economy. In this context, Japan's regional posture evolved from a "low posture" (cautious, humble) to an overweening "high posture" by the end of the 1980s. As noted earlier, so great was Japanese economic dominance that Japanese firms as a group could veto the building of a non-Japanese steel mill in Thailand. More broadly, the exports of the littoral countries of Asia were increasingly merely components of the Japanese economic machine. Southeast Asians benefited from the dynamism stimulated by Japanese investment, trade, and good management, but they also resented their own gradual subordination.

The emergence of China transformed the regional economy from imminent Japanese hegemony to multilateral competition. China became a regional economic power, but it did not supplant Japan. Toyota remained as strong as ever and in fact continually became stronger. Meanwhile, China's openness to foreign direct investment drew the United States and Europe back into Asia on a truly competitive scale. The Asian economic game became at least a four-power game (at least, because South Korea and Taiwan also increased their roles), rather than an exercise in Japanese hegemony. This had a liberating effect on all the regional economies.

Moreover, even when considered by itself, the Chinese role was quite different from the Japanese role. Japanese firms virtually always held the commanding heights of technology and finance. Within Japanese firms and joint ventures, Japanese managers typically occupied most of the top roles. (This was quite different from the typical U.S. and European strategy of quickly devolving senior local management positions to local people.) Chinese firms, in contrast, are often the bottom of the value chain—for instance, supplying basic parts or assembly for a Taiwanese computer company. In 2003, 84 percent of all Chinese technology exports were those of foreign companies with operations in China.[27] The big companies often had Taiwanese or Singaporean or Korean ownership or management. Indeed, the large U.S.

---

[27] A study by Professor Chen-yuan Tung of Taiwan's National Chengchi University showed that in the first half of 2003, 84.3 percent of China's technology exports were those of foreign-invested companies (see "Cross-Strait Interflow Prospect Foundation," *China Economic Analysis Monthly*, Vol. 4, August 2003, p. 3).

and European companies attracted to Asia by the China boom typically did not follow the Japanese pattern of having expatriates dominating senior management; they localized as quickly as possible, for cost and cultural reasons. All this transformed Asia's economy away from potential Japanese hegemony.

As Fareed Zakaria has noted, "China's growth strategy has been different from Japan's. When Japan rose to power, it did so in a predatory fashion, pushing its products and investments in other countries but keeping its own market closed. China has done the opposite, opening itself up to foreign trade and investment. The result: growth in countries from Brazil to Australia increasingly depends on China, making it indispensable to the world."[28]

This was extraordinarily welcome in most of Asia, where wartime resentments of Japan had not had time to fade before resentments of Japanese economic dominance set in. This is little understood in the West, particularly in the United States. Western geopolitical strategists fly to Thailand and ask local military counterparts whether they are concerned about the rise of China. The answer is yes, of course. They fly home thinking there is consensus about the view of China as a threat. But the fundamental political fact about the rise of the two powers is that South Koreans and Southeast Asians distrust China less than they distrust Japan.[29] As small countries, they inherently fear big countries. They have suffered waves of Chinese immigration for generations, and they suffered Maoist subversion for three decades, from 1949 to 1979. But they had their freedom of action curtailed by Japan, first through military action, then through economic

---

[28] Fareed Zakaria, "Mishandling the China Challenge," *South China Morning Post*, August 9, 2005.

[29] This is most true in South Korea, as discussed in the section on Korea in Chapter Five. The unwillingness of most of America's staunchest allies to take sides with Japan against China is a central fact of U.S. relations with Asia. In 2005, for instance, the Australian parliament's committee dealing with foreign affairs and defense spent time with me discussing how they could communicate to uncomprehending counterparts in Washington that while they were willing to allow many joint military exercises on Australian soil, they would adamantly oppose any joint military exercises involving Japan. The United States probably has no ally other than Britain that is more loyal than Australia.

and financial domination, for most of the 20th century. As the United States aligns itself fully with Japan, this is consequential background.

The China-Japan Relationship

> We should be prepared to a certain degree and not expect too much that neighbors should always be on good terms.
> —*Japanese Foreign Minister Taro Aso*[30]

Prior to the 20th century, direct Chinese-Japanese conflict occurred only rarely, but 20th-century Asia was dominated by Japanese (and, to a lesser extent, European) predations against a weak China and a weak Korea—the Asian equivalent of Franco-German rivalries in Europe. Following World War II, the United States was absolutely determined to prevent a recurrence of this fatal conflict. Its strategy for accomplishing this was to combine disarmament of Japan with initial occupation and later a military alliance that protected Japan against any combination of Soviet threat, Sino-Soviet alliance, or Chinese threat. The U.S.-Japan alliance became the principal instrument for ensuring that the great Asian rivalry would not resume. As noted elsewhere, China largely accepted it as such.

Throughout most of the postwar period, Sino-Japanese relations have been quite tolerable, albeit with considerable volatility. For most of the period since at least the mid-1970s, Chinese officials and officers have privately acknowledged the value of a U.S.-Japanese alliance that maintained stability.[31] But the relationship has nonetheless been quite sensitive, with occasional flare-ups.

---

[30] Speaking on national television in Japan, quoted by Thomas Plate, "Thoughts That Deserve to Be Disguised," *Pacific Perspectives*, February 22, 2006. Thomas Plate is a professor at the University of California, Los Angeles (UCLA) and a syndicated columnist. This column was received by e-mail.

[31] This comment is based on numerous personal interviews, beginning with Chinese military officers assigned to the United Nations in the 1970s. For a Chinese scholar's summation of this, see the quotation from Wu Xinbo on pp. 133–134. One of the remarkable aspects of

As noted earlier, the irritants causing these flare-ups have included periodic Japanese approval of textbooks portraying a revisionist view of World War II, senior Japanese officials' visits to the Yasukuni Shrine, competing claims to the Senkaku/Diaoyutai Islands, Chinese naval intrusions into Japanese waters (most notably by a nuclear submarine in July 2004), and Chinese drilling in seabed areas that Japanese officials believe might drain natural gas reservoirs in disputed territory. Periodically, too, Chinese student nationalism wells up in anti-Japanese demonstrations that the government usually suppresses. The students' criticism is ostensibly directed at Japan, but some part of the frustration is often directed implicitly at the Chinese government itself. All of this is part of the normal background of Japanese-Chinese relations, which for most of the post–World War II period have proved quite manageable. However, the beginning of the new century has seen an escalation of tensions.

Japan's government has sought always to be ahead of the United States in relations with China and has mounted an anxious, angry diplomatic offensive whenever the United States seemed to get out in front. Thus, when Nixon secretly organized his February 1972 trip to China, Japan mounted a very large-scale, very angry offensive.[32] Similarly, when Clinton visited China in 1998 without stopping in Tokyo on the way back, Japan mounted another such offensive—even though Clinton had previously visited Japan twice and had strengthened the military alliance, while visiting China only once for symbolic and minor commercial purposes. In 1998, unlike 1972, the Japanese offensive became part of a serious partisan divide in the U.S. presidential

---

these connected shifts in U.S. and Chinese policies is that many U.S. officials were not aware of the strong Chinese support for key U.S. alliances and military bases and therefore did not know what they were abandoning.

[32] At the time, I was spending a great deal of time on Japanese issues, as well as having written one consulting paper in support of Henry Kissinger's secret 1971 trip. I absorbed and accepted the full weight of the Japanese denunciations at the time. Many of these are recounted in William H. Overholt, "President Nixon's Trip to China and Its Consequences," *Asian Survey,* Vol 13, No. 7, July 1973. I now regard that account as having drastically underestimated the value of the trip because I was so overwhelmed by the antagonistic Japanese reaction. Japan did have reason to complain at the way the United States held Japan back, then rushed ahead itself, but the scale of the reaction was disproportionate.

election of 2000, which was marked by Republican charges that the Clinton administration was too soft on China and too inattentive to its Japanese ally. Japanese institutions mobilized a bitter, highly personalized campaign against the Clinton administration. As an officer of a Japanese bank, I attended a number of private-sector briefings where the efforts of President Clinton and his treasury secretary, Lawrence Summers, to persuade Japan to further stimulate its economy were bitterly described as efforts to totally destroy the Japanese economy and eliminate a competitor once and for all. These views had no connection to reality, but they were strongly held and strongly proselytized, and they led to very strong support by right-wing Japanese interests for the election in the United States of a successor to Clinton who would repudiate Clinton's policies.

The new Bush administration, accepting the view, codified in the Armitage Report,[33] that the Clinton administration had slighted Japan

---

[33] *The U.S. and Japan: Advancing Toward a Mature Partnership*, Institute of National Strategic Studies Special Report, 2001. That report, a bipartisan, high-level document, nonetheless became a major campaign bludgeon against the Clinton administration's Asia policies. It is the pivotal expression of the George W. Bush administration's early views on Asia policy. Ironically, it is an exact parallel to the 1992 Clinton campaign's denunciations of President George H.W. Bush's excessive coddling of China and the Clinton team's demand for removal of China's MFN trade privileges. I comment extensively on it here because of its historic importance. It expresses inter alia concern about U.S. policymakers' excessive focus of attention on China and singles out as *positive* developments the indicators of rising Japanese nationalism and concern for military power and territorial claims: "The political system is risk-averse. But the successor generations of politicians and the public-at-large also recognize that economic power alone will no longer be enough to secure Japan's future. Moreover, the Japanese public, by giving official standing to the national flag and anthem, and in focusing on such territorial claims as the Senkaku Islands, has evidenced a new respect for the sovereignty and integrity of the nation state." It would be an interesting exercise to ascertain whether there is any other document in modern U.S. diplomacy that treats the rekindling of territorial disputes and nationalism as a positive thing. The document's policy recommendations focus on Japanese rearmament and a stronger military partnership, rather than, for instance, taking the view that the end of the Cold War had brought new opportunities for reducing regional military competition and putting resources into new diplomatic and economic initiatives: "Japan's prohibition against collective self-defense is a constraint on alliance cooperation. Lifting this prohibition would allow for closer and more efficient security cooperation." It speaks of the U.S.-UK relationship as the proper model for the U.S.-Japan partnership. Intriguingly, for such a high-level document, it contains a strikingly inaccurate description of China's policy: "Beijing let it be known in no uncertain terms that it regarded

and overemphasized relations with China, pointedly replaced China specialists in senior Asia policy positions (e.g., assistant secretary of state and senior director for Asia of the National Security Council) with Japan specialists[34] and engaged in a major effort to strengthen the U.S.-Japan alliance against a background of China-directed announcements that the U.S. military would move from a Europe focus to an Asian focus and from a land-warfare focus to a naval-warfare focus. Japan declared for the first time in its December 2004 National Defense Program Guidelines that its potential enemies were China and North Korea. In that same month, Prime Minister Koizumi announced that he would invite former Taiwan President Lee Teng-hui to visit Japan. Japanese military officers began making comments to the effect that if Taiwan formally became part of China, it would constitute a vital threat to Japan's sea lanes:

> "If you assume conditions are balanced now," said Admiral Koichi Furusho, the former chief of staff of Japan's Maritime Self-

---

the U.S.-Japan partnership as an important element of a broader effort by Washington to constrain its regional diplomacy." In reality, what the authors reference is Beijing's much more limited objection to the 1996 U.S.-Japan agreement to strengthen military cooperation. Beijing strongly opposed an expansion of Japan's military role but was not objecting to the partnership, the alliance, or even, most of the time, the bases.

[34] One of the most reliable ways to detect shifts of policy and priorities is to watch the allocation of people. In the United States, when the Bush administration took office, all the top foreign-policy and national-security positions were filled by individuals with a military background and all top Asia positions were filled with Japan specialists, usually replacing China specialists. People with economic expertise were notably missing. During Bush's second term, the appointment of former U.S. Trade Representative Robert Zoellick as deputy secretary of state reflected some concern that economics was being neglected. Zoellick gave many speeches that were music to Asian ears, but his ability to affect national priorities remained limited, and he resigned after being denied promotion. In Japan, during Prime Minister Koizumi's administration, the "America School" became dominant in the Ministry of Foreign Affairs, and the "China School" (those trained in Chinese language) suffered a drastic loss of position and prestige. Within the North America Bureau, according to interviews, the number of positions dealing with military affairs expanded substantially, while those dealing with political and economic affairs contracted.

Defense Forces, "they would collapse as soon as Taiwan unifies with China. The sea lanes would turn all red."[35]

In February 2005, the military and foreign-affairs leaders of the United States and Japan formally included assuring peaceful settlement of the Taiwan problem as a goal of the U.S.-Japan alliance. Although the wording of the latter was deliberately innocuous,[36] the implications were momentous in Chinese eyes—as the Japanese proponents of the agreement had intended them to be. In March 2005, the Japanese government announced that it would end development aid to China in 2008, long before China achieves the normal aid cutoff level of $5,000 per capita.[37]

In April 2005, triggered by Japanese government approval of a new revisionist textbook but heavily influenced by the February U.S.-Japan agreement, Chinese students engaged in the most serious and violent anti-Japanese riots in recent decades. (The vehemence of Chinese government responses encouraged the students, even though the government belatedly reined them in.) Chinese scholars began expressing the view that the U.S.-Japan alliance no longer served to stabilize

---

[35] Quoted by Norimitsu Onishi and Howard W. French, "Chinese Warships Remind Japanese of Challenge on High Seas," *International Herald Tribune* (Asian edition), September 12, 2005, p. 3. For a more detailed articulation of the official rationale behind this argument, see Tomohiko Taniguchi, "A Cold Peace: The Changing Security Equation in Northeast Asia," *Orbis*, Summer 2005, p. 456.

[36] "In the region, common strategic objectives include: Encourage the peaceful resolution of issues concerning the Taiwan Strait through dialogue," Joint Statement, U.S.-Japan Security Consultative Committee, Washington, DC, February 19, 2005. The United States has long been committed to ensuring a peaceful resolution of the Taiwan problem, so that is not a change. But bringing the problem under the explicit purview of the alliance with Japan, together with the Japanese government's recent designation of China as a potential enemy, was a major step. Japanese government officials emphasized in private that this was intended to send China a major signal about Japan's posture. Interestingly, Japanese government officials said in private conversations that the Japanese side initiated the idea of such a clause in order to send a strong message to China, while people on the U.S. side indicated that the United States initiated the idea in order to remove any ambiguity about the involvement of the alliance in the event of conflict.

[37] See, for instance, David Pilling and Richard McGregor, "Japan Says to End Development Aid to China," *Financial Times*, March 17, 2005.

relations in Asia but instead constituted a direct threat to China. Typical of Chinese scholarly and official reactions is this view from an associate dean at Fudan University:

> For years, many Chinese analysts regarded the U.S.-Japanese alliance as a useful constraint on Japan's remilitarization. Developments since the mid-1990s and especially during the past few years, however, have convinced them that the alliance has become an excuse for Japan to pursue a more active security policy. . . . Indeed, as Beijing continues to expand its material power and influence in Asia, Washington has sought to balance China's rise through its campaign to return Japan to a "normal nation." Contrary to past policies, the United States is now driving rather than constraining Japan's rearmament. In the foreseeable future, short of a major adjustment of U.S. regional security strategy, the U.S.-Japanese alliance will act as a propellant of, rather than as a cap on, Japan's military development. At least as far as China is concerned, the bright side of the U.S.-Japanese alliance seems to be gone.[38]

Energy security has become another dimension of rivalry. China increasingly depends on imported oil from the Middle East. Unlike the United States, which has its own navy to assure its lines of supply from the Middle East, and Japan, which can rely on the U.S. Navy, China has no such assurance and could find itself terribly vulnerable in the event of a conflict. In response to this, China has sought to diversify and ensure its sources of supply, most notably through a pipeline from Russia that would connect to China's refining and distribution center at Daqing. But Japan intervened late in the game and initially outbid China and for a while persuaded Russia to create a longer and more expensive pipeline that would bypass China and connect to the Pacific Ocean. Although the project began primarily as a Japanese Foreign Ministry effort to improve relations with Russia, it evolved into

---

[38] Wu Xinbo, "The End of the Silver Lining: A Chinese View of the U.S.-Japanese Alliance," *The Washington Quarterly*, Vol. 29, No. 1, Winter 2005–2006, pp. 119–120.

an effort primarily to prevent China from having such a large direct source of supply.[39]

Each country tends to take a nationalistic view of the deterioration of Japanese-Chinese relations. China, joined by South Korea and to a certain extent by key Southeast Asian countries, blames the emergence of right-wing Japanese views that revise history and seek to rebuild the military. Conversely, the Japanese perceive China as flexing its muscles by asserting an unreasonable right to tell Japanese what history books they can use and what shrines they can visit. In the United States, opinion spans the range from joining the Japanese in just blaming Chinese muscle-flexing to seeing inappropriate nationalistic reactions by two immature Asian powers. U.S. scholars rightly view the Chinese government as having no standing to criticize inaccurate Japanese history textbooks until Chinese history textbooks tell the full and accurate story of the Korean War and of the cost in lives and suffering that Mao Zedong's policies visited upon his Chinese subjects.

In fact, all three powers have contributed to the new dynamic.[40] Ham-handed Chinese denunciations of greatly exaggerated versions of Japanese textbook and shrine developments, as well as Chinese naval intrusions into Japanese waters and Chinese drilling for seabed gas, have seriously alienated Japanese opinion. The 2005 riots made the Chinese appear to the Japanese as uncivilized; ever since, many Japanese have referred to China as "unstable."

Conversely, Japan certainly had to expect reactions from its neighbors when its prime minister started visiting the Yasukuni Shrine regularly and when a strengthened alliance was pointedly directed toward China. While the Asian principals have to take responsibility for their

---

[39] This is based on a presentation by a leading U.S. energy expert at RAND on March 3, 2006, citing conversations with Japanese officials who stated that the main reason for diverting the pipeline was that the future of Asia was at stake. As this is being written, the latest agreement is to build the pipeline to the Chinese border and then build a further link to the coast only if the supply justifies it.

[40] For a useful summary of the deterioration of Sino-Japanese relations, including a good chronology and tactical recommendations, see Minxin Pei and Michael Swaine, *Simmering Fire in Asia: Averting Sino-Japanese Strategic Conflict*, Washington, DC: Carnegie Endowment for International Peace, Policy Brief No. 44, November 2005.

own contributions to the new dynamic, it is crucial to note that changes in U.S. policy have also made major contributions. The old "cork in the bottle" strategy of averting a renewal of Sino-Japanese rivalry had virtually vanished as a core concern of U.S. policy in Asia during much of the George W. Bush administration and has revived only as a peripheral concern. The principal institution that once implemented such concern, the U.S.-Japan alliance, has been revised in ways that exacerbate the problem rather than resolving it. The revision began when the George H.W. Bush administration criticized Japan for offering only financial support in the 1991 Iraq war and greatly accelerated when the George W. Bush administration pushed for Japanese rearmament and support in various conflicts. The George W. Bush administration has been so focused on strengthening the military alliance with Japan that it has overlooked the strengthening of the far right in Japanese politics, the damage to constitutional law, and the exacerbation of Sino-Japanese rivalry. The gratuitous polarization of Asia, at a time when the end of the Cold War and the transformation of China's policies created a historic opportunity to reduce conflict, is one of the major new structural features of post–Cold War Asia.

There is, moreover, a further structural change in the triangular U.S.-Japan-China relationship that distinguishes the new Asia sharply from the old. The Cold War was marked by a broad congruence among the military, political, and economic dimensions of the U.S. relationship with Asian powers. Most important positive military business was between the United States and Japan. Most important positive political business was between the United States and Japan. Most important positive economic business focused on the U.S.-Japan relationship. Equal and opposite, the Soviet Union provided the negative side of these dimensions.

On one hand, in the new Asia, the U.S.-Japan military dimension becomes stronger and stronger. On the other hand, when one looks at the East Asian political agenda other than Taiwan, the principal issues are increasingly managed by a U.S.-Chinese bicondominium. North Korea is primarily a U.S.-Chinese issue, as are the war on terror, regional crime, regional proliferation of WMD, regional human trafficking, and, increasingly, Pakistan. Likewise in the economic sphere, the principal promoters of freedom of trade and freedom of invest-ment are the United States and China, with Japan and India dragging behind. On genetically modified foods, the United States and China are the world's number one and two inventors, producers, and consum-ers, and they are actively opposed by Japan, India, and the EU.

This is another major structural change in the new order. The countries and the institutions are the same, but the content of rela-tionships has changed. To those schooled in Cold War assumptions about how things are supposed to work, President Clinton's increasing attention to business with China seemed an inexcusable ideological deviation. Thus, the fact that within months of taking office, Presi-dent George W. Bush was doing the same thing caused considerable disgruntlement in some quarters. Underlying this was not ideological deviation or selling out, but rather a new reality to which Cold War assumptions and institutions have not yet adapted. We shall return to this theme repeatedly: There is a new alignment of U.S. interests in Asia with which Cold War institutions and ideology have been unable to cope. Indicative of the new era is the February 2007 deal constrain-ing for a while Pacific Asia's most difficult and dangerous problem, North Korean nuclear proliferation. To the consternation of tradition-alists, the deal resulted from close U.S.-Chinese collaboration, with Japan in angry opposition.[41]

Given the antagonism that has emerged in the Japan-China rela-tionship, it may be appropriate to conclude this chapter with an issue on which the news from both Japan and China is positive, despite mutual accusations to the contrary. It has become popular in China to worry about the rise of a new 1930s-style militarism in Japan, and it has become fashionable on the right in the United States and Japan to muse about the likely emergence in China of some analog of 1930s-style Japanese fascism. Regarding the former, I have already noted that Japan's military budget so far remains constrained to 1 percent of GDP, and it is worth adding to this that most Japanese military officers and

---

[41] In several interviews, senior Japanese officials demanded to know why the Bush adminis-tration had sold out to North Korea and abandoned the sounder policies of ultraconservative John Bolton.

national-security officials are firmly committed to democratic politics at home and moderate policies abroad. Regarding both, the crucial point is that militaristic fascism arose in both Japan and Germany due to massive economic and social crises. The Japanese were hungry, and against all the inward-looking tendencies of Japanese culture, many were moving, out of desperation, to places like Brazil and the Philippines to become farmers and gardeners. The current era of mutual prosperity is not conducive to that kind of desperation in either Japan or China. Moreover, there is no power vacuum of the kind that existed in China during the first half of the 20th century to invite the attentions of would-be imperialists.

Serious conflicts may occur, but they will not occur out of the kinds of dynamics that existed in the 1930s. It is not impossible that an adventurous leadership could come to power in China. It is not impossible that a right-wing Japanese government will overreach regarding Taiwan or Korea. It is not impossible that China and Japan could clash over conflicting seabed claims. But the conditions for the rise of 1930s-style regimes will recur only if there is a massive failure of globalization and an economic collapse, not if the successful rise of Japan is followed by the successful rises of China and India.

CHAPTER FIVE

Smaller Places, Decisive Pivots: Taiwan, Korea, Southeast Asia

Taiwan

> Striving for negotiations, preparing for war, not fearing delays.
> —*Chinese President Hu Jintao's summary*
> *of China's Taiwan strategy*[1]

Big-power maneuvering over the status of Taiwan is absolutely crucial to Asia's future geopolitics, so this discussion pays particularly detailed attention to Taiwan.

The island of Taiwan lies 90 miles off the coast of China. Most of its population migrated over a long period of time from the mainland of China, and the majority speak a version of the dialect of Fujian Province. The Dutch occupied Taiwan from 1624 to 1662. At the end of that period, the Ming Dynasty was collapsing, and its last remnant, led by Koxinga, or Cheng Cheng-kung, fled to Taiwan and captured it. In 1683, the new Qing Dynasty defeated Koxinga and conquered the island. Subsequently the Qing Dynasty treated Taiwan as a prefecture of Fujian Province, but because of difficult communications and transportation, Qing rule was loose. Dissidence was frequent.

In 1895, Japan forced China to cede Taiwan in perpetuity as part of the settlement of the Sino-Japanese War. This was the first colonial

---

[1] Quoted in Andy Gudgel, "The PLA Shapes the Future Security Environment," Carlisle, PA: U.S. Army War College, and Washington, DC: The Heritage Foundation, Colloquium Brief, September 2005, p. 2.

thrust of Japanese empire, followed by the conquest of Korea in 1905, the Twenty-One Demands on China in 1915, and later by the full invasion of China and Southeast Asia and the attack on Pearl Harbor. Japanese rule ended in 1945 with Japan's defeat in World War II.

Like other colonies, Taiwan was returned to its original master, and the original master was assumed to be China. At the Cairo Conference in 1943, the allies agreed that Taiwan should be returned to China as represented then by Chiang Kai-shek's Guomindang Party. China subsequently descended into full civil war. Chiang attained control of Taiwan in 1945, at the end of World War II, and as his Guomindang was gradually defeated by the Communist Party on the mainland, his supporters began to flood to Taiwan; he formally moved his government to the island in 1948–1949. The Taiwanese did not welcome the enormous influx of mainlanders, and the tension resulted in a huge demonstration and bloody repression on February 28, 1947, that left the Guomindang fully in control but also left a bitter legacy; at least 18 times as many people were killed in that melee as were killed around Tiananmen Square after June 4, 1989.

To the new rulers in Beijing, the flight of Chiang Kai-shek to Taiwan was an exact rerun of the flight of Koxinga three centuries earlier.

It was the policy of the U.S. government at the time to let the Chinese civil war proceed to its logical conclusion, namely, eventual defeat of the Chiang Kai-shek government by the new communist government in Beijing. However, the North Korean invasion of South Korea in June 1950 changed this, because Washington saw the invasion as the first gambit in a potential global communist thrust led by Stalin with Mao's support. The United States therefore cordoned off the Taiwan Strait, protecting the Guomindang government and recognizing it as the government of all of China. The United States continued that policy and carried much of the world with it until it changed recognition to Beijing in 1979. The United States then offered to ensure that Taiwan retained a seat in the United Nations, but the Taiwan government refused, insisting that there could be only one government of China.

The Leninist Guomindang government in Taiwan gradually liberalized until it was holding completely free elections, but the Guomindang Party controlled many of the nation's large businesses, exercised full control of the (wholly government-owned) banks, had intricate control of patronage and political networks at the village level, and controlled most of the media, so Guomindang victory in the elections was mostly assured. However, at the end of two terms, the first freely elected president, Lee Teng-hui, used the residual power of the old Leninist presidency to impose on the party a weak candidate, Lien Chan, to succeed himself, despite the far greater popularity of a competing candidate, James Soong. This split the Guomindang and opened the door for the opposition party, the DPP, to take the presidency. Together, the two fractions of the Guomindang considerably outpolled the DPP, but the DPP became the ruling party. Its candidate, Chen Shui-bian, had expanded his party's share of the vote by presenting himself for years prior to the election as a moderate who would not press for Taiwan's independence, but once in office he moved gradually in the direction of independence and indeed asserted frequently that Taiwan already was a sovereign and independent nation.

The mainland screed is that the people of Taiwan came from the mainland, had been ruled by the mainland for centuries, were forcibly colonized by Japan, and, like other colonies, were supposed to be properly returned to their rightful owner, China.

The Taiwan independence screed is that China never really ruled Taiwan, or ruled it only in name, that the mainland has not controlled the island for a century, and that Taiwan's superior democratic system makes it deserving of sovereignty and independence.

Only a small proportion of Taiwanese (typically well under 20 percent, up from about 8 percent 20 years ago) have ever indicated in polls that they want to assert independence, but they overwhelmingly reject the idea of being ruled by the mainland's communist system. The number who are unreservedly in favor of unification has always been substantially smaller than the number who favor independence.[2]

---

[2] There are many polls of Taiwanese views. The most easily available are from the Mainland Affairs Commission, a Taiwan government agency that has a heavy pro-independence

Between these polar views, Taiwan's polity is consistently and over-whelmingly moderate. The independence-minded DPP won in 2000 only because the Guomindang split and the presidential candidate presented himself as a moderate; his associates spent a good deal of time explaining that the party leadership no longer wanted to push for independence, but that it didn't want to try to change the inde-pendence clause of the party constitution because that would alienate the party's activist base.[3] According to private polls, President Chen was headed for defeat in 2004 but was saved by a sympathy vote when a would-be assassin grazed his stomach with a bullet just before the vote. The incident was marked with many peculiarities, and the assas-sin conveniently committed suicide, denying the police a chance to interview him. In that election, Chen scheduled a referendum on a measure rebuking China for stationing so many missiles opposite Taiwan. Voters who participated in the election picked up ballots for candidates and voted, but so many refused to vote on the simultaneous referendum ballots that the referendum did not meet the requirements

---

propaganda orientation. The best are probably from Gallup, but Gallup does not publish most of its polls. One recent poll, a telephone survey with the usual difficulties of telephone surveys but representative of findings regarding the ratio of independence sentiment to uni-fication sentiment, was the ERA Survey Research Center poll of April 27–28, 2005, which asked:

> "In our society, some people say that Taiwan should become independent quickly, some say that Taiwan should be unified quickly with China, and others say that the status quo should be preserved. Which do you agree with?" The findings were:
>
> – 16.0% wanted to be independent quickly
> ‑ 7.4% wanted to keep the status quo and then work toward independence
> ‑ 41.2% wanted to keep the status quo and then watch what happens
> ‑ 9.7% wanted to keep the status quo forever
> ‑ 7.8% wanted to keep the status quo and then unite with China
> ‑ 6.1% wanted to unify with China quickly
> ‑ 11.9% answered "don't know/no response."

See http://www.zonaeuropa.com/20050528_1.htm for a translation or http://www.zonaeuropa.com/20050528_1.htm for the original Chinese version.

[3] I personally participated in discussions with party leaders along these lines.

of validity; in other words, Taiwanese voters firmly rejected the effort to draw them into an exercise designed to provoke China. All this is important not as a partisan matter but because it illustrates the most important feature of Taiwan politics: the fundamental pragmatism and moderation of the Taiwanese electorate. There is a Taiwanese identity. There is commitment to Taiwan's democracy. But there is very little Serb- or Kosovar-style fanaticism in Taiwan politics. People want both democracy and peace. They want the status quo, which embodies both.

Since 1979, most of the world's governments recognize only the People's Republic of China (PRC), not the government in Taiwan, but most would oppose, at least diplomatically, forcible conquest of Taiwan by the mainland government. Although governments rarely spell out the reasons for their recognition decisions, most governments (1) lean toward the mainland interpretation that after the expulsion of the Japanese colonizers, Taiwan reverted to China; (2) agree with the Taiwan government that its superior economy and democratic government deserve respect; and (3) prefer to fudge the sovereignty issue in order to avoid a war. Scholars and political activists on various sides criticize these views in intricate detail, but that is today's political reality.[4]

In the years of Mao Zedong and Chiang Kai-shek, occasional overtures for peaceful unification notwithstanding, the mainland's policy was to invade Taiwan if necessary to achieve early unification, and Taipei's policy was to invade the mainland and unify China under Guomindang rule. Soon after reform began, China changed its policy of pushing for early, forceful unification, and much later the Taiwan government changed its policy of claiming to be the legitimate ruler of the mainland.

In January 1979, Deng Xiaoping proposed a deal whereby Taiwan would accept Chinese sovereignty, and in return, China would "respect

---

[4] For a Taiwan independence reading of history, see Hsueh Hua-yuan, Tai Pao-tsun, and Chow Mei-li, *Is Taiwan Chinese? Taiwan: Taiwan Advocates,* 2005. For a right-wing Japanese view, which is rather similar, see http://www.taiwandc.org/hst-1624.htm, in particular its conclusion: "Taiwan does have a history, and Taiwan has never been an integral part of China."

the existing social and economic realities there." In September 1981, China spelled out the details of this offer, including commitments to maintain Taiwan's economic, social, and political systems and even allow it to retain its own military.[5] (The catch regarding the military was that once Taiwan had accepted that it was under Chinese sovereignty, Beijing would have a legal right to ban foreign arms sales.)

Taiwan rejected that offer, and Deng made a similar but truncated offer one year later to Hong Kong: Hong Kong could retain its separate economic, social, legal, political, and currency systems for 50 years. However, unlike the offer to Taiwan, the Hong Kong offer reserved for Beijing the right to write Hong Kong's constitutional document (the Basic Law), to interpret the Basic Law, and to approve the appointments of Hong Kong's senior government officials. In addition, Beijing guaranteed Hong Kong only 50 years of autonomy, whereas the offer to Taiwan had no expiration date. Beijing did not demand the right to rewrite Taiwan's constitution, and it did not seek the right to approve Taiwan's senior officials.

China's reform-era approach to Hong Kong and Taiwan provides the sharpest possible contrast to the way other countries dealt with territories that they believed belonged to them. India, for instance, simply marched its military into Goa, which had been ruled separately from India far longer than Hong Kong had been ruled separately from China, and absorbed it into the existing Indian system.

The Chinese strategy was to modernize China over a period of decades and to demonstrate sincerity about "one country, two systems" over a period of half a century. Then, Chinese leaders believed, China would be far more like Taiwan, the Taiwanese people would accept the sincerity of "one country, two systems," and unification would be peaceful and mutually agreeable. Beijing reassured anyone who asked that this was its peaceful intention, but it reserved the right to use force if Taiwan declared independence.

---

[5] For a summary of the Chinese offer and the broader Chinese view on Taiwan, see the Chinese Ministry of Foreign Affairs website, "A policy of 'one country, two systems' on Taiwan," http://www.fmprc.gov.cn/eng/ziliao/3602/3604/t18027.htm.

In Western media and parliamentary debates, one frequently hears the assertions or assumptions that China wants to impose the communist system on Taiwan and that China hopes to use military force to subdue Taiwan. At least since January 1979, both of these assertions have been the opposite of the truth. Moreover, China's promise not to impose its system on Hong Kong or Taiwan does not result from a sense that it would like to impose the communist system on them but has to compromise that desire because it can't implement it. Quite the opposite. China could have retaken Hong Kong and imposed its system at any time by simply turning off the water. In fact, Beijing has seen Hong Kong as a superior kind of economy from which it can learn. Deng remarked after the Hong Kong deal was done that they had made a mistake: Instead of ensuring Hong Kong's autonomy for a half-century, they should have done it for a century.

In the case of Taiwan, reformist Beijing's argument has consistently been, rightly or wrongly, that in half a century, mainland China will have caught up to Taiwan, and therefore the Taiwanese people would feel comfortable joining China. Since 1979, no Chinese official has ever argued either that Taiwan would become more like China or that such an evolution would be desirable. Although no Chinese official could ever use these words, for obvious reasons, for the past 27 years mainland China's government has assumed the superiority of the Taiwan system. In the view of the communist government, Beijing's job is to catch up with, not to change, Taiwan.

On the economic and social aspects, there would be no debate at all in China about this. On the political aspects, there is a broader range of opinions, but at the highest levels of the current leadership, the general view has been that Taiwan's political system is something Beijing needs to study, to learn from, and in important respects to emulate. Contrary to a good deal of writing in Western media, Chinese leaders have not questioned Taiwan's right to democracy or to a directly elected president.[6] China's top leaders have ordered studies of what China can learn from Taiwan, Japan, Mexico, and other govern-

---

[6] Particularly in 1996, during the big confrontation over President Lee's visit to Cornell (discussed below), and during the two direct elections of President Lee, many Western media

ments where the electoral system was opened up but a dominant party remained in power for long periods. They have funded a Washington, DC–based scholar, known in the United States as a critic of China, to examine the lessons they can learn from Taiwan's liberalization. To take one noteworthy example of dialogue about such things, at a conference in which I participated, we were having a debate about Taiwan; an associate of the current leadership said about Lee Teng-hui, "Of course we hate what he did in cross-strait relations, but we admire the way he took Taiwan politics to a new level."[7] As another example, after a typical Sino-American debate about Taiwan, in which I had offered several alternative scenarios for Taiwan, a senior Communist Party official took me aside and said, "Bill, you forgot one scenario." I said, "Oh, what's that?" He said, "One country, one system: democracy."

All of this points to a remarkable convergence. The Taiwanese people will defend their democracy, but the vast majority have no stomach for provoking a conflict with China over formal independence. Conversely, China will fight against any formal declaration of independence but has long committed to preserving Taiwan's democracy (something the Taiwan government of DPP President Chen Shui-bian has systematically sought to obscure). Most of the world recognizes Taiwan as part of China or accepts that both Taiwan and the mainland are part of one China but would oppose any pressure against Taiwan democracy or any forcible subjugation. The United States might well intervene militarily to prevent any forcible subjugation but has warned Taiwan that it is not sovereign and not independent; that Washington's only legal requirement is to sell Taiwan adequate weapons, not to actually defend it; and that in that light, Taipei should not provoke Beijing by attempting to alter the status quo. All these positions are broadly consistent and could provide the basis for a peaceful settlement.

---

stated as fact that China objected to direct election of a Taiwan president. That was simply not true.

[7] Influential Chinese obviously can't express admiration for Taiwan's more-advanced political system for public consumption in China, and consequently I cannot quote names or other details. Regrettably, there are many situations like this. In this case, a number of distinguished U.S. scholars were present.

That, however, is not how events have appeared in recent years. What has happened?

When President Lee Teng-hui took office, he set about making important changes. Domestically, he sought to create an independent Taiwanese sense of identity. He curtailed the teaching of Chinese history in Taiwan's schools and substituted a nationalistic version of Taiwanese history. His government conducted a massive disinformation campaign to convince Taiwan's people that China was not honoring its "one country, two systems" promises to Hong Kong. (One publication of the Mainland Affairs Commission listed more than 150 alleged violations, none of which was a true violation.) These efforts to create a new Taiwanese identity achieved considerable success.

Internationally, President Lee sought to reverse the declining international recognition of his government through a clever tactic called "vacation diplomacy." He would request a visa for a personal visit to a small country, emphasizing that the visit was purely personal. Meanwhile, his government would spend large sums in the country in support of his request. In one small country after another, his request was accepted, he visited, and afterward he proclaimed each visit as a huge diplomatic triumph for international recognition of Taiwan. By 1995, he was ready to try this in the United States.[8] Cornell University, Lee's alma mater, received a large donation, and shortly thereafter, Cornell invited Lee to speak. He requested a visa for a purely personal visit as an alumnus, and the Taiwan government spent millions of dollars mobilizing political support for his request. China adamantly opposed this, and the U.S. media had virtually no information about the extensive international campaign of which this was a part. The center of gravity of the reaction among Americans was that China had no right to dictate to the United States who could receive a U.S. visa for a personal visit to an alma mater. The Department of State had promised China that the visa would not be issued, but at the last minute, con-

---

[8] For a detailed view of the diplomacy around this Taiwan gambit by a leading authority and former U.S. diplomat, see Alan D. Romberg, *Reign In at the Brink of the Precipice: American Policy Toward Taiwan and U.S.-PRC Relations,* Washington, DC: Henry L. Stimson Center, 2003.

gressional pressure forced a change of policy. Lee visited Cornell, then went to a gala reception with supportive congressmen and declared a huge diplomatic victory over China, just as he had done in the smaller countries. China overreacted egregiously, flinging rhetoric and missiles across the Taiwan Strait until the missiles were coming fairly close to Kaohsiung Harbor, Taiwan's biggest port. By March 1996, a U.S. carrier task force showed up nearby, and a shocked China got the message that such behavior would lead to confrontation with the United States. China's behavior created an image around the world of a dangerous, aggressive, militaristic country. Lee's strategy had proved scalable to the most powerful country in the world, and Beijing's ugly reaction only amplified Lee's victories.

As a result, Beijing's confidence that time was on its side faltered. The leaders' assumption had been that China would grow its economy and evolve its institutions faster than Taiwan would and that by mid-century, China would be so much like Taiwan that the Taiwanese would feel comfortable with peaceful unification. But if Lee Teng-hui could create a new sense of independent Taiwanese identity in the short run and could finesse Beijing diplomatically with the United States, then the game might be over before Beijing achieved its long-run development goals. There ensued a period of angry warnings, confrontational politics, and a large military buildup opposite Taiwan. Zhu Rongji's angry public rant against the danger of a DPP victory in the 2000 election, quite unusual for him, reinforced the 1996 image of a hostile, angry, aggressive China.

The arms race between the Chinese buildup opposite Taiwan and the U.S. buildup of capabilities to cope with a military threat to Taiwan became increasingly serious. In Beijing, the arms race was seen as a defensive reaction to a newly provocative policy from Taipei and to Washington's willingness to play along with that policy. In U.S. national-security circles, the Chinese military buildup became widely cited, wrongly, as evidence that China's strategy focused on military conquest of Taiwan.

On May 20, 2000, the first president from the independence-minded DPP took office in Taipei. In January 2001, the Bush administration took office, proclaiming much stronger support for Taiwan.

"Whatever it takes" was the new president's answer to a question about what he would do to defend Taiwan. In 2001 also, Japan got a new, more nationalistic prime minister, Junichiro Koizumi, and in January 2002, Makiko Tanaka was forced to resign as Japan's Foreign Minister, after which the China School's influence in the ministry began to collapse. China's position was weakening catastrophically, and its Taiwan experts were doing a great deal of soul-searching. They were very open in acknowledging that they had hurt themselves badly through the missiles in 1996 and the self-defeating rhetoric in 2000, but they weren't sure how to proceed.[9] They had to back off from the harsh tactics, but they still needed to draw a firm line. They didn't know what the right balance was.

In May 2002, some Taiwan experts in Shanghai responded positively to an American from Harvard University who argued that the arms race was becoming expensive and dangerous for both sides and that it was time to try to reverse the arms spiral. The leading expert in Shanghai flew to a Track Two meeting in Beijing in July to ask a former top U.S. diplomat and others whether it was really true that the United States might look favorably on a proposal to reverse the arms race. The Americans unanimously affirmed that it was a good idea. The Chinese worked remarkably swiftly and got their proposal for Beijing to pull back its missiles opposite Taiwan and for the United States to reciprocate by reducing military sales to Taiwan ready for presentation at the Bush-Jiang summit in Crawford, Texas, on October 25, 2002. The Bush administration rejected it completely, for two reasons. It was easier for China to move the missiles back to the strait than it would be for the United States to ramp up military sales quickly. And the United States had promised in July 1982, as part of the Six Assurances,[10] that it would not negotiate such things over Taiwan's head.

---

[9] This account is based on interviews I conducted at the time.

[10] The Six Assurances are:
1. The United States will not set a date for termination of arms sales to Taiwan.
2. The United States will not alter the terms of the Taiwan Relations Act.
3. The United States will not consult with China in advance before making decisions about U.S. arms sales to Taiwan.
4. The United States will not mediate between Taiwan and China.

These were valid reasons, but the U.S. response could have been to treat this as the opening round of a series of negotiations and to persuade Taipei to join the lead in offering counterproposals. Instead, the message was clear: Washington and Taipei were emphatically not interested in discussing arms control. Indeed, arms control had pretty much disappeared from the lexicon of U.S. diplomacy. The Americans who had assured the Chinese that the United States would be interested came from a previous era of U.S. diplomacy and had unwittingly misled the Chinese.[11]

As the Jiang Zemin administration came to an end and the Hu Jintao administration assembled for its inauguration in March 2003, a tremendous struggle occurred over Taiwan policy, with some of the old guard demanding very harsh policies toward Taiwan (and Hong Kong) and others insisting on the need for new approaches. In the end, the new administration settled on a policy of bigger carrots and bigger sticks. On March 14, 2005, the National People's Congress passed an Anti-Secession Law,[12] entrenching legally what had always been the Chinese position, namely that if Taiwan declared independence,

---

5. The United States will not alter its position about the sovereignty of Taiwan, which is that the question is one to be decided peacefully by the people themselves, and will not pressure Taiwan to enter into negotiations with China.
6. The United States will not formally recognize Chinese sovereignty over Taiwan.

[11] I was the one who initiated the idea in Shanghai that it was time for the Chinese to try arms control. Former Undersecretary of State Michael Armacost and former National Intelligence Officer for Asia Ezra Vogel were among the several Americans at the Track Two meeting in Beijing who affirmed that an effort to initiate arms-control negotiations would be likely to draw a positive response.

[12] See "Full Text of Anti-Secession Law," http://www.china.org.cn/english/2005lh/122724. htm. The law provides for the possible, not definite, use of force under three conditions: effective declaration of Taiwan independence; occurrence of some event that decisively separates Taiwan from the mainland; or the prospects for unification become hopeless. Neither the Anti-Secession Law nor any other law or decision has ever set a deadline for unification. In the 1990s, the belief spread through much of the world that Jiang Zemin had set such a deadline, but that story was invented by a Hong Kong columnist and picked up uncritically by a wide variety of newspapers. This is a prominent example of a phenomenon (see footnote 14 in Chapter Eight) widespread in the Western press: Negative stories about China do not require standard fact-checking. The U.S. government checked this story very carefully, and national security officials told anyone who asked about it that it was false.

China would attack. That was the bigger stick, and it created an outcry around the world. Then came the carrots. Beijing invited two leaders of the opposition, representing a majority of Taiwanese voters, to visit Beijing and address the people of China through television, followed by a series of cross-strait trade and transport concessions, speeches with warmer rhetoric than in the past, and in early 2006, an offer of a panda for a Taiwan zoo. These soft approaches, in very sharp contrast to the tone of earlier years, had a very large impact. Taiwan President Chen's popularity plummeted to below 10 percent, possibly the lowest of any elected leader in the world. His prime minister and cabinet resigned, with the prime minister citing differences over policy toward the mainland. Chen tried to mobilize his base by calling for more control over Taiwanese investment on the mainland, but the majority of such investors were DPP members who bitterly resented his attempts to control their businesses. The chairman of the DPP resigned and left the party—the third of the past three chairmen to do so. The most credible DPP candidates for the subsequent presidency moved toward the center, toward the kinds of non-provocative positions that had been the key to Chen's original chance of getting elected. Taiwan politics was re-equilibrating, with the broad center of the spectrum increasingly in control once again.

Meanwhile, more than 5 percent of the population of Taiwan had moved to the mainland to work. That does not reverse the heavily successful efforts to create a new Taiwanese identity, but it means that former President Lee Teng-hui's effort to reduce and minimize cultural ties has no chance of future success. As I took executives on investment tours of Taiwanese companies operating in the areas around Shanghai and Hong Kong, I found none who like the mainland's political system but many, probably a majority, who like living and working in China and may stay indefinitely. As a member of the board of a venture capital company focused on China, I absorbed the lesson so many companies have learned: If you want to build a company for transfer to the mainland, don't build a management team in Hong Kong, where the culture has evolved into a Sino-British hybrid that is partly incompatible with China. Build it in Taiwan, where the management culture is essentially identical. If you have a company in Taiwan, don't take it to

Hong Kong. Take it to the mainland, where the cultural assumptions are the same.

Beijing is now returning, slowly, to more comfort since it believes that time is on its side. It is probably right, although the argument that Taiwan's economic dependence on the mainland will give Beijing irresistible political leverage is almost certainly wrong. Economic dependence cuts two ways; Taiwan needs low-cost inputs from the mainland, while the mainland is completely dependent for technical exports on Taiwan's technology, funding, and management. But cultural ties will grow.

Unless Beijing returns to a harsh approach, the momentum of the Lee/Chen drive for formal independence has probably been broken for the indefinite future. Barring some mainland economic catastrophe, China's economic and cultural ties around the world will grow faster than Taiwan's. In the advanced countries, including the United States, the lobbying gap will after a few years begin to close rapidly. Currently, Taiwan-related companies have a huge economic presence in countries such as the United States, and they can legally donate to political campaigns and in many ways exercise political influence. China lacks such presence and lacks the knowledge to use it, but this will not be the case for long.

As a result of all these developments, there are two dynamics in place. Politically and economically, the conditions of convergence for a peaceful settlement, or a peaceful balance, have returned. Neither the Guomindang nor the DPP will sell out Taiwan's democracy, freedom, or prosperity. A more relaxed China can bide its time. While basically following the same cross-strait policies as his predecessors, President Bush has made the rules of the game much more explicit than his predecessors did: The military defense of Taiwan against any aggressive attack is much more explicit. The warning to Taiwan not to provoke is much more explicit. All this creates a better opportunity for a peaceful deal than Taiwan has had for decades. Its negotiating leverage is higher now than it is ever likely to be in the future.

But there is another dynamic, the dynamic of military competition. As the mainland builds up its missiles and adds modern jets and ships to its forces, the United States not only builds up its forces, but also, because the time for reaction gets shorter and shorter, must integrate those forces ever more tightly with Taiwan's. Simultaneously, the U.S.-Japanese alliance becomes more integrated and more focused on Taiwan, and right-wing Japanese politicians who are determined to press for an independent Taiwan become increasingly influential. Meanwhile, back in the United States, the possibility of war with China over Taiwan has become the only justification for a new generation of high-performance aircraft and ships. One of the world's most enormous industrial lobbies becomes increasingly focused on hyping the China threat in order to justify more than $100 billion per year of business that would otherwise evaporate.

The future of Asian geopolitics hinges, to a greater extent than on any other feature of the modern world, on which of these two dynamics becomes dominant. They cannot coexist indefinitely. At some point, continuation of the military competition will force a virtually complete restoration of the old U.S. military alliance with Taiwan, while Japanese politicians increasingly trumpet the right of Taiwan to be formally independent, and no Chinese government could survive the popular anger that would result from such a situation. Chinese leaders will be forced to act.

A Sino-American war over Taiwan would likely become one of history's more devastating conflicts. China cannot afford such a war. Its fragile financial system would quickly collapse or would engulf the economy in hyperinflation. The arrangements that Japan and the United States agreed to in 1996 and 2005, and the formal announcement of the alliance's engagement in the Taiwan issue, mean that Japan and Japanese territory would be involved in large-scale war from the start of any conflict. Barring absolutely brilliant Chinese military moves, the United States would almost certainly win the initial conflict overwhelmingly. But Taiwan would be devastated, and however great the U.S. victory, the initial conflict would not be the end of it. Anyone who has spent long periods of time in China, as I have, knows that the population will mobilize around the issue and accept great sacrifices. Sporadic major warfare could go on for decades. The outcome would be catastrophic for all participants. Ironically, this may actually be a sound reason for hope that both sides will avoid conflict. Mutual deterrence and the moderate rationality of the overwhelming majority of the Taiwanese people augur reasonably well for avoiding conflict. It is worth reiterating the central point: People in Taiwan would fight to avoid the imposition of a communist government, but Beijing has no desire to impose such a government. Only a small minority of Taiwanese would support a push for early independence, and many of them would probably support it only because they have been lulled into the false belief that such a thrust would not actually risk war. Taiwanese society is overwhelmingly dominated by sensible people who will not sacrifice millions of lives over the color of a flag.

A political rapprochement between Taipei and Beijing could create an era of China-Taiwan prosperity and a U.S. peace dividend larger than the one that resulted from the end of the Cold War. Either dynamic is possible. The outcome will be determined by leaders, not by inevitable historical processes.

Korea

> A positive and cooperative China-U.S. relationship is thus essential for a smooth transition toward a unified Korea let alone peaceful coexistence of the two Koreas.
>
> —*Sung han Kim*[13]

> At some point, a unified Korean Peninsula could cause some complications for the U.S.-Japan relationship. Korea has a robust population, relatively young. A unified Korea would have a huge military. And Korea would be a country that, very fairly, has often been described as a "shrimp among whales." I wouldn't blame Koreans if they were to decide that they do not want to be a "shrimp among whales." The desire to end that role that history seemed to impose on them would be understandable.
>
> —*Former U.S. Deputy Secretary of State Richard Armitage*[14]

---

[13] "Peace Regime on the Korean Peninsula and the ROK-US Alliance: Peace and Non-Proliferation on the Korean Peninsula," *IFANS Review,* Vol. 13, No. 2, December 2005, p. 63.

[14] Richard Armitage, Interview, *The Oriental Economist,* March 2006, p. 15.

Korea has long been the classic "man in the middle," caught among the swirling big-power rivalries of Japan, China, Russia, and the United States. Weak and divided for more than a century, it has attracted these conflicts into itself rather than being able to repel them. As a result, Korea has been the site of big-power warfare in 1895, 1905, and 1950 and has been on the verge of such warfare a number of times since, including 1994 and 2005–2006.

One logical stratagem for such a country is to ally with a big power far away, and indeed that has been South Korea's position for half a century, closely allied to the United States while maintaining a more-or-less hostile attitude toward Japan, China, North Korea, and the Soviet Union until relatively recently. While this is a sensible tactic, it is laden with tension, because South Korea's vital American ally has generally felt closer ties to Japan, the still-disliked ex-colonial power, than to South Korea itself.

Post–Cold War developments are changing Korea's strategic context. North Korea, which in the 1960s seemed politically and economically superior and possessed considerable international support, now appears hapless. Table 1 shows the transformation of the intra-Korean balance, with GDP stated in current U.S. dollars adjusted for purchasing power and population in millions.[15] The Republic of Korea (ROK), i.e., South Korea, has simply overwhelmed its rival economically, and

Table 1
Ratios of North and South Korean GDP and Population

	GDP (PPP[a]) ($ billions)	Population (millions)
South Korea	965.3	48.8
North Korea	40	23.1
Ratio[b]	24.1	2.1

SOURCE: *CIA World Factbook*, 2006 (http://www.theodora.com/wfb/index.html#CURRENT).

[a]PPP = purchasing power parity.

[b]This is probably the lowest respectable estimate of the ratios of the sizes of the two economies. The CIA figure is rounded up to the nearest $10 billion. Some estimates place the ratio well above 30.

---

[15] Source: *CIA Factbook,* https://www.cia.gov/cia/publications/factbook/.

such economic disparity eventually renders North Korea's relative military position hopeless. South Korea, now a member of the Organisation for Economic Co-operation and Development (OECD) with a per capita income well over $10,000, faces a North Korea whose people have starved in large numbers and whose national debts have been in default since 1974.

Beyond the intra-Korean balance, China and Russia, long North Korea's closest allies, are now closer to Seoul than to Pyongyang, notwithstanding the 1961 defense treaty between China and North Korea. Seoul's American ally has acquired far greater military superiority than in the past. In short, North Korea has suffered economic defeat, diplomatic defeat, and balance-of-military-power defeat. North Korea can impose huge loss of life and destruction of property by attacking Seoul, which lies close to the demilitarized zone (DMZ), but only as part of an act of suicide.

North Korea has not gently acceded to defeat. It is reduced to smuggling drugs, alcohol, and weapons, accepting humanitarian food aid, and making military threats as a way of keeping its regime alive. But, like a poker player holding only a pair of deuces, it plays its cards with desperate bravado. It seems irrational and is unreliable not because its leader is crazy (he isn't) but because the desperate situation requires a new stratagem every week. Since the early 1990s, its main card has been the threat of nuclear weapons. In the wake of the September 11 attacks, the United States is hypersensitive about terrorists being potentially able to buy WMD from North Korea. Likewise, Japan is extremely sensitive to Korean hostility (North and South alike), and Prime Minister Abe became Prime Minister by taking a strong stand on North Korean kidnappings of Japanese citizens. South Koreans have a different set of sensitivities, focused on the risk that U.S.-initiated warfare could engulf them. As a result of all this, the policies of hapless Pyongyang have greatly facilitated the rightward shift in Japanese politics, enhanced Japanese adherence to the U.S.-Japan alliance, divided the United States from South Korea, and greatly complicated the Japan-China-U.S. relationship.

Since the 1980s, North Korea's former principal ploy, the threat to attack South Korea with conventional forces, has gained little traction, so the threat of nuclear weapons has become the ploy of choice. In 1994, the Clinton administration came close to war in response to the prospect of Pyongyang being on the verge of nuclear capability. In the event, pressure from the United States and China,[16] together with a promise to deliver safer forms of energy, led North Korea to accept foreign monitoring of its plutonium-producing facilities.

At the beginning of the George W. Bush administration, it appeared that North Korea was pursuing a highly-enriched-uranium strategy that eventually would produce nuclear weapons even though the plutonium facilities were under international inspection. The United States reacted strongly. In response, Pyongyang renounced the 1994 agreement and expelled the inspectors. There ensued a standoff in which the Bush administration refused to talk directly to the North Koreans and refused to negotiate in detail until they conceded all the main points. The administration was determined to raise the ante until Pyongyang paid attention. Pyongyang, desperate for U.S. recognition and security guarantees, was determined to raise the nuclear ante, first through terminating inspections, then through missile tests and an eventual nuclear-weapon test, until the administration paid attention. This was not an auspicious dynamic.

The Chinese strategy was to entice the North Koreans into a Chinese-style peaceful economic reform, while putting the lid on Pyongyang's nuclear ambitions through diplomatic démarches and occasional economic pressure. South Korea's strategy was to deplore U.S. threats and entice the North into economic engagement. In the end this spaghetti bowl of conflicting strategies led to North Korea's acquiring multiple nuclear weapons, with the embarrassed Chinese acknowledging that their strategy had failed and the embarrassed Bush administration reverting to an updated version of the Clinton administration policies that it had earlier denounced.

The South Korean strategy contributed little because it provided no strong penalties for North Korean misbehavior. The initial Bush-

---

[16] The United States threatened military force. China applied diplomatic pressure and engaged in such ploys as having "technical difficulties" in delivering vitally needed oil to North Korea for a short demonstration period.

administration strategy failed because it was built on a bluff. Tied down in Iraq, the United States lacked a credible military option, and in any case, the potential harm to South Korea from implementing a military option was beyond anything the South could reasonably be expected to tolerate. Most of the rest of the world was not willing to support the U.S. refusal to talk directly to the North Koreans, nor was it willing to support refusal to negotiate until the North Koreans had agreed to all the important points in advance. The Chinese strategy had both sticks and carrots, but getting North Korea to emulate China's reversal of economic and foreign-policy strategy was not politically credible in the short run; Deng Xiaoping, always a critic of Maoist policies, could repudiate virtually everything Mao stood for, but Kim Jong Il was, after all, the son of Kim Il Sung and could not repudiate his father without repudiating his own legitimacy and his son's.

The best of a set of unpalatable options was to bribe the North Koreans just enough to keep the nuclear program from expanding and to deter them from selling WMD by vowing nuclear retaliation if terrorists were to acquire North Korean weapons, while allowing the Chinese and South Koreans to seduce them economically at a very slow, piecemeal rate. There is no way that the North Korean regime can survive indefinitely with the social opening that would be required, but it remains to be seen whether the regime will transform internally or implode.

Notwithstanding Northern bravado, South Korea's victory is real, but as this inauspicious recent history suggests, victory has brought South Korea strains as well as triumph. The relative diminution of North Korea's threat, the emergence of friendly big powers on two sides of the peninsula, and the emergence of a highly diversified trade pattern have given Seoul more room for maneuver, and a less frightened population increasingly demands that the new freedom be used. Feeling less threatened, South Koreans have begun to explore ways of interacting peacefully with North Korea, both economically and politically. Fear and anger over the risk that the Bush administration would initiate a devastating war has revived an interest in eventual (but not immediate) unification that had previously gone dormant, along with a sense of intra-Korean brotherhood. This popular reaction to the perceived risk of war was heightened by the coincidence of the Bush administration's threats with its decision to pull U.S. troops back from their exposed position on the DMZ. Although there were sound military reasons for the redeployment—and in fact a strong argument that, overall, the redeployment would strengthen the U.S.–South Korean position—many South Koreans thought the United States was reducing the exposure of its own troops and increasing the risks to South Koreans just when it was raising the risk of war.

One of the clichés that has arisen in analyzing South Korea's new, somewhat strained, international position is that its trade with China now exceeds its trade with any other country. That statistic is true as far as it goes, and if one includes a substantial part of its trade with Hong Kong as trade with China proper, it is clear that China is substantially South Korea's biggest trade partner. However, as Figure 4 shows, it is hardly dependent upon any one partner. This is a picture of a country with sufficiently balanced trade that it cannot be blackmailed or manipulated by any one partner. That is particularly true because in

Figure 4
South Korea's Trade Relationships

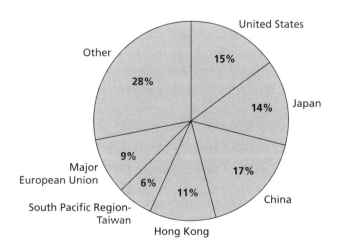

many of its trade and investment deals with China, South Korea is in fact technologically, financially, or managerially dominant.[17]

This is a picture of a country whose trade gives it options, a country with more options than in the past rather than fewer. It is not in any way a picture of a country that can be forced by economic dependence on China to change its international alignments.

Other forces are changing its American ally. In the aftermath of 9/11, the United States is intensely concerned that North Korea, in desperate economic shape, might sell WMD to a terrorist group or a Middle Eastern enemy of the United States. It is tying its Asia security policy ever more closely to Japan. And it is restructuring its forces worldwide to emphasize lean mobility.

The changes created by these trends strain the old U.S.–South Korean alliance. Just when the United States and Japan are inclined to take a tough, confrontational line with North Korea, South Koreans feel more comfortable than they once did exploring non-confrontational options, and they desperately fear that confrontation over the North's nuclear programs might lead to war. The disparity between, on the one hand, rising U.S. and Japanese fears of North Korean nuclear weapons being sold to terrorist groups or being used to blackmail Japan and, on the other hand, declining fears in South Korea of direct conflict with the hapless, bankrupt, starving North lies behind the public-opinion polls showing that, however outlandish this may seem to many Americans, the majority of South Koreans see U.S. President George W. Bush as a greater threat to peace than hereditary, militaristic, confrontational North Korean dictator Kim Jong Il.

Just when the United States is making its Asia security policy ever more reliant on Japan, South Korea is nervous about the direction Japan is taking; notwithstanding a strong earlier effort by former President Kim Dae Jung to improve the Korea-Japan relationship, and notwithstanding improved cultural ties, the year 2005 will be best remembered for Koreans cutting off fingers to demonstrate their anger over revisionist Japanese textbooks and prime-ministerial visits to the

---

[17] On technological relationships, see Somi Seong, Steven W. Popper, and Kungang Zheng, *Strategic Choices in Science and Technology: Korea in the Era of a Rising China*, Santa Monica, CA: RAND Corporation, MG-320-KISTEP, 2005, esp. pp. 31ff.

Yasukuni Shrine. Paradoxically, the decline or vanishing hostility of other old adversaries (the DPRK, Russia, and China, respectively) frees South Koreans to express their concerns about Japan. As the poll results reproduced in Table 2 indicate, South Koreans' views of Japan are three times more unfavorable than those of China or the United States, they see the Japanese military buildup as twice as threatening to Asia's peace as its Chinese counterpart, and they think Japan presents more than four times the threat to their country's security that

Table 2
Polls of Adult South Koreans' Attitudes Toward Other Countries

Is your overall opinion favorable or unfavorable?

Country	Favorable	Unfavorable	Neither/Don't Know	Total (%)
Japan	7.8	63.4	28.8	100.0
China	20.0	24.4	55.6	100.0
U.S.	20.9	24.9	54.2	100.0

Which country do you feel is most threatening to the security of South Korea? Please choose one.

Group	Japan	North Korea	U.S.	China	Iraq	Other	No Threat Exists	Don't Know/No Response	Total (%)
Total sample	28.1	46.1	17.3	6.7	0.4	0.1	1.2	0.1	100.0

What factors do you think will threaten peace and stability in East Asia? Choose two among choices.

Group	The Korean Peninsula	Territorial Disputes	Japanese Military Build-up	Terrorism	Presence of U.S. Forces	Chinese Military	Tensions over Taiwan Strait
Overall (%)	55.0	36.7	29.8	26.2	21.9	15.7	13.9

SOURCE: Polls of adult South Koreans, Dong-A Ilbo, March 2005 (http://www.mansfieldfdn.org/polls/poll-05-2.htm).

China does.[18] In 2005, according to a presentation at RAND by a top South Korean official, South Korea requested that the ROK-U.S. alliance formally designate Japan as a potential enemy—in the way that Japan had designated China as a potential enemy. The United States, of course, emphatically refused, but the incident showed the intensity of the strains in the triangular relationship and the potential cost of Washington's overwhelming reliance on the U.S.-Japan alliance at a time when an increasingly nationalistic Japan is antagonizing its neighbors.

South Koreans also fear that the new mobility of U.S. forces based in Korea means that those forces might be used to defend Taiwan in a war with China, engaging them alongside a country they see as an enemy (Japan) against a country they see as favorably as they see the United States (China). Many South Koreans see Korea and China as the two Asian countries that have suffered from unfair division. Not surprisingly, the United States is adamant about its right to deploy its forces elsewhere when needed, and South Korea's President Roh Moo Hyun is equally adamant that such regional deployments will not be tolerated.[19]

---

[18] A systematic set of polls of South Korean foreign-policy attitudes can be found in Norman D. Levin and Yong-Sup Han, *The Shape of Korea's Future: South Korean Attitudes Toward Unification and Long-Term Security Issues,* Santa Monica, CA: RAND Corporation, MR-1092-CAPP, 1999. Levin and Han found that South Korean views of Japan were moderating, but that appears to have been a blip. Polls before that time and since have shown a striking antagonism toward Japan, and this is consistent with my own personal experiences during visits over a period of 35 years. At the height of the Cold War, when North Korean soldiers were killing South Koreans at the DMZ, infiltrating the South, and even attempting to kill South Korea's president, senior South Korean officials often said North Korea was a problem, but Japan was the enemy. In 2005, Japanese textbook revisions precipitated angry riots in South Korea during which some participants cut off their own fingers to prove how strongly they felt.

[19] "'I clearly state that the U.S. Forces Korea should not be involved in disputes in Northeast Asia without our consent,' [South Korean President] Roh said at an Air Force Academy commencement ceremony on Tuesday [March 8, 2005]. . . . It was the first formal response from the country's leader to a U.S. plan to use its troops in South Korea as a regional force, with missions to handle conflicts outside the peninsula." ("Roh Tells U.S. to Stay Out of Regional Affairs," *Washington Times,* March 11, 2005, p. 16.) South Korea's Yonhap News Agency carried additional details on March 8, 2005.

South Korea's strategic dilemma increasingly resembles the old riddle, What happens when an irresistible force meets an immovable object? The country's need for a distant, powerful ally, the United States, in the face of its feuding, powerful neighbors remains a consensus among South Korea's elite, but the fact that the United States is betting its relationship with the region completely on Japan, which South Koreans have always seen as the biggest long-run threat to themselves, and specifically building up the Japanese military, which is profoundly feared in South Korea, creates an exquisite dilemma for South Korean leaders. This dilemma is multiplied by the increasing focus of the U.S.-Japan alliance on China as a potential adversary, since the South Koreans have a relatively favorable view of China, and they know China's consent will be required if Korea is to be peacefully unified.

Many analyses of the parlous state of the U.S.–South Korean relationship have emphasized generational change and other domestic factors. Certainly, there has been generational change of various kinds, including the maturation of a generation that has no memory of the Korean War and the emergence of leaders who were formerly outside the establishment. There is now a deep and potentially volatile divide in South Korean politics, a legacy of the ruthless years of building a fractured nation under threat, a serious wound that has not healed. But anyone who meets with those who have dominated South Korean foreign policy since the beginning of the Park Chung Hee era, as I have, knows that the basic concerns about the direction of the alliance are widely shared. Koreans agree about very few things, and they are as outspoken about their disagreements as anyone on earth. Their unusual unity regarding what they see as the errors of U.S. policy underlines the reality that the scope of discontent over the current relationship with the United States derives not primarily from new leaders or from generational change, but rather from the exquisitely painful strategic dilemma that South Korea faces.

Korea's situation is more dramatic than that of other allies, but it is widely shared throughout a region where, except in Taiwan, distrust of Japan generally runs higher than distrust of China. This in turn creates a potential future problem for Washington, which tends to assume that allies' perceptions and concerns about China and Japan automatically parallel its own. That Cold War assumption holds little reality in the new era.

South Korea's strategic uncertainty further magnifies all these problems. North Korea might become unstable. It might collapse. It might test a nuclear weapon, or threaten Japan with one, or sell one to a terrorist group. An opportunity might arise to achieve either gradual or sudden unification with fellow Koreans in the North. In these circumstances, Seoul desperately needs a strong ally, but it needs one whose strategy is congruent with its own needs. The result so far has been a consensual reaffirmation of the alliance with the United States but also an equally consensual, if somewhat quieter, anger with the United States.[20] This situation could break in multiple directions.

Which of the many potential outcomes actually occurs will depend on developments in North Korea and the attitudes of South Korea, Japan, China, and the United States. Russian views are less important. Developments over Taiwan will be crucial to Chinese and U.S. positions.

All the key powers, including the United States, China, Japan, and North and South Korea, as well as Russia, are agreed that they do not want war and that any sudden transformation of the Korean peninsula would run a high risk of war. All the powers except North Korea agree that a nuclear North Korea is unacceptable. In the tradeoff between these two agreed goals, the United States (and perhaps Japan or key parts of Japan's national-security establishment) is willing to

---

[20] At one conference I attended before the February 2007 agreement, unfortunately one where the rules prohibited detailed attribution, the speakers included Korean leaders representing several quite different governments that covered much of the last half-century and, in each case, individuals who have strongly identified their own cause with the United States. One after another, they spoke of their frustration, disappointment, and anger over the direction of U.S. policies. These feelings, usually muted in public statements, show that the fundamental problem is conflicting strategic needs, not just generational change or the different ideological tone of the current government. The basic differences from U.S. policy are arguments that (1) the United States should not make threats it can't deliver on (because its troops are bogged down in Iraq); (2) if anything is to be accomplished, sticks must be accompanied by carrots; (3) the United States must talk directly to North Korea; (4) delegating pressure on North Korea to China is self-defeating because the North Koreans have such a strong nationalistic reaction to any Chinese pressure; and (5) siding regionally with Japan against China makes no sense.

run a much higher risk of war because it is far more concerned about proliferation of North Korean nuclear weapons to terrorist groups and direct nuclear threats to Japan. The United States would also welcome a North Korean collapse, short of war, leading to the unification of Korea under South Korean auspices. South Korea and China are more worried about any sudden collapse of North Korea, with or without war, because they fear floods of refugees and possibly a spillover of actual conflict that could harm their own economies and destabilize their societies.

Notwithstanding the near-consensus hope for a relatively smooth or stable outcome, the stability of North Korea is something no combination of powers can assure. A recurrence of famine, greater awareness in North Korea of how much better life is in South Korea, a split in the North Korean elite leading to civil war, or any combination of these could suddenly destabilize North Korea.

In the long term, the only stable outcome for Korea is a unified Korea, and for the foreseeable future any unified Korea would have to be under South Korean leadership. For this reason, it is worth exploring in detail the conditions under which Korea could be unified.

As a practical matter, such an outcome would require Chinese consent. No analyst has yet invented a persuasive scenario under which unification could occur in the face of determined Chinese opposition. Chinese consent, in turn, is largely linked to developments over Taiwan.

The division of Korea and the division of China are linked both historically and in the present. As we have noted earlier, the Truman administration originally intended to let the Chinese civil war take its course to unification of Taiwan under Mao, but Mao's backing of the Soviet-inspired North Korean invasion of South Korea led Truman to seal the Taiwan Strait. The separation of Taiwan is the price China pays for its role in the Korean War. The continued division of Korea is more arguably a price the United States pays for its inability or unwillingness to deal with the winning side in China a half-century ago.

In the present, China's principal goal in Korea is stability, and that goal would be served by a unified Korea. Moreover, there is a much more immediate linkage: The Bush administration has wanted to avert any unnecessary tension with China over Taiwan because it needs Chinese help with North Korea. However, China fears that a Korea unified around Seoul and allied with Washington would threaten China regionally and along the shared Yalu River border if conflict flared over Taiwan. Therefore, China will oppose unification under South Korean auspices unless its concerns about the impact of a unified Korea allied to the United States on Taiwan are assuaged. They might be assuaged by an agreement that U.S. troops would remain in the southern part of the peninsula or that they would never be used in a Taiwan contingency (something the current South Korean government already wants to insist on). Or a regional settlement of both the Korean problem and the Taiwan problem might make the U.S. bases in Korea superfluous.

Why would China even consider a serious risk of unification of Korea under Seoul? Because a divided, unstable, and nuclear Korea constitutes a serious danger to China. China's leaders have recognized for the past quarter-century that they have a vital interest in stability on the Korean peninsula, and they have acted time after time to preserve stability and avert a nuclear North Korea. Since the mid-1970s, Chinese officials have privately ridiculed North Korea and feared the dangerous adventures of Pyongyang's leaders. Since at least the mid-1990s, Beijing has developed deep economic and political ties with Seoul. South Korea exports more to China than it does to the United States, and Beijing's leaders trust Seoul's leaders more than they trust Pyongyang's.

There is a myth that Beijing is as close to Pyongyang as lips to teeth—not surprising, because China used to use exactly that language to describe the relationship. Despite China's massive military intervention in the Korean War and a formal defense treaty dating from 1961, Pyongyang has alienated Beijing politically and ideologically, and Beijing has occasionally taken strong actions against North Korea, such as demanding hard-currency payments that Pyongyang could not afford or temporarily curtailing oil supplies. Beijing sometimes perpetuates the myth of closeness publicly because it needs a working relationship with Pyongyang, but in fact, since the 1990s, Beijing has had much closer and more-positive relations with Seoul economically, diplomatically, and strategically. Some in the United States perpetuate the obsolete characterization because they resent Beijing's unwillingness to line up with U.S. confrontational policies on North Korean nuclear issues. For U.S. media, the relationships have sometimes proved too subtle. But anyone who talks with the U.S. diplomats directly involved knows that time after time, Beijing's "good cop" approach has helpfully and deliberately complemented the U.S. "bad cop" in crises with Pyongyang.

There are three reasons why Beijing fears the unification of Korea under Seoul: ideological embarrassment over the collapse of a fellow communist regime, the convenience of having a malleable regime next door, and fears of the U.S.-Korea alliance becoming a gigantic security threat on China's Yalu River border.

The embarrassment should work the other way now. While there was a time when China and North Korea were similar autarkic, totalitarian regimes fomenting revolutionary instability all over the world, since the late 1970s, they have moved in precisely opposite directions. North Korea has remained largely autarkic, socialist to the point of starving a substantial part of its own population, and fully totalitarian, and it has persisted in a foreign policy based on threats of war and on trade driven by military exports. In contrast, China has become an economy more open and globalized than Japan; a polity that, while still a dictatorship, has steadily expanded the personal freedom of its citizens; and an advocate of stability in all the Asian countries where previously it fomented upheaval. The typical Chinese family has more than one television, while the typical North Korean family has a relative who has starved to death. Today what should be embarrassing for the Chinese government is any suggestion that these regimes are of the same type. There are few in China who do not see the ideological issue this way.

Regarding the second reason, the convenience of having a regime next door that is more malleable than South Korea, it has been a long time since Beijing found Pyongyang more convenient to deal with than Seoul. North Korea's nationalism toward China is prickly and antagonistic. Chinese foreign-policy leaders agonize over how to persuade North Korea to back away from dangerous military tactics and foreign policies, including, most notably, progress in building nuclear weaponry. China called the North Korean nuclear explosion in October 2006 "brazen." China tries private threats, cuts in oil deliveries, and even large-scale military maneuvers near the border, but nothing seems to work. South Korean diplomats complain about U.S. reliance on Chinese pressure to resolve the nuclear issue, saying that North Korean hostility toward China makes Chinese pressure automatically counterproductive. China has no such problems with South Korea.

The security issue is more difficult. With an arms race escalating around Taiwan and a large, potent U.S. force in South Korea, loss of the North Korean buffer would potentially bring a heavily armed Seoul-Washington alliance to China's border and free all U.S. forces in Korea for use in a Taiwan contingency. For Beijing, these are serious and legitimate concerns.

If those concerns could be assuaged, then China would have an interest in pressing for decisive resolution of the Korean conflict, even if this risked the likely eventual disappearance of the North Korean regime. The risks created by North Korea are greater for China than they are for the United States, and they increase inexorably with each passing year. North Korean weapons get more dangerous. Potential connections between global terrorist groups and dissidents in China's Xinjiang province multiply. The risk of U.S. military intervention in North Korea rises. The risk that China would be affected by warfare, by nuclear and chemical and biological fallout, and by vast floods of North Korean refugees steadily increases. Chinese leaders need to accept the danger of delay and draw hard conclusions—now.

The security issue need not prove insuperable. The scale of U.S. forces in South Korea is substantially, although not exclusively, a response to the danger of war between South and North Korea. If Korea were unified, the U.S. military presence could be seriously reduced. It could certainly be confined to the southern part of the peninsula. U.S. Secretary of Defense Donald Rumsfeld indicated an intention to move U.S. forces on the DMZ further south and to reduce the total U.S. force based in Korea.

Chinese fears that the U.S. alliance with a unified Korea would constitute a serious threat could be further assuaged, and the U.S. need to maintain and increase forces directed at China could be reduced, by reduction of tensions over Taiwan. In return for an agreement by China to limit aid to North Korea, the United States could promise that it would not abandon its current status quo policy on Taiwan. President Bush had, as of early 2006, entrenched this policy more explicitly than any other U.S. president. But this sound policy always seems under threat—from a new U.S. president, from the power of the Taiwan lobby in the Congress, or from a reaction to some unforeseen event. This basic policy has survived seven presidencies because it fits the national interest, but it is always under assault. If the U.S. government can show some kind of credible, ratified long-term commitment, the dividend can be enormous, especially in Korea. A more detailed scenario to this effect is outlined in Chapter Nine of this volume. For now, the key point is that the North Korea and Taiwan problems are joined at the hip.

Southeast Asia

A group of small countries in Southeast Asia has long played a dispro-portionate role in regional and global politics and economic forums. During the Cold War, the members of ASEAN[21] constituted an anti-communist bulwark that proved crucial to the future of the region. Ostensibly only an economic organization, ASEAN tied together a half-dozen threatened countries in a way that provided a sense of common identity and shared purpose at a difficult time. Underneath the blan-ket of economic cooperation, ASEAN cultivated common positions on international political issues and facilitated joint military training. The economic exchanges proved politically decisive. By serving as a trans-mission belt for the lessons of economic and institutional development, both from the Asian-miracle countries to the north and among them-selves, they spread the Asian economic miracle to their members. With the exception of the Philippines, they enjoyed an economic takeoff that

---

[21] ASEAN was formed in 1967 with U.S. encouragement by Indonesia, Malaysia, the Philippines, Singapore, and Thailand, with Brunei joining in 1984 and four others (see pp. 173–174) in the mid-1990s.

followed in the footsteps of Japan, South Korea, Taiwan, Hong Kong, and Singapore.

As in Northeast Asia, the economic takeoff proved to be the key to stopping the spread of instability and communism, as well as Islamic fundamentalism. Prior to the takeoff, all these countries had serious communist insurgencies and tribal divisions. Indonesia had the world's third largest Communist Party and the world's largest Islamic fundamentalist movement, along with innumerable tribal conflicts. Soon after the economic takeoff began, the tribal divisions eased; the Indonesian government was able to minimize the communist movement after its bloody suppression in 1966; after a brief period of repression under Suharto, Indonesia's Islamist movement became moderate and ceased its demands for an Islamic state; and governments throughout the region gradually defeated their communist insurgencies. In contrast, Laos, Cambodia, and Burma, where economic growth had not taken off, succumbed to tribal divisions and communist movements; and the Philippines, which, although a member of ASEAN, never adopted the economic reforms or made the infrastructure investments necessary for a "miracle" takeoff, has never been able to completely defeat either its communist or Muslim/tribal insurgencies.

Notwithstanding the world's current focus on Arab Muslims, the ASEAN countries also have great weight in the global development of Islamic politics. Indonesia has the world's largest Muslim population. Malaysia is the world's most successful diversified Muslim economy and the most successful Muslim democracy. (It has oil, but unlike Saudi Arabia, Kuwait, and the other Middle Eastern oil states, it also has highly diversified successes in agriculture and manufacturing.) Had Indonesia, Malaysia, and Thailand failed to develop, moderate Islam would be much weaker today globally, and radical Islam would have spread much faster and much further.

ASEAN's cohesion and success in turn made it the swing vote in global multilateral trade negotiations. The takeoffs of its formerly impoverished countries provided the United States, the World Bank, and the IMF the intellectual ammunition and political support needed to persuade much of the rest of the developing world to go along with economic liberalization.

While ASEAN created itself through local efforts and outspokenly eschewed alignment with any of the big powers, the United States encouraged its development—after abortive attempts at other incarnations of regional organization (MAPHILINDO and ASPAC)—for national-security reasons. Given the anticolonial orientation of Indonesia in particular and the foreign-policy sensitivities of Malaysia and others, a bloc that was U.S.-backed and Western-oriented but focused on economic cooperation could be more inclusive than a traditional military alliance. Indeed, the economic association, ASEAN, proved effective and enduring, while the overt military alliance, SEATO, quickly fell into disrepair. Alliances with the Philippines and Thailand, quasi-alliance cooperation with Singapore, and close collaboration with Indonesia and Malaysia were nonetheless important to U.S. success in the Cold War.

The United States was the principal outside political beneficiary of ASEAN's success, because it encouraged the group's formation and put a huge effort into the advisory, aid, and institution-building programs that underlay these countries' economic success. The U.S. contribution was omnipresent and unmistakable. Aid missions were large and important. Ambassadors spent their time not only on diplomacy and military efforts, but also on the intricacies of institution-building, public-administration training, trade liberalization, foreign-debt management, land reform, foreign-investment rules, and all the intricate difficulties of transforming some of the world's most impoverished peoples into what became the Asian miracle.

The connection to political orientation was quite direct, most notably in the region's most important country, Indonesia. The Indonesian post-colonial mentality was relentlessly anti-Western. Sukarno was as fervently anticolonial and anti-American as Mao Zedong. Even the military, where the United States had some traction, was bitterly divided and unstable in its orientation—for example, the Indonesian air force had strong pro-communist sympathies. But the military's 1966 obliteration of the communist movement was perpetuated by economic success, and the periodic outbreaks of Islamist violence moderated in direct proportion to the improvements in living conditions. U.S. education and institution-building programs underlay the emergence of the Berkeley Mafia (so-called because so many had doctorates in economics from the University of California, Berkeley), which managed the country's economic takeoff and effectively provided the core national strategy for the regime until shortly before Suharto fell more than three decades later. Eventually, President Suharto was able to strike an explicit deal with the largest of the Islamic movements, Nahdatul Ulama, in which he agreed that Islamic leaders could participate as individuals in politics as long as they confined their religious activities to the social realm. Parenthetically, some radical Islamist groups reemerged following the economic crisis of 1998, but not on anything like the threatening scale that preceded the economic takeoff.[22]

This kind of experience, multiplied throughout Southeast Asia, added up to a large, strategically located population that served as a highly effective quasi-ally of the United States throughout the Cold War. It is worth underlining the geographic scope of this group: Indonesia alone covers an area equivalent to the region bounded by London, Moscow, Stockholm, and Algiers—and, unlike Central Asia, it has a large population.

Since the mid-1990s, ASEAN's international political role has become less and less clear-cut. Four developments have intervened: the Asian crisis, the expansion of ASEAN, the war on terror and the war in Iraq, and changes in the roles of the United States and China.

In 1997 and 1998, the Asian miracle turned temporarily into the Asian debacle. In what became known as the Asian crisis, Thailand and Indonesia suffered financial collapses and economic recessions that were comparable to the Great Depression in the United States, but compressed into two brutal years. Banks collapsed, property and stock markets collapsed, currencies collapsed, the countries' most prestigious

---

[22] The nearly perfect correlation in Indonesia between economic success and the decline of the Islamist movement, and vice versa, needs to be studied by American analysts who are convinced that there is no connection between poverty and Islamist radicalism. The fact that radical Islamist leaders and suicide bombers are frequently not poor does not provide conclusive evidence against such a correlation. Similarly, Mao Zedong and his fellow leaders were not poor, and the anti-bourgeois rhetoric of Maoism could be summed up as "We hate your freedoms," but Maoist radicalism evaporated as soon as the Chinese people were given opportunities to rapidly advance their standards of living. Maoism was rooted in poverty and cultural despair.

companies collapsed, unemployment rose, and health and social welfare declined. This was a particularly terrible shock for populations that had come to believe that superior economic performance and rapidly improving standards of living were endowed by their DNA.

Indonesia had been the unofficial but universally acknowledged leader of ASEAN. Indonesian leaders guided the trade talks, eased difficult political tensions, and almost alone managed such things as the conflicting seabed and territorial-waters claims that bedevil the region (including its relations with China). Indonesia suffered more from the Asian crisis than any other country, and its financial collapse and political chaos crisis shattered its regional leadership position. With divided politics and a foundering economy, Indonesia lacked both the prestige and the domestic cohesion needed to lead the region. Its early post-Suharto leaders had little understanding of foreign policy or international economics. Importantly and symbolically, President Megawati Sukarnoputri fired the team that had so successfully managed the territorial-waters issues, and nobody who was effective replaced it.

Similarly, Thailand had been the unofficial but acknowledged deputy leader of ASEAN, with aspirations to manage the regional economic affairs of Indochina (Burma, Laos, Cambodia, and Vietnam) as well. It had made intricate currency arrangements to ensure that it would become the Southeast Asian regional financial center. Precisely those currency arrangements brought down the Thai financial system. Thus, neither the leader nor the deputy leader was any longer in a position to lead ASEAN, and there were no alternatives—the Philippines was too mismanaged, Singapore too Chinese, Brunei too small, and Malaysia under anti-Western Prime Minister Mahathir both too small and too distant from the ASEAN consensus. By the turn of the century, new member Vietnam, with a large enough population to give it political weight, had become by far ASEAN's most dynamic economy, but its politics, its aggressive history, and its low level of economic liberalization precluded its being accepted—for now—as the group's leader.

The second critical development was the expansion of ASEAN to include Vietnam (1995), Laos and Myanmar (1997), and Cambodia (1999). This fundamentally altered what had been an implicit anti-communist alliance. Now three out of ten members of ASEAN were communist countries, and one (Burma) was an anti-Western tribalized dictatorship, more like an African nation than a Southeast Asian one, whose government inflicted some of the worst human-rights abuses ever experienced. ASEAN and the United States differed fundamentally on whether the right approach to Burma was to isolate it (the U.S. position) or to seduce it (ASEAN's position). All this created tensions with the United States.

Third, the war on terror and the war in Iraq agitated many of Southeast Asia's Muslims. This caused Indonesia and Malaysia to distance themselves a bit more from U.S. foreign policy, and it seemed to inspire a higher level of domestic dissent in the Muslim communities of southern Thailand. It drove the financially imperiled, sometimes unstable Philippine government, unable to manage by itself, into a much closer relationship with the United States.

Fourth, beginning with the Asian crisis of 1997–1998, the relationship of the United States to ASEAN changed decisively. Traditionally, Thailand had been a close ally and had come to expect strong U.S. support, but when the Asian crisis began with the collapse of Thailand's currency regime on July 2, 1997, congressional restrictions imposed after the 1994 bailout of Mexico prevented the kind of decisive U.S. intervention that could have moderated Thailand's financial collapse. Moreover, the IMF, perceived in Asia as working closely with the Clinton Treasury Department, underestimated the severity of Thailand's crunch and imposed austerity measures that, instead of the predicted zero growth, led Thailand's economy to contract by an extraordinary 12 percent in 1997 and 1998.[23]

---

[23] Calculated from CEIC data, using 1988 constant prices. The IMF demanded that Thailand, a country facing financial and economic implosion, run a deflationary fiscal surplus and forecast that this would lead to a growth rate of zero. When it led instead to depression, the IMF reversed itself and prescribed a fiscal deficit of 2 percent of GDP. In international conferences, IMF officials acknowledged the difference between their 0 percent forecast and the actual result in Thailand. For a disquisition on the ill consequences of the IMF programs, see Joseph E. Stiglitz, "The East Asia Crisis," chap. 4 of *Globalization and Its Discontents*, New York: W. W. Norton, 2002. For the details of the IMF programs, see "The Asian Crisis" in *International Monetary Fund, Annual Report 1998*, pp. 23ff. I prepared a particularly detailed report on the Thai crisis and its aftermath, with perspectives that are generally

Similarly, in Indonesia, the United States was unable to offer decisive help, and again, the IMF, perceived rightly or wrongly in Southeast Asia as working closely with the Clinton Treasury Department, made a crucial error. It demanded that a group of insolvent banks with close links to the Suharto family be shut down, in itself a quite reasonable decision, but it failed to provide for safeguards to support the remainder of the banking system. The Indonesian population, seeing that even banks linked to the ruling family could collapse, lost all faith in the banking system, which then suffered a broad collapse. The banking-system collapse in turn was catastrophic for the economy.

Malaysia responded to the crisis by pegging its currency to the U.S. dollar, and Prime Minister Mahathir bitterly blamed Western speculators, singling out Jews as perpetrators. Both his economic and his political positions antagonized the United States, and Vice President Al Gore prominently attacked his policies at a meeting in the Malaysian capital. The ASEAN reaction was that Mahathir had been too provocative, but that Gore had unacceptably infringed Asian conventions of hospitality.

The outcome of these developments was a broad ASEAN disillusionment with the United States as a patron and protector. In parallel, although not to the same degree, Washington had more disagreements with the new ASEAN, most notably about ASEAN's embrace of Burma and the possibility that Burma might at some point have a turn as a formal leader of the organization.

In this context, the George W. Bush administration came to power in 2001 believing that the Clinton administration had relied far too heavily on economic policy and that more emphasis was needed on military security.[24] Foreign policy in the new administration was dominated by officials with a military background, including both the secretary of state and the deputy secretary of state. The 9/11 al Qaeda attack on the World Trade Center ensured even more intense focus on national security in the relatively narrow sense of military security. The

---

overlooked in the academic literature, in William H. Overholt, *Thailand: Reform at a Stately Pace,* Hong Kong: Nomura Securities, July 8, 1999.

[24] As noted earlier, this is a central theme of Mann, *The Rise of the Vulcans,* op. cit.

core strategy of the United States had shifted away from the Marshall Plan/Asian-miracle focus on economic and social development protected by the military, to an emphasis on military security, with multilateral economic development as a secondary or tertiary appendage.

Within economic policy, the U.S. emphasis shifted heavily to the promotion of bilateral free-trade agreements (FTAs), rather than the more onerous task of promoting successful global multilateral liberalization. FTAs are advantageous to large countries like the United States, but they provide drastically fewer advantages for small trade partners like Southeast Asian countries. Extremely complex Rules of Origin, catalogued in hundreds of pages of intricate requirements designed by domestic interest groups in the countries involved, determine products' eligibility for free-trade status; it is relatively easy for a wide range of big-country products to clearly satisfy the Rules of Origin, but small, open economies like those of Singapore or Australia typically provide one or two steps in a long value chain. As a result, many of their products cannot meet the Rules of Origin requirements, and for many more products, the documentation requirements are so onerous that companies pay the tariffs rather than trying to benefit from the FTAs.[25] Moreover, within FTA policy, the United States decided to give heavy priority to those countries that supported the war in Iraq, notably Singapore, Australia, and South Korea, rather than giving economic considerations their traditional preeminence. These changed priorities magnified the ASEAN disillusionment that had begun with the Clinton administration's disappointing policies during the Asian crisis.

Simultaneously, China, the latecomer to Eastern Asia's obsession with economic development, was moving to put economic development through multilateral trade and investment liberalization at the core of its foreign policy.

Southeast Asian disillusionment over this drastic change in U.S. priorities was exacerbated in the cases of predominantly Muslim Indo-

---

[25] I am indebted to Professor Ross Garnaut for both the analysis of the different impacts of FTAs on small countries and the fact that many Singaporean and Australian companies find it less costly to pay the tariffs than to undertake the costly effort to prove that they satisfy the Rules of Origin requirements.

nesia and Malaysia by perceptions (possibly unfair, but deeply felt) that the war in Iraq and the war on terror had strong anti-Muslim components.

Movements in the tectonic plates of international relations become identified by diplomatic quakes. In this case, the shifting positions of the United States and China produced a diplomatic quake when Presidents Bush and Hu addressed the Asia-Pacific Economic Cooperation (APEC) meeting in Bangkok[26] during October 2003 and subsequently both addressed the Australian parliament in Canberra. The general reaction in Asia to both speeches was that President Bush had given a pre-reform Chinese speech, focused on geopolitics and specifically the war on terror at a conference traditionally devoted to economic issues, while President Hu had given the traditional U.S. speech, focused on mutual economic development through multilateral reform. The speeches in themselves were not earth-shaking; what was important was that they were seen as dramatically highlighting changes that had occurred in the positions of the two powers.

The Bush effort to shift priorities at the 2003 APEC meeting punctuated the decline of an organization for which the United States had had great hopes. APEC, founded in 1989, had much broader membership than ASEAN, incorporating Northeast Asia as well as Southeast Asia, and much of South America as well. The U.S. hope was that this broad organization of Pacific Rim countries could lead a vast integration of Pacific Rim economies and in the process give the United States a major political as well as economic leadership role over the world's most dynamic economies. Instead, APEC went into drastic decline in the Bush years. The parallel security-related organization, the Asian Regional Forum, experienced the same decline.

---

[26] These events were widely noted in Asia. The major television networks all carried extensive segments on the Bush-Hu speeches and Asians' reactions to them. (I was one of those asked to comment.) They were less noted in the United States but not completely ignored. See, for instance, Fareed Zakaria, "Bush's PR Problem," *Washington Post,* December 2, 2003, p. A27. In the month following the APEC meeting, I attended several top-level conferences in Asia, and the speeches were frequently referred to as punctuating a historic turning point.

The decline of organizations that the United States had once fostered resulted from a deliberate choice by the Bush administration, which preferred ad hoc coalitions of the willing. Advocates of this view argued that the only effective organizations in Asia were coalitions like the six-power talks organized to deal with North Korean nuclear issues and the tsunami-relief coalition. They found organizations like ASEAN to be squishy talk shops, in contrast to norm-setting formal organizations like NATO or the OECD or the Organization of American States (OAS), and that American officials such as the secretary of state simply no longer had time to participate in such talk shops. Moreover, Asian organizations had proliferated into an unmanageable conglomeration: ASEAN, ASEAN+3, ASEAN+3+3, the ASEAN Regional Forum (ARF), and many others. They even argued that "China is good at multilateral organization, and we Americans are not, so we should not try to compete with them."[27]

The alternative view, to which I subscribe, was that not only was the United States good at managing multilateral organizations, it built its whole victory in the Cold War around its successful support of them—NATO, the Marshall Plan, the EU, the development banks, and many others, including Asian organizations such as ASEAN. What had failed in Asia was a formal regional military alliance, SEATO and any possible successor, and an administration focused on military issues had difficulty seeing the broader benefits of non-military organizations. While institutions like ASEAN did not fit the preconceptions of a U.S. formal organization, they have been essential in institutionalizing all the learning mechanisms that spread the Asian miracle. They have institutionalized forms of security cooperation that, given the diversity of the countries concerned, could not have been accommodated in a formally structured organization that was required to set official common norms. They have played an enormously important role in the success of global trade negotiations. Much of the reason for the morass of unmanageable organizations was the lack, for the first time in modern history, of U.S. leadership. In the end, the new

---

[27] This paragraph summarizes a presentation by National Security Council Director for Southeast Asia Holly Morrow at RAND on May 21, 2007.

policy reflected the administration's focus on the war in Iraq and other Middle East issues at the expense of East Asia, a subordination of economic arrangements such as FTAs to the mobilization of support for the war, and a broad unwillingness to compromise U.S. freedom of action by participating at top levels in multilateral organizations.

This alteration of U.S. policies in favor of coalitions of the willing and bilateral rather than multilateral agreements tied in with a broader global failure of multilateral trade talks and a weakening of multilateral organizations. Disillusioned Latin American regimes turned away from schemes for expanded free trade with the United States, and the emergence of several extreme populist regimes in South America, most notably that of Hugo Chavez in Venezuela, confounded any hopes for broad economic integration and political concord. And East Asian countries decided they needed a broad organization to discuss their interests without the overbearing presence of the United States.

Hence another modest quake in the shifting role of Southeast Asia came in December 2005, with the first East Asia Summit. The original proposal for a gathering of Asian leaders that would exclude the United States had come many years earlier from Prime Minister Mahathir of Malaysia. Mahathir had a post-colonial chip on his shoulder, and his proposal had a specifically anti-American content that was for many years rejected by the Asian consensus and fiercely resisted by the United States. After the Asian crisis, China, Japan, and a number of other Asian countries began actively pushing the development of regional programs that would have a specifically Asian identity to counterbalance the influence of the United States and the IMF. Japanese proposals for regional currency swaps, regional trade agreements, a common regional currency, and a regional emergency fund all had this political thrust. Some Southeast Asian leaders expressed privately the hope that, even if such proposals had a limited chance of being effective in the short term, they would lead to the creation of a regional secretariat that could counterbalance the United States and the IMF.[28]

---

[28] These were, for instance, the central themes of a conference organized by the Japanese Ministry of Foreign Affairs in Hakone in June 2002. I was the invitee from the United States.

In the early discussions, ASEAN leaders were determined to exclude Australia and New Zealand because they were too close to the United States.

These ideas had to overcome two problems, however: the opposition of the United States and the rivalry between Japan and China as to who should serve as the regional leader. Chinese proposals for multilateral liberalization were much more attractive to Southeast Asia than were Japanese proposals for a spider web of (very protectionist[29]) bilateral FTAs between Japan and individual countries, so the Japanese faced the problem of ensuring that China would not become the unofficial leader. After years of discussion, these problems were resolved by bringing India into the group as a further counterbalance to China and by allowing Australia and New Zealand to join in order to reduce U.S. opposition. In addition, the economic proposals were tailored to be consistent with the IMF. The bottom line was that after two decades of rejecting the idea, Asia finally agreed on a regional summit meeting that would exclude the Americans. The first summit occurred in Kuala Lumpur on December 14, 2005, with ten ASEAN members plus China, Japan, South Korea, Australia, New Zealand, and India.

All of this was led by the ASEAN group, which had the swing votes, since neither China nor Japan would accept a group in which the other held leadership and since India was not big enough economically or open enough to bid for leadership. The way the organization developed underlined the continued importance of ASEAN. It underlined the fact that, for all their disagreements, China and Japan agreed on creating an Asian identity and regional structures that exclude the United States. Holding the summit in Kuala Lumpur made explicit the connection to Mahathir's original idea that Asia needed an organization from which the United States would be excluded.

This did not imply the emergence of an overall anti-American posture either for ASEAN or for the Asian summit. Indeed, almost all

---

[29] Japanese "free-trade agreements" institutionalize Japanese protection of much of its agriculture, plus other key industries. The ban in the Japan-Singapore FTA on any Singapore exports of products such as orchids and goldfish has become the symbol of those agreements for Southeast Asians.

the participants welcome and actively encourage a strong U.S. military and economic presence to balance Japan and China. India, a member of the new group, has been simultaneously conducting a major rapprochement with the United States (as well as with China). What it did symbolize was the traditional American allies putting some distance between themselves and the United States. ASEAN and South Korea are no longer appendages of U.S. foreign policy, and both explicitly reject the view that they are allies of the United States against China. All still want the United States in the region to counterbalance China and Japan, but the Cold War content of the relationships has been evaporating. As a recent Army War College and State Department conference report summarized the situation, "The United States remains much more powerful than China in Asia and has the added advantage of being seen by ASEAN leaders as Asia's 'least distrusted power'. . . . ASEAN states generally seek [a] more diversified range of contacts, partly to avoid a situation of having to choose between the United States and China."[30] In short, Southeast Asia has not become anti-American and there is no suggestion that it will, but most of the traditional allies are far more independent now. Crucially, even Japan is maneuvering to create Asian structures independent of the United States—provided they are not dominated by China.

The United States continues to have Cold War–style quasi-alliances with Singapore and the Philippines, the two relatively peripheral members of ASEAN. Singapore is seen as only a partial member of the ASEAN team because it is viewed by its neighbors as too Chinese, and the Philippines is peripheral because it has not made the leap into the modern world economy. Both are perceived by Asian neighbors as having sold out, Singapore by having signed a free-trade agreement with the United States rather than insisting on a multilateral agreement, the Philippines for being too much of a diplomatic and cultural appendage of the United States and insufficiently Asian. Even the prime

---

[30] Corazon Sandoval Foley, "Contending Perspectives: Southeast Asia and American Views on a Rising China," Colloquium Brief, Strategic Studies Institute, Army War College, reporting on conferences held in Singapore, August 22–24, 2005, and Washington, DC, November 3, 2005.

minister of Singapore, which has for half a century been the most reliable U.S. ally in Asia, took the opportunity of a 2007 summit meeting with President Bush to urge a U.S. posture more balanced between China and Japan. Thus the U.S. ties are strengthening mainly in the military dimension and mainly with the relatively peripheral players in ASEAN, and even they are advocating more balance between the U.S. relationships with China and Japan.

On the other side of the ledger, Vietnam has joined the Asian miracle. It is doing the kinds of liberalization that created "miracle" economic growth in the other dynamic Asian economies, and it has, better late than never, shifted its focus from conquest of its neighbors to domestic economic reform. Its large population and dynamic economy will in time make Vietnam a major influence on the region. Its shift of priorities in favor of economic development means that it is no longer threatening to its neighbors (although it has not abandoned effective political domination of Laos), and it is no longer threatening to the principal objectives of U.S. foreign policy. In fact, as relations continue to evolve, Vietnam could become a major asset to U.S. foreign policy in the region. Singapore's Kishore Mahbubani has argued that "Vietnam is the world's last great reservoir of love for the United States"[31]—a surprising development, given the intensity of the Vietnam War, but an accurate reflection of popular Vietnamese sentiment.

Other countries and organizations are rapidly filling the vacuum left by the United States. China saw an opportunity and has consolidated its position with ASEAN. In 2002, it promoted and accepted a Code of Conduct for behavior regarding disputed territorial waters and seabed areas in Southeast Asia. In 2003, it effectively joined ASEAN's Asian Free Trade Area (AFTA) and conducted a highly successful diplomatic friendship campaign in the region. In 2004, China agreed with ASEAN on a phased reduction of tariffs beginning in 2005 and leading to the complete elimination of tariffs by 2010. Whether that goal would prove achievable remains the subject of reasonable debate. What is beyond doubt is the way it repositioned China's relationship

---

[31] He said this in a keynote address to the Advisory Board meeting of the RAND Center for Asia Pacific Policy on June 2, 2006, in Singapore.

to ASEAN. China began by opening its markets faster than promised and delivered substantial economic benefits to ASEAN countries, for instance, conveying substantial benefits to Thai agriculture. China's membership in the ASEAN agreement to create a free-trade area gives ASEAN the backbone it has lacked since the Asian crisis weakened Indonesia and Thailand.

At the same time, China, following an internal diplomatic guideline, "Never lead," provided that backbone and outflanked Japan without in any way threatening or subordinating ASEAN. Effectively, it just became an associate of ASEAN, without any leadership role or even official membership. It did not engage in the hardball negotiations typical of U.S. and Japanese trade negotiations, but for the most part just joined an existing deal. It has been opening its markets to ASEAN products faster than promised. Now it is playing the role the United States played for most of the post–World War II period as the primary supporter of ASEAN's aspiration to prosperity and prestige through multilateral economic liberalization. Having accepted an exceptionally rigorous WTO accession agreement, China has little to lose by moving a step further to complete free trade with its neighbors. Having opened its markets wide to the ASEAN countries, it will be increasingly integrated with them, and the sense of shared interests will probably expand.

This does not, however, imply, or even risk, ASEAN becoming a tributary or ally of China. None of the ASEAN countries finds that option attractive. All of the original members of ASEAN except tiny Brunei have more sophisticated political systems than China and regard China's system as unattractive. All of the original members except the hapless Philippines have economies and social systems far more advanced than China's. (Indonesia risks falling behind but is more advanced on most institutional indicators.) Most of both the original and new members remain conscious of China's pre-reform subversion and meddling in their domestic politics and are vigilant against even a remote risk of future recurrence. ASEAN's decision to invite Vietnam to join reflected a conscious decision that the group needed Vietnam to balance China. A reviving Indonesia, with its vast territory, large population, and determination to lead the region, still zealously guards against any hint of emergent Chinese hegemony. Even more than other countries in the region, Indonesia has powerful antibodies to any hint of strong Chinese assertion. Rightly or wrongly, most Indonesian politicians continue to hold Chinese meddling partly responsible for the conspiracies that led up to the country's great bloodletting of 1966–1967, and recurrent outbreaks of domestic tension between the country's majority population and its tiny, economically dominant Chinese minority are much more severe than in other Asian countries. Moreover, Indonesia's determinedly independent posture is now reinforced by the remarkable rise of a Vietnam whose ancient and successful record of fighting off any Chinese attempts at subordination is buttressed by both a powerful military and an economy taking off at the same rate as China's. In short, the United States has lost stature, and China has gained it, but that does not presage Chinese dominance.

Japan's position in Southeast Asia remains strongly influential, but Japan has lost its previous dominance. It remains the region's largest foreign investor by a large margin, while China has become the largest trade influence. Southeast Asians now see China rather than Japan as more inspiring in its dynamism and economic decisiveness and as more supportive of their desire for multilateral trade and investment liberalization. Southeast Asian financial elites are conscious that the Asian financial crisis was in part an epiphenomenon of Japan's domestic banking crisis, which forced the banks to drastically and suddenly cut their loans to Korea and Southeast Asia. The competition among China, Japan, the United States, and, to a lesser extent, India and Europe causes a few problems but on balance suits Southeast Asian leaders just fine as they maneuver to ensure their continued autonomy from all big powers.

ASEAN has to be counted as a Cold War institution that has successfully adapted to a new era. It has done so through drastic transformation. It responded to China's reversal of priorities and to the Soviet collapse by expanding to include three communist neighbors. By doing so, instead of persisting in old ideological and power rivalries, it co-opted Vietnam, now the region's most dynamic nation, into a peaceful and diplomatically cooperative relationship of great economic and strategic value. Hammered by the Asian crisis and by a downgrading in U.S. priorities, it acquired new backbone by entering into an association with China in which China simply accepted ASEAN's economic program rather than engaging in complex negotiations requiring compromises of ASEAN's organization or goals. Although it has abandoned old ideological antagonism and embraced old enemies, ASEAN has sacrificed none of its own organizational integrity, none of its economic agenda, and none of its members' security relationships with the United States.

CHAPTER SIX

The Aspiring Power and Its Near Abroad: India and South Asia

India

Indian civilization has been one of the most pervasive and important influences on human history. To the east, throughout the area we know as Confucian civilization, Indian-derived Buddhism has been an omnipresent influence; in Japan, at the point of Confucian civilization most distant from India, when a family member dies, Buddhist rites are the norm. To the west, and indeed throughout the world, Christianity exhibits a multifaceted Indian legacy. The early Christian church was structured on Indian models. Every Catholic who prays the rosary is following an Indian tradition.

Like China, India has the advantages and disadvantages of a huge, complex society. The principal disadvantage is that these societies are difficult to manage, and both countries have paid a heavy price in parts of the 20th century for those difficulties. The principal advantage is that they are both cosmopolitan societies, comfortable with different kinds of people, benefiting economically from diasporas that have spread to every populated part of the world. In both cases, the diasporas have until recently fared better than the population at home who were burdened by huge socialist bureaucracies; as a result, the diasporas have enormous ability to bring back wealth, technology, and market connections that are relatively lacking at home.

India's and China's diversities are both vast, but they differ in kind. China assimilates diverse groups into a common Confucian culture despite a diversity of dialects, physical types, and cultural origins;

although they conquered China, the Manchus and most of the Mongols became part of the melting pot. India accumulates diverse groups, which identify themselves as Indian but retain highly distinctive cultures to a far greater extent. These different diversities have shaped the late-20th–century political choices of their respective countries. China's relative homogeneity has enabled it to manage the society, for a time, as if it were a business corporation. India's distinctive cultures and castes have been more amenable to management through the interest-group accommodations of democracy.

In order to understand the challenges India faces, it is useful to do some systematic comparison with China. These two huge societies have quite different traditions of governance. In China, for many centuries, the ideal (starting a bit below the emperor) has been uniform meritocracy in a highly centralized polity. If a peasant boy speaking some distant dialect could pass the requisite exams, he could rise to high office. Of course, in practice, there were many deviations from this standard, and the actual social structure generally gave overwhelming advantages to some groups in preparing for the exam, but the standard set the tone of society and actually did achieve much of the meritocracy that it was designed for. The meritocracy enabled Chinese rulers to manage vast populations and territories, and when the meritocracy eroded, the dynasty typically came to an end. Likewise, the highly centralized order tended to deteriorate over time but, like meritocracy, remained the accepted organizing principle.

This tradition has carried over into the era of reform communism, which has tried with considerable success to manage China as a business. Each mayor, each party secretary, has business goals to achieve—so much economic growth, so much employment growth, so much local investment, so much foreign investment. Local goals are roughly aligned with national goals, and those officials who exceed their targets gain rapid promotion. Technocratic merit is supposed to be accompanied by political loyalty, as it was in the days of emperors, but the balance between "red" and "expert" has shifted overwhelmingly in favor of "expert" during the reform years. The main problem of running a country like a business is that of ensuring that everyone is included and that economic adjustments don't have too severe an impact on certain groups. China has had difficulty with this and is trying to adjust; the new slogan is "harmonious society."

India's tradition has been to accommodate every group by giving it an assigned place in the society and economy. Traditional Indian society divided the population into castes, which had assigned social roles and economic tasks. The advantage for the caste member was that he or she had an assured place. The disadvantage lay in being confined to that place. Modern India has sought to end the institution of castes—with great success in certain places like Bangalore and in the most modern companies, like Tata Consultancy, but limited success in much of the country. (Even in the major cities, the marriage ads in the newspapers are organized according to caste.) Today, whereas China seeks fairness by trying to ensure basic education and equal access to the college entrance exams, India seeks fairness by democratic patronage and by assigning large numbers of school places and government jobs to traditionally disadvantaged groups. By law, 22.5 percent of government jobs and school places in India are assigned to formerly disadvantaged groups. A law passed in 2006 would have increased that to 49.5 percent had not the courts disallowed it on the narrow ground that the numbers were based on obsolete statistics.

These differences in social practice, in concepts and strategies of fairness, and in structures of government pervasively influence every aspect of India and China, including economic growth and foreign policy.

India's governing elite believes deeply not only in the greatness of its civilization but also in the greatness of India's proper geopolitical role. Its leaders see India as a future great power and demand that the world acknowledge its current and future importance. Moreover, India exists in a feisty neighborhood and shares the feistiness of its neighbors. But however great its past civilization and future potential, for many centuries India has been subordinate to other powers. For the past half-century of independence, its poverty and economic stagnation have condemned India to a position of weakness and pretense. Nehru's eloquent assertion of national dignity was belied by the malnutrition and shortened life spans that his inward-looking, socialist, bureaucratized economic policies caused. His emphatic assertions of non-alignment were belied by the reality of economic and political alignment with the Soviet Union. Poverty defined both India's social reality and its international standing.

Now India is becoming the latest member of the Asian economic miracle—with some qualifications. For much of the post-independence period, India had been stuck with what became jocularly known as "the Hindu rate of growth," namely about 3 percent of GDP per year, a fraction of the 7 to 10 percent typical of the Asian-miracle economies. Then, starting in 1991, two things happened. First, India's leadership was shocked by an imminent foreign-exchange crisis. Second, it was shocked by the consistently superior economic growth of China. In reaction, the government removed much of the "license raj," the layers of regulation that hampered domestic economic activity, and began to open up the economy internationally, following lessons learned from China. The result has been Indian growth rates that are higher, more consistent, and more sustainable (see Figure 5). (While the 1980s saw substantial growth, that growth was based on unsustainable domestic-budget deficits and unsustainable current-account deficits.)

The reform program and the higher growth rates seem to be politically sustainable. Both the previous Bharatiya Janata Party (BJP)–led government and the current Congress Party–led government have endorsed the same broad directions of reform. Both the emergent technology sector (in Bangalore and elsewhere) and the center of gravity of traditional industry (the Confederation of Indian Industry, the major steel companies) have accepted liberalizing reforms as the way forward. Broad segments of the population, primarily in urban areas, have benefited. There is a noticeable change of tone from despair to optimism in the streets of the major cities (Delhi, Mumbai, Bangalore, Chennai).[1]

---

[1] One of the striking things about the Asian-miracle takeoffs is how the results can be seen on the visages of strangers walking down the streets. In India's major cities, the pre-1995 tone of life was fatalistic despair. In Shanghai, through the early 1980s, what one saw as people went trudging home at night was a deep, forlorn weariness. Now one sees confidence on the faces in Delhi and Mumbai and extraordinary energy on the faces in Shanghai. These changes occurred decades earlier in Seoul, Singapore, Taipei, and Bangkok. Throughout China, despite the vast inequalities and serious remaining areas of poverty, this change in tone is pervasive, because every region and sector has been lifted to some degree. In India,

Figure 5
Real GDP Growth in India

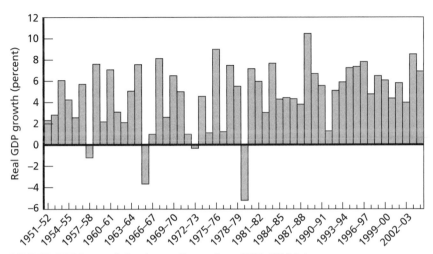

SOURCE: CEIC Domestic Product at Factor Cost, 1993–1994 Prices
(http://www.ceicdata.com).

While there remain residual concerns about broad swaths of the population, especially in northern India, that have been left out, India seems to have acquired a workable consensus on economic reform.[2]

That consensus should mean continued high growth rates relative to what India has achieved in the past. However, because India has not provided infrastructure and education to the degree that the principal East Asian miracle economies did, India will not likely sustain the 10 percent growth rates that typified the early decades of economic takeoff in Japan, South Korea, Taiwan, and China. India's exports, inward foreign direct investment, major roads, port capacity, and the like remain

---

where large areas remain untouched by reformist dynamism, one must be more careful about generalizing.

[2] This judgment will be tested by the partially successful efforts of the Communist Party, which is a member of the governing coalition, to stifle such reforms as privatization. If it slows reform too much and is not replaced, the judgment on effective reform consensus will have to be revised.

at levels that are a fraction of those in China (see Table 3). But 6 to 8 percent does seem sustainable.

Over the next decade, the disparities in education, infrastructure, and liberalization are not likely to be rectified, so China's lead is likely to increase. If the gap between the two countries decreases during that period, it will be because China stumbles in political or financial reform, not because India is able to catch up sustainably with China's current pace.[3]

The consequences of India's economic acceleration are substantial. For business, it enlarges the India market so substantially that soon no company will be able to label itself truly global without a substantial Indian operation. That puts India far ahead of Brazil and Russia and into the same "must be there" category as China, a huge change from India's previous position. For geopolitics, growth on this scale, combined with continued lackluster growth elsewhere in South Asia, will ensure India's overwhelming dominance on the subcontinent and will raise its global stature. These constitute major changes in the international landscape.

That being said, for the next decade, most of such impacts will be limited to the subcontinent. India will not have a large enough military to affect events in most of Central Asia, Southeast Asia, or East Asia. Its economic influence will continue to be vastly overshadowed by that of Japan and China, and this is not a subtle difference. While some division of labor will begin to emerge at the margin with China, India's

Table 3
China and India: Exports, GNP, Foreign Direct Investment, and Foreign Reserves in 2006 (in $ billions)

	GNP	Exports	FDI	FX Reserves
India	782	233	20	152
China	2,638	969	69	1,066

SOURCE: CEIC, using period average exchange rates, US$1 = Rp45.3025; US$1 = RMB7.9735.

---

[3] For a contrary view, see Yasheng Huang and Tarun Khanna, "Can India Overtake China?" *Foreign Policy*, July–August 2004. My reply appears as a letter in the following issue.

trade and investment patterns will not provide a predominant influence, except in the very limited sectors of business-process outsourcing and high-end related activities, outside South Asia. The geopolitical environment of Asia outside the subcontinent will largely be shaped by Japan, China, and the United States, not by more distant India.

Many demographers believe that in a decade this could begin to change. As it approaches the year 2020, Chinese society will be graying to an extent that could inhibit rapid growth. Because India has had no counterpart of China's one-child policy, Indian society will not be affected by a comparable degree of graying, so India will have a window of demographic opportunity to begin catching up with China and perhaps eventually surpassing it. From that perspective, the second half of the century could be India's. But India can take advantage of that window of opportunity only if it engages in transformative efforts to improve its education and infrastructure. With one-third of India's population illiterate, including half of its women, there are vast segments of Indian society that are completely unprepared to compete in a globalized world, and this could conceivably mean a future crisis in some regions. There are still vast areas of India where most people are skinny, malnourished, virtually uneducated, and possibly vulnerable to harm rather than benefit from a globalizing world. That being said, there are hopeful signs, at least concerning the infrastructure, but these are as yet too small to validate predictions of transformative change.[4]

Conversely, China's demographic squeeze notwithstanding, productivity improvements and faster urbanization could offset many of the negative consequences of its falling ratio of workers to nonworkers.[5] Having fully considered the implications of the demographic squeeze, China has nonetheless recently recommitted itself to the one-child policy. India is betting on having large numbers of workers.

---

[4] These statements about demography, infrastructure, and education are based on unpublished RAND documents by Julie Kim (infrastructure), Ying Liu and Krishna Kumar (education), and Julie DaVanzo and Cliff Grammlich (demography). My view of the economic implications of the demography, however, differs from that of DaVanzo and Grammlich.

[5] This argument is made by Helen Qiao, "Will China Grow Old Before Getting Rich?" Goldman Sachs, Global Economics Paper 138, February 14, 2006, online at https://portal.gs.com.

China is betting that it will be more important to have more highly educated workers with proportionately better infrastructure and less strain on the environment.

We can predict that, on balance, India's regional geopolitical role and its role in global business will be much larger than it has been, but to go beyond that and predict that India will have a role comparable to or larger than China's would strain the evidence.

Some analysts have put a great deal of geopolitical weight on India's being a stable democracy, whereas they believe China's authoritarianism to be inherently unstable, thus ensuring India a brighter future than that of China. Certainly, China will have to change, but Taiwan and other East Asian examples show that a smooth transition from a Leninist system to a more open polity is not just possible but has happened consistently in the previous Asian-miracle economies. Taiwan, a model for China, is a particularly persuasive case of transformation from a Leninist system to a democratic system; through the early 1980s, it was much more Leninist and much more repressive than China is today. (To take one example, Taiwan was still assassinating dissidents in the 1980s, including Henry Liu, who was assassinated outside his home in Daly City, California, in 1984.) Conversely, India's apparent reformist consensus is quite auspicious, but those who believe that democracy assures rapid economic growth need to reflect on the experience of the Philippines and other pre-modern democracies.

Indian democracy has held India together, a remarkable achievement, and has inhibited the radicalization of India's Muslims, another remarkable achievement, and it now appears to be consistent with an extended period of rapid growth. India's legal system contributes to the prospects for sustained growth. Beyond that, political structure is a poor guide to economic prospects. India's electoral politics has encouraged consumption at the expense of investment and has encouraged patronage to outweigh efficiency—to the great detriment of, for instance, the country's primary schools and its welfare programs, whose efficiency is shockingly poor. Indian federalism has permitted experimentation, although not as effectively as China's provincial structure, but has inhibited coherent national infrastructure and educational development. The balance of effects on economic development is unpredictable. Democracy does not ensure superior economic performance compared with that of the Asian-miracle economies, all of which were authoritarian until they reached relatively high levels of economic development (see Figure 6). I shall comment in more detail on this later; for now, it is worth noting that even those studies that tout the superior performance of democracies list the Asian-miracle economies as exceptions to the rule.

The effects of Indian democracy on economic performance are sometimes perverse compared with what Western theories typically presume. In a society where poverty deprives much of the population of the ability to understand politics or to organize for political influence, democratic elections frequently provide elites with unfair advantages. Society becomes extremely unequal, unfair, and sometimes inefficient. This occurs dramatically in education, where until recently almost twice as many Indians (3.5 percent) as Chinese (2 percent) received tertiary education, but almost all Chinese became literate, while half of all Indian women and many Indian men remained illiterate. In India,

Figure 6
Comparative Economic Growth in South Asia and China

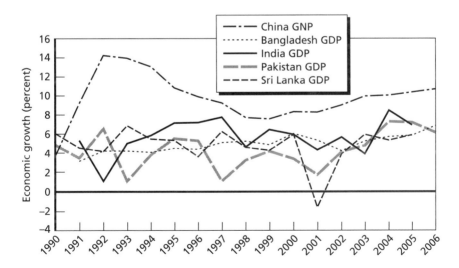

the elite gets elected to parliament and subsidizes its children's higher education.

In this society, the teachers union is an elite, and most of the population lacks the resources to organize a counterweight. Studies have revealed that, as a result, in many areas the teachers show up for class only a few days a week and the parents have no recourse. Ironically, the workings of Indian democracy remove accountability from such elite groups. This and patronage politics account for the otherwise inexplicable result that India spends proportionately about twice as much on primary and secondary education as China does but gets radically inferior results.[6]

Related political problems affect India's infrastructure development. India builds far more roads than China, 2.5 million kilometers versus 1.8 million,[7] but only 57 percent of India's roads are paved, compared with 91 percent of China's. China builds more first-class expressways each year than India has built in all the years since independence. And whereas China's roads are built according to a coherent national plan, with local officials held strictly accountable, India's are a hodgepodge of local roadways that do not form an efficient national network. Moreover, China's expressways are built according to the highest international standards (in many cases superior to those in the United States), whereas even India's main intercity roads are generally of extremely low quality. Decentralized politics and funding based on political patronage account for the differences. The Philippines and Mexico display the Indian pattern of low-quality roads built according to electoral patronage, while South Korea, Taiwan, and Singapore display the careful planning and high-quality implementation that China is emulating.

Similarly, India lags in providing health care. Both China and India take good care of their elites—the best hospitals in Mumbai and Shanghai can compete with most of the best in the developed world.

---

[6] These comments on education derive from a forthcoming RAND paper by Ying Liu and Krishna Kumar. The links to the politics are my inferences based on similar experience in the Philippines and other third-world democracies.

[7] These data are from unpublished work by RAND colleague Julie Kim.

In fact, India is becoming a center of "health tourism" to which citizens from rich Western countries travel for high-quality but extremely low-cost treatment for serious diseases such as heart ailments. Both countries have inferior health care for the poor, but the life expectancy of the average Indian woman is only 63 years, while that of the average Chinese woman is 74. (The corresponding figures for men are 61 for Indians and 70 for Chinese.) These startling mortality figures reflect an absence of such things as basic sanitation in India and the fact that India's poor are even poorer than their counterparts in sub-Saharan Africa.

There are strong movements in India to improve performance in all these areas, and the pressures for improvement are having important positive consequences. But the more decentralized, elitist, and patronage-ridden structure of Indian politics makes it difficult to catch up with the performance of the East Asian–miracle economies, including China.

Nevertheless, India's current economic achievement is remarkable, and as a result, India is on the way to overwhelming preeminence on the subcontinent, not by force of arms or by size, but because of its political stability and gradually accumulating economic advantage. Its economic growth is not startlingly better than that of Pakistan or Bangladesh, but its political stability and attractiveness to investment are so superior that it is fair to project steady relative gains.

India is also overtly determined to be preeminent. Its relations with neighbors have been rough. It invaded and absorbed Goa, absorbed Sikkim, fought two wars with Pakistan, recently came to the brink of nuclear confrontation with Pakistan, intervened to ensure Bangladesh's division from Pakistan, incited a civil war in Sri Lanka and then sent an expeditionary force to quell it, has continual low-level exchanges of fire across its border with Bangladesh, and in general has remained on difficult terms with most of its neighbors. India's navy, which includes several small carriers and plans for more, as well as plans for nuclear ICBM-carrying submarines, asserts itself far from India's shores, even to the shores of Africa and into the South China Sea, while China has no comparable force and no comparable plans. And India asserts its determination to be able to project its naval power in the Malacca Strait and beyond, where it has no obvious trade or security interests but would be positioned to interdict China's trade. Unlike China, which has no foreign military bases, India has built an air base in Tajikistan and has plans for military logistics and other cooperative military relationships with Iran, Tajikistan, Kazakhstan, Uzbekistan, Malaysia, Indonesia, Singapore, Thailand, Laos, Vietnam, South Africa, Oman, the United Arab Emirates (UAE), and Myanmar.[8] It demanded U.S. acknowledgment that it has military interests in an "extended strategic neighborhood" from the Suez Canal to the Strait of Malacca and encompassing Central Asia.[9] India takes a very assertive posture toward China, including at sea, while China pays so little attention to India that the subject doesn't arise in most foreign-policy or security discussions.[10]

South Asia at the turn of the century was more like Southeast Asia a half-century ago, with all countries making claims upon their neighbors. India itself until recently behaved more like an impoverished version of its Soviet mentor, lavishing resources on military-related sectors and dominating its neighbors, than like one of the economics-obsessed East Asian countries. Only in the past few years has India shown signs of substituting economic priorities for geopolitical ones in the way that happened among the smaller East Asian countries and then in China. The past few years have seen India press for better relations with Pakistan and China and shift noticeably toward economic priorities. The trends are auspicious but still preliminary. Unlike China, India has not

---

[8] See Stephen J. Blank, *Natural Allies? Regional Security in Asia and Prospects for Indo-American Strategic Cooperation*, Carlisle, PA: Army War College Strategic Studies Institute, 2005. The list of countries is drawn from p. 22.

[9] Ibid., p. 17.

[10] Some writers assert otherwise. For instance, Robert Blackwill, former U.S. Ambassador to India, attributes the Chinese building of airfields in Tibet to hostile intentions toward India (see "The India Imperative," *The National Interest*, No. 80, Summer 2005, pp. 9–18). However, Chinese airfields in Tibet are fully explained by security needs in Tibet itself, and top Indian policymakers I have interviewed do not share Blackwill's view of China's intentions. Indian military deployments belie the notion that they feel terribly threatened by China. Chinese foreign policy conferences rarely even have India on the agenda. The two countries collaborate, often against U.S. interests, on virtually every aspect of energy security.

actually compromised on its key border disputes, most notably with Pakistan over Kashmir. Unlike China, which firmly denies any ambition or prospects to become a great power, India openly demands to be called a great power (see Table 4).

The most auspicious development of this kind has come in India's relations with China, which have long been disputatious. In 1962, the two fought a brief border war. Historically, China has supported India's enemy, Pakistan, with arms and diplomatic backing. India was long a protégé of the Soviet Union, which was China's greatest enemy. China and India had little mutual trade or investment. Today these conditions have changed. The border is quiescent—far more quiescent than the borders with Bangladesh and Pakistan—and under sympathetic negotiation, although not resolved. Pakistan, an unstable state, the world's greatest harbor of jihadists and the world's greatest source of WMD proliferation, has become a pain in the neck for both, with rivalries greatly downgraded. Sino-Indian trade and investment are rising rapidly, and India's early trade surplus with China gave Indians the confidence that they can open up and compete with anyone.

India has conducted a great rapprochement with the United States, but it has also made many gestures of friendship to China, has

Table 4
Are Democracies More Peaceful?

China	India
• Denies having great-power ambitions	• Insists on entitlement to great-power status
• Has compromised 12 of 14 land border issues	• Border disputes with most neighbors
• No foreign bases as a matter of principle	• Seeks foreign bases; has one in Tajikistan
• Naval ambitions focused on Taiwan, close seabed issues	• Naval ambitions from the Persian Gulf to the South China Sea to Africa
• Rarely intervenes in neighbors, supports stability	• Intervenes frequently in neighboring countries
• Friendly relations with most neighbors	• Difficult relations with most neighbors
• Serious seabed issues	• Serious watershed, sea-boundary issues

signed a friendship treaty with China, and has become an observer in the Shanghai Cooperation Organization (SCO), the regional security organization sponsored by China with the support of Russia and various Central Asian states. Responding to India's new stature, disconnected from the old Soviet Union, and Pakistan's dubious and conflicted role regarding nuclear proliferation and the war in Afghanistan, the United States is now leaning heavily toward India while doing the minimum to keep Pakistan on board regarding the logistics of the Afghan war. Japan has abandoned its posture of equidistance toward the two countries and is leaning toward India. China, like the United States, is tilting toward India while hanging onto a positive relationship with Pakistan. Although various fears and rivalries remain, it is difficult to imagine a scenario today in which India and China would go to war. In this area as in others, India has started later than China, but the shift to economic priorities may be under way.[11]

Like other countries, India could experience surprises. Its poorer areas could revolt against the adjustments required by globalization. Its bureaucracies, particularly the country's teachers, might prove capable of resisting the demands for modernization and effectiveness and could thereby slow down India's economic progress. War with Pakistan, either conventional or nuclear, could drain India financially. Anti-Muslim moves by the BJP or RSS could spark religious polarization and internecine conflict on a scale that would inhibit growth. On a more optimistic note, some breakthrough could give reformist leaders control of parliament and sweep away the obstacles to rapid implementation of the leaders' programs for privatization, liberalization, and opening of the economy; then economic growth could accelerate beyond current levels.

Any of these surprises could happen, but our baseline scenario is that Indian politics will continue in a business-as-usual-fashion, gradual reform will continue to produce 6 to 8 percent real GDP growth, and

---

[11] I am indebted to an unpublished presentation by my colleague Rollie Lal, "South Asia and Strategic Shifts in Asia," May 24, 2004, and to an as-yet-unpublished paper of hers, "India and South Asia," July 2005, for insights about how unlikely Sino-Indian war is and about how Indian leaders' priorities are beginning to shift. However, she should not be held responsible for the particular elaboration of those arguments that I have used here.

the country will avoid serious warfare. In that scenario, India becomes much more important than it has been, particularly for business, but it does not become a primary determinant of Asia's geopolitical future for the next 15 years unless China falters.

India's future will be determined primarily by two things:

- The leadership's ability to overcome interest-group resistance to reforms.
- The leadership's willingness to continue reorienting the country's priorities away from geopolitical conflict in order to focus on economic development, as the East Asian miracle economies have done. It has begun this process, particularly through its rapprochement with China and its improvement of relations with Pakistan. But the test will be whether it moves toward compromise over Kashmir and settles its other conflicts with neighboring countries, as China has done. Meanwhile, the United States has been pressuring India in the other direction, to take a more expansive and forceful view of its international role.

Pakistan

Pakistan has in the past been India's great rival. In the future, it may be a source of trouble for India, particularly over Kashmir, but it has not been making the transition to a priority for economic development as quickly as India, and as a result its future role will likely be as a sore spot rather than a rival. Unlike China and the other East Asian states, Pakistan has for most of recent history chosen to give military expenditures priority over economic development and to give territorial (Kashmir) and geopolitical (Afghanistan) ambitions priority over education and infrastructure. It has not attempted to institutionalize its domestic governance; rather, the military has moved to dismantle the major parties and other institutions that provided the country with some political skeleton. Instead of trying to compromise its international conflicts and moderate its international risks, Pakistan has chosen intransigence over Kashmir and a high-risk strategy of relying on militant groups and nuclear weapons for security. Instead of trying to stabilize its international environment, it continues to try to destabilize the Karzai government in Afghanistan. It has aligned itself with Sunni militant groups in a way that alienates Iran, Russia, and other Central Asian countries. Pakistan's traditional big-country supporters, the United States and China, while not abandoning it, have both announced friendships with its great enemy, India, and both have become concerned about Pakistan's roles in spreading nuclear proliferation and Islamist radicalism. If the time comes when the United States no longer needs Pakistan's support for operations in Afghanistan, U.S. perceptions of Pakistan could alter from "vitally needed ally" to "intersection of the axes of evil." Seldom has such a large country found itself in such a precarious strategic position.[12]

Pakistan's trajectory is unpredictable; that is the nature of uninstitutionalized polities. What is much more predictable is Pakistan's relative stature compared with India, unless (see below) there is a drastic change in Pakistan's priorities. The Indian government is rapidly moderating politics, institutionalizing the functions of government, devoting higher priority to economic development, eschewing provocative international positions, and successfully wooing Pakistan's former big allies, the United States and China, while Pakistan at best moves more slowly. With Bangladesh stagnating in poverty, corruption, and divisive politics, and Sri Lanka and Nepal riven by civil war, the easily predictable outcome is a subcontinent dominated by India.

There are some preliminary signs that Pakistan's government is beginning to shift its priorities. The current economic team is quite capable; there are plans to expand investments in education, health, rural credit, and microfinance; and the budgets for those functions are rising, while (still disproportionately large) military budgets are declining somewhat. If priorities were to continue to shift, and if development plans turn out to be well-implemented, the scenario for Pakistan would be far brighter.

---

[12] My knowledge of Pakistan is heavily derived from a series of essays by Christine Fair, including an unpublished essay, "War and Escalation in South Asia: Pakistan," dated July 2005. Fair, however, should not be held responsible for my stark descriptions. My description of new reformist economic priorities comes from official sources and conversations with development consultants.

Pakistan could reform successfully—a challenging scenario that would involve changes as great as those that have occurred in China. Or it could enunciate brilliant reform plans but fail to implement them. In the worst case, President Pervez Musharraf could be assassinated, Islamic fundamentalists could seize control of the government, and Pakistan could spin into tribalized, terror-prone chaos.

The South Asian Subcontinent

While India is moving in the right directions and increasingly dominating its region, the subcontinent remains dangerous and volatile. South Asia remains where East and Southeast Asia were three to four decades ago. Even inside India, domestic violence remains at a high level, with 58 insurgencies and flare-ups of ethnic, religious, and union violence reminiscent of the situation in Thailand around 1970. Nepal has a major guerrilla insurgency, like Malaya or the Philippines in the 1950s or Thailand in 1960. Sri Lanka has an ongoing civil war. Pakistan and Bangladesh remain highly tribalized, like Burma today or Indonesia in 1960, with governing institutions that depend more on personalities than vice versa. By looking at how Southeast Asia and China evolved, one can see what would happen if India's current emulation of East Asian development priorities and practices were to continue and to spread to its neighbors. By looking at how the Philippines trapped itself in a previous age and failed to move forward with its neighbors, one can see what will happen if South Asia fails to make the transition: tribalization, zero-sum politics, persistent desperate poverty, ideological and religious strife, pockets of radicalized insurgency.

CHAPTER SEVEN

Russia and Its Near Abroad

Russia: Canada with Testosterone

> We've been so desperate to hold together the tatters of our own
> "near abroad" that we failed to notice that we have now become
> part of China's "near abroad."
>
> —*Andrei Piontkovsky,* Moscow Times, *August 15, 2005*

> Putin goes to a restaurant with the leaders of the two houses of
> parliament. The waiter approaches and asks Putin what he would
> like to order.
> "I'll have the meat."
> "What about the vegetables?"
> "They'll have the meat too."
>
> —*Russian joke*[1]

The Soviet Union was weakened by many developments, including
important political ones, but it ultimately collapsed because it ran out
of money. The costs of giving the military first call on every sector of the
economy, of controlling one empire in Eastern Europe and another in
Central Asia, of maintaining incompetent allies from Cuba to Angola,
of fighting proxy wars in Vietnam and Ethiopia and a direct war in
Afghanistan, and of pouring more and more money into more and

---

[1] Lynn Berry, "Did You Hear the One About Putin and the Jellied Meat?" *Los Angeles Times*,
July 16, 2006, p. M6.

more inefficient state enterprises at home amounted to one of history's most dramatic cases of imperial overstretch.[2]

The political costs of running out of money and having to retract proved far greater for the Soviet Union than they would have been for an ordinary country, because the Russian empire and the Soviet Union defined themselves, drew their identity from, the majesty of an ever-expanding empire. Without this identity, Russia didn't know what it stood for, who its people were, or what its boundaries should be.[3]

The contrast with China could not have been more dramatic. Reformist China carefully contracted its foreign-policy ambitions and military priorities in order to focus on increasing the prosperity of its people. Visitors to the Soviet Union and China in the late 1970s and early 1980s already noticed that, although Soviet per capita GNP was far higher than China's, Chinese markets were filled with fruits and vegetables and consumer goods, while Soviet citizens rushed out and formed long lines whenever such things were rumored to be available.[4]

Soviet leaders made a series of fatal errors. First, Gorbachev's predecessors, faced with decades of evidence of accumulating economic

---

[2] It is particularly important to stress the economic aspect because so many popular accounts in the West emphasize the political drama to the complete exclusion of the economic. For instance, see David Remnick's prize-winning and otherwise admirable history of Soviet collapse, which manages to completely ignore economic issues (David Remnick, *Lenin's Tomb: The Last Days of the Soviet Empire*, New York: Random House, 1993). This is roughly comparable to writing a history of the end of World War II without mentioning the superior U.S. industrial capacity.

[3] On this point, see Dmitri Trenin, *The End of Eurasia: Russia on the Border Between Geopolitics and Globalization*, Washington, DC: Carnegie Endowment for International Peace, 2002, especially chap. 1 of pt. 1, "The Spatial Dimension of Russian History." This brilliant book has pervasively influenced my view of Russia beyond what individual footnotes can convey.

[4] My parents led some of the early student exchanges with both the Soviet Union and China, and their astonishment at the higher standards of living in urban China became a standard part of their slide shows. This fundamental difference—that the Soviet Union poured its treasure into foreign adventures, while China's priority was taking care of its people (albeit sometimes with disastrous Maoist schemes)—never penetrated Western consciousness. Even today, much of the writing about China, particularly by Western geopolitical strategists, ignores this overwhelmingly important point.

problems and even declining life expectancies, just muddled along without making the kinds of drastic system changes that Chinese leaders made after they realized the scale of their predecessors' errors. Brezhnev slept while his empire crumbled. Soviet Communism included profound ideological commitment. Chinese history over the last two centuries is a series of experiments to find something that works—and rejection of anything that does not. Then Gorbachev and his successors, facing imminent economic collapse, made two colossal errors. First, they focused on politics rather than economics as their first priority. For years prior to the collapse, I gave briefings contrasting Deng Xiaoping's priorities with Gorbachev's priorities (see Table 5).

Of course, there were important differences between urbanized, industrialized Soviet society and rural, agriculturally driven Chinese society, but Gorbachev's politically driven priorities had no hope of solving the fatal problem of Soviet financial stringency or of creating the jobs that might have stabilized Soviet society.

Gorbachev's fatal failure of priorities was fully supported by establishment opinion in the West, as was the second fatal decision that set the structure of Russian society for a long time to come, namely, the decision to base economic reform on a version of shock therapy. What became known as the Washington consensus supported the attempt to change from a socialist economy to a capitalist one overnight. The implicit assumption behind this strategy was that if you destroyed socialist institutions, working markets would somehow magically appear. But burning down a wooden house does not make a brick house magically appear. One has to build it, and that takes a great deal

Table 5
Deng's Priorities vs. Gorbachev's Priorities

Deng's Priorities	Gorbachev's Priorities
1. Agriculture	1. International politics
2. Light industry	2. Domestic politics
3. Heavy industry	3. Heavy industry
4. Domestic politics	4. Light industry
5. International politics	5. Agriculture

of time. Market economies are exceedingly complex mechanisms that require laws, institutions, lawyers, analysts, national information networks, and much else. Creating them takes many years.

These errors had many consequences, but four are particularly noteworthy. First, the unnecessarily magnified collapse of living standards and sense of disorder caused by the shock-therapy approach left large segments of the population dubious about the competence of the new system and nostalgic for the order and seeming competence of the old system to ensure that there would be food on the table. The latter two factors seriously damaged the confidence of much of the public in both democracy and market economics.

Second, the socialist governing elite has a monopoly of the information, skills, and regulatory levers that lead to success in a deregulating economy. In China, even with its gradual pace of reform, emphasis on local initiative, and priority for jobs and popular welfare, this problem has created tens or hundreds of thousands of local millionaires based on privileged access to training, information, and regulatory power. The resulting issues, defined as corruption and inequality, became a major divisive force in Chinese politics. But in Russia, the problems became orders of magnitude worse because of the decision, under Western advice, to transform ownership overnight. The sudden distribution of shares of state enterprises to a population desperate for immediate income and almost completely lacking the information and skills to value the shares ensured that the economy would end up controlled by a handful of billionaires.

Third, the effect on politics is similar. In the Asian-miracle economies, democratic politics develops from the grassroots upward and over a substantial period of time. The result—for instance, in Taiwan, South Korea, Thailand, and even Indonesia—is parties with deep connections to a vigorous civil society. In Russia, democratic politics paralleled the market economics. Small elites had all the resources, and the system became a caricature of vulnerability to narrow interest groups and corrupt manipulation.

Fourth, the combination of social disorder, lack of market rules and institutions, and narrowly based politics ensured the rise of a gangster economy. Just below the billionaires is a vast network of gangs, political-business conspiracies, and assassination plots.[5]

These problems, along with the sudden and unexpected loss of the empire that had defined and legitimized Russia for five centuries, led to "the semi-disintegration of Russia, where weak regions co-exist uneasily with a weak center."[6] This induced a profound popular longing for powerful authority to stop the disintegration, stop the disorder, stop the crime, and control the billionaires. These concerns were exacerbated by the extension of NATO to the edge of Russia, Western encouragement of the color revolutions (the current jargon for democratic upheavals that Russia and China perceive as mainly sponsored by the United States) in Ukraine and elsewhere, and the insertion of apparently permanent U.S. bases into Central Asia. These circumstances rendered virtually inevitable the emergence of a somewhat authoritarian figure like Putin, with a mandate to consolidate central political authority, manipulate the law in the absence of established institutions to control the billionaires and crime gangs, and vigorously defend Russia's (ill-defined) interests abroad. Europe and the United States, having exaggerated Russia's earlier conversion to democracy and welcomed it into the G-8, have since vigorously criticized Putin's infringement of democratic principles and market principles but have been slow to acknowledge even to themselves the way their own advice and actions contributed to the conditions that nurtured the Putin regime. Russia is not the first country to have this experience: The West frequently gives bad advice and then holds the advisee rigorously accountable for the consequences.

Putin's semi-authoritarianism is probably the most innocuous of the possible outcomes. Given Russia's identity crisis, the innumerable conflicts among and within its 89 distinct regions, and the combination of tribal and big-power conflicts that swirl throughout the

---

[5] See Paul Klebnikov, *Grandfather of the Kremlin: The Decline of Russia in the Age of Gangster Capitalism*, New York: Harcourt, 2000, for a detailed account of the influence of gangsterism. As if to prove his point, Klebnikov himself was subsequently assassinated.

[6] Trenin, op. cit., p. 239.

Commonwealth of Independent States (CIS), the absence so far of cataclysmic conflict bespeaks considerable moderation and sensitivity. The principal alternatives are worse. A disjointed democracy manipulated by gangsters and billionaires hiding behind demagogues could be much worse. The military regime that would shortly follow such a manipulated democracy definitely would be much worse. The keys for the future are whether the regime moves toward fairer distribution of economic resources or toward consolidation of such resources under one permanent political faction; whether it moves toward increasing or decreasing economic competition; whether it moves toward increasingly law-based means of regulating the economy or toward more manipulation of laws to consolidate political control of it; whether it moves toward competitive political parties with deep roots in the population or toward politics manipulated by narrow economic interests; and whether the leadership focuses on economic revitalization of European Russia or diffuses its resources in efforts to manage or dominate the politics of former components of the old Soviet Union.

The ease with which control over a natural-resource–based economy can be concentrated in a few hands and then used to dominate national politics will provide a serious temptation. Equally tempting will be the ease with which Western interventions in neighboring countries and Islamic terrorism could be blamed for problems in the "near abroad" and manipulated to concentrate political power in a few hands. At this point, notwithstanding Vladimir Putin's semiauthoritarianism and selective prosecution of billionaires, Russia could go either way.

Future historians will probably see U.S. and EU encouragement of the color revolutions as positive for the countries in question but costly in terms of Russia's relationship with the West, and above all, in terms of whether Russians see themselves as dealing with problems of their own making or problems incited from abroad. There is a risk that such historians will have to write that the thrust to establish permanent U.S. bases (as opposed to temporary ones for the war in Afghanistan) in Central Asia was gratuitous for Western security but drove China and Russia together and gave demagogic Russian politicians an opportunity to justify more interventionist policies in the former Soviet region than would otherwise have occurred.

For the time being, Russia is becoming China's and the EU's Canada—a heavily armed Canada on testosterone that has lost its way. During the Cold War era, Canada served as a buffer between the United States and the Soviet Union and as a quarry for the U.S. and Japanese economies. Its small population and small economy made its role diminutive in all other areas. Russia's economy is now about the same order of magnitude as Canada's. It is a vast buffer between China and the EU and a quarry for China and the EU. Although Russians have good education and high-technology capabilities, Russia is fundamentally a third-world producer of raw materials, with little other impact on the world economy. In purchasing-power terms, it is comparable in size to Brazil, Canada, or Mexico (see Figure 7). Without PPP adjustments, Russia's economy appears even smaller than this. To be sure, continued high energy and raw-materials prices will boost the Russian economy, as they will Canada's, but over time, the key

Figure 7
Russia's GDP Relative to Other Nations in 2004 (in PPP)

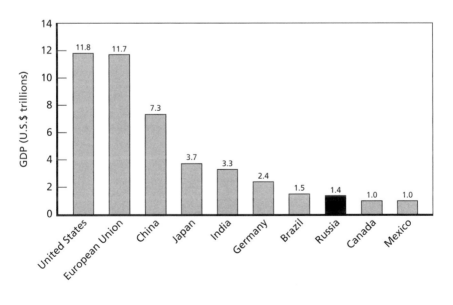

to economic success will be the economy's ability to adopt and innovate modern technologies. A recent RAND study, not yet published, by Richard Silberglitt and Philip Anton, predicts that in the future, Russia will have more difficulty absorbing new technologies than China or India will. To those accustomed to Cold War fears of Russian military technology, it was once almost unimaginable that serious analysts could even contemplate Russia being less capable of absorbing technology than India.

To be sure, Russia has a larger population than Canada, but it is small relative to China and the EU, and it is destined for historically rapid demographic decline. It is graying rapidly. As Nicholas Eberstadt has made clear, "Russia and Poland, for their part, will likely have populations more aged in 2025 than Japan's today: that is to say, they will be 'grayer' than any population within the human experience has yet been."[7] His calculations show that death rates for Russian men have risen by 40 percent since the mid-1960s. He quotes U.S. Census Bureau projections that Russian life expectancy will be less than that in India, Pakistan, or Bangladesh through 2025. Murray Feshbach, one of the most respected U.S. demographers, forecasts that Russia's population will decline from 145 million in 2003 to 101 million in 2050.[8] Like Canada, Russia must constantly fear an exodus of its most talented people to more economically and culturally dynamic neighbors. Its lack of distinctive contemporary cultural attractions, notwithstanding a past history of great art, music, and literature, as well as a major variant of Christian religion, further limits its prospective international role.

Compared with Canada, Russia's noteworthy strength is its nuclear weapons, combined with the strength of its military in comparison with those of its small neighbors. But the nuclear weapons have little practical utility in a world of big powers that lack designs on Russian territory, and its relatively large military has difficulty both in keeping up with other big powers and in dealing with the insurgencies

---

[7] Nicholas Eberstadt, "The Graying of the 'Emerging Markets': Population Aging in Today's Low-Income Countries," Washington, DC: American Enterprise Institute, unpublished.

[8] Murray Feshbach, "A Country on the Verge," *The New York Times*, May 31, 2003.

and terror attacks typical of warfare in Russia's neighborhood and hinterlands. Russian forces can deter attacks on Russia and can be decisive in local conventional conflicts. They can shift balances in Central Asia. They can arm neighbors. But they cannot be decisive in the principal issues of modern Asia: North Korea, Taiwan, the war on terror, keeping the sea lanes open (or closing them). The Russian military is at risk of chronic, debilitating, humiliating preoccupation with local conflicts such as the interminable bloodletting in Chechnya.

Russia's weaknesses, compared with Canada's, are equally noteworthy. So far, it lacks domestic consensus on either economic or political structure, it lacks a confident relationship with its neighbors, and it lacks a confident cultural identity. Russia eternally needs to become part of Europe but fears submerging its identity in European culture. It needs to focus its attention on building up its own economy and polity but cannot resist detailed engagement in the affairs of the vast territories and populations and intrigues of the old Soviet empire. It needs to accommodate China's power and benefit from China's economy but is terrified of China's population and economic dynamism. Putin's reassertion of government control over Russia's biggest companies, at the expense of Russia's private sector and foreign companies, helps him consolidate power at home but will ultimately weaken Russian power by depriving the economy of needed investment, technology, and entrepreneurship. Within these ambivalences, it has neither made choices nor agreed on sustainable balances.

Abutted by an EU with a relatively stagnant economy and a relatively incoherent foreign policy and a China with clear direction, Russia is most susceptible to Chinese influence. Russia's greatest opportunities reach across Central Asia, and its greatest vulnerabilities lie there as well. With virtually negligible Russian population in the vast area north of China, Russia needs to accommodate with China and to reinsure by having important friends abroad.

In the vise between China and the EU, Russia becomes geographically the natural ally of Japan or the United States. But it has an important territorial dispute with Japan, and it fears both the U.S./EU crusade for democracy and the intrusion of U.S. military power into its "near abroad." These conditions could change. Japan could decide to settle with Russia, as China did. More likely, the U.S./EU alliance could fragment. Russia could become more confident in its own politics, or it could disengage from concern about the political structures of neighbors such as Ukraine or Kazakhstan. It could become decisively more worried about China than about the U.S. ideological challenge, or it could accept the role of China's Canada. Any of these shifts would tilt the political alignment of a substantial fraction of the earth's geography.

In short, Russia has many choices, and it has made none of them. The Soviet Union lost the Cold War, and Russia repudiated its Stalinist heritage, but Russia remains trapped within a modified Cold War framework. Geopolitically, the worst possible outcome is the one contemporary Russian leaders have slipped into, namely, to be a marginal power with real enemies at home and no real allies abroad. Although it abandoned Cold War aggressiveness and Leninist ideology and settled its border dispute with China, Russia, like former quasi-ally India, has not yet decisively shifted its priorities away from international engagements in order to focus on domestic economic development. If it decisively cuts its losses in the "near abroad," its economic growth, life expectancy, and international influence will eventually be much greater. But that remains in doubt.

Even with its politics stabilizing somewhat and its economy improving somewhat, as is occurring now, Russia is in play. Although it has little power to direct events, its many available choices and its ability to shift local balances in a volatile Central Asia assure it a place at the table. As and if the post–Cold War architecture begins to melt, Russia's posture has more room to shift than that of any other substantial player except Korea.

Russia and China

The Russian-Chinese relationship has always been crucial to Asian politics, and it will be more complex and important than ever, now that Central Asia has fallen out of the former Soviet Union. The ancient power vacuum has recurred, and the Great Game has resumed.

As the new century begins, these two powers, traditionally conflictual, have found much in common. In 2005, they finally compromised their age-old border dispute. Trade has been rising fast, fed by Chinese desire for weapons and raw materials and by Russian need for manufactured goods. They share fears of Islamist extremism, of the regional drug trade and human trafficking, and of organized crime. They both seek stability, China because it wants to focus its resources on domestic economic development, Russia because any instability in the region can feed back into instability at home. For this reason, both fear color revolutions.

In the background of all these shared interests are intense Russian fears that China will in some sense come to occupy much of the vast, nearly empty space that lies between European Russia and the Chinese frontier. The vastness of Siberia contains a population smaller than that of tiny Hong Kong—and declining rapidly. Mongolia, with a territory larger than Western Europe, has a population comparable to that of Hong Kong. Adjacent are not only China's vast population, but also its clear economic superiority. There are no signs of Chinese territorial acquisitiveness; indeed, it has just abandoned its ancient claims. But Russian fears run quite deep.

The balance between the shared interests and the fears is held by the United States. Russia fears an expanded NATO, China a potential U.S. containment policy; both have concerns about the U.S.-India ten-year "strategic framework on defense."[9] Both have border problems with Japan. Both have intense concerns about their own territorial integrity and therefore take very strong stands regarding sovereignty and non-interference in internal affairs. For that reason, China supported Russia's position on Serbia, and Russia strongly supports China's position on Taiwan. Along with most other regional countries, they share a strong antagonism toward the idea of permanent U.S. military bases in Central Asia; in foreign-policy costs, the U.S. bases in Central Asia are by far the most expensive in the world. In sum, what has shifted

---

[9] "New Framework for the U.S.-India Defense Relationship, signed on June 28, 2005 in Washington DC by Minister of Defense of India, Pranab Mukherjee & Secretary of Defense of the United States, Donald Rumsfeld" (http://newdelhi.usembassy.gov/ipr062805.html).

the balance between fear and shared interests in favor of the shared interests is mutual concern about U.S. bases, U.S. ideological antagonism, and U.S. activism in Iraq and elsewhere. If these were to change, change in the postures of Russia and China—and in the relationship between them—could come quickly, so the United States has a great deal of leverage. To date, it has squandered that leverage through policies, such as moving NATO right up to the Russian border and seeking to build permanent military bases in Central Asia, that ensure a strong Sino-Russian sense of common interest.

Between the two, while confronting both, the United States has treated Russia far better than it has treated China. Washington welcomed Moscow into the G-8 club of advanced democracies, and President Bush developed a personal friendship with President Putin. The reason for the better treatment is that Russia elects its president, whereas China does not. China takes better care of its people, establishes friendly relations with most of its neighbors, keeps its military at home, accommodates democracy in Taiwan, and systematically compromises its border issues, while Russia, rather authoritarian despite its elections, actively sponsors military conflicts in the former empire, stations its military in parts of the former empire and uses it to suppress local autonomy, and actively tries to repress democratic movements in key parts of its "near abroad." The United States has far more areas of both economic and geopolitical cooperation with China than it has with Russia.

These distinctions highlight the tradeoffs between an ideological U.S. policy that regards election of the top leader as the most important criterion for relatively friendly relations and a potential alternative policy that might emphasize peaceful behavior and rapid progress in the well-being of the country's people. It has become common for U.S. political speeches and concrete policies to laud democracy, defined rather narrowly as election of the top leader, without mention of these potential tradeoffs, which are quite severe in both Russia and India. Conceptually, the tradeoffs are brushed aside, using statistical arguments that democracy facilitates both development and peace, but in the concrete behavior of the key nations in Asia, this correlation is conspicuously absent. Perhaps it would be more fruitful to base policy on the actual behavior of countries rather than on theoretical and statistical arguments about how political scientists believe the countries should be behaving. Perhaps it would be useful to have a very concrete debate about whether election of a leader or peaceful behavior is more important when the United States chooses its friends.

The combination of shared interests and shared concerns about U.S. policy have led China and Russia to jointly sponsor the SCO. Originally, after the collapse of the Soviet Union, Russia hoped to continue to treat the Central Asian components of its former empire as part of a club, the CIS, that Russia would continue to manage. The important borders would not be Russia's borders with CIS countries such as Kazakhstan, but the borders of the CIS with outsiders like China. Russia, its leaders hoped, would continue to guard the outer borders of the CIS and would be able to manage the CIS club to some extent. That concept soon proved hopeless and became diluted to something like a Monroe Doctrine for Central Asia, but even that quickly proved unsustainable. Having acknowledged its inability to manage or corral the CIS by itself, Russia has decided to collaborate with China in the SCO. The two have transformed the SCO from a paper club into something that resembles a real institution for security cooperation. Except for U.S. bilateral alliances, the SCO is becoming the broadest regional security organization in Asia. This is discussed in more detail below.

Meanwhile, the dynamism of India and (mainly) China is having an effect on the world economy that may come to outweigh all other aspects of the Chinese-Russian relationship. Because of the incremental demand for energy and other raw materials, the prices of Russia's principal exports have climbed to a level that has flooded Russia with money. Only a few years away from a financial collapse, Russia finds itself with foreign-exchange reserves accumulating at a pace never previously imagined. The country's major cities are filled with shiny new cars for the first time ever. Whether this bounty will overflow into political appreciation remains to be seen, but by floating the Russian economy, China is helping to stabilize Russia and potentially augment its weight in world politics beyond what analysts would have once imagined possible.

Central Asia

> Uzbekistan is well down the path of self-destruction followed by such countries as Burma, Zimbabwe and North Korea, in which an elite prospers while the majority lives in worsening poverty. Even as European governments and the U.S. have encouraged regional development, Tashkent acts as a persistent spoiler and presents a growing threat to its neighbors, with refugees and drugs spilling over its frontiers. The other four Central Asian states and Afghanistan are all relatively weak and vulnerable. Kyrgyzstan was profoundly shaken by the arrival of fewer than 500 refugees. . . . Tajikistan has been hard hit by border closures and trade restrictions. Even relatively prosperous Kazakhstan could be seriously troubled if violence were to drive Uzbeks across its border.
>
> —*International Crisis Group*[10]

> Gandzha was like Batumi, a sprinkle of globalization with criminal overtones over a carcass of Soviet-era poverty. There may be no crueler kind of capitalism than the post-communist variety.
>
> —*Robert D. Kaplan*[11]

Central Asia comprises vast spaces, tiny populations, arbitrary boundaries, poverty, primary loyalties to clans and ethnic groups rather than to nations, lack of consensus about political structure, internecine Islamic conflicts, and powerful, disputatious neighbors. Running throughout the region are very large-scale drug trade, human trafficking, organized crime, and trafficking in dangerous weapons. This is a recipe for guaranteed instability. The conflicts, the trafficking, resource competition, and Russia's sense of residual ownership tend to drag the big powers in.

The big powers that influence this region play with different currencies. China's currency is economic magnetism, offset somewhat by

---

[10] International Crisis Group, "Uzbekistan: In for the Long Haul," Asia Briefing No. 45, February 16, 2006 (http://www.crisisgroup.org/home/index.cfm?id=3952&l=1).

[11] Robert D. Kaplan, *Eastward to Tartary: Travels in the Balkans, the Middle East, and the Caucasus*, New York: Vintage, 2001, p. 261. Even though this statement is about Azerbaijan, Kaplan's comment clearly applied to post-Soviet Central Asia as well.

Central Asian indignation over the repression of the Uighurs and other Islamic minorities in China's northwest. Turkey offers a model of moderate Islamic modernization that reinforces cultural ties to a region containing many speakers of Turkic languages. Iran offers a model of fundamentalist political triumph, offset somewhat by economic problems and social discontent. Russia has raw military power, with credibility bruised by Chechnya, and a history of bringing secular stability to the region that inspires nostalgia in some, fervent nationalist and religious hatred in others. The United States has military power, with credibility somewhat bruised by Iraq, and democratic ideology that is even more bruised by Iraq. Democratic values are becoming influential but do not particularly redound to the advantage of the United States, because of perceptions that the United States seeks to impose its values by force, that its primary interests in the region are geopolitical rather than developmental, and that it is at war with Islam. India and Japan both wish to play, but neither has sufficient currency of any kind to occupy a full seat.

Currently, struggles for political influence interact with a struggle for control of resources, particularly oil. National leaders focus heavily on who will own particular oil fields and what paths oil and gas pipelines will follow. To Americans, it is not clear that ownership of oil fields and control of pipelines convey significant advantage in an era of globalized oil markets, but Chinese, Japanese, and Indians believe intensely that their future security depends on such ownership and control. As a result, these countries frequently contend with one another, constantly pay premium prices for control of oil, quickly invest in high-risk situations, and damage the prospects for various kinds of potential collaboration such as cooperative bargaining with OPEC, cooperative development of new technologies, and cooperative development of reserves. The struggle may be silly, but the struggle is nonetheless real. India and China have created a largely cooperative energy strategy with each other, while Japan has characteristically isolated itself.

As in the game of "rock, paper, scissors," none of these powers has a decisive edge for all occasions. Nobody can win complete control. The stakes and the nature of the game shift unpredictably.

In this context, all parties are concerned about instability, and all the established governments are concerned about Islamist upheavals. The United States has responded to this concern about stability by inserting its military into bases in Kyrgyzstan and, for a time, Uzbekistan. Russia initially tried to create institutional structures through the CIS and the Collective Security Treaty Organization, but these efforts have faded in favor of a Chinese-initiated structure, the SCO. The SCO, comprising China, Russia, Uzbekistan, Kazakhstan, Kyrgyzstan, and Tajikistan, with India, Pakistan, Iran, and Mongolia as observers, remains loose, but it reflects shared values of stability and local control in the face of Islamic insurgencies, U.S. military presence, and color revolutions. It has a secretariat based in Beijing and a Regional Anti-Terrorism Structure (RATS) based in Tashkent, and it is forming a Business Council. Its concern about potential U.S. dominance is expressed in language of rejection of "monopoly or domination in world affairs" and in calls for a "just and rational new multipolar international order." It has endorsed the use of Central Asian bases by the international coalition trying to stabilize Afghanistan but has called for a deadline to be set for ultimate withdrawal from such bases.[12]

So far, the organization has been reactive and not particularly effective. A large joint Chinese-Russian military exercise in August 2005 provided an explicit counterpoint to the February 2005 2+2 announcement of the Japan-U.S. alliance. India's observer status in the SCO counterbalances its rapprochement with the United States, and Pakistan seeks to balance the new U.S.-India alignment through engagement in the SCO. The SCO's advantage is that it is the one multilateral security organization that ties together much of the region.

That having been said, the region's predominant characteristic is not the emergence of stable regional institutions, but rather their absence. If the United States adopted a friendlier stance toward either Russia or China, the SCO might crack or take on a quite different character. If the United States withdrew its military from Central Asia, the

---

[12] The July 6, 2005, declaration endorsing the use of bases but calling for a withdrawal deadline is published on the website of the SCO (http://www.sectsco.org).

SCO would lose an important source of cohesion. A successful terrorist attack on a U.S. base could suddenly alter alignments. If developments in one of the Central Asian states pit Russian and Chinese interests against each other, with, for instance, a traditional pro-Russian apparatchik on one side of a power struggle and a key Chinese economic interest on the other, the SCO could crack. Relatively small amounts of money or military power can change the internal balance of Central Asian states very quickly, and the struggle for control of resources raises the emotional temperature whenever such shifts occur.

The current geopolitical dynamic of the region is based on widely shared opposition to a dominant U.S. role and to widely shared concern about Islamist extremism. It is easy to imagine a different dynamic.

A distinctive aspect of the new Great Game is that the stakes may not mean very much outside the perfervid imaginations of the players. Ownership of various oil fields and oil companies may not in fact mean very much except that the players get very excited about it. (Many U.S. analysts argue that modern history is replete with evidence that ownership provides neither assurance of continued supply nor assurance of stable prices.) If the SCO were to become a very effective organization, the negative consequences for the United States might well be minimal—a color revolution or two marginally retarded—and effective collaboration against narcotics trafficking and Islamist extremists might be a major advantage for all states, including the United States and the EU. U.S. bases in the region may very well convey little advantage to the United States and little disadvantage to either Russia or China, but in each case, the pursuit of the Great Game can have consequences for big-power relationships even if the stakes in the Central Asian games themselves are minimal.

The revival of the Great Game introduces random influences into the larger geopolitics of Asia. Something could happen here that would suddenly escalate tensions or shift alignments in ways that nobody could have predicted the week before. In this situation, there is a powerful argument for the big powers not to let their prestige, their armies, or their economic interests become engaged any more than is absolutely necessary. But current evidence indicates that this powerful argument is not persuading the key governments.

For the United States, the key strategic decision has been the local corollary of the George W. Bush administration's global decision to focus primarily on military issues as the core strategic concerns and secondarily on early democratization, at the cost of abandoning America's traditional priority focus on economic and institutional development. This means that U.S. goals in Central Asia are perceived locally not as a partnership for development protected by the military, but rather as part of a raw struggle for geopolitical preeminence. In turn, this means that the stabilization and pro-American engagement that succeeded in South Korea and Southeast Asia cannot be replicated for the United States in Central Asia. As with the shift in Southeast Asia, it is now China that is focusing on the mutual-development game in the way that the United States formerly did elsewhere in Asia, and it is China that is building limited but credible regional institutions in the way the United States once did. As a result, if China can avoid a broad conflict with Islam stemming from its unrest in Xinjiang, it stands to gain more than any of the other players in the new Great Game. In this context, the advantages that the United States gains from its military presence in Central Asia could well prove evanescent.

In Central Asia, as in Korea and Southeast Asia, China is winning disproportionate influence with a weak hand, and the U.S. is losing influence despite a strong hand, not so much because of a brilliant or insidious Chinese strategy but rather because the U.S. has regressed to a pre-modern overemphasis on the military in the age of the Asian economic miracle.

CHAPTER EIGHT

The United States and the New Asia

My argument is that if China continues to grow economically, it will translate that economic might into military might, and it will become involved in an intense security competition with the United States, similar to the security competition that existed between the United States and the Soviet Union during the Cold War. That intense security competition, in my opinion, is unavoidable. . . . Why should we expect that China won't have a Monroe Doctrine, when we have a Monroe Doctrine? . . . I think that we'll go to considerable lengths to slow down Chinese economic growth.

—John Mearsheimer[1]

[T]he center of gravity in Asian regionalism has shifted over the past decade from trans-Pacific forums to pan-Asian venues. The Asia-Pacific Economic Cooperation has been largely supplanted by ASEAN+3 as the locus of practical projects to foster Asian trade liberalization and monetary cooperation. At the same time, multilateral trade negotiations—in which the United States has historically played a central role—have lost momentum, while bilateral and regional free trade agreements among Asians have rapidly proliferated. . . . [All this] suggests that the United States is heading for a more modest role in Northeast Asia. The relative

---

[1]   Interview with Harry Kreisler, University of California, Berkeley, April 8, 2002 (http://globetrotter.berkeley.edu/people2/Mearsheimer/mearsheimer-con6.html).

power of others is expanding; U.S. interest and influence in the
region appears to have waned.

—*Former U.S. Under Secretary of State Michael Armacost*[2]

The U.S. position in Asia is founded on several strategic realities that
have changed little over the years. Most Northeast and Southeast Asian
countries want a strong U.S. role, including especially a military presence, in the region to balance China and Japan. This includes Japan
wanting the United States in the region to balance China; most of the
time, it has included China wanting a strong U.S. presence to balance
the former Soviet Union and now Japan, but as noted earlier, this is
changing. All the non-communist Southeast Asian countries definitely
desire a strong U.S. presence. The attitudes of Vietnam, Cambodia,
and Laos are unclear, and Burma just wishes all the big powers would
go away, but of these, only Vietnam matters, and Vietnam is no longer
hostile and indeed might one day be America's strongest supporter in
Southeast Asia. Attitudes in the Indian subcontinent are more complex. Pakistan long welcomed U.S. support against India and welcomes
its current support tied to the war in Afghanistan, but the relationship
could change quickly. India is no longer hostile to the United States
and welcomes the benefits of new-found amity, but it does not feel the
kind of vital requirement for a U.S. presence that Japan or Indonesia does. On balance, there is overwhelming support for continuation
of a strong U.S. military presence in East Asia and substantial support in South Asia. In addition, all of Asia acknowledges U.S. military
preeminence.

Asian countries admire U.S. democracy. Even those, most notably China, that have different systems and do not believe the model is
appropriate for themselves at this moment acknowledge it as a highly
advanced, smoothly functioning system that connects the people to
the government in a way that ensures stability. To reiterate the phrase
employed by the U.S. State Department rapporteur quoted earlier, the

---

[2] Michael Armacost, "The Mismatch Between Northeast Asian Change and American
Distractions," in *NBR Analysis—Emerging Trends, Dormant Interest: Developments in Northeast Asian Politics,* Vol. 18, No. 1, January 2007, p. 12.

overwhelming majority of Asian countries view the United States as the "least distrusted" of the big powers.

At the same time, U.S. foreign policy must adapt to a number of crucial changes that have occurred. The Soviet threat has disappeared, and Russian influence in East and South Asia is now quite limited. Japan has lost its economic dynamism, its regional economic dominance, and most of its regional leadership role. China has become the region's most dynamic economy and has shifted from a policy of destabilization to a policy of joining the system. Islamist terrorism has emerged as a major regional issue and has become a source of consensual collaboration; with negligible exceptions (e.g., Burma), the whole panoply of Asian governments is willing to cooperate with the United States in attacking Islamist terrorism. Even predominantly Islamic countries such as Indonesia and Malaysia that disagree with U.S. Middle East policy have strong motivation to collaborate against terrorist attacks.

Adapting to China's Rise

The greatest dilemma in U.S. policy is how to respond to China's dynamism and, correspondingly, to Japan's loss of its leadership role. There are two basic stances that the industrial democracies can take toward China's dynamism.[3] Given the core U.S. post–World War II strategy of incorporating as much of the world as possible into its principal institutions and of promoting stability in Asia, one obvious stance is that China's reform period constitutes one of the three greatest successes in the history of modern American foreign policy, along with the recovery and stabilization of Europe and the incorporation of Japan and the Asian littoral states into the U.S.-designed system. The rise of one-sixth of the world's population from poverty, the stimulus of having another big prosperous economy in the world, and the disappearance

---

[3] What follows is an attempt to encapsulate briefly a very complex debate. There is some following for every imaginable permutation of views on China. For a reasonably comprehensive overview of the permutations, including citations that cover the most prominent literature, see Aaron L. Friedberg, "The Future of U.S.-China Relations: Is Conflict Inevitable?" *International Security*, Vol. 30, No. 2, Fall 2005.

of the power vacuum that caused so many tragedies in the 20th century are all, in this view, causes for rejoicing. This perspective emphasizes the drastic changes that have occurred in China since Mao's time, the parallels of Chinese development with Taiwan's development, and the rapid pace of not only economic but also political change in contemporary China. It underlines the trend that Asian states that have discovered the virtues of rapid development have become less interested in territorial issues and expansionist or ideological foreign policies.

The alternative perspective, more popular in the Western media and in the national-security establishments shaped by the Cold War, is that the Cold War effectively continues; that today's China is just a continuation of Mao's China; that because it is ruled by a Communist Party, today's China must be aggressively expansive like the Soviet Union of yesterday; and possibly that any rising power will inevitably cause violent disruption of the system. This perspective perceives an unbridgeable ideological gulf between the democracies and any communist country. It argues, based largely on European and Japanese experience in a previous era, that any rising power necessarily constitutes a threat to the United States and the international system and that, moreover, non-democratic countries are inherently more likely to engage in conflict than democratic countries, and therefore China is a danger.

Those who take a positive view of China's rise, with its emphasis on stability and joining the system, have to acknowledge that the future remains uncertain. While China's leaders have so far had the wisdom to evolve both their economics and their politics in the way that Taiwan's and South Korea's leaders did before them, albeit with long lags, it cannot be a foregone conclusion that future leaders will manage China's extraordinary banking, migration, unemployment, medical, pension, corruption, and political-evolution problems successfully. Nor is it a foregone conclusion that the advanced industrial democracies will continue to manage globalization in a way that will continue to seduce China into joining the system. Certainly, whatever the economic and strategic benefits of China's success, the democracies will continue to be appalled and repelled by its authoritarianism and numerous abuses of human rights.

Those who take a negative view of China's dynamism divide into two principal camps. Many realists, led intellectually by John Mearsheimer,[4] argue that any rising power will inevitably challenge the reigning power and pose a threat to the stability of the established international system. Mearsheimer even argues that, based on a historical analysis, the United States should intervene to stop or slow China's rise. This negative realist view has had powerful advocates inside the U.S. national-security establishment.

There are, however, fundamental problems with this mechanistic view of rising powers. One is the problem of identifying who would be the threat according to this theory. The Japanese and EU economies are still much larger than China's, and as it expands and integrates, Europe seems to be a rising power, indeed a much bigger, albeit somewhat inchoate one, than China. The principal EU countries sometimes have more differences with U.S. foreign policy than China has. A demographic squeeze beginning between 2015 and 2020 or any of a series of financial, employment, or demographic problems could restrict China's ability to continue to grow at anything like current rates, so it could become less dynamic at a time when it will still be quite poor. Does this mean that the EU is the threat? Or Japan, which still has a much larger economy than China's, along with far greater ability to project military power overseas? Or, if rapid growth is the criterion, does it mean that India will be the threat? (Realist theory holds the domestic structure of a rising power to be unimportant to its inevitable destabilizing threats, so the democratic peace argument cannot be used by realists to eliminate the EU and India.) Most of those who argue that China is a threat hold, contradictorily, that India's rise is a wonderful benefit, and some even argue enthusiastically for high-tech arms sales to India. But if India continues to succeed, and if China is slowed down a decade hence by its graying demography, then India will be the faster rising power and, according to realist theory, possibly the big threat.

---

[4] For a condensed version of Mearsheimer's views, see Zbigniew Brzezinski and John J. Mearsheimer, "Clash of the Titans," *Foreign Policy*, No. 146, January-February 2005, pp. 46–49. For a detailed theoretical argument, see John J. Mearsheimer, *The Tragedy of Great Power Politics*, New York: W. W. Norton, 2001.

In addition, these realist theorists tend to ignore the past half-century's experience that rapid Asian development and modern military technology have created a huge incentive for successful countries to focus inward on economic reform rather than outward on territorial expansion. There is, moreover, a moral problem with arguing that the United States should deliberately slow the economic progress of one-sixth of the human race. Such slowing would entail depriving millions of people of education, of adequate incomes in their old age, and of medical attention that often means the difference between life and death, compared with what they would have had if rapid economic growth had continued. To adopt a policy with such devastating human consequences on the basis of an academic theory would raise the most profound moral issues, comparable to those involved in war crimes. Not surprisingly, no U.S. president has seriously considered such a policy, despite Mearsheimer's confident prediction.

A second brand of negative theory focuses on ideology, holding that non-democracies are more likely to be aggressive than democracies. Although it is usually not made explicit, this argument is often used most vehemently by those who believe that because it is ruled by communists, China must be the successor to the aggressive policies of the old Soviet Union. U.S. theorists of democracy have increasingly argued that democracies are both more peaceful and more successful at economic development. However, Asian countries have consistently proved to be exceptions to these rules, if indeed they are rules. The most successful Asian economies, most notably South Korea, Taiwan, Singapore, and British and Chinese Hong Kong, but also Thailand and now Vietnam, have consistently been authoritarian until they created societies with large, highly educated middle classes; they have typically transitioned to democracy afterward, rather than experiencing rapid growth because of democracy. The region's leading developing democracies, India and the Philippines, have lagged counterparts such as China, South Korea, Taiwan, Hong Kong, Singapore, and Thailand that were mostly quite undemocratic during their economic takeoffs.[5]

---

[5] The conclusion that democracies are more successful at economic development is derived by a transparent statistical sleight of hand, which works as follows. All non-democracies,

Malaysia, perhaps a partial exception, was a democracy under martial law until recently, and it has consistently been ruled by a typical East Asian coalition of elite groups so powerful that no successful challenge was likely, regardless of free elections. Likewise, democratic India has been far slower to settle both hostile international relationships and violent internal conflicts than its initially more authoritarian East Asian counterparts. (At last count, India's Northeast had 58 insurgencies, rather like Thailand or Indonesia 40 years ago, and serious problems with virtually all of its neighbors, rather like China 30 years ago or Indonesia 40 years ago. As noted earlier, India has been much slower to try to settle border problems with its neighbors and much faster to resort to armed conflict than has China.) Even Japan, for a half-century the model of peace, has been totally intransigent about settling border issues with its neighbors, while China has made many compromises.

U.S. presidents have consistently abjured grand theories, and all since Nixon have eventually settled on a pragmatic approach that encourages China when it seeks to join the system, deters China when it seems to threaten the peace (as in the Taiwan crisis of 1996), and keeps the U.S. military powerful just in case it should be needed in the future. This pragmatism has persisted through the diverse presidencies of Nixon, Ford, Carter, Reagan, Bush I, Clinton, and Bush II, so it has proved robust. It is threatened primarily when the president's power slips relative to that of the Congress or when national-security institutions pursue policies that are relatively disconnected from the pragmatic view of the president.

In sum, policy toward China has been consistently pragmatic, but Cold War images have persisted. Moreover, national-security policy, in theory a hedge, has increasingly treated China as a likely enemy. U.S.

---

including developmental authoritarian states, fading empires, exploitative dictatorships, tribal autocracies, military dictatorships, totalitarian states, civil wars, and others are lumped together and the average taken. This average is then compared with the growth of democracies, to the benefit of the latter. This is like taking the average beauty of European women of all ages and comparing it with the average beauty of American 18-year-olds, then drawing the conclusion that American women are invariably more beautiful than European women. Such sleight of hand on any less politically correct subject would be unpublishable. Moreover, some of these analyses take the Asian-miracle economies out and list them as exceptions, thereby further skewing the analysis.

military forces have engaged in a vast shift of resources toward Asia, mostly without citing China explicitly as the target but quite clearly focused on China contingencies. The acquisition of the coming generation of high-tech aircraft and fighting ships is based on the China-threat theory. The huge tilt toward Japan since 2001, the explicit focusing of the U.S.-Japan alliance on the Taiwan problem, the rapprochement with India, and the argument for permanent acquisition of bases in Central Asia are all based in part on the presupposition of a China threat, so much so that the "hedge" often seems to overwhelm what is supposedly the core policy of enticing China to continue to buy into the existing international system.[6]

Cold War Images and Post–Cold War Policy Anomalies

Within the pragmatic pattern, there are several anomalies that indicate strains between the momentum of Cold War assumptions and the reality of the post–Cold War environment. First, as noted in Chapter Two, U.S. presidents tend to come into office with powerful Cold War images and policy prescriptions, then modify them after about 18 months as they become exposed to the realities of dealing with China. Reagan campaigned to upgrade relations with Taiwan, then after experiencing relations with China, signed a remarkable 1982 agreement that promised never to upgrade the value or technological level of arms sales to Taiwan as long as cross-strait relations remained peaceful. His actual experience of dealing with China and Taiwan led him to a different understanding than the knee-jerk Cold War view typical of political campaigns.

Likewise, Clinton came to office demanding that China's MFN trade privileges be revoked, as a way of improving human rights in China, then abandoned that policy during his second year and ended up praising China as a "strategic partner." Once in office, he became

---

[6] For the most current official statements on the issues addressed in this paragraph, see the relevant sections of U.S. Department of Defense, *Quadrennial Defense Review Report*, February 6, 2006, and President of the United States, *The National Security Strategy of the United States of America*, Washington, DC, September 2002.

aware of the great strategic value of China's support in, for instance, dealing with North Korea, and he learned that taking away China's trade privileges would do more harm than good. Taking away MFN privileges would have devastated Hong Kong, Taiwan, and the liberal coastal areas of China, while strengthening China's conservatives, considerations that immediately came to light when a sitting president had expert advisors and was dealing with concrete problems but that didn't surface in the rhetorical heat of an electoral campaign.

Similarly, President George W. Bush came to office after a campaign that bitterly attacked Clinton's concept of strategic partnership with China and variously characterized China as a strategic adversary and a strategic competitor. This translated into substantial hostile reorientation of military planning at the beginning of his administration (from land focus to sea focus, from Europe focus to Asia focus, a promise to do "whatever it takes" to defend Taiwan, and a leaked notion of retargeting strategic nuclear weapons toward China). Soon, however, President Bush was praising China's support for the war on terror, neglecting to mention ally Japan in that connection, characterizing China as a "strategic ally" in that war, and warning Taiwan while standing on the White House steps with Chinese Premier Wen Jiabao in December 2003. Again, this change of view resulted from exposure to the reality that on most of the big Asian issues, China is an essential and cooperative partner.

This pattern has afflicted all recent U.S. presidents except George H.W. Bush, the only one who came to office with a primary expertise in foreign affairs and specific expertise on China. The pattern results from the powerful hold that Cold War images have on much of politically active America, in contrast to what presidents quickly learn once they take office and confront the realities of doing business with China. China's cooperation against the Soviet Union strongly influenced Reagan's views. China's help on North Korean nuclear issues, along with strong economic ties and a range of political issues discussed elsewhere in this book, strongly influenced Presidents Clinton and George W. Bush. After coming to office, all presidents are exposed to the weight of expertise on China in the CIA and the Departments of State, Defense, and Treasury, where expertise has overcome the superficial images that predominate in the media, political campaigns, and parts of Congress. The key point here is the consistent dramatic difference between the superficial images of China when a president takes office and the reality he discovers when he is actually in power. This exposure to reality greatly conditions not only direct policy toward China, but also the balance of policy toward Taiwan-China and Japan-China issues. But much of the public and much of the political elite lack this presidential experience and maintain the inertia of Cold War views. Within parts of the professional military, which must prepare for China contingencies but often has extremely limited exposure to a broader range of China-related considerations, the inertia of Cold War views remains formidable. On the other hand, parts of the professional military, such as the Pacific Command (PACOM), have direct dealings with China and sometimes have as sophisticated an understanding of China as anyone has; indeed, successive PACOM commanders are among those in the United States having the most balanced and thoughtful comprehension of China.

What happens in political campaigns is a throwback to the verities of the Cold War, with political leaders trying to excite their potential followers by stirring up the emotions that were inculcated in the Cold War era. That emotional stimulus is, of course, greatly facilitated by powerful interest groups, most notably weapon and trade lobbies, that stand to profit from continuation of Cold War patterns of behavior and spending. But when the new president takes office, he faces real problems that don't respond to the old medicine, so he changes his approach.

As noted earlier, the same phenomenon occurs in other areas. Secretary of Defense Donald Rumsfeld made a heroic organizational effort to create a more efficient Cold War–style military and succeeded to an extent that few would have predicted possible. But it was a costly example of preparing to fight the last war, and his force was not prepared for the wars it did have to fight. Likewise, the Armitage Report, discussed earlier, was a clarion call to return to the verities of the Cold War alliance with Japan. It resulted in some improvements in U.S. military ability to cope with a Taiwan crisis, but it exacerbated a gratuitous polarization of Asia, and it substituted ineffectual Japanese military support in the second Iraq War for vitally needed financial support in the first. It replaced the senior China experts in the State Department and on the National Security Council (NSC) staff, only to find six years later that the top China specialist was back to running the NSC Asia staff and the assistant secretary of state for East Asia was spending his time on a collaborative effort with China to put in place a deal with North Korea that Japan refused to support. Such are the exigencies of a transitional era in which vigorous efforts to restore old verities become overwhelmed by new realities. Every few years, there is a new version of King Canute—the Reagan proposal to upgrade relations with Taiwan, the Clinton proposal to remove China's trade privileges, the Armitage Report—but ultimately, King Canute cannot push back the tide of history.

The second anomaly concerns the patterns of post–Cold War relationships. During the Cold War, U.S. military, political, and economic relations all aligned quite positively with Japan and quite negatively with the Soviet Union. That made for consistent policy, for congruence among the political, economic, and military aspects of policy—in accordance, for instance, with Carl von Clausewitz's adage, "War is a continuation of politics by other means."

Likewise, during the Cold War, the alliances with Japan and South Korea were mutually reinforcing, notwithstanding old hatreds between the two allies. U.S. bases in Japan were vital to South Korea's security, and the U.S. forces in South Korea kept the threats farther away from Japanese territory.

In the post–Cold War period, the alignment of relationships is less consistent. During the early years of the new century, Washington has consistently strengthened the alliance with Japan, while increasingly doing its most important constructive Asian political and economic business with China. Dealing with the war on terror in Asia has been heavily a U.S.-Chinese collaboration—with China in a position to be much more helpful than Japan and much less ambivalent than Indonesia. Trying to roll back North Korea's nuclear program has been primarily a U.S.-China collaboration. Dealing with regional crime, regional drug trafficking, and regional human trafficking has been primarily a U.S.-China collaboration. Except on the Taiwan issue, Asian geopolitics has increasingly become a U.S.-China bicondominium, with Japan and Russia in relatively more-passive support roles.

In economic relations, the new pattern is even more striking. The chief protagonists in promoting free trade have been the United States and China, with Japan, Russia, and Europe dragging their feet; China's membership in the AFTA agreement with Southeast Asia actually puts it ahead of the United States in promoting multilateral free trade. In promoting freedom of investment, the chief protagonists have been the United States, Europe, and China, with Japan and India very reluctantly dragged along far behind. In arguments over genetically modified organism crops—an absolutely crucial issue, both economically and politically—the United States, the number one producer, innovator, and consumer of such crops, and China, the number two, have aligned against Japan, Europe, and India.

In short, the post–Cold War era has seen a huge tension between the direction of military alignment and the direction of political-economic alignment. To be sure, the issues of shared commitments to human rights and democracy provide an ideological tie between the United States and Japan, but this does not relieve the tension between a military alliance increasingly directed at China and a political and economic relationship in which China is becoming America's principal collaborator. Clausewitz would not approve.

This tension is paralleled throughout the region by traditional allies and quasi-allies who, although they all welcome a strong U.S. military presence to counterbalance China and Japan, generally distrust Japan more than they distrust China and therefore are wary of a U.S. policy founded on a tight alliance with Japan that (1) specifically targets China and (2) replaces the old emphasis on suppressing Chinese-Japanese rivalries with policies that enhance Chinese-Japanese conflicts. Southeast Asian leaders express disquiet about the U.S. over-emphasis on the relationship with Japan and the targeting of China as an adversary. As noted earlier, Singapore, the most consistent supporter of the United States in Southeast Asia for many decades, took the occasion of a summit with President Bush in May 2007 to insist strongly on the need for balance in U.S. ties with China and Japan.[7]

In the Cold War era, the U.S.-Japan and U.S.–South Korea alliances were overwhelmingly complementary—old antagonisms between Japan and Korea notwithstanding. Particularly in the early Cold War era, both China and the Soviet Union were serious threats to both Japan and South Korea, so the rationale for what amounted to an integrated triangular U.S.-Japan–South Korea alliance was almost beyond question. However, in the post–Cold War era, neither Russia nor China threatens South Korea, and both are closer to South Korea than they are to North Korea, despite some occasional Chinese language designed to maintain its good-cop relationship with Pyongyang. As competing rivalries diminish, South Korean concerns about Japan become more prominent. As the U.S.-Japan alliance becomes ever tighter and becomes more targeted on China and the current Japanese political leadership increasingly adopts a view of history anathema to Koreans, the South Korean government finds itself torn between the vital necessity to maintain an alliance with the United States and the vital necessity to avoid getting dragged into a gratuitous (from the perspective of Korean national interests) conflict with China. U.S. determination to have its troops in South Korea available for a Taiwan contingency and South Korean determination not to risk involvement in such a conflict could one day break the alliance.

A third anomaly is that the greatest beneficiaries in Japanese domestic politics of the U.S. pressure to rearm and to target China

---

[7] "Singapore's prime minister has urged the US to maintain ties with both China and Japan because south-east Asian nations do not want to 'choose sides'" ("Singapore PM warns US over China," May 5, 2007, http://news.bbc.co.uk/2/hi/asia-pacific/6627361.stm). To emphasize a point made earlier, there is a curious phenomenon in much of the U.S. national-security community's dialogue with the smaller Asian countries. Focused on the military aspect of policy, officials travel around Asia and ask, Do you want an American military presence to balance any possible future problem with China? The answer is invariably yes, virtually everywhere, and that is interpreted in important quarters in Washington to mean that Southeast Asians and Koreans are afraid of China and support the U.S. targeting it. But every public-opinion poll and almost every wide-ranging conversation with leaders of these countries indicates that they have greater concern about Japan than about China and considerable unease about the way the U.S. military obsesses over China.

as a potential enemy—namely, the harder portions of the Japanese right—are those who have the most nationalistic attitudes toward the United States. The Yushukan's portrayal of World War II as an honorable and heroic liberation of Asia from Europe and the United States is ultimately as unacceptable to Americans as it is to Chinese, Koreans, Filipinos, Malaysians, Singaporeans, British, and Dutch; it is just less publicized in the United States than it is in Northeast and Southeast Asia. For this part of the Japanese political spectrum, resentment of the United States has never been far beneath the surface. It came out in the assertions of U.S. incompetence and decline in the late 1980s, and it blossomed with the assertions in the late 1980s that Clinton and Treasury Secretary Lawrence Summers were trying to destroy Japan economically and that Clinton's single visit to China, following two visits to Japan, was a betrayal of the alliance with Japan. Discounting that part of the left that is never likely to govern Japan, the hard right is the least likely part of the Japanese political spectrum to accept indefinite subordination to U.S. foreign policy and indefinite retention of U.S. bases. The natural long-term allies of the United States are the center of the political spectrum and the moderates who predominate in the Ministry of Foreign Affairs (except current minister Aso) and indeed in the overwhelming majority of the Japanese public.

The hard right in Japan is also the part of the political spectrum most likely to oppose U.S. efforts to settle the principal Northeast Asian conflicts, namely divided Korea and divided China. A very broad consensus of U.S. political leaders and policy experts would welcome peaceful unification of Korea as the best solution to the Korean problem. Likewise, most would welcome some kind of peaceful, mutually acceptable one-China deal between Taiwan and the mainland that would firmly preserve Taiwan's democracy and freedom. While such solutions would be acceptable to the center and left of the Japanese political spectrum, those who visit the Yasukuni Shrine often take the view that a divided Korea and an independent Taiwan are vital Japanese national-security interests. This view has now spread well beyond the extreme right and could one day put Japan and the United States at loggerheads in the manner of the current U.S.–South Korean tension over the policy toward North Korea. (Most of the Japanese population would have little stomach for fighting China to ensure an independent Taiwan; the implicit assumption on the right seems to be that the United States or the U.S.-Japan alliance could protect a Taiwan that was going independent. Whatever the implicit rationale, supporting a Taiwan independence movement would inevitably lead to war.)

From the domestic political perspective of the alliance partners, the latest evolution of the U.S.-Japan alliance constitutes an alliance between U.S. conservatives, who believe that China must be the successor of the Soviet Union because it is communist, and Japanese conservatives, who see China as a threat to Japan's rightful dominance of Asian politics and economics. In addition to these beliefs, which are mostly genuine, these positions represent powerful interests. The Japanese right can attain power and rearmament only if fear of China pushes the Japanese public into support of the right's power and the military's rearmament. The U.S. right can continue its emphasis on military expenditure, particularly on new high-tech ships and planes, at the expense of domestic expenditure only if there is a serious emerging threat, and China is the only candidate. Therefore, both believe in, and have a vital political and economic need for, the China threat. The longer-term problem is that the U.S. right needs the China threat in order to keep fighting the Cold War indefinitely, whereas the Japanese right needs the China threat in order to keep fighting World War II indefinitely. These two needs will clash in public opinion if the American public becomes aware of the view of World War II that the Japanese right is promoting. More important, they clash in policy if a U.S. president decides that to maintain peace, he must solve the problems of Taiwan and divided Korea. They clash in military interests when Japan has sufficiently rearmed to feel it doesn't need U.S. bases anymore. Recent joint Japanese-American military exercises designed to enhance Japan's ability to assert its claims to the Senkaku/Diaoyutai Islands are inconsistent with neutrality over Japan's and Korea's conflicting claims to Tokdo/Takeshima Island, where the basis of Japan's claims is similar.[8] The Armitage Report's call for the United States to commit itself

---

[8]   South Korea has exercised control over the island for most of the period since World War II. Japan seized control at the time it colonized Korea and has claimed sovereignty ever since.

to defense of the Senkaku Islands betokens an unreflective Cold War mentality. If the United States does not commit itself to solving Asia's numerous seabed and territorial-waters claims on the basis of broad principles and compromise rather than ideology and Cold War legacies, the problem will become unsolvable throughout Asia.

It may be possible for a while to finesse these differences between U.S. interests and the Japanese right wing, but the differences concern the decisive issues in Asian geopolitics. It may be that Japanese domestic politics will in the future water down the influence of the hardliners, but the current trend is for this part of the Japanese political spectrum to have more and more control of Japanese national-security policy, regardless of public opinion, with strong implicit support from the United States. The cycle of conflict with China continuously strengthens the hardliners' hand and broadens their public support. A continuous increase in their role initially strengthens the U.S.-Japan partnership, because Japan cannot today confront China or even South Korea by itself, but indefinite continuation of the same trend would eventually break the alliance, because dependence on the United States offends the Japanese right wing's nationalism and historic resentments.

Changing Priorities: The Perils of Dominant Military Priorities

Some of the greatest post–Cold War changes come from changes in American priorities. As the new century began, the Bush administration seemed to abandon a half-century tradition that put economic development, along with military deterrence, at the core of U.S. strategy in Asia (as well as in the rest of the world). As noted in the Southeast Asia section above, these new priorities, following closely after the

---

In the second week of April 2006, responding to a Korean intention to give Korean names to seabed features near the island, Japan announced a survey mission to Tokdo/Takeshima in order to be able to propose Japanese names. This followed up a Japanese prefecture's assertion in 2005 that the island was part of the prefecture. In response to the Japanese announcement of a survey, South Korea mobilized a considerable naval flotilla on April 19, 2006. Japan deferred the survey, while South Korea promised to defer proposing Korean names.

Clinton administration's inability to support Indonesia and Thailand during the Asian crisis, have fundamentally weakened the U.S. relationship with Southeast Asia. They preclude the possibility of following in Central Asia the kinds of policies that led to success in East and Southeast Asia. U.S. aid is now at 0.15 percent of gross national income (GNI), making the United States proportionately the least generous donor of any large country; even that small contribution is heavily diluted, because most of the aid is devoted to a handful of Middle East countries, and most of the rest is allocated with heavily political priorities rather than a focus on economic development.[9]

The ranking of aid priorities shown in Figure 8 greatly overstates actual U.S. aid to developing countries as traditionally understood, because a high proportion of U.S. aid is earmarked for Israel, a developed country that does not need economic aid, and Egypt, as an incentive to keep the peace. For contrast, relative rankings in military expenditure are shown in Figure 9.

These developments have weakened U.S. ties to the principal Southeast Asian countries and have created a partial vacuum that China gladly filled. Subsequently, the United States has strengthened military ties to the non-core countries, Singapore and the Philippines, while sacrificing much of its quasi-alliance relationships with the core of ASEAN, Indonesia and Thailand. (Military relationships with Indonesia did strengthen, but the overall relationship weakened.)

One of the consequences of the dominance of U.S. policy by individuals whose primary career experience has been military is that the U.S. role in Asia has become organized so predominantly around the U.S.-Japan alliance and the requirements for military bases that other forms of regional organization have been neglected. I have noted

---

9 For a concise comparison of the programs of the advanced countries and a graph of major donors derived from OECD figures, see Sang-sik Oh, *ODA Policies of Advanced Nations and Related Tasks for Korea*, Institute of Foreign Affairs and National Security, South Korea, Policy Brief No. 2005-7, November 2005. Aid is now far less important than private capital flows, and it is less important to third-world economic development than it was in the past, but poor countries still require assistance and advice and infrastructure assistance, so the ratios of generosity remain a valid indicator of a rich country's priority for stimulating economic progress. The United Nations target for foreign aid is 0.75 percent of GDP, almost five times the U.S. level.

Figure 8
Aid to Developing Countries in 2005

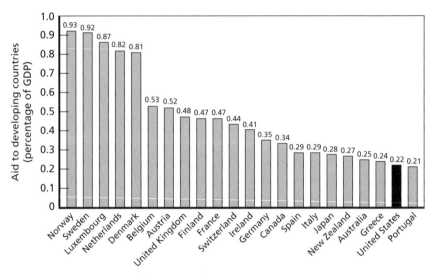

SOURCE: Organisation for Economic Co-operation and Development, *OECD in Figures,*
2006–2007, Paris: OECD Publications, 2006 (http://www.oecd.org/infigures).

the downgrading of economic priorities and the unofficial, but clear, diplomatic downgrading of ASEAN. In the section on Southeast Asia earlier, I elaborated the official rationale for the very recent U.S. disinterest in building regional Asian economic and security organizations. Feeling that the U.S.-Japanese alliance is sufficient, Washington has both explicitly and implicitly discouraged other forms of regional organization. ASEAN and others are constantly proposing new organizational efforts (e.g., ASEAN+3, to bring China, Japan, and South Korea into a common regional economic and political forum). Koreans and others lament the absence of a regional security organization to bring, at a minimum, Japan, China, Russia, the United States, and South Korea into structured security relationships and security dialogues. Officials in Seoul and others have hoped that the six-party talks, focused on the North Korean nuclear threat, could evolve into a regional security organization, but Washington has given scant encouragement.

Figure 9
Military Expenditures in Developed Countries in 2005

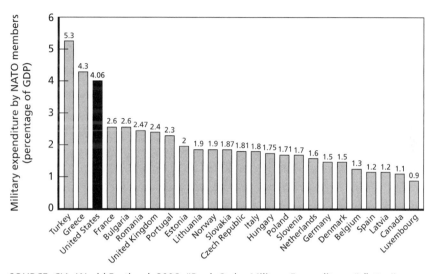

SOURCE: CIA, World Factbook 2006, "Rank Order-Military Expenditures" (http://www.cia.gov/cia/publications/factbook/, as of November 14, 2006).

Likewise, most U.S. energy experts, as well as many of their Asian counterparts, see no hope for transforming regional energy-security conflicts into cooperative consumer relationships unless Washington takes the lead in forming a regional organization, and much hope for success if it does, but no initiatives come out of Washington. These possibilities are neglected by Washington because of an obsession with military security and with strengthening the U.S.-Japan alliance. The trumpeted new relationship with India thrives because it is seen (in Washington, but emphatically not in Delhi) primarily as an adjunct to military security, particularly vis-à-vis China, supplementing the U.S.-Japan alliance.

Similarly, as conflicting seabed and territorial-waters issues become critical, there is little hope of resolving them without a sustained effort by a regional organization with considerable leadership from Washington. As noted earlier, if Washington takes the view that this is predominantly a Japan-China issue to be handled through the U.S.-Japan alliance, rather than a structural issue to be resolved throughout the region according to some general principles and broad compromises, the only likely outcome is disastrous confrontations.

The U.S.-Japan alliance is unquestionably the most valuable item in the U.S. Asia-policy toolkit. Moreover, when the national-security establishment focuses on the issue of military alliance and military bases, it is just doing its job. The problem is that there are other jobs to be done, including some that balance the role of the military, and the domination of other institutions by military priorities and military experts threatens to overwhelm other vital functions.

A number of consequences flow from this syndrome. Most dramatically, the gratuitously conflictual struggle over energy security threatens to get out of control due to a lack of regional discussions and regional understandings that should come from a regional organization with U.S. leadership. For instance, India is actively planning for a possible naval war with China over access to energy and resources. China is buying oil companies around the world at high prices that will likely damage the Chinese economy sometime in the future, just as Japan's over-the-top purchases of U.S. companies and real estate in the 1980s proved damaging. Japan is trying to hamper China's efforts to diversify its energy sources through a pipeline to Russia. With a regional organization and U.S. leadership, all these countries could be focusing on cooperative bargaining with OPEC, cooperative development of new energy technologies, cooperative development of stockpiles, and cooperative defense of the sea lanes.

Second, old organizations such as ASEAN are migrating away from U.S. influence, U.S.-favored organizations such as APEC and ARF are decaying, and new institutions such as the East Asia Summit and the SCO are emerging to fill a vacuum that need not exist. The absence of generous development programs for Central Asia means that Washington incurs the political cost of seeking military bases in the region without the political benefit of being seen as a strong promoter of improved living conditions and national strength. Even in a purely military analysis, this balance of priorities is probably counterproductive, because the bases would be more welcome if they were seen more as a buttressing of local aspirations and less as a self-interested bid for global power. Paradoxically, Washington is greatly increasing its military power but sharply degrading its political influence. Improved economic support would cost only a fraction of gratuitous weapon systems. Throughout Asia, the talk is of declining U.S. influence. Nobody in Asia doubts that the United Sates is the world's biggest military power, the world's biggest economy, and the world's greatest cultural influence, but it is seen as a declining power because it is pre-occupied elsewhere, it has weakened relationships with key quasi-allies, it has lost its image as a partner in nation-building, events in the Middle East have weakened its moral standing, and it has allowed its leverage through organizations other than the U.S.-Japan alliance to wither.

The syndrome poses particular risks to the relationship with China. Declared U.S. policy toward China is to welcome it into the family of nations as long as it behaves and to conduct a lot of important business with it (e.g., on North Korea, terror, drugs, trade), with a big hedge in case Beijing does not behave. The military, of course, has the duty to focus on the hedge; that is a difficult and perilous duty, and the military is right to worry over it and to demand the resources for effective deterrence and defense. At the same time, and this is where the problem arises, the military also has a duty not to undercut the first part of the policy. Sometimes, however, the leadership of the Department of Defense risks becoming a lobby for treating China as an enemy, restoring an overt alliance with Taiwan, and supporting Japanese right-wingers in their Taiwan ambitions.

Related to this, for most of modern history, the United States has had important, albeit only privately stated, Chinese support for its bases in Asia because the Chinese felt that the bases in Japan reduced the risk of revived Sino-Japanese conflict, the bases in South Korea contributed to stability on the peninsula, and so forth. Chinese support persisted for decades despite ongoing disagreements about Taiwan. Now the United States is losing that support because of the way the U.S.-Japan alliance and other factors are being managed.

In this way as in others, excessive focus on maximizing the ability to accomplish military missions can undermine the nation's broader ability to accomplish even its specifically military missions. On one hand, as long as the military has the mission of defending Taiwan in a potential conflict, it must have the resources to be decisive in such an eventuality. On the other hand, the chances of actually having to fight over Taiwan are very low, while the chances of needing Chinese support, or needing facilities that Chinese pressure could deny the United States, in a wide variety of other contingencies are very high.

Similarly, a U.S. effort to be perfectly prepared for every imaginable contingency in Central Asia, China, and the Middle East by seeking bases in Central Asia could well risk consolidating the SCO into an enduring Sino-Russian-Central Asian alliance with an anti-American core. Thus, even the narrow military-security interests of the United States might be enhanced by reintroducing a broader range of priorities into U.S. policy.

Finally, even the military is rediscovering the dangers of seeing issues only with a military eye and neglecting the economic aspects of policy. One thoughtful Marine Corps colonel who held a number of high-strategy posts recently concluded:

> We must adapt our security agencies to become more than merely a one-armed Cyclops. Too often we look at the world through a single lens, a military lens. This perspective, along with our well-developed single military arm, distorts our ability to advance all of our security needs. We do need our military might, but we need more than a military lens to anticipate future threats and secure our interests. We also need a strong State Department, with the capacity to help foreign governments build adequate forms of governance and the institutions to serve their people. We need law enforcement experts, people who can help with economic development and infrastructure, and for we Americans who know how to reestablish the rule of law and judiciary mechanisms in foreign countries that lack experience with these fundamentals. Until we do this, we'll just be a one-armed Cyclops, and we'll continue to win many battles, but never establish a better peace anywhere.[10]

---

[10] Frank G. Hoffman, "Normalcy," distributed electronically by the Foreign Policy Research Institute, May 12, 2006 (www.fpri.org).

Globalization and the Downgrading of Economic Priorities

In addition to weakening U.S. diplomatic leverage with ASEAN and depriving the United States of a potential winning strategy in Central Asia, the downgrading of priority for economics comes at a crucial moment in the development of globalization.

What has come to be called *globalization* began, in the post–World War II period, with the Marshall Plan, encouraging increasing integration of the European economies and of Europe's economy with America's, and with a similar opening to Japan. Gradually, through incentives, argument, and pressures, much of the world was persuaded, primarily by the United States, to participate more and more in this integration. The defeat of the Soviet Union, the stabilization of non-communist Asia from Japan to Indonesia, and the reversal of China's strategy from ideological destabilization to stable integration all relied primarily on this U.S. strategy. The prosperity of today's world, including both the prosperity of the advanced industrial democracies and the radical reduction of poverty in China, India, and Southeast Asia, is in large part the consequence of this U.S.-sponsored economic globalization. The United States succeeded because all U.S. presidents emphasized this strategy and devoted the attention that was required to make it succeed. Often in the past, success has seemed to be in jeopardy. For instance, many commentators believed the Uruguay round likely to fail; it involved 123 countries and, from gestation of the idea in 1982 to completion in 1994, took more than a decade, including seven and a half years of politically difficult, economically complex negotiations. But it did succeed, because of the determination of American and European leaders.

By the middle of the first decade of the new century, a pervasive backlash against globalization had developed. France led the backlash in Europe, as it has always done, but the defeat of the EU Constitution was a huge blow. Simultaneously, the United States was caught up in one of its periodic anti-Asian frenzies, but this time the president was in a politically weak position vis-à-vis Congress; since all presidents are free traders and all congresses, representing local constituents, are protectionist, this dangerously tipped the balance. China's support for globalization helped, but India and Brazil continued to lead an ideological anti-globalization backlash at WTO meetings. Much of the world had grown complacent, taking the advantages of the globalized trading and investment system for granted, while special interests from Korean rice farmers to North Carolina textile manufacturers to a spectrum of French protectionists became increasingly organized and vocal.

In this context, the U.S. downgrading of economic priorities was not the only problem or even the main problem, but it became potentially the decisive problem. A series of changes altered the globalization balance at the margin. The shift by both Japan and the United States from a strategy of multilateral liberalization to bilateral FTAs further dissipated the already weak momentum toward a successful Doha trade round. The Bush administration's decision to allocate FTAs in relation to countries' support for the war in Iraq further downgraded economic priorities. The partial alienation of ASEAN weakened one of the most important diplomatic links. The absence of a foreign policy that made a centerpiece of efforts to uplift the developing world from poverty changed for the worse the context in which poor countries were asked to make politically painful economic concessions. Above all, the absence of focused, energetic U.S. leadership on the issue made a huge difference; that leadership had been sustained all through the Cold War and all through the Vietnam War, but it was overwhelmed by the smaller challenges of the war on terror and the war in Iraq.

It remains to be seen whether the trend toward increasing global economic integration and the resultant prosperity are actually at risk. The potential consequences if they turn out to be at risk are so grave that most commentators do not even want to contemplate them. If we do see a reversal of globalization, future historians will recount a confluence of many unfortunate tendencies from different parts of the world. But the far-reaching consequences of a slackening of U.S. leadership, of a decisive shift of U.S. priorities, would certainly be a major part of any such account.

The Costs and Benefits of Promoting Democracy

Along with enhancing the role of the military and reducing the role of economic support and institution-building in its global policies, the Bush administration has attempted to raise the priority of democratization. At his second inauguration, President Bush said that "it is the policy of the United States to seek and support the growth of democratic movements and institutions in every nation and culture, with the ultimate goal of ending tyranny in our world." The sharp end of this policy seems to be directed primarily at the Middle East, and its intended application to Asia is unclear, but "in our world" is pretty comprehensive. While the United States has always supported democratization in Asia, in the Cold War era democratization always took a back seat to economic development, regional institution-building, and military security. South Korea, Taiwan, Thailand, Singapore, and Indonesia, among others, emphasized security and economic development and ignored Washington's exhortations to democracy, or to greater democracy, when they felt their national interests dictated otherwise. For instance, when Park Chung Hee of South Korea launched his coup against the weak and despised but democratic government of his predecessor, President Kennedy ordered him back to the barracks, but Park ignored Kennedy.

The Northeast and Southeast Asian path from impoverished, chaotic weakness to socialist authoritarian unity to prosperous, secure, market-oriented economies with a demanding middle class that forces the political elite toward industrial democracy has worked well. Most Northeast and Southeast Asian elites see this path as developmental, and for the most part, they see China, rightly or wrongly, as following a similar path. They are all proud of their democracies, but they disagree profoundly with the Manichean view common in Washington that Leninist systems like China and democratic systems like their own are on opposite sides of an unbridgeable chasm that divides good from evil and can be crossed only by the baptism of a plunge into political revolution. Any senior policymaker in Asia today can remember when Taiwan was a great deal more Leninist than China is today, and most are conscious that most of Asia's successful democracies evolved from authoritarian socialist beginnings. With few exceptions (such as the DPP leadership in Taiwan and parts of the Philippine political spectrum), their developmental view of the differences between China and themselves leads them to be quite fearful of the risk that Washington might turn rhetoric into policy and attempt to pressure China counterproductively into premature democratization. The pressure might, in their view, provoke a reaction that would ultimately retard democratization. It might, in their view, provoke gratuitous international conflict; the precedent of Iraq worries them. Successful pressure for premature democratization might, in their view, leave China in the condition of parlous stagnation that has been the fate of the Philippines and until recently of India; that would return Asia to the evils of the 20th century political vacuum in China.

America's successful Asian partners are conscious that if the current administration's democratic aid criteria for the Millennium Challenge Account had been applied to them, the Asian miracle would never have been funded.[11] South Korea, Taiwan, Indonesia, and Thailand would have been ineligible for support that made a life-and-death difference to each of them. Taiwan, a partially socialist economy with a repressive Leninist polity considerably worse than that of today's China through the early 1980s, was the worst of the bunch; it would certainly have been excluded from aid and might well have collapsed and been taken over by Maoist China. Japan would have been isolated in Asia, hence vulnerable and much more divided internally, as well as more likely to accept an Asian version of Finlandization. The outcome of the Cold War in Asia could have been disastrously different.

The case for treating democracy as a prerequisite of aid rests on the theory that democracies are better at economic development than non-democracies. This conclusion is reached by comparing the economic growth of democracies with that of non-democracies; the latter category lumps together empires, several categories of individual dic-

---

[11] For the case that democracy should be a prerequisite of aid, see Joseph T. Siegle, Michael M. Weinstein, and Morton H. Halperin, "Why Democracies Excel," *Foreign Affairs*, September/October 2004. Siegle, Weinstein, and Halperin acknowledge that the key Asian countries constitute exceptions to their argument that democratic countries perform better economically.

tatorships, single-party states, warring African tribal systems, Asian developmental authoritarian regimes, and much else. The outcome of the analysis is determined by its inappropriate lumping of all non-democratic regimes into a single category. That outcome, not surprisingly, is that democracies outperform, but the Asian developmental authoritarian systems are exceptions. If the analysis had been structured differently, comparing the economic growth of developmental authoritarian regimes with all others, the outcome would have been even more striking, and we would have learned the lesson that aid should go only to developmental authoritarian regimes. Asian leaders generally do not go through the statistics, but they know that the American conclusions conflict radically with their own experience and that the current American policy conclusion, institutionalized in the Millennium Challenge Corporation, would likely, if it had been implemented in 1960, have led to U.S. loss of the Cold War in Asia.

Today, China is following in Africa the policies that were successful for the United States in East Asia. The United States, which has in the meantime turned away from its own successful policies, has orchestrated a storm of criticism of China for being an unprincipled supporter of dictators. The Chinese respond that they are just trying to spread to Africa the good fortune that fellow Asians have experienced and express concern that the Americans are trying to impose policies that consistently failed when they were tried in Asia. They argue that successful democracy and successful reduction of corruption have almost always come after a considerable amount of economic development and that trying to reverse the natural path of evolution ensures failure. (Parenthetically, in systematic interviews in Beijing on this subject during March 2007, all the interviewees explicitly viewed successful democracy as a good outcome.) There are, in fact, some valid points on both sides of this debate, because aspects of the African situation may differ from the successful Asian miracles, but the U.S. public fury and overdone national-security concern directed at China for following the old, successful U.S. development approach betoken much more than rational calculation of what would help the Africans most.

Thus, ironically, for all these reasons, the developing world's most stable and vigorous democracies view with considerable anxiety and occasional dread the forceful democratic rhetoric coming out of Washington. Democratic ideals abound in Asia; Asian democracies are typically more stable and successful than their counterparts in Africa and Latin America; democratic countries in Asia consistently deliver improvements in standards of living that their Latin American and African counterparts fail to deliver; democratic movements are making real headway in parts of Central Asia; and various kinds of elections, transparency, and accountability arrangements are progressing even in China, but there is little support among U.S. allies in Asia for the notions that pre–middle-class democracies are better at economic development or are inherently more peaceful or that U.S. intervention would be helpful in promoting democracy. The combination of the Iraq war and assertions about democracy that are inconsistent with the Asian experience have considerably devalued the soft power that American democratic ideas yielded for the United States during the Cold War. Increasingly, the United States is seen to be exploiting democratic rhetoric in pursuit of cold geopolitical advantage, rather than promoting genuine concern for the freedom of Asian people.

Putting all these changes together, while the post–Cold War United States has far greater relative military power than it has had at any time in its history, its geopolitical leverage in east Asia has declined precipitously. The U.S. military relationship with Southeast Asia has improved—especially with the Philippines, Singapore, Indonesia, and Malaysia—and much of the national-security establishment equates that with an improvement in the overall relationship. But, as has happened with South Korea, where the U.S. military posture has also strengthened, the overall ability of the United States to obtain needed support in difficult situations has sharply deteriorated. That means neither that China has replaced the United States nor that it is likely to do so. But U.S. ties to South Korea and Southeast Asia have become far more ambivalent, and China has reversed its earlier belief that U.S. alliances in Northeast Asia serve Chinese interests by stabilizing Asia. The principal Asian countries, including core American ally Japan, have combined to ensure that they will for the first time have their own regional institutions that exclude the United States. Confidence in the competence and good faith of the IMF and the U.S. Treasury to help emerging Asian countries manage crises has attenuated significantly since the Asian crisis.

The United States can reasonably hope that gains with India will eventually offset losses with South Korea and Southeast Asia. Certainly, having warm ties with India and having a dynamic Indian economy are a tremendous improvement over India's old links to the Soviet Union and advocacy of socialist, protectionist economics. The improvement of the living standards of about one billion people, the addition of a major new source of demand growth for the world economy, and the reduction of suspicions between the two great democracies are unquestionably valuable achievements. But whether the new ties will provide the United States with either economic or diplomatic leverage on major issues remains more a hope than an assurance. India's international economic policies are improving, but unlike ASEAN's and China's, they remain a drag on global negotiations over free trade, free investment, and issues such as genetically modified crops. Indian geopolitical ambitions remain a throwback to the early 20th century. India has welcomed diplomatic warmth and practical concessions from the United States but has as yet reciprocated little in concrete support; in the meantime, it has warmed its ties with China, occasionally hinting to Beijing that it can help contain U.S. power in Asia. It has decided to hold joint military exercises with China, and it has become an observer in the SCO.[12]

More broadly, the U.S. strategy of giving priority to economic and social development, along with military protection, that worked such wonders for U.S. policy in Western Europe, Northeast Asia, and Southeast Asia has not been attempted in Central Asia, and the predominantly military strategy has so far not yielded results comparable

---

[12] For a fulsome view of the India-U.S. relationship by the ambassador who implemented the U.S. rapprochement with India, see Robert D. Blackwill, op. cit. Blackwill sees no ambivalence in India's relations with the United States and China, promotes the sale of high-tech weapons to India, thinks that India's plans for four aircraft carriers (heavily China-directed, according to him, and pressing into the South China Sea) are a good thing even though India faces no substantial sea challenges, and is sure that if China builds an airfield in Tibet, it must be directed against India. Blackwill's views typify the reality of the heavy anti-China thrust of many recent U.S. policy developments.

to those of its predecessor. It is in fact difficult even to imagine that it has a chance of achieving such results. The implications of the U.S. shift from a balanced economic/military strategy to a predominantly military strategy are very strong in Southeast Asia, where they move ASEAN from a quasi-allied role to something approaching equidistance between the United States and China, but they are overwhelming in Central Asia. With such a strategy, the United States has virtually no chance of "winning" there, in any of a range of reasonable definitions of that term, and it has little chance of stabilizing the region in any foreseeable period of time. A military-focused strategy creates a vacuum in which Soviet military power, Iranian theological influence, and, above all, Chinese economic attraction will have relatively free rein for the indefinite future. This is exactly what would have happened if the United States had abandoned vigorous nation-building efforts in Indonesia in 1967 and decided to rely exclusively on the military.

In short, some principal Cold War institutions persist, and images and assumptions from that era persist. But they persist in truncated form and they play very different roles in a setting drastically different from the Cold War era. While the fundamental U.S. interests— namely, security, prosperity, and democracy—are eternal, the priorities among them are radically different from those in the Cold War era, and the consequences are radically different. While the U.S. military may be the same military, its role is totally different once the economic, nation-building, and regional institution-building counterparts have withered. The U.S.-Japan military alliance and the U.S.-China political-economic bicondominium are increasingly in tension—gratuitous tension because it was not necessary to overtly target the U.S.-Japan alliance against China, to bring Taiwan under its scope, or to abandon a half-century of efforts to ensure Japanese-Chinese amity. The U.S. alliances with Japan and South Korea are in potentially fatal tension. The U.S.-Japan alliance was once the solution to the problem of Sino-Japanese rivalry but now is an accelerator of the problem. The vast national-security literature that has arisen about the threat of Chinese penetration of Africa and Latin America is almost completely a legacy of Cold War images of an aggressive Soviet Union, completely disconnected from the current reality that China is not seeking to export its political model and is not seeking foreign bases or military allies. U.S. assumptions about the long-run purpose and durability of its bases and alliance with Japan are in tension with the assumptions held by the principal Japanese supporters of rearmament and of a focus on China. All this means that, while the direction of change is difficult to forecast confidently, fundamental change has already happened and far more is likely.

The nature and direction of change could be critically affected by unpredictable events. U.S. or Japanese elections could alter priorities in either country. Military conflict over North Korea, Taiwan, or some sudden Central Asian event could shift or consolidate alignments very quickly. The outcome of the distant war in Iraq could reinforce U.S. confidence or create a durable disillusionment with military activism. Either China or India could suffer reversals that would affect domestic cohesion and lead to sharply different foreign policies.

The remaining Cold War institutions increasingly resemble stretched rubber bands, but we can't discern precisely how tightly each is stretched. Reasonable people can disagree on how tightly the bands are stretched or how important each is. And we do not yet know which of the rubber bands will be tweaked by events or the order in which they will be tweaked.

Because it is not possible to confidently predict exactly how these rubber bands will relax their tension, we have to resort to alternative scenarios, the subject of the next chapter. Before I launch into scenarios, however, it is important to recall the enormous momentum that foreign-policy doctrines and institutions have, even when they are obsolescent. The No Entangling Alliances doctrine of George Washington's farewell address ended only after the expensive lessons delivered by two world wars. The canonical version of the Truman Doctrine ended only with the painful experience of Vietnam.

The power of great foreign policies derives from powerful ideas, powerful institutions, and powerful lobbies. The past two presidents of the United States, and three of the last four, came to office with Cold War images and policy proposals that had to be quickly revised. Both the liberal and conservative wings in Congress (which can be appropriately represented by their respective leaders, Rep. Nancy Pelosi, Democrat from California, and former Rep. Tom DeLay, Republican from Texas) continue to advocate such views, and there is a strong move in parts of the Congress to take China policy away from the White House. Most of the U.S. media reports on Asia, conservative and liberal alike, align more with Cold War images than with the realities analyzed in this chapter. As one would expect, institutional and lobbying momentum is also enormously strong. For a decade, the U.S. Department of Defense has been making an enormous effort to be prepared to fight, more efficiently, more swiftly, and with fewer casualties, the kind of war that it would have had to fight during the Cold War—and it has accomplished that task with great success but at great cost to its ability to wage the kinds of wars and peacekeeping that have actually been its task for the entire generation since the Soviet Union collapsed. China has become a proxy for the old Soviet Union, and the China threat becomes particularly vivid each autumn when budgets are being decided. If the nation were to decide that the United States does not in fact face a serious risk of all-out war with China, the new high-tech ships and planes would be unnecessary, and the defense budget could decline by about 20 percent. That evinces a $100+ billion lobby for the Cold War view of Asia. The U.S. union movement and a broad range of trailing-edge businesses (textiles, furniture, various kinds of manufacturing, etc.) unite in order to promote Cold War images and policies as a way to inhibit economic competition from China; they are, however, offset by America's biggest and most successful companies, most of whom profit from relations with China. The Taiwan lobby, which is the second most powerful foreign lobby operating in the United States, is just one of several other powerful lobbies pushing in the same direction.[13] All of this is perfectly normal at the end of any foreign-policy

---

[13] To take a non-defense case, note the heat that was generated over the China National Offshore Oil Corporation's (CNOOC's) 2005 attempt to buy control of Unocal. This was presented—frantically—in Congress and the U.S. press as if it raised great national-security issues, even though Unocal controls only 1 percent of U.S. oil and China was willing to commit in advance that the Unocal oil would stay in the United States. (In any case, it was hard to imagine how, in the event of a crisis, China would exercise real control of oil located in California.) The real issue was whether a U.S. company would have to pay several billion dollars more than its earlier bid to match the Chinese offer; it was cheaper to fund a lobbying and media campaign. Analysts of all stripes who look at the drivers of China

era, and that is why most foreign policy "doctrines" end with the country hitting some kind of wall.

Beyond specific interest-group pressures, U.S. foreign policy toward Asia is often affected for substantial periods by a kind of hysteria. In the mid-1970s, after the Vietnam War, much of the American public, indeed much of the highly educated and politically active American public, became convinced that all small, authoritarian countries must be like Vietnam. The result, a Carter campaign promise to withdraw U.S. troops from South Korea, would have been catastrophic both for peace and for human rights if it had been implemented. Implementation actually began before some new intelligence estimates provided an excuse for discontinuance. Any thoughtful analysis of the countries involved would have led immediately to the conclusion that the withdrawal was a terrible idea, but lack of knowledge plus post-Vietnam fear plus populist moralism and the demagogic pressures of a political campaign almost overwhelmed a very fundamental national interest.

In a more direct parallel with today, during the 1980s, rapid Japanese economic growth and the penetration of Japanese competition into complacent U.S. industries such as cars and steel led to a wave of hysterical concern that the United States would not be able to keep up with Japan. After all, Japan had lower wages, was more efficient, and had better industrial relations, higher company morale (those inspiring corporate songs to sing each morning), and special techniques like quality circles, industrial policy, the industrial convoy system, and the main

---

policy emphasize the important and rising role of lobbies and political contributions. See, for instance, Philip C. Saunders (a pro-Taiwan analyst at the Institute for National Security Studies of the U.S. National Defense University), "Long-Term Trends in China-Taiwan Relations: Implications for U.S. Policy," *Asian Survey*, Vol. 45, No. 6, November/December 2005: "Some members of Congress have also found support for Taiwan to be a useful fundraising tool, despite the potential negative impact on relations with China and cross-strait stability. The role of domestic politics has become particularly important on issues such as arms sales, which affect U.S. domestic economic interests. Domestic politics also affects U.S. declaratory policy on Taiwan, which frequently appears to be aimed at domestic constituencies rather than an international audience. This introduces an element of instability into U.S. policy because short-term political incentives can undermine longer-term interests" (p. 986).

bank system that made Japan invulnerable to competition and gave Japan superiority over the United States. Japanese imitations undercut American brands. Japan kept its currency undervalued and its interest rates low, and it had a 30 percent savings rate, all of which gave Japanese companies huge advantages that hapless Americans seemingly could never compete with.

As the United States had to close inefficient steel mills, and as the Japanese bought up Rockefeller Center, the Pebble Beach country club, Los Angeles hotels, and seemingly all the nice homes in Hawaii, U.S. companies and unions demanded protection, and pundits forecast the Japanese taking over everything. By the late 1980s, the Tokyo stock market had capitalization equal to 47 percent of all world stock markets combined, and the land under the emperor's palace was worth as much as all of California. Clearly, the Japanese were supermen and the United States could not compete.

Within a few years, it became clear that Japanese industrial subsidies to certain companies and sectors were now doing more harm than good to Japan; that as Japan's economy became more prosperous, Japanese wages rose and the low-wage advantage largely disappeared; that Japanese protectionism damaged the competitiveness of Japanese industry; that the only highly competitive sectors in Japan were cars, consumer electronics, and video games; that manipulated banks invariably headed for insolvency; that artificially inflated capital markets were doomed to catastrophic collapse; that the main bank and convoy systems just dragged the good companies down along with the bad; and that the huge, terrifying wave of Japanese investment in the United States amounted to only a small fraction of British or even Dutch investment. Gigantic industrial conglomerates fed by governmentally guided bank loans could not compete with more agile, more innovative U.S. firms funded by competitive markets. Japanese companies that had used cheap funding to outbid U.S. companies had helped America twice—first by paying Americans too much, and second by having to sell their acquisitions back at fire-sale prices. By 1991, the hysteria of the 1980s seemed silly and just disappeared from conversation.

Japanese success was the most critical factor in the U.S. victory in the Cold War in Asia. Japanese prosperity provided enlarged markets and stimulation, benefiting the whole world economy. Japanese success gave U.S. consumers cheaper socks, better cars, cooler stereo sound, and a better choice of small cars during periods of high gasoline prices. It goaded bloated industries into producing better cars and better steel at lower prices. These were the principal consequences of Japanese success. When the Japanese economy slowed, it was bad for the entire world, and the U.S. government pleaded with the Japanese government to stimulate its economy into greater dynamism. But to read the popular press, congressional debate, and much of the relatively scholarly literature of the 1980s, one would have thought that Japanese success threatened both U.S. power and the American way of life. America was fortunate that national-security concerns had mobilized and empowered the executive branch of government to constrain congressional protectionism and occasionally even to try to calm popular fears.

Less than a decade after the hysteria over Japan ended, the hysteria over China began. A cheap currency was giving China unfair advantages. Government-directed loans were giving Chinese companies unfair trade advantages. Cheap loans were giving Chinese companies an unfair advantage in buying up U.S. industry, while Chinese restrictions prohibited U.S. investment from most sectors in China.[14]

---

[14] There is a vast literature on each of these points, but the one about Chinese restrictions on foreign direct investment deserves a footnote both because it is more esoteric and because of the point it can illustrate. See U.S. Senator Charles Schumer, "China's One-Way Street on Foreign Direct Investment and Market Access," August 18, 2005, available at http://www.senate.gov/~schumer/SchumerWebsite/pressroom/record_print.cfm?id=260470. The report leads with the sentence, "The Chinese government does not allow any foreign company to own a majority stake in almost any domestic Chinese enterprise." This is the exact opposite of the truth, as is much of the rest of the report; foreign companies have bought tens of thousands of Chinese companies and can do so in the majority of sectors. China is much more open to such purchases than Japan or most developing countries. This is not a subject where opinions are divided; it is a factual matter that no expert would dispute. It would be virtually impossible to get away with issuing such a report about Britain or Germany, because the level of media and public knowledge of the subject would imply immediate recognition of the falsehood, and prevailing standards would force immediate retraction. But the levels of knowledge and the standards are completely different on Asian subjects. In leading newspapers and magazines, on domestic subjects, the slightest error in, for instance, an executive's title warrants a retraction. On Asian subjects, written complaints about serious, substantive errors frequently elicit no response. Readers who want historical examples from the most reputable publications might consult *The New York Times* Week in Review photo

Cheap wages would allow China to take over all the manufacturing in the world. China and India were each graduating many times the number of engineers that the U.S. produced. Unfair Chinese competition was costing the United States millions of manufacturing jobs. Today, all one has to do is replace "Japan" with "China" in the political hysteria over Chinese government-related companies trying to buy into the U.S. market.

The reality, of course, was that if the Chinese currency had been completely freed, capital outflows might well have led its value to decline, any imaginable revaluation that occurred would not have yielded significant extra jobs for the United States, U.S. job losses were

---

essay on Hong Kong published in the Sunday edition exactly a year before the July 1, 1997, handover of Hong Kong, and a profile of Hong Kong Governor Chris Patten published in *The New Yorker* before the handover. Both contained pervasive, gross factual errors that no Asian college freshman could have gotten away with. See John Newhouse, "Tweaking the Dragon's Tail," *The New Yorker*, March 1993, pp. 89ff. For instance, Newhouse says that "of the Legislative Council's sixty members eighteen could be directly elected . . . (The other members are appointed)." That leaves 42 appointed members, which is 32 more than reality. Such errors pervade the article, all in ways derogatory to China, in the magazine known for the most meticulous editing in America. Both articles elicited numerous protests, including mine, but no retractions were published. More broadly, in the years before the 1997 handover, almost every major publication in the West published articles suggesting that an increasing brain drain was draining Hong Kong of talent and that huge numbers of Hong Kong residents were moving to Singapore. The truth was that the number of people emigrating was vastly outnumbered by the number immigrating, that the number emigrating steadily declined as the handover approached, and that only a handful of Hong Kong people emigrated to Singapore, while thousands of Singaporeans migrated to Hong Kong. The Singapore International School in Hong Kong had to be built to take care of the children of all the Singaporean immigrants to Hong Kong. The brain drain myth was propagated year after year, when the actual numbers were readily available, not because of any media conspiracy but simply because it was taken for granted that almost any negative assertion about China must be true. The parallel today is the almost universal assertion that the loss of several million U.S. manufacturing jobs is entirely due to Chinese competition. Any economist knows that much, probably most, of that decline is caused by rising productivity—for instance, the fact that the number of labor hours required to build a car has declined from 40 to 15. The impact of these distortions on public opinion is enormous. Suppose, for instance, that Senator Schumer and the leading newspapers all bombarded the Ohio public with the news that giant British corporations were taking over the best American retailers while prohibiting U.S. companies from investing in any sector in Britain. The anti-British reaction would be very strong, except that most of the public has enough knowledge of Britain to reject the allegation instantly.

mostly caused by productivity improvements rather than by China, U.S. unemployment was lower than what economists once thought frictional unemployment (the unemployment necessarily generated by changes in the structure of a growing economy) to be, government-directed banks were even more damaging to China than they had been to Japan, China was more open to U.S. investment than all but a handful of developing countries, Chinese manufacturing exports to the United States were only a few percentage points of total U.S. manufacturing, U.S. manufacturing output was steadily growing, only 10 percent of Chinese engineers could pass the minimum qualifications for any job at a multinational corporation, and the prospects for survival of many U.S. companies such as General Motors depended heavily on the large profits they were making in China. But such analysis rarely appeared in the media or in congressional debates.[15]

Much of the hysteria is paid for by the lobbying and media efforts of unions and of businesses in trailing-edge sectors. The hysteria gets far more intense over Asian issues because the public knows more about Europe and is more comfortable with nearby Latin America. Media hype can exaggerate far more on subjects about which most of the audience knows almost nothing. If Brazil or Spain were suddenly suc-

---

[15] That it fails to appear is not an accident, nor does it result from unavailable information. When the Chinese company Lenovo sought to buy IBM's laptop computer division, "Think," the Lou Dobbs show on CNN, called RAND for an expert to interview. Referred to me, CNN made an appointment to send a camera crew over in the afternoon. Just before lunch, Dobbs's assistant called me and said she wanted to do a "pre-interview." She asked me whether the purchase would transfer important technology to the Chinese and whether it carried important national-security risks. I replied that laptop-computer knowledge is a commodity, that the majority of laptops were already made in China, and that therefore there was no substantial national-security risk. She immediately said that they had found somebody else to do the interview and that the appointment with me was canceled. Dobbs subsequently interviewed Richard d'Amato, famous for his hostility to China, who confirmed that the deal involved major technology transfers and national-security risks. Subsequent review of the facts by very conservative U.S. officials, including some from the U.S. Department of Defense, confirmed that what Dobbs and D'Amato told millions of viewers was wrong. The deal was allowed to proceed. The subsequent effort by CNOOC to buy Unocal was derailed by a massive public-relations campaign paid for by corporate interests to convey the false premise that the deal would endanger U.S. energy security—even though, as noted earlier, Unocal carried less than 1 percent of U.S. oil and CNOOC had promised in advance to leave all of that in the United States.

cessful, the hysteria would not be nearly so great as that generated with reference to Japan or China. The combination of ignorance, residual racism, and free-spending lobbies is powerful.

The hysteria factor deserves attention because it could prove decisive at some point of delicate political balance. Normally, an executive branch with enormous expertise led by a powerful presidency, together with a strong political center in the U.S. Congress, keeps the hysteria from damaging the country. Asia policy has in fact been remarkably robust. Japan policy remained steady from Truman through Clinton, through Republicans and Democrats alike, including times of hysteria. China policy has remained remarkably stable from Nixon through the present. But there remains a residual risk that a polarizing Congress and a weakened presidency could come together and break the mold. If it did break, the whole process of globalization and peaceful Asian development could shatter.

The year 2005 was a delicate and dangerous year. The French and Dutch voted against the EU Constitution, basically as a protest against globalization. (The phantom danger to jobs of "the Polish plumber" was the symbol of French rejectionists.) The rise of populism in some Latin American countries, most notably Venezuela, along with the foreign-policy strains between the Bush administration and the larger Latin American states, doomed any hopes for large-scale multilateral trade liberalization with Latin America. In the United States, the year began just after Secretary of State Colin Powell's December 2004 declaration that U.S.-China relations were in better shape than ever before and steadily deteriorated into a period of China-bashing that resembled the worst period of Japan-bashing. The war in Iraq weakened the free-trade-oriented presidency and strengthened a more protectionist Congress, and then the November 2006 elections brought to power a new Congress with many key committees dominated by more-protectionist figures. The Doha round of trade talks seemed to be going nowhere. Throughout the world, the globalization process was at risk.

The degree of this risk is debatable, but it is higher now than it has been in the past. With Japan, protectionist lobbying was offset by the national-security requirement to support the U.S.-Japan alliance. For

China, national-security budget pressures and arms-industry lobbies reinforce protectionist lobbying instead of offsetting them.

The Need for an Attitude Transplant

Notwithstanding the constant battering of public opinion by the union lobbies, the fading business lobbies, the military preoccupations, and the ideological punditry of both the left and the right of the political spectrum, supplemented by sporadic bouts of hysteria, the underlying story of Asia has been and is extraordinarily positive for the United States. Japanese success and the Asian miracle did not destroy U.S. manufacturing and leave Americans unemployed. They made Americans richer and won the Asian Cold War for the United States. Toyota turned out to make better cars than Ford, but Microsoft turned out to make better software than NEC. That division of labor enriched everyone and gave Americans better cars and Japanese better software. Employment even in the car industry stayed high precisely because the United States adjusted and because Japanese companies needed to build factories in the United States to stay competitive.

Notwithstanding an entire generation of lobbyists' warnings about the loss of all U.S. manufacturing industry to Japan and China, U.S. manufacturing output continues to grow, and the United States is predominant on the commanding heights of the modern manufacturing economy: aircraft (Boeing), infrastructure construction (Caterpillar), pharmaceuticals, the highest-value specialty steels and petrochemicals, and so forth. America's overwhelming success, in contrast with France and Japan, results precisely from its willingness to adjust to the international market.

Likewise, the rises of India and China are achieving American goals. Notwithstanding a whole generation of warnings that, successively, Japanese, Chinese, and Indians were going to take away all American jobs, U.S. unemployment is presently at 4.5 percent, significantly lower than what economists once believed was the minimum frictional unemployment. The countries with high unemployment, such as France, are those that have followed the protectionist prescriptions of the protectionist lobbies and hysterical columnists.

From the Truman administration to the Bush administration, the core foreign-policy goal of the United States in Asia has been to promote stability. The stabilization of Japan through its economic miracle of 1955–1975 and the switch of China from a force promoting instability to one promoting stability in the interest of domestic economic development have ensured U.S. success in achieving that goal. China's joining and supporting the panoply of institutions that the United States set up after World War II is a victory that was simply beyond imagination a generation ago.

Likewise, Americans, along with most of the world, have long seen the reduction of poverty and its consequent human suffering as one of the noblest goals of mankind. The emergence of the majority of Chinese, Indians, and Southeast Asians from subhuman conditions of life to the greater health, longevity, education, and general dignity to which they can aspire today makes the achievements of this era among the greatest in human history. The average Chinese lived only to age 41 in 1953 but in 2005 could expect to live 72.7 years. For decades, Americans have said that they cared deeply about such things, but somehow such facts get lost in the rhetoric of the China (and India) threat. In the face of all these extraordinary benefits and achievements, it is remarkable that the United States and much of the West view these victories as dreaded threats. That distorted perspective is achieved through incessant lobbying and propaganda that can be put in perspective only by strong leadership at the highest level. The core of the U.S. and European intellectual and political and economic establishment understands the real history, but throughout the West, the voices of optimism and clarity are ironically much weaker than they were in the dark and threatening days of the Cold War.

CHAPTER NINE

Scenarios for the Future

The benign American world order conceived by Franklin Delano Roosevelt and Winston Churchill and launched by President Harry Truman in 1945 has been responsible for the unprecedented global peace and prosperity of the past 60 years. Despite its enormous contribution to humankind, this world order is likely to die in our lifetime.

—Kishore Mahbubani

The previous chapters described the major features of the Cold War period in Asia and the major features of the post–Cold War era. In the post–Cold War era, most of the images and institutions of the earlier era persist despite the disappearance of the Cold War itself. What might a post-post–Cold War Asia look like in 10 to 20 years?

When we attempt to peer that far into the future, we have no hope of predicting exactly what will happen. Our vision of the future is not like a laser beam, which could pinpoint one exact outcome; rather, it is like a wide-angle flashlight illuminating a range of different possibilities. Instead of trying to predict, I shall try to tell a few stories that span much of the range of possibilities. It isn't even possible to provide probabilities for the different scenarios. Which story/scenario eventuates will be decided by political leaders, and the central purpose of writing scenarios is to induce leaders to ponder which path they want their country or the world to travel. Such pondering may well change the probabilities. After relating some principal scenarios, we can examine a few surprises (less likely, but not impossible, outcomes or events) that widen the range still further.

One of the crucial decisions made in writing scenarios is the choice among all the hundreds of political, economic, and military trends about what the most important drivers and characteristics of future scenarios will be. If one gets it wrong, this is most likely where one will get it wrong, so these choices are crucial.

Based on the preceding analysis, the most important features of future scenarios should almost certainly be the relationships among the United States, Japan, and China. India is coming up in the world, but its economy is so much smaller and less open than those of the big three and it is geographically so far from Asia's center of geopolitical gravity (assuming Korea as the center of geopolitical gravity) that it is not going to be a primary determinant of Asia's architecture in the next two decades. Likewise, Russia is not one of the big players; its population and economy are too small, and the crucial area of Russia near the Asian center of geopolitical gravity is depopulated and further depopulating. The border conflict with China has been resolved, and the border conflict with Japan seems unlikely to become a major determinant of the regional architecture.

Other parts are, of course, important. India is important because it is big and increasingly dominates the subcontinent. Pakistan is important because it can implode or become a regional cancer from which proliferation and fundamentalist radicalism metastasize. Korea is important because it is right in the middle and because its division is an invitation to regional conflict. Taiwan is important for the same reason. Indonesia is important because it is huge and because it is the world's largest Islamic country. Vietnam is important because it is a moderately large, cohesive country with both a powerful military and one of the world's fastest-growing economies. But being important is different from being a dominant feature of the region's architecture. These important countries are important because what they do may affect relations among the cornerstones of the region's architecture, namely, Japan, China, and the United States. Events in these smaller or more peripheral but nonetheless important countries may—indeed, probably will—prove decisive, but what they will be decisive for is relationships among the big three.

This is already very different from the Cold War era, when the regional architecture was bipolar. The United States and the Soviet Union were the cornerstones, and everything else was important to the degree that it affected the Soviet-American relationship. Japan was important as a U.S. ally, China as a sometime ally, sometime enemy of the Soviet Union. Indonesia and Vietnam were important because their volatility seemed to threaten to change the Soviet-American balance. India was a quasi-ally of the Soviet Union, ASEAN a quasi-ally of the United States.

It is also different from the turn-of-the-century period, when the world seemed unipolar, with the United States dominant militarily, economically, and culturally. The United States remains the biggest in all three dimensions, but it squandered its dominance. The more-distant relationships with South Korea and Southeast Asia, the deliberate decision by the military to target China disproportionately to any threat, and getting bogged down in Iraq and other Middle Eastern conflicts have made the difference between being dominant and being big. (The newly warmer U.S. relationship with India is precisely balanced by India's newly warmer relationship with China.) Now things are much, much more complicated than they were in either the Cold War or the immediate post–Cold War period. The unipolar moment of U.S. dominance was an evanescent footnote of the turn of the 21st century.

Scenario 1: Business as Usual

What many national-security planners in all three of the big powers seem to plan for is a scenario in which relationships among them remain fairly similar to what they recently have been, with details and relative weights changing quite gradually.

In this scenario, the Cold War institutions, especially the U.S. alliances with Japan, Australia, and South Korea and the quasi-alliance arrangements with Singapore and the Philippines, remain in place. The central lines of tension are between the advanced democracies and the residual major communist state, China. Several structural changes distinguish the post–Cold War structure from the Cold War structure. One, which future historians may see as the most important, is the ramping up of the U.S.-Japan alliance, with an expanded Japanese military role and an increasing focus on China. More obviously, in this scenario, the Soviet Union is gone as a major antagonist and is replaced by a Russia that is neither a big antagonist nor a substantial ally of either the United States or China. It is mainly influential in Central Asia, mainly focused on keeping itself together and keeping China, the United States, and Islamic fundamentalism from dominating its old haunts in Central Asia. India, the other substantial Asian power, attempts to remain friendly with all significant powers while gradually increasing its domination of South Asia and its naval expansion into Middle Eastern, Southeast Asian, African, and Chinese waters.

Globalization continues, however gradually, and that gives the greatest advantages to the United States and China. India, Vietnam, and Southeast Asia continue to grow relatively rapidly as they continue to gradually open themselves; among this group, the really big winner is Vietnam, whose combination of rapid growth and diplomatic moderation gives it a steadily rising role within ASEAN. This scenario assumes that China continues to reform rapidly enough to stay ahead of the risks created by financial-sector weakness, urbanization, inequality, unemployment, and, after 2015, a graying society. It assumes that India's elite is able to overcome opposition to further reform by reactionary groups (including the Communist Party) and to avoid dangerous polarization between the parts of the country that are prepared to benefit from globalization and those that are not.

Our earlier findings suggest that there are critical sources of instability in this scenario. One is that tensions between South Korea, on one hand, and Japan and the increasingly anti-China thrust of the U.S.-Japan alliance, on the other, could lead to South Korea's departure from the alliance with the United States and the ejection of U.S. troops. That could indeed happen, but it would not change the basic structure of the scenario.

Another problem with this scenario is the pressure for a shift to a more positive relationship with China created by the shifting balance of U.S. practical interests. We have seen how the China policies of the Reagan, Clinton, and George W. Bush administrations all underwent sharp alteration between the beginnings of those administrations and the second year, due to presidential recognition of the need to do important business with China and the ability to do that business successfully. Shared interests in the North Korea problem, global terrorism, regional crime, regional drug trafficking, regional human trafficking, regional and global trade liberalization, regional and global investment liberalization, genetically modified crops, and a number of other problems lead both sides toward a closer and more stable relationship. As the volume of U.S.-Chinese business increases, the pressure from U.S. business for a stable relationship will rise, and a China lobby will gradually emerge to offset, at least partially, the Taiwan lobby; the Taiwan lobby, meanwhile, is increasingly divided, reflecting the growing division in Taiwan domestic politics over relations with the mainland.

In the face of these pressures, what keeps the U.S.-Japan alliance and the other core aspects of the post–Cold War structure viable? Ideological affinity, the momentum of old institutions, and powerful lobbying networks certainly provide some glue. But the latter two are features of all important policies; momentum explains momentum only until the time that it doesn't—the time when some events cause a fundamental reconsideration.

The role of ideological affinity is more complicated. Chinese foreign policy once was very ideological; Mao wanted to promote communism in neighbors such as Thailand and even in distant countries such as Tanzania and the United States. Today, ideological motivations in Chinese foreign policy are marginal. China is not attempting to sell communism to any other country; its leaders do have some fear that color revolutions in Central Asia might have some contagious effect on China, and Jiang Zemin did make the occasional random visit to places such as Havana. But the thrust of Chinese foreign policy is better symbolized by the facts that Beijing is much more comfortable with Seoul than with Pyongyang and that it strongly opposed the Maoist guerrillas in Nepal for fomenting instability.[1]

Ideology plays a much more substantial role in U.S. foreign policy, as indicated, for instance, by President George W. Bush's 2005 State of the Union address, which emphasized an intent to spread democracy everywhere. Wilsonian proselytization of democracy has always appealed to significant segments of the U.S. foreign-policy elite, and certain aspects of that proselytization, with very practical consequences, have workable consensus support in the United States— for instance, U.S. support of color revolutions, U.S. support of pro-democracy non-governmental organizations (NGOs) around the world, and recently, the tying of the Millennium Challenge aid program to measures of democratization. But historically, the promulgation of democracy has rarely been decisive in structuring U.S. relations with the rest of the world; put another way, the lack of democracy has rarely by itself been a cause of enmity with the United States unless it was combined with egregious abuses of other kinds. (Saddam Hussein's Iraq and early 1990s Serbs had other issues. A series of Tiananmen Square–type events would put China in that category, but that is not the current trend.) Moreover, throughout much of U.S. history, the U.S. desire to promote democracy has been magnified by the fact that the world's democracies as a group were experiencing a confrontation with an ideologically aggressive opposing coalition—monarchists, fascists, communists. For the first time in more than a century, no opposing ideology other than jihadist Islamism is trying to defeat the democracies as a group. Jihadist Islamism has different consequences; it does not specifically threaten democracies, but rather unites almost all countries, including most Muslim countries and non-democratic countries such as China, against the common terrorist threat. That reduces the incentive for ideologically based policies in the United States. Nevertheless, the United States currently does have a strong proselytizing thrust in its foreign policy, and to the extent that this thrust continues,

---

[1] Until 2005, China supported Nepal's king against the Maoists on grounds of stability. Relatively late in the day, when it became clear that the king could not in fact provide stability, it joined India and others in supporting the democratic movement against him.

it supports the combination of a strong alliance with Japan, warmth toward India, and a negative posture toward China.

That leaves the Taiwan problem, the arms lobby, and the recurrent U.S. hysteria about Asia that affected Americans' images of Japan in the 1980s and affects their images of China today. Each of these is potentially significant, but the core is the Taiwan problem. If the Taiwan problem were somehow resolved, the arms lobby would lose much of its argument, and the hysteria would lose much of its funding. There is no other comparable issue. This business-as-usual scenario therefore rests, like a huge inverted pyramid, on the Taiwan issue. Resolve that issue, and the balance in the U.S.-Japan-China triangle will start evolving very rapidly. However, there is no reason at the moment to believe that the Taiwan issue is headed toward early resolution, so these considerations do not reduce the plausibility of the scenario.

There is a third problem with the indefinite continuation of this scenario. Suppose the Taiwan problem does not get resolved and the Taiwan Strait arms race therefore continues. As China continues to acquire more missiles, more modern ships, and more modern planes, the time available for the U.S. military to rescue Taiwan from a hypothetical war becomes shorter and shorter. The result has been closer and closer coordination between U.S. military plans and Taiwan military plans, together with ever more urgent U.S. efforts to get soldiers and equipment where they can be delivered quickly to Taiwan. This process can go on for a while with limited political consequences, but not indefinitely. At some point, successful defense of Taiwan will require effective integration of the U.S. and Taiwan militaries. Otherwise, the United States and Taiwan will have to concede defeat. Alternatively, if such integration exceeds a certain threshold, such as stationing U.S. troops in Taiwan or actively supporting a Japan-Taiwan quasi-alliance, China will have to react or concede defeat. In either case, the post–Cold War business-as-usual scenario collapses.

Put another way, the business-as-usual scenario is potentially destabilized by four paradoxes. U.S.-China political-economic relations are becoming deeper and deeper, and under Bush and Hu the politics of the Taiwan problem seems to be under much better control, but the military dynamics of the Taiwan Strait arms race are heading toward a crisis. The United States is becoming ever more militarily dependent on Japan but ever more economically and geopolitically allied with China. Possibly the greatest era of peaceful prosperity in world history has been built on the foundation of post–World War II globalization, and the United States has been the greatest beneficiary of that globalization, but the United States and much of the world seem weary of globalization and at risk of turning against it. U.S. economic, military, and cultural power have reached a pinnacle, but U.S. influence in Asia has been declining sharply. All of these are critical reasons why we must examine other potential paths into the future.

Scenario 2: Cold War II

Two kinds of tensions in the business-as-usual scenario generate the possibility that business as usual would break down. These tensions result in two obvious alternative scenarios, a renewed Cold War and a reversal of alliances.

In the Cold War II scenario, the United States elects a leadership with strong ideological views—either of the right-wing anti-communist variety or the left-wing human-rights strain. (In contrast, on China issues, all recent U.S. presidents, Republican and Democrat alike, have adopted centrist, managerial views.) U.S. foreign policy continues to be dominated by military considerations and military means. The United States acquires more bases in Central Asia.

In Japan, right-wing leaders and anti-Chinese views continue to strengthen. The U.S.-Japan alliance focuses ever more heavily on Taiwan. Japanese national-security leaders come increasingly from the school that asserts an independent Taiwan as a vital national-security interest. Japanese military officers become far more numerous and conspicuous in Taiwan than they are today, and they become deeply involved in joint planning and joint military exercises with Taiwan's military.

Chinese leaders become divided about politics, divided about the economy, and divided about foreign policy, with the result that it is impossible to move forward decisively in any area. Failure to take decisive action on banking and government budget problems slows the economy, and popular discontent rises. It becomes impossible for any leader to push hard for political liberalization, so the leadership response to rising discontent and unrest becomes increasingly repressive. From abroad, Beijing seems an increasingly distasteful partner. From Taiwan, the prospect of moving closer to the mainland also becomes very distasteful. In response to Taiwanese disdain, Beijing reverts back to its pre-2005 strategy of relying primarily on threats to corral Taiwan.

The Chinese military buildup opposite Taiwan reaches a level at which a sudden strike against Taiwan would be very difficult for the United States to stop without forces already in place in Taiwan. The United States responds by integrating its forces increasingly with Taiwan's forces. It also begins issuing statements that if China attacks Taiwan, all of China will be considered a target for military retaliation. Beijing responds with a warning that, in that case, U.S. cities would become fair targets for Chinese nuclear weapons.

In this atmosphere, cooperation on issues such as North Korea and intelligence against terrorists gradually breaks down. The United States puts more and more restrictions on Chinese trade and investment, and American companies, fearful of being caught by sanctions or even a military clash, increasingly forgo business in China. Incentives for cooperation decline. Sources of tensions rise. Within a decade, the United States, China, and Taiwan are engaged in a full Cold War, with South Korea (for anti-Japanese reasons), Southeast Asia, and Central Asia (for largely economic reasons) largely leaning toward China and India largely leaning toward the United States.

Scenario 3: Reversal of Partnerships

In this, the most radical of the scenarios posited here, suppose that Japanese politics continues its rightward trend. The next prime minister and his successors not only visit the Yasukuni Shrine and endorse revisionist textbooks, they also explicitly praise the museum of the Yasukuni Shrine and its view of World War II as a heroic crusade to liberate Asia from European and American colonialism.

Meanwhile, U.S. relations with China continue to develop positively both on major regional political issues and on global economic issues. More and more, the U.S. president needs China's support around the world. China refines its village-level elections and begins to hold elections in all towns, with clear indications that cities and provinces will follow shortly. The Communist Party starts to allow open factionalism, and top officials are increasingly chosen by competitive vote based on their policy views and factional membership. Repression of all kinds lessens, and the courts begin to act more competently and (gradually but steadily) with somewhat greater independence. China remains a long way from Western democracy, but the trend toward something resembling Mexico's old PRI or Japan's LDP becomes unmistakable, softening U.S. and European suspicions.

A new generation of U.S. foreign-policy and national-security officials has less-fervent Cold War convictions and becomes accustomed to dealing positively with its Chinese counterparts. South Korea, Southeast Asia, and Australia become more outspoken in their insistence that they will oppose any war stimulated by a Taiwan bid for independence. The Chinese policy, begun in 2005, of seducing Taiwan with economic opportunities and political invitations, rather than just threatening it, makes increasing inroads; a decisive repudiation of the DPP in the 2008 elections destroys the illusion (always an illusion, but in some quarters a strong one) that Taiwan's people will support provocative independence policies that risk war. The new Taiwan government removes most restrictions on investment in the mainland, the economy booms, and prosperity is enhanced by the fact that Taiwan companies and investors no longer need to stash their money in the Cayman Islands to circumvent the old restrictions.

Hence the rationale for a more and more hostile U.S. military posture weakens. The China lobby grows and the Taiwan lobby remains split between DPP and Guomindang factions, but the United States remains politically committed to the defense of Taiwan against any unprovoked attack.[2]

Within Taiwan, the DPP loses the 2008 election to a candidate from a unified blue movement. There remains no substantial interest in unification, especially early unification, with the mainland, but the push toward independence subsides.

The arms race continues, and the U.S. president's military advisors warn him that China will soon have the ability to launch a stunning first blow, followed by a rapid amphibious attack. Unless the U.S. military has a substantial presence in Taiwan itself, it will be unable to get to Taiwan fast enough to avert defeat. In order to carry out its assigned mission, it absolutely must base substantial forces in Taiwan. The president's political advisors warn that this would be a return to the explicit U.S.-Taiwan alliance that the U.S. promised to end in 1979 and that China would have to react in the strongest fashion. Anyway, they say, now that China has returned to its pre-1996 relaxed view of the timing of unification, there is no sign at all that China would launch an unprovoked invasion. The military advisors express a more ominous view of China's intentions but more persuasively insist that intentions are beside the point. If the president tasks them to defend Taiwan, he must ensure that they have the capability to do so; China's capabilities, not its intentions, must, they argue, be the principal weight in the calculation. Without an integrated military alliance, they cannot do what the president wants.

The president orders his military advisors to prepare detailed plans for the alliance they require and simultaneously tells his political advisors to prepare a plan for negotiations.

Some weeks later, the president calls in Taiwan's top unofficial official in the United States and simultaneously has the head of the American Institute in Taiwan (AIT) brief Taiwan's president. The message for Taiwan is that the United States will remain committed to defending Taiwan against any unprovoked invasion, but the arms

---

[2] The United States has no legal obligation to defend Taiwan, and the Taiwan Relations Act requires only the sale of adequate arms, but the sense of political obligation is pervasive and under this scenario remains so.

race is reaching a dangerous point, and that neither China nor Taiwan wants to provoke or attack the other, but the current situation cannot continue. Either it is going to become explosive or some deal is going to have to be made. Since China's power is rising and its diplomatic support among its neighbors continues to rise, Taiwan now has the greatest bargaining power it will ever have. The U.S. president says that if Taiwan wants continued support from the United States, it must now make a good faith effort to reach a sustainable deal with the mainland. He says that he wants a detailed list of every assurance Taiwan would need in order to make a permanent deal with the mainland.

The Taiwan leadership makes a point of appearing very upset, but it grasps the reality of the strategic balance, and it needs U.S. support. From South Korea to Singapore to Australia, with only Japan (and possibly the Philippines) as an exception, the neighbors have made it clear that they will not support Taiwan independence; they will not support a Chinese invasion, but they will not allow use of their facilities or waters for any war with China if Taiwan moves toward independence and provokes a conflict. The one-China policy has become by this time accepted by every country in the world except two tiny Central American countries, two tiny South Pacific countries, and two of the smaller African countries, all of which dilute the importance of their diplomacy by alternating recognition of Taipei and Beijing depending on who offers the biggest bribe that year. Taiwan's bargaining power is as great as it will ever be and will steadily be eroded, so it is time to make a deal—as long as its real autonomy is protected and as long as its president can defuse potentially violent reactions from the island's small but determined group of independence activists by telling them that the United States imposed the deal.

After he receives Taiwan's reply and deals as best he can with the congressional outcry over leaks that suggest some kind of untoward pressure on Taiwan, the U.S. president meets the Chinese president in connection with a United Nations conference. The U.S. president tells his Chinese counterpart that however much they would both like to avoid a crisis over Taiwan, one is coming. One way or another, big changes are coming. The Chinese president responds that his advisors have told him the same thing.

Both presidents also want to talk about Korea. The Korea problem has been a sporadic crisis since 1950. The nuclear issue has become greater and greater since the early 1990s. The six-party talks have sputtered on and off for more than a decade, but the situation has just gotten worse. The United States, hobbled by a decade of fighting in Iraq and by public disillusionment, is desperately concerned about Pyongyang's nuclear weapons but has no credible military options, particularly in the face of South Korea's determination to build bridges to the North rather than destabilize it. Now North Korea is headed into another famine. The drain on China is becoming worse. The pressure on Pyongyang to sell nuclear weapons to the highest bidder is becoming inexorable. As a neighbor of North Korea, China has a great deal more to lose from this situation than the United States has. The Chinese president says that his country and the United States have learned to cooperate on virtually the whole range of global issues. They are enriching each other. They are restraining nuclear proliferation together. They are liberalizing global trade and investment together. But their relations have for six decades been troubled by the divided-country problem. It is time to solve the problems of divided China and divided Korea before the Taiwan arms race and the North Korean famine and nuclear sales create unmanageable crises. The two presidents agree in principle that they have to make whatever hard decisions are necessary.

The U.S. president hands China's president a 20-page list of guarantees that Taiwan's president has demanded. If China will provide those guarantees through an international treaty, the United States will endorse the one-China concept unreservedly and will drastically reduce military sales to Taiwan. In this, he is aided by a movement in congressional elections away from the ideological polarization that characterized the beginning of the new century and back toward a more normal strong center. The Chinese president reads the list carefully and says that almost all of the items on it are just details of what China had already promised in September 1981. But, chuckling, he promises never to refer to the results as "one country, two systems." In addition to the detailed guarantees, he says, China will treat the Taiwan government as an equal government within one China. Both sides will change their flags to a common flag. The name People's Republic of

China will be eliminated. Both the mainland and Taiwan can hence-forth say they are part of "China" but can maintain their distinctive identities under names to be discussed later. China, he says firmly, will not accept an international treaty about a part of its domestic terri-tory but will make a declaration to the United Nations covering all the points. Moves toward further democratization of Hong Kong and a rigorous analysis of China's handling of its promises to Hong Kong will reassure all concerned that Beijing will keep those promises, even if sometimes in a restrictive, literal fashion.

In turn, the U.S. president promises to gradually curtail arms sales to Taiwan; under the Taiwan Relations Act, if the prospects for peace improve, he has the right to do this. He acknowledges that this will be tumultuous and difficult, but he has already spoken with key congres-sional leaders. He reminds the Chinese president that any breach of the agreement will cause an irreparable breakdown of Sino-American relations. The Chinese president says that, of course, he knows that, but there would be no reason for China to break an agreement that gives it what it has always wanted.

Turning to Korea, the two sides emphasize what they have long agreed: North Korea is incompetent and a danger to the region and to itself. Neither Beijing nor Seoul wants a disruptive unification, but Seoul wants unification and Beijing can live with unification as long as it does not risk war or a flood of refugees across China's Yalu border with North Korea. The United States wants unification even if it is dis-ruptive. Beijing agrees to gradually curtail all aid to North Korea and to require hard currency for all purchases as long as Seoul, helped as necessary by its allies, replaces that aid. This leaves North Korea com-pletely dependent on South Korea, which can gradually do a seduction and buy-out of it. China and the United States will jointly guarantee the security of South Korea and provide a declaration of non-aggression toward North Korea as long as it does not expand its nuclear weapons program or sell WMD.

The U.S. president raises the delicate issue of U.S. bases in Korea. China's president responds that China has long respected the stabil-ity that the U.S. military presence brings to Asia but in recent years has been very concerned that U.S. forces in Northeast Asia have been increasingly targeted at China. With the Taiwan and divided-Korea issues off the agenda, that is less of a concern, but China needs some assurances. After lengthy discussion, they agree on those assurances, including assurance that the U.S. forces in Korea will never be moved into what is now North Korea and that they will not be targeted at China, including Taiwan. China's president reminds the American president anxiously that he will have as difficult a time selling the U.S. bases in Korea to his colleagues as the U.S. president will have persuading pro-Taiwan factions in Congress that he is satisfying the requirements of the Taiwan Relations Act.

The U.S. Congress and public react with stunned incredulity when the president goes on national television to announce the agreement. Not since Nixon met Mao or since Reagan agreed with Gorbachev on the goal of eliminating nuclear weapons has an American president made such an audacious move. But the American public rallies around a president who acts decisively, and this, together with advance briefings of key members of Congress, enables the president to rally the center and defeat the wild opposition from the far right of the Republican Party and the far left of the Democratic Party.

The U.S. president prepares to fly to Japan to explain the deal to his Japanese allies. But Japan's right mobilizes against this. Since 1895, when Japan acquired Taiwan, and since 1905, when it conquered Korea, the Japanese right has felt some sense of ownership of those areas, expressed now in the conviction that an independent Taiwan and a divided Korea are essential buffers against China. Amid riots, the Japanese prime minister tells the U.S. president that, regrettably, this would not be a favorable time to visit Japan. Within a year, the United States finds itself complying with a Japanese request to remove its bases from Japan.

The United States and Japan do not become enemies, but relations remain frosty and suspicious. Southeast Asians and Koreans rejoice at the removal of the biggest threats to peace in their region, and as a result, U.S. relations with both groups improve to the best level since 1995. Chinese relations with both also improve; this is a win-win situation.

The geopolitical game evolves into a geoeconomic game. The success of the most-open economies, namely the United States, China, and Southeast Asia, worries Japan and Europe, which increasingly align with each other to block global Sino-American initiatives. India is clear that it wants to be on the winning economic side, so it increasingly aligns with the Sino-American bloc. Latin America, always protectionist and now disillusioned with the United States over immigration issues, increasingly aligns with Europe and Japan on global economic policy but is careful to ensure that it can sell its raw materials to the booming U.S. and Chinese economies. Russia, torn between the protectionist demands of an increasingly Latin American social structure and its total dependence on Chinese markets, remains ambivalent, not a swing vote but a player that is not sure which goal to run toward.

Scenario 4: U.S. Disengagement

The United States has never dealt with a world in which China, India, and Japan were simultaneously strong. Today, all three appear strong. The last vestige of the weaknesses that ensured conflict in the 20th century is the division of Korea; while South Korea is strong, the Korean nation is divided. In a world where all three big Asian countries are headed toward strength, it is not at all impossible that over time they will decide that U.S. bases are an anachronism. Historians of a generation from now would then look back and say that the Northeast Asian bases were a product of World War II, sustained by the Cold War but inevitably an anachronism in the 21st century.

In this scenario, by 2007, South Korean leaders may decide that the Taiwan Strait arms race is clearly headed toward some kind of turning point, and they may believe that U.S. forces in Korea are being restructured for use in a looming Taiwan contingency. At the same time, disagreements with the United States over policy toward North Korea may have escalated. The continued presence of the U.S. bases in South Korea would now become vulnerable—vulnerable to an incident in which Koreans are accidentally killed during practice maneuvers, vulnerable to a dispute over location or payments, vulnerable to an angry confrontation in which the United States demands an end to the Pyongyang regime while Seoul persists in subsidizing that regime—in short, vulnerable to any kind of event that could prod leaders to say, "This just isn't working."

Over a much longer period of time, the new dynamic that has been driving the U.S.-Japan-China triangle could go much further than anticipated. The United States continues to prod Japan to expand its military role, helping the Japanese right. The Japanese right becomes more assertive, revising more textbooks, visiting the Yasukuni Shrine more often and praising the Yushukan museum on each visit. China has more anti-Japanese riots. Both sides parade their rising naval power. More and more of the Japanese public becomes convinced that China is aggressive, uncivilized, and dangerous, so they give more and more support to the right wing. Japanese military budgets, not just missions, break through their hitherto low ceilings, and the world is amazed at how quickly Japanese power increases; the mobilization base that Japanese governments since the 1950s have created has always been underappreciated, and Japan's technological superiority over its Asian neighbors becomes manifest in military, as previously in civilian, areas. Japan's overwhelming naval superiority over China gives Japan confidence that ultimately it can deal with China.

Nationalist pride rises, and nationalist Japanese governments increasingly question their dependence on the United States. They assert themselves on China policy and on Korea policy. They increasingly emphasize regional organizations that exclude the United States or are not dependent on it. Washington is shocked that a nationalistic Japan is not behaving like the Asian version of Britain that they expected. Differences between the U.S. desire to unify Korea and this Japanese government's determination to keep it forever divided become the most prominent disagreement. More and more politicians support those who, like the Okinawans, want to get rid of U.S. bases or impose severe limits on them.

Meanwhile, in this scenario, the American public has been wearied by an endless, fruitless Iraq conflict, a rapidly escalating guerrilla war in Afghanistan, and a succession of other crises that drain morale and overstretch the government budget. Politicians from both parties begin to call for a retraction of overseas commitments. Questioning begins to spread about why the United States should bear the burden of defending a Japan whose leaders are saying that their fight against the United States in World War II was a valiant regional liberation and who seem to be pursuing a gratuitous conflict with China.

Eventually, without formally severing the alliance, Washington and Tokyo agree that the troublesome bases will be removed.

This leaves the United States without bases in Northeast Asia, but Southeast Asians are still anxiously seeking to retain an American role in protecting them from both China and Japan. The United States could retain bases or quasi-bases in Southeast Asia without incurring any great risks or great costs, so post-Iraq war-weariness would not greatly affect such a posture. In this scenario, the United States reverts to a balancing role between the big powers, rather like Britain's attitude toward continental Europe during the post-Metternich era, but possibly from a very weak position compared to its British analogue. For that matter, it is very similar to the role it played during the Cold War, before the post–Cold War policy of leaning with Japan against China set in. The United States would then see its primary task as ensuring that neither big Asian power had cause or ability to attack the other—rather than weighing in on the side of Japan and accelerating the conflict. Although still formally allied to Japan, the United States increasingly sees the Sino-Japanese conflict as obsolete nationalism and balances the two powers according to circumstance.

This scenario entails powerful nationalist antagonisms, with a very nationalistic Japan confronting very nationalistic Chinese and Koreans. Although the United States would attempt a balancing role, in fact, U.S. ability to moderate Sino-Japanese territorial-waters and seabed conflicts, as well as potential conflicts over Central Asia, would be minimal. This kind of Japan would push powerfully for Taiwan independence, and this kind of China would be likely to react in exceptionally brittle fashion. This could easily be the most dangerous scenario.

Scenario 5: Revitalized, Peaceful, Balanced Globalization

> In congressional testimony earlier this year, [U.S. Pacific Commander Admiral William] Fallon argued that the United States should seek to collaborate more with China and not presuppose that China would compete with the United States in a Cold War–like contest. "It's been our desire to work with China to find areas where we might move forward with constructive relationships," he said before the Senate Armed Services Committee in March.
>
> —*Chris Johnson*[3]

In the United States, the generation that accedes to power has defining experiences other than the Cold War. The new leaders look across the Pacific and see the U.S.-Japan alliance as a vital relationship, a bond sustained for more than a half-century and the most powerful foreign-policy tool the United States has in Asia. But the new leaders also put great value on the relationship with Korea and understand that Korea, as the region's crossroads and the site of three great-power wars in a century, must be respected as strategically vital and an important civilization. They see a need to respect the desire among Koreans for national unification and the need for some ultimate resolution to Korea's divisions, even if powerful factions in the Japanese national-security establishment are determined to keep Korea permanently divided and weak. And as they try to solve the region's numerous political problems (Korea, Taiwan, terror, drugs, human trafficking) and take advantage of the region's great opportunities, they recognize that China is an indispensable partner.

With this more-balanced perception, the United States continues to emphasize that the U.S.-Japan alliance is America's most important bond in Asia, but it also emphasizes that military ties with one country cannot be allowed to overwhelm other kinds of relationships and ties with other countries. The United States continually upgrades its forces in Japan, and it does not stand in the way of Japan's military normalization, but it ceases to demand faster Japanese rearmament and stops

---

[3] Chris Johnson, "Chinese Forces Invited to Observe Valiant Shield Exercise in Pacific," *Inside the Navy*, May 22, 2006.

counseling, implicitly as well as explicitly, the Japanese to amend their Constitution or to take actions inconsistent with their Constitution. It discourages rather than encourages Japan from designating China as a potential enemy and involving itself militarily with Taiwan

The United States, Japan, Korea, China, and Indonesia convene an international conference to address territorial-waters and seabed disputes. Such disputes involve nearly every Pacific Asian country in quarrels that are systemic rather than confrontations of good and evil. Japan's dispute with Korea over Tokdo/Takeshima Island is not a confrontation of good and evil, nor are Thailand's disputes with Vietnam and Cambodia. The administration in Washington understands that the conference has no chance of success if the United States arbitrarily sides with one party to the problem, Japan, so it participates in the conference as a party interested in any fair and mutually acceptable outcome, not as an advocate of one of the disputants. This entails a decisive shift away from the one-sided Armitage Report's encouragement of Japan to be more assertive of its claims.

Using this approach to seabed issues as a central symbol of its new stance in Asia, the United States systematically and conspicuously refrains from actions that would polarize Japan and China. Instead of encouraging Japan to designate China as an enemy, it discourages such action. It makes clear to right-wingers in Japan that efforts by them to support Taiwan independence will strain ties with the United States. Through private meetings and encouragement of congressional speeches, the United States makes clear that it frowns on the rewriting of history in ways that blame the United States for World War II and denies what Japanese troops did in China. By doing this while improving military coordination with Japanese forces, while strengthening Japan's defense against North Korean risks, while enhancing intelligence cooperation, while collaborating more closely with Japan on global issues, and while supporting Japan's desire for a United Nations Security Council seat, the United States returns to a posture that actively seeks to avoid polarization among Asia's big powers rather than, as has happened in the first few years of the new century, enhancing gratuitous polarization.

The United States takes the risk of conflict over seabed issues as an opportunity to revitalize regional political institutions by using them to address real issues rather than downgrading them to sporadic pulpits for military issues such as the war in Iraq and the war on terror. The revitalization of APEC and the founding of a new regional security institution evolved from the six-party talks, combined with a parallel effort to revitalize multilateral economic liberalization, gradually come to provide a regional architecture that is balanced and consistent with the complex realities of the region. Active dialogue and concrete decisions made through these institutions gradually reduce polarization in Asia, especially Northeast Asia, and also gradually restore the leverage the United States had lost by downgrading involvement in regional institution-building.

The new regional institutions agree on the necessity for a common strategy to stabilize Central Asia. The key to that stabilization is the same as the key to the stabilization of Southeast Asia in the 1960s: promotion of rapid economic development, education, and institution-building. The United States announces that as its contribution to this effort, its aid program will fund a collaborative study by Japanese, Indian, Chinese, Russian, Korean, Indonesian, and U.S. think tanks of how Southeast Asia was stabilized despite the chaos, ideological division, and Muslim fundamentalist movements during the post–World War II era of decolonization, and it will devote $20 billion per year from its military budget to "national-security stabilization programs" designed to implement the lessons of Southeast Asian success in Central Asia. Washington pledges to withdraw all its military bases from Central Asia if others will do likewise. China, Japan, and Korea, which have no overseas bases, readily assent. Some Russians see the pledge as an American ploy to weaken them, but national leaders eventually decide that having U.S. troops out and diminishing any future risk of Chinese bases is worth it. India becomes angry at having to give up its base in Tajikistan and its ambitions for more, but it eventually accedes to the consensus.

Rather than seeing China through Cold War lenses, this generation of U.S. leaders acknowledges that China has made more compromises in settling problems with its neighbors than either India or Japan has and has made more progress in developing friendly relations with its neighbors as well. Therefore, while still abhorring China's domestic abuses of human rights, the U.S. leaders stop treating China as a likely aggressor and cease to make it the focus of one of world history's greatest military buildups. The stated strategy remains the same—entice China to become a responsible stakeholder and hedge in case it doesn't—but the practice comes to acknowledge that since 1979, China has in fact been a force for regional stability and has shown no signs of aggressive military ambitions. Military strategy and national strategy become integrated for the first time in the new century. U.S. military forces in the region remain strong enough to be the powerful hedge they are intended to be, but the use of an exaggerated China threat as an excuse for continued maintenance of a Cold War–style military diminishes. Spending on ships and aircraft that had been rationalized by an exaggerated China threat diminishes, and attention shifts to the kinds of conflict the United States actually faces in the 21st century. As a result, U.S. military power becomes much more effective for the conflicts it actually faces globally and much more respected than it was in 2006.

The U.S. leaders become determined to find a peaceful resolution to the Taiwan problem and determined to maintain a military posture adequate to deter any adventurism that might arise in Beijing, but they recognize that China has no desire to change the freedom and democracy of Taiwan's system and no desire to incorporate Taiwan formally in the foreseeable future. They pursue an arms-control dialogue with Beijing and encourage the more-balanced diplomacy of China that eventually succeeded the foolish missile-throwing of 1996 and the threatening rhetoric that characterized the Jiang Zemin era. In this, both the United States and China are assisted by the electoral repudiation in Taiwan of the provocative moves that characterized the eight years of Chen Shui-bian's accidental and accident-prone presidency.

As the Taiwan problem calms down, China becomes more relaxed in negotiating over North Korea and in particular over Korean unification. As many Chinese foreign-policy leaders have long acknowledged in private, China's core interest in regional stability would be served by a unified Korea, which would have to be a Korea largely dominated by South Korea, since it has the peninsula's larger population, dominant economy, and dominant international recognition. U.S. and Chinese perspectives gradually converge around this understanding. Chinese aid to North Korea diminishes. South Korean aid to North Korea rises, leaving the Korean problem increasingly in the hands of Koreans. The newly revitalized regional institutions, in a less-polarized regional environment, find it much easier to impose tough sanctions on North Korean threats and WMD programs and also much easier to agree on carefully targeted economic aid programs to reward North Korean good behavior and domestic reforms.

In Japan, setbacks to both political and economic reform in the post-Koizumi era lead to a sense of stagnation. The public becomes fed up with both stagnation at home and isolation abroad. A new generation of leaders begins to appear, offering a new vision of the future: a Japan that is more open and competitive economically and more cosmopolitan socially; a Japan that will show the world how to manage a more mature society with, among many other things, far more flexibility and dignity for women and older people; and a Japan that reaches out to its neighbors the way China has. The new leaders demand that Japan take the lead in solving the agricultural deadlock in global trade negotiations. The post-Koizumi/Abe era sees a rejection of the emphasis on designating China as a potential enemy, forming military bonds with Taiwan, visiting the Yasukuni Shrine, and praising the revisionist history of the Yushukan. This reversal is led by Japan's major businesses, organized around the Keidanren, and by a group of leading politicians who by 2006 had become increasingly outspoken against the trend toward antagonizing China.

In China, the government is sobered by the very large losses of potential foreign direct investment and aid that result from its excessive promotion of nationalism and its tolerance of anti-Japanese riots. Humiliated by foreign scholars from all over the world who point to the flaws in its own textbooks, Beijing quiets its rhetoric about Japan's much smaller number of revisionist textbooks. Pressured by the United States and by countries all over the world, and persuaded by the rebalancing of Japanese foreign policy, China also backs off from some of its nationalist excesses toward Japan.

The inauguration of a new administration in Washington is followed quickly by the passage of bills that impose high tariffs on China and demand labor and environmental standards that virtually all of the developing world rejects. As those bills proceed through Congress, stock markets around the world begin to crash. The overnight loss of several trillion dollars of investment value sobers the mood in the major capitals. World leaders meet and agree on a coordinated campaign to remind their countries that all the prosperity and political stabilization of the previous half-century depended upon the gradual freeing of trade and investment. A summit meeting of Japan, China, Korea, and ASEAN agrees that a half-century of increasing prosperity and political stabilization are at risk. These are the countries that benefit most from globalization, and they have the most at risk if protectionism spreads. They agree to move toward a free-trade area, welcoming any other country or region that wants to join. Markets rebound.

Of all the scenarios presented here, this is the only truly stable one. It requires a certain amount of cooperation from each of the major parties, but it can in fact be quite resilient in the face of a fairly wide range of issues and behaviors. There is certainly enough good will and good sense in all the major countries to make such a scenario work if the region is led in that direction. The core of Japanese public opinion and the leadership of the pinnacle of Japanese industry strongly desire such a scenario, even if a highly outspoken, well-organized part of the national-security establishment and the right-wing political establishment do not. The center of gravity of Chinese foreign-policy thinking is the peaceful-rise approach, not nationalist provocation of Japan, even though a broad spectrum of Chinese youth and part of the national-security establishment take a more aggressive stance. The broad center of the American political spectrum, including the leadership of the business and intellectual communities and every president from Richard Nixon through George W. Bush, strongly supports the policies required by this scenario, even though the most conservative Republicans, the most liberal Democrats, a wide range of declining businesses and unions, and the arms lobby prefer to demonize China. The core requirement of the scenario is that the United States play a flexible, pragmatic, balancing role, that it lead in reducing the roles of ideology, nationalism, polarization, and demonization, rather than enhancing them.

This scenario could lead to an era of prosperity and peace unparalleled in world history. It could do so even if many of the individual assumptions (e.g., a regional FTA) were weakened considerably. Success does not require achievement of nirvana. Sound policies in the half-century after World War II have provided a considerable foundation of existing success. All that is required for future success is to build gradually on that foundation: more open economies, more prosperity, stronger regional institutions, more reduction of ideological thinking, more emphasis on mutual understanding. All that is required for failure is further polarization, further protectionism, and further downgrading of economic and human needs to enhance military priorities.

Scenario 6: Crisis of Globalization

In this scenario, the year 2005 turns out to have been a turning point in world history. As noted earlier, in Europe, anti-globalization sentiment (e.g., French fear of "the Polish plumber") led to rejection of the EU Constitution. Latin American populism in some countries and disillusionment with the United States in others killed earlier opportunities for multilateral liberalization. The Doha trade round became moribund, presaging the first defeat of a major global trade round since World War II. In the United States, 2004 had ended with the U.S. Secretary of State saying that Sino-American relations were in the best shape ever, but 2005 saw steadily decreasing presidential prestige and steadily increasing influence of congressional protectionists. The big companies that had defended China against, for instance, removal of its trade privileges in 1993 went silent out of anger over intellectual-property violations, while the unions and sunset industries seized an opportunity to impose their protectionist agenda. As a consequence of this domestic shift, anti-China fever set the tone in Washington, even though the shifting balance had almost nothing to do with China or Asia. This was universally noted, but everyone expected life to go on along pretty much the same track.

In 2008, the mood continues to sour, unexpectedly worsened by events in China. President Bush's political influence and ability to ward off congressional protectionism continue to weaken. In China, a rising tide of popular protests finally coalesces into a massive demonstration against land seizures in Sichuan. The police intervene, lose control, and fire on the protestors, with many casualties—all captured on film by Fox News. Given the resultant combined political and economic sourness toward China in Washington, a bill to punish China by imposing very high tariffs passes both houses of Congress. The French government spreads concern that the U.S. tariff will mean that a flood of formerly U.S.-bound Chinese goods will be diverted to the EU, so the EU passes restrictive quotas. Japan follows suit. China retaliates against the United States, which responds with quotas that supplement the tariffs.

As happened at the end of the 1920s when the Smoot-Hawley tariff proceeded through Congress, the U.S. stock market experiences successive crashes, taking all other major world stock markets with it. Fearful Asians stop buying dollars, causing U.S. and global interest rates to rise and housing markets to fall. Throughout the world, prices rise in anticipation of coming inability to import cheap goods, and employment falls as consumers buy fewer goods and businesses invest less.

The hardest-hit economies are the most open ones—the smaller economies of Asia, Taiwan, Hong Kong, Singapore, South Korea, and Malaysia, followed at some distance by Indonesia and Thailand. All experience severe recessions. Taiwan and Hong Kong, because of their total dependence on production in China, are thrown into severe depressions. Taiwan's politics become chaotic, with the greens attacking the blues for promoting integration with the Chinese economy and a witch hunt being waged against major industrial companies that have invested heavily in the mainland. The Philippines, less globalized but more fragile financially, becomes insolvent, and the democratic government is overthrown by a dictator promising to bring order and competence to a nation chronically beset by corruption, division, and incompetence.

As growth declines, the raw-materials prices fall off a cliff. Indonesia, the core of Southeast Asia and especially dependent on raw-materials prices, suffers a financial crisis and elects a populist, anti-Western, Islamist government. The Russian economy suffers the most spectacular collapse among the larger countries, and Australian terms of trade become the worst in the nation's history. Radical declines in oil prices shatter the Saudi, Iranian, and Iraqi economies, possibly leading to political upheaval in all three. Brazil and Mexico suffer debt crises.

China is less affected than the smaller countries but far more affected than Japan or most of the rest of the developing world, because it is so much more open. Hence, China suffers a wave of business collapses unprecedented in modern history, with the private sector particularly devastated. The business collapses pile new bad loans on top of the existing mountain of bad debt carried by the banks, and the government bails them out at the cost of inflation exceeding 50 percent. Even then, millions of people fall into severe privation. As in Taiwan, many intellectuals and much of the public blame the government for allowing the economy to become dependent upon hostile foreigners. Social order and government stability become questionable; little Maoist uprisings appear in many provinces. The principal alternative is not market democracy, but a return to socialist principles and hostility to the West.

India is hurt by spreading protectionism, but because it is both a continental economy and relatively closed, it is hurt proportionately less than anyone in East Asia. However, its progressive areas such as Bangalore are disproportionately damaged, and Indian reform loses its momentum. Its growth rate falls back to the range of 2 to 3 percent.

Japan, the EU, and the United States soon find that they have a problem. Their controls on imports from China fall heavily on goods from their own companies that are assembled in China for export to each other. They begin demanding that exceptions be made for those goods or for goods that have only limited dependence on Chinese parts. As they argue over this insoluble problem, tempers flare. France, Greece, and others use various excuses to backpedal on EU rules. The United States and the EU quarrel about agriculture and many detailed rules. Previously, these would have been resolved, and there would have been forward movement. But the determination to resolve issues and move forward seems to have evaporated.

Later historians look back and argue that the result was inevitable. The EU was structurally too weak,[4] and the defeat of the EU Constitution was, they say, just the first crack in a crumbling foundation. In the United States, gradual political polarization beginning in the early 1990s and spiraling out of control after the turn of the century so weakened the center in the U.S. Congress that it could no longer defend the national interest against the relatively small but well-organized and well-funded interest groups of the right wing of the Republican Party and the left wing of the Democratic Party.

The political counterpart of spreading global protectionism is nationalism, exacerbated by universal anger over rising prices, rising unemployment, falling growth, and the enormous loss of wealth from the crashes of stock markets, bond markets, and property markets. In Asia, this nationalism would have two overwhelmingly important aspects: The United States as world leader would be blamed for much of the collapse, and U.S. bases would be expelled, except possibly from South Korea and Australia. Sino-Japanese antagonism would escalate. In Southeast Asia, frictions over seabed issues would rise.

The world would find itself in a position reminiscent of the early 1930s. Europe would not, however, be on the precipice of a great war. East Asia might find itself drifting toward Sino-Japanese conflict.

Surprises

The above scenarios attempt to explore the range of alternative major structures that post-post–Cold War Asian geopolitics might form. They do not, and cannot, cover all possibilities, nor can they cover many important details within themselves. Scenarios are designed to probe the range of possibilities. Since policymakers in major countries have some leverage over the direction the world takes, such scenar-

---

[4] For an argument along these lines, see Laurent Cohen-Tanugi, "The End of Europe?" *Foreign Affairs*, November/December 2005, pp. 55ff.

ios may help them think about the choices they make. Do they, for instance, want to run the risk of the globalization-collapse scenario? To the extent that they find themselves in some variant of one of the scenarios, they can consider the dynamics of the scenario and perhaps achieve a more successful outcome for their country within it.

There are two important qualifications to this exercise. The first is that the scenarios are not entirely mutually exclusive. In any of the first three scenarios, there is a risk that a set of economic decisions could send the world careening into the globalization-collapse scenario.

Second, a number of lower-probability events could greatly affect the evolving structure of Asian geopolitics. I outline a few of these below. These are developments that are relatively unlikely to happen but would be very consequential if they did.

China Sticks to Globalization Despite Globalization Collapsing Elsewhere

Suppose the globalization-collapse scenario occurs, but China, following an initial inclination to reciprocate other countries' protectionism, decides to continue opening its economy. This would be the economically rational policy, but domestic political pressure would probably force Chinese leaders to follow the protectionist trend. Suppose, however, that brilliant, committed leaders could find a way to finesse those pressures. The Chinese economy would then become an irresistible magnet for its neighbors, and the integrated combination of China and its neighbors would, after the initial shock, greatly outperform the rest of the world. (I define "neighbors" as any nearby countries that reciprocated China's openness. Most of the smaller countries would. Japan almost certainly would not, due to nationalistic antagonism. India's position would probably be ambiguous.) The neighbors would rightly see China as their economic savior. The result, if long continued, would be a shift in the global balance parallel to what once happened between Europe and Islam.

When Islam was the open, globalizing culture, it was the dynamic, high-technology, politically expanding culture of its day, and Europe was the protectionist, insular, backward culture. As their positions reversed, with Islam turning insular and Europe turning outward,

Europe became dominant. A comparable shift between China and the rest of the world due to a globalization collapse elsewhere is unlikely, but it is not impossible and deserves reflection. China has already replaced the United States as the principal advocate of multilateral economic liberalization, a reverse the conventional wisdom of a decade ago would have regarded as ludicrously improbable. This is probably the only scenario in which China would achieve the kind of global power that sensationalist journalists project from its rise; ironically, it results from the antidote many of them, along with many U.S. legislators, recommend, namely, protectionism in the United States and Europe. The anti-China lobby would make China the greatest of the powers.

Failure of Chinese or Indian Reform

I have emphasized the momentum of Chinese reform and the gathering momentum of Indian reform. Continuation of reform and rapid economic growth in both places does seem probable, but it is not inevitable. Chinese leaders could lose their reformist courage and fail to push through economically necessary but politically painful reforms. As this is written, a new generation of Chinese leaders is confronting the need to take very painful measures or else risk a classic Asian financial bubble and ensuing collapse. We don't yet know whether they will pass this test. They could also fail to keep political reform reasonably synchronized with economic reform.

Similarly, Indian leaders could find their reformist drive stopped by recalcitrant opposition in the legislature or by revolt in the more backward provinces.

In either case, the reform failure would be politically consequential. A sharp economic setback or a prolonged slowing of growth would severely weaken the central leadership, empower reactionary and xenophobic leaders, and create a zone of geopolitical vacuum rather than the zone of strength that has been emerging.

Emergence of an Aggressive India

Unlike many of its East Asian neighbors, India has only begun to emerge into the modern Asian world, in which a focus on domestic economic growth leads to a muting of international ambitions and a determination to settle differences with neighbors. The counterpart to China's settlement with Russia would be an Indian willingness to settle with Pakistan over Kashmir; so far, there is no real inkling of compromise. If India's reform succeeds over a sustained period of time, we would expect it to follow the East Asian pattern. But if key neighbors (Bangladesh, Pakistan, China) were to weaken sharply in the near term, India's ambitions to be a great power, which have always been strong but have always been thwarted by the lack of capability and opportunity, could conceivably evolve toward severe pressure on its neighbors to submit to Indian hegemony. If China were to weaken while India was in this kind of expansionist mode, handling the consequences of an expansionist India would become a major issue for other world powers.

Emergence of an Aggressive China

China is much farther along in the process of refocusing its priorities from great-power ambitions to domestic economics than India is, but a setback over Taiwan, a clash with Japan, or the emergence of a different kind of leadership could create a different China. At the end of the Jiang Zemin era, some of the old leaders pressured their successors very hard to take a tough line on Taiwan, Hong Kong, and seabed drilling and to suppress Zheng Bijian's peaceful-rise theory. After initially bowing to those pressures, the new leaders set a more moderate course, but the incident was a warning that Deng Xiaoping's legacy is not completely ensured. The emergence of a China that demanded real control of Taiwan and settlement of seabed and territorial-waters issues disproportionately in its favor, and one that sought to enforce such claims by military force, would ensure the movement of the world into a new–Cold-War scenario.

Local Wars of Global Consequence

It would actually not be terribly surprising if events in Pakistan, North Korea, or Central Asia spun into warfare that involved the big powers. A North Korean leadership on its last legs could threaten to attack Japan and could set off a nuclear weapon after lobbing it into the sea several hundred miles past Japan to demonstrate its capabilities. Or Pyongyang's leaders could get caught selling WMD to al Qaeda.

Pakistan could disintegrate or turn into an aggressive, nuclear-armed Islamist terrorist state. Warfare could break out in one of the countries of Central Asia, and one or more of the countries could disappear, possibly dragging big powers into the fray. One could write a scenario for Russian-Chinese enmity based on such warfare, particularly if allies of one country were to seize and nationalize oil fields belonging to the other.

CHAPTER TEN

Conclusion

The law that key institutions and images of one era survive into another era appears to be the political analogue of physics' law of conservation of momentum. Old ideas burn themselves into the mind and can be excised only by some searing experience. Old institutions struggle to survive and mobilize supportive interest groups. Sometimes they transform themselves in ways that serve the national interest and sometimes they don't, but always they seek ways to justify themselves, to mobilize political and economic support, and to reshape themselves for survival. This is bedrock human behavior, and the Cold War institutions are no different from others.

ASEAN is a Cold War institution that has adapted itself in the face of multiple challenges. Organized with the support of the United States to create a barrier to Soviet, Chinese, and Vietnamese communist expansion, ASEAN was seen by its own leaders as a collaborative mechanism for enhancing the members' prosperity through economic integration, increasing the small countries' international security in the face of challenges from far bigger countries (primarily the Soviet Union and China), improving domestic security through exchange of intelligence and techniques, and magnifying their global diplomatic clout by banding together. The ASEAN leaders welcomed U.S. support against the communist international and domestic threats but always maintained their own autonomy.

With the fall of the Soviet Union and the evolution of China into a supporter of stability rather than a fount of subversion, ASEAN risked losing its reason for existence. With the Asian crisis and the resultant crippling of Indonesia and Thailand, it lost its leadership. With the change of U.S. priorities away from economic development, it lost its sugar daddy. But it adapted to an era of non-ideological politics by expanding its membership to include former opponents, and it incorporated the new economic dynamism and new peaceful diplomacy of Vietnam. It continued to pursue its free-trade goals and to advocate its members' interests through the WTO. While continuing to be an association of small countries asserting themselves collectively in the midst of big powers, it allowed China to join its goal of a free-trade area, thereby gaining market access and pursuing its multilateral trade and investment goals in an era when the United States and Japan had shifted to disadvantageous (for small countries) pursuit of bilateral FTAs.

In adapting to the post–Cold War world, India and China had the disadvantage and advantage that their traditional institutional arrangements and images were shattered by the emergence of the new era. India lost its principal patron and model, the Soviet Union. China now had neither the Soviet alliance nor the galvanizing Soviet enemy nor the assurance that "socialist" systems would survive. Hence India and China entered the new era with the disadvantage of having lost their traditional institutional roots but with the more important advantage of facing the future relatively unburdened. Their strategic situation today is like their telephone systems: They have the disadvantage of not having a nation connected by millions of miles of copper wire but the advantage that they can now build wireless systems without the burdensome legacy of all that copper wire.

Russia, in contrast, has kept groping for some semblance of the old order. The CIS, the concept of the "near abroad," the on-again off-again interference in the politics of Central Asia and the new Eastern Europe all revealed an inability to shake off the presuppositions of the past and come to clear terms with the new era. Russia, in short, is the extreme example of a country still so hobbled by the past that it is unsure of its domestic economic strategy, its domestic political strategy, or its foreign policy, indeed of its identity.

The United States is a far more complex case, liberated by the collapse of its Soviet opponent, invigorated by a vibrant domestic economy, empowered by a military-industrial complex that dwarfs all competitors, but inhibited in the effective deployment of its extraordinary power by the drag of old ideas and old institutions and even more by an imbalance that has developed among them.

Those ideas and institutions have evolved in striking ways, but institutional maintenance has been the core theme. The foreign-policy team that took office at the dawn of the new century was led almost exclusively by a group of defense experts determined to maintain the defense budget and the defense establishment but to make more-unfettered use of it in the new environment—unfettered by the old Soviet adversary, unfettered by many traditional State Department concerns, and unfettered by traditional economic priorities. The result was a strong resurgence of military spending and of technological development of the kinds of extremely advanced naval ships and military aircraft that would have been particularly useful in a conflict with the old Soviet Union. The new team explicitly rejected the idea that the demise of the principal old adversary in Moscow should lead to a decline in such resource allocations. China and al Qaeda have become the excuses for this institutional maintenance, but the requirements of conflicts and potential conflicts with al Qaeda and China would lead defense budgets and technologies in substantially different directions, at substantially lower cost.[1] China now provides the sole rationale for developing and acquiring the most advanced and fabulously expensive air and naval platforms.

The use of China as a proxy for the old Soviet Union is a severely stretched rationale for continued development of the military budgets, high-tech platforms, and strategic plans and is diverting resources away from the real challenges of the new era. Unlike the Soviet Union, China is not trying to impose its system on the world or indeed on any other countries and is not expansionist. Taiwan is not Munich;

---

[1] This has been the near-consensus reaction of professional analysts outside the current administration. See, for instance, Michele A. Flournoy, "Did the Pentagon Get the Quadrennial Defense Review Right?" *Washington Quarterly*, Vol. 29, No. 2, Spring 2006, pp. 67–84. On the use of al Qaeda to justify unrelated expenditures, see David Gompert and James Dobbins, "Outside View: A Far Too Costly Pentagon," *United Press International*, February 27, 2006.

if it were, China would be claiming Singapore, Malaysia, and much else, and it would not have devoted so much energy to settling its land borders. There are real issues surrounding Taiwan, and military officers are right to be concerned about them and demand the resources to cope with them. But China has been the region's big country most supportive of stability among its neighbors, the country most willing to compromise regarding its boundaries, and the country most directly helpful to the United States on the big regional political and economic issues, from North Korea to genetically modified foods. In this context, the assertion that the United States needs to mobilize vast new technologies for war with an aggressive China goes well beyond hedging; it is the voice of interest groups, ideology, and institutional maintenance, not evidence.

Just as striking as the triumph of the U.S. Cold War military system is the withering of what had seemed like its dual Siamese twins, the economic development and regional institution-building programs that were the recipe for success in the Cold War. The United States has not seen a smooth continuation of those Cold War institutions; rather, it has seen a blossoming of its military and ideological programs.

Just as the military has displaced much of the role formerly played by the diplomats and the economic-development advisors and in the process has changed its role in U.S. policy, the U.S. alliance with Japan has overshadowed the other institutions and instruments of U.S. policy in Asia. Alliance with a disarmed Japan was once the instrument that protected Japan from China and also protected China from Japan. The institution that long ensured Sino-Japanese peace has now become an instrument that accelerates Sino-Japanese antagonism. Perhaps more important, the domestic political correlate in Japan of a broader military role—namely, the continuing rise to power of a nationalistic Japanese right wing—may turn out to be inconsistent with U.S. hopes to turn Japan into its Asian counterpart of British partnership, sharing a common worldview and values and accepting U.S. regional dominance for the indefinite future. There is a real risk that future historians will look back at our era and say that the decisive foreign-policy decisions Washington made at the turn of the new century concerned not Iraq, not the war on terror, but rather the reignition and acceleration of Sino-Japanese rivalry. It is hoped that this will not occur. The degree to which Japan alienated its neighbors under Koizumi shocked many Japanese opinion leaders and led Prime Minister Abe to make a successful pilgrimage to China, as well as an unsuccessful one to South Korea, at the beginning of his new administration. But Abe offered only words, not new policies, and the elite that has come to power with him may not sustain the moderation.

Throughout the Cold War, the U.S. alliance with Japan was fully consistent with alliance and quasi-alliance relationships with most of the significant countries of the Asian littoral—from South Korea to Indonesia. But the new, overweening U.S.-Japan alliance is fraying American relationships with other allies. Most notably, the U.S. alliance with South Korea is at risk of being torn asunder by the conflict between South Korea's eternal need for a distant defender and its fear of being dragged into a gratuitous war with North Korea or with China, as well as by the U.S. decision to bet its entire Asia policy on rearming Japan, Korea's old antagonist.

Likewise, the United States has not yet worked out the proper balance in Southeast Asia between, on one hand, servicing Southeast Asians' strong desire for a powerful U.S. military presence to protect them against China and Japan and, on the other hand, respecting Southeast Asian distaste for a policy that promotes Japanese power and, in their view, needlessly provokes China. Even Australia, America's second most loyal ally after Britain, sees U.S. policy in this light and is determined not to be part of it. While the U.S. military presence is highly desired by Southeast Asians, Washington's de-emphasis since 2001 on economic policy in the region cedes steadily growing regional influence to China. Over time, that gradual shift in the balance will imply that Washington must either accept eventual Chinese preeminence, reconsider its relative priorities between military and economic policy, or raise the level of military presence and tension to offset its diplomatic decline. Much of the current national-security establishment in Washington expresses fear of being forced out of Asia by China. In recent years, China has indeed made disproportionate gains. But this is not because it forced the United States out. It is because Washington insisted that a reluctant China take the lead on

North Korean nuclear issues, because Washington deliberately stepped back from Asian regional institutions and created a vacuum into which China stepped, and because Washington reduced its priority for multilateral economic liberalization and created another vacuum into which China stepped. China's disproportionate success in both Asia and Africa has come from adopting policies that were the core U.S. strategies in winning the Cold War. The United States had a patent on those strategies but turned the intellectual-property rights over to China.

Japan's initial response to the failure of its bids for Asian predominance, through military means in the first half of the 20th century and through economic means in the second half, has been to make the U.S.-Japan alliance a substitute for an Asia policy. The Koizumi administration inaugurated the new century by doing what Japan needed most: rejuvenating economic growth and initiating reform of the political system. Those priorities were absolutely correct. These successes did, however, come at the expense of adopting a foreign policy that has to various degrees alienated all of its neighbors except Taiwan. Koizumi spoke often of managing China and South Korea "through the U.S. alliance." In this process, Japan's Asia policy became in substantial part the instrument of a small but superbly organized and financed group that essentially advocated a return to some of the rationalizations of the first half of the 20th century. The hallmarks of this group were rearmament; disregard for the sensibilities of Koreans, Chinese, Southeast Asians, Australasians, and, at the margin of consciousness, knowledgeable Americans and Europeans; rationalization of colonial-era aggressions; and renewed pursuit of efforts to organize the region in ways that would minimize U.S. and Chinese influence. The effect of these tendencies was to tilt the balance of Asian sympathy to China, thereby defeating Japan's own goals. This policy strain was totally dependent on U.S. military support but was not ultimately pro-American. The right wing in Japanese politics seeks to organize an Asian currency that would be dominated by the yen, in order to weaken Chinese and U.S. influence, and it enthusiastically supports efforts to create Asian economic institutions and an East Asia Summit that exclude the United States. It is utterly opposed to U.S. goals regarding Taiwan and unification of Korea. It vilifies the U.S. role in World War II and ultimately would lead to a Japan that could do without U.S. bases and the U.S. alliance.

Such policies have not been institutionalized. The vast majority of the Japanese public opposes any rapid rearmament and would like peaceful relations with China. Most of the Japanese do not understand the implications of the 2+2 Declaration of February 2005 and the official designation of China as a potential enemy, if they have even heard of them. Most would not share the strong feelings about Taiwan independence and indefinite continuation of a divided Korea. Most of Japan's foreign-policy experts, including virtually all of the diplomats an American meets, express confusion and concern about why Prime Minister Koizumi insisted on visiting the Yasukuni Shrine, along with a desire to dampen Sino-Japanese tensions. Japan's biggest businesses and largest business organizations oppose actions that would further inflame relations with China. A number of Japan's leading political figures would, if they came to power, act quickly to improve relations with Japan's neighbors. Prime Minister Abe did so, after this book was initially written, while telling friends that the reason he did not need to visit the Yasukuni Shrine was that his reputation as an adherent of that credo was already so firmly established. Given the peaceful, conciliatory center of gravity of Japanese public opinion, the future of Japan's Asia policy is by no means set on a firm course of nationalist alienation of Japan's neighbors.

None of this is to suggest that China is innocent or less to blame for Sino-Japanese tensions. It is not. Its naval probes into Japanese waters, its destructive riots, and its exaggeration of the history-textbook issue make it fully as culpable as Japan. The noteworthy difference between the policies of the two countries is that Japan is alienating the majority of its neighbors, while China is winning more and more support, not for its excesses in relations with Japan, but for its generally collaborative and empathetic economic and political postures toward its neighbors. Similarly, India has a very assertive, very nationalistic foreign policy, but unlike Japan, it has been continuously improving relations with China, with the United States, and even with Pakistan. India's foreign policy is not inherently peaceful, and it is certainly not pro-American in any strong sense. India's leaders are wisely establishing good relations ("strategic partnerships") with all the big powers and not disillusioning any who want to believe that they are more special than the others. By being closer to both the United States and China than those two powers are to each other, India wisely maximizes its own leverage. Both the Indians and the Chinese are playing the geopolitical game with far more finesse than their American and Japanese counterparts.

The arms race in the Taiwan Strait cannot be perpetuated indefinitely without a crisis; this is not based on a general (and often false) proposition that arms races necessarily lead to conflict, but on the specific situation in the strait. Within a very few years, this will require a decision either to fully ally with Taiwan and initiate a new Cold War with China or to broker a cross-strait deal.

Change is coming. Old ideas, most notably late–20th century U.S. caricatures of China and Japan, have persisted long after the underlying reality changed. Lessons drawn by academics from study of the era that predates modern Asian economic dynamism and destructive modern military technology are being used to justify potentially life-and-death decisions in an entirely different context. World history's most powerful military continues to be organized to fight the last war—and justified by caricatures of China that risk unnecessary strife. An outsized effort to hedge against an unlikely conflict will almost certainly constrain future U.S. presidents from obtaining desperately needed Chinese support in a wide variety of far more-likely conflicts. The delicate balance of global forces for and against globalization could be tipped, at the margin, in the wrong direction by inattention to economic priorities and gratuitous stirring up of hostility toward China.

Asia needs regional organizations that can seriously address the most important regional issues. It has a whole portfolio of organizations—ASEAN, ARF, APEC, and so forth, plus budding associations such as ASEAN+3 (ASEAN plus Japan, South Korea, and China)—but these organizations lack the ability to affect major regional issues because some don't have the United States as a member and those that do are not being taken as seriously by Washington as they once were. For leaders in Washington, as for leaders in Tokyo, the U.S.-Japan alliance has become a substitute for broader institutional structures and detailed policies, a big tree that casts such a large shadow that everything else is deprived of sunshine. To observe this is not to denigrate the importance or value of the big tree or to completely neglect Washington's search for other bilateral military relationships or Tokyo's search for dominance in Asian economic relationships; rather, it is to note that special efforts are required to provide sunshine to other vitally needed plants.

Local organizations are emerging to fill the empty space left under the big tree. The SCO, the East Asia Summit, the ASEAN Plus efforts, and the Chinese association with the AFTA all have value for their members. Bilateral FTAs are similarly filling the vacuum left by Washington's and Tokyo's fading commitment to multilateral trade liberalization. But those agreements cannot provide a full substitute for regional organizations that include the United States and focus the attention of the members' top leaders on resolving vital regional issues. Moreover, in the absence of sustained top-level U.S. engagement, at least some of these organizations are likely to evolve in ways that frustrate U.S. goals.

The six-party talks over North Korea, for all the frustrations of dealing with North Korea, provide the kind of forum that the big powers need in order to address Northeast Asian issues. This structure could be broadened to address Taiwan and regional territorial waters and seabed issues too. That structure could be either embedded in a larger regional forum that would address similar pressing issues for Southeast Asia or coordinated with a parallel forum in which, for instance, the concerned powers would seek a structural solution to the rising tensions over territorial-waters and seabed issues. Similarly, Asia needs a common approach to trade. If the Doha trade round is destined to fail, then Pacific Asia, which has more to gain or lose than any other region from the progress or breakdown of the globalization process, needs to organize a collective approach.

The alternatives to regional structures that include vigorous U.S. participation have serious negative consequences. The proliferating, highly politicized competition to negotiate (misnamed) bilateral free-trade agreements presages an eventual breakdown of the trading system. Leaving the omnipresent territorial waters and seabed disputes to fester as resource competition rises virtually ensures eventual conflict. Seeing those disputes through the lens of the Japan-U.S. alliance certainly ensures conflict. If Sino-Japanese disputes over disputed waters and islands are to be handled by U.S.-Japanese training for amphibious landings, how will the United States handle identical conflicts between South Korea and Japan, or between Malaysia and the Philippines, or between Thailand and Vietnam? The Armitage Report's one-sided approach to this many-sided problem and the corresponding posture that was subsequently put in place could conceivably be seen by future historians as the key decision that tipped the world away from a new era where seabed issues were settled in the way East Asia settled its ancient land-border disputes toward one of rising tensions, military conflict, and more generally destructive conflictual approaches to problems of the global commons (seabeds, fisheries, environmental degradation, global warming), rather than collective cooperative approaches based on broad principles and a spirit of compromise.

This study has examined the fundamental regional and national trends that underlie the future of Asia and Asian-American relations. These trends are far too complex and indeterminate to permit firm predictions, so it has suggested, by no means comprehensively, some alternative scenarios and potential surprises. Those scenarios show a wide variety of possible outcomes of the trends. Some of these lead to peace and prosperity, others to the risk of war.

Likewise, the study has looked at the institutional structures and relationships by which nations try to channel the trends in desirable directions. If anything is clear, it is that much of the institutional infrastructure of the Cold War has fallen away. Some of this is good, most notably the disappearance of the terrible bipolar nuclear and ideological confrontation that defined the Cold War; whatever today's difficulties, the area of confrontation has narrowed and the area of consensus has greatly widened with China's and Russia's acceptance of the majority of Western economic and international norms. Some of it is bad, namely the truncation of U.S. and others' efforts to bring peace and stability to the world through economic development. The effort to preserve and justify Cold War military organizations by using China as a proxy for the old Soviet Union is a potential source of great mischief. As some key economic and diplomatic Cold War institutions have withered, military considerations have expanded to occupy much of the space partially evacuated by economic and diplomatic priorities, and the U.S.-Japan alliance has expanded to an extent that withers other institutions and priorities. The fault here lies not with the military leaders, who are doing their assigned jobs, but with the civilian leaders who have failed to confront the realities of a new age and to proffer to their citizens the wonderful possibilities of this new age.

We remain in a period of inertia from a bygone era. What greater irony could there be than the fact that the solution of the 20th century's bloody strife over Chinese and Korean weakness and the uplifting of hundreds of millions of Indian and Chinese peasants and workers from a century of subhuman poverty could be envisaged by a very wide range of Western political leaders of both the right and the left as primarily a fearful economic and geopolitical threat? What greater strategic irony could there be than the end of the Cold War leading to a rising priority for the military, a declining priority for mutual economic effort, and a renewed polarization of Asian geopolitics? Who could have imagined that America's achievement of the pinnacle of world economic power, the pinnacle of world military power, and the pinnacle of world cultural influence would be accompanied by a marked decline in its Asian political influence?

A world with a coherent and prosperous China is a good world, not a bad one. A world where China has joined all the major U.S.-nurtured institutions and is promoting stability is a U.S. and Western triumph beyond the farthest-fetched imagination of only three decades ago. A world where the poverty of two billion people in China and India is being eliminated at the cost of some slowing of wage growth in the West is one of the greatest triumphs of the human condition in all of world history. The fact that Indian and Chinese demand has spectacularly improved African, Indonesian, and Brazilian terms of trade, after nearly two decades of seemingly inexorable decline and impoverishment, provides real hope that Asian success will result in a reduction of poverty elsewhere. The fact that U.S. unemployment is at one of the lowest levels in half a century is an occasion for celebration, not for angry rhetoric about loss of jobs. Indian and Chinese leaders have instilled confidence, hope, and excitement in a context of poverty and still-daunting problems. Supported by reactionary interest groups, far too many U.S. and Japanese leaders have managed to instill fear and anxiety in a context of geopolitical victory and the greatest prosperity in human history. In either country, a leader who can communicate the extent of today's global success and instill a vision of greater peace and greater prosperity building on that success, rather than managing to convince citizens that their victory is actually an imminent defeat, could inspire his or her for nation and the world for decades.

Change is coming. The forms that change may take will be determined not by mechanistic forces of history, but rather by leaders' decisions.

Bibliography

Abramowitz, Morton, and Stephen Bosworth, *Chasing the Sun: Rethinking East Asian Policy*, New York: Century Foundation Press, 2006.

Agakimi, Hikari, *"We the Japanese People"—A Reflection on Public Opinion*, Japan Institute of International Affairs Commentary No. 2, May 22, 2006. Online at: http://yaleglobal.yale.edu/display.article?id=7444

Alexander, Arthur, *In the Shadow of the Miracle: The Japanese Economy Since the End of High-Speed Growth*, Lanham, MD: Lexington Books, 2002.

Armacost, Michael, "The Mismatch Between Northeast Asian Change and American Distractions," in *NBR Analysis—Emerging Trends, Dormant Interest: Developments in Northeast Asian Politics*, Vol. 18, No. 1, January 2007, p. 12.

Armitage, Richard, Interview, *The Oriental Economist*, March 2006, p. 15. Online at:
http://agonist.org/20060325/interview_with_richard_armitage

Armitage, Richard, and Joseph Nye, *The U.S. and Japan: Advancing Toward a Mature Partnership*, Washington, DC: Institute for National Strategic Studies, Special Report, 2001.

"The Asian Crisis," International Monetary Fund, *Annual Report 1998*, pp. 23ff.

Barnett, Thomas P.M., *The Pentagon's New Map: War and Peace in the Twenty-First Century*, New York: G. P. Putnm's Sons, 2004.

Benedict, Ruth, *The Chrysanthemum and the Sword*, Boston, MA: Houghton Mifflin, 1989 (originally published in 1946).

Berger, Suzanne, and Richard K. Lester, *Global Taiwan*, Cambridge, MA: Massachusetts Institute of Technology, 2005.

Bergsten, C. Fred, Takatoshi Ito, and Marcus Noland, *No More Bashing: Building a New Japan-United States Economic Relationship*, Washington, DC: Institute for International Economics, 2001.

Berry, Lynn, "Did You Hear the One About Putin and the Jellied Meat?" *Los Angeles Times*, July 16, 2006, p. M6.

Blackwill, Robert D., "The India Imperative," *The National Interest*, No. 80, Summer 2005, pp. 9–18.

Blank, Stephen J., *Natural Allies? Regional Security in Asia and Prospects for Indo-American Strategic Cooperation*, Carlisle, PA: Army War College, Strategic Studies Institute, 2005.

Boucher, Richard, "Encourage the Peaceful Resolution of Issues Concerning the Taiwan Strait Through Dialogue," Joint Statement, U.S.-Japan Security Consultative Committee, Washington, DC, February 19, 2005.

Bowen, Roger W., *Japan's Dysfunctional Democracy: The Liberal Democratic Party and Structural Corruption*, Armonk, NY: M. E. Sharpe, 2003.

Brzezinski, Zbigniew, and John J. Mearsheimer, "Clash of the Titans," *Foreign Policy*, No. 146, January-February 2005, pp. 46–49.

CEIC Data Company. Online at:
http://www.ceicdata.com

Chang, Gordon C., *The Coming Collapse of China*, New York: Random House, 2001.

Chen, Shuxun, and Charles Wolf, Jr., *China, the United States, and the Global Economy*, Santa Monica, CA: RAND Corporation, MR-1300-RC, 2001. Online at:
http://www.rand.org/pubs/monograph_reports/MR1300/

Chinese Ministry of Foreign Affairs, "A policy of 'one country, two systems' on Taiwan." Online at:
http://www.fmprc.gov.cn/eng/ziliao/3602/3604/t18027.htm

Chinese People's Political Consultative Conference, "Full Text of Anti-Secession Law." Online at:
http://www.china.org.cn/english/2005lh/122724.htm

Chou, Marylin, and William H. Overholt, "Foreign Policy Doctrines," *Policy Studies Journal*, Vol. 3, No. 2, Winter 1974.

CIA World Factbook, November 2005. Online at:
http://www.cia.gov/cia/publications/factbook

Cohen-Tanugi, Laurent, "The End of Europe?" *Foreign Affairs*, November/December 2005, pp. 55ff.

"Confess and Be Done with It," *The Economist*, February 10, 2007, pp. 41–42.

"Cross-Strait Interflow Prospect Foundation," *China Economic Analysis Monthly*, Vol. 4, August 2003, p. 3.

Curtis, Gerald L., *The Logic of Japanese Politics: Leaders, Institutions, and the Limits of Change*, New York: Columbia University Press, 1999.

"Democracy Will Come Slowly, Says Wen," *Agence France Press, Online*, September 6, 2006. Online at: http://www.afp.com/home/

Eberstadt, Nicholas, "The Graying of the 'Emerging Markets': Population Aging in Today's Low-Income Countries," Washington, DC: American Enterprise Institute, unpublished manuscript, 2005.

Fair, Christine, "War and Escalation in South Asia: Pakistan," Santa Monica, CA: RAND Corporation, unpublished paper, July 2005.

Feith, Herbert, *The Decline of Constitutional Democracy in Indonesia*, Ithaca, NY: Cornell University Press, 1962.

Ferguson, Niall, *Colossus: The Rise and Fall of the American Empire*, New York: Penguin Books, 2004.

Feshbach, Murray, "A Country on the Verge," *The New York Times*, May 31, 2003.

Flournoy, Michele A., "Did the Pentagon Get the Quadrennial Defense Review Right?" *Washington Quarterly*, Vol. 29, No. 2, Spring 2006, pp. 67–84.

Foley, Corazon Sandoval, "Contending Perspectives: Southeast Asia and American Views on a Rising China," Carlisle, PA: Strategic Studies Institute, Army War College, Colloquium Brief reporting on a conference held in Singapore, August 22–24, 2005, and Washington, DC, November 3, 2005.

French, Howard W., and Norimitsu Onishi, "Chinese Warships Remind Japanese of Challenge on Seas," *International Herald Tribune* (Asia-Pacific edition), September 11, 2005.

Friedberg, Aaron L., "The Future of U.S.-China Relations: Is Conflict Inevitable?" *International Security*, Vol. 30, No. 2, Fall 2005.

Fukuyama, Francis, *The End of History and the Last Man*, New York: Free Press, 1992.

"Full Text of Anti-Secession Law." Online at: http://www.china.org.cn/english/2005lh/122724.htm.

Gompert, David, and James Dobbins, "Outside View: A Far Too Costly Pentagon," *United Press International*, February 27, 2006.

Grinter, Lawrence E., "Avoiding the Burden: The Carter Doctrine in Perspective," *Air University Review*, January-February 1983.

Gudgel, Andy, "The PLA Shapes the Future Security Environment," Carlisle, PA: U.S. Army War College, and Washington, DC: The Heritage Foundation, Colloquium Brief, September 2005.

Hoffman, Frank G., "Normalcy," Philadelphia, PA: Foreign Policy Research Institute, May 12, 2006. Online at: http://www.fpri.org/enotes/20060512.americawar.hoffman.newnormalcy.html

Huang, Yasheng, and Tarun Khanna, "Can India Overtake China?" *Foreign Policy*, July-August 2004.

Hua-yuan, Hsueh, Tai Pao-tsun, and Chow Mei-li, *Is Taiwan Chinese?* Taipei: Taiwan Advocates, 2005.

Hughes, Christopher W., *Japan's Reemergence as a "Normal" Military Power*, London: International Institute of Strategic Studies, Adelphi Paper 368-9, 2005.

Hunter, Shireen T., *Central Asia Since Independence*, Washington, DC: Center for Strategic and International Studies, 1996

Iinuma, Yoshisuke, "After Koizumi," *Oriental Economist*, Vol. 74, No. 1, January 2006, p. 11.

IMD World Competitiveness Yearbook 2007. Online at: http://www.imd.ch/research/publications/wcy/index.cfm

Institute of Higher Education, Shanghai Jiao Tong University, "Academic Ranking of Universities Worldwide—2005." Online at: http://ed.sjtu.edu.cn/rank/2005/ARWU2005Main.htm

International Crisis Group, "China and North Korea: Comrades Forever?" Crisis Group Asia Report, No. 112, February 1, 2006.

———, "Uzbekistan: In for the Long Haul," Asia Briefing No. 45, February 16, 2006. Online at: http://www.crisisgroup.org/home/index.cfm?id=3952&l=1

———, "Kyrgyzstan: A Faltering State," Crisis Group Asia Report No. 109, December 16, 2005.

———, "Repression and Regression in Turkmenistan: A New International Strategy," ICG Asia Report No. 85, November 4, 2004.

———, "Tajikistan's Politics: Confrontation or Consolidation?" ICG Asia Briefing, May 19, 2004.

———, "Is Radical Islam Inevitable in Central Asia? Priorities for Engagement," ICG Asia Report No. 72, December 22, 2003.

———, "Central Asia: A Last Chance for Change," ICG Asia Briefing Paper, April 29, 2003.

Ishihara, Shintaro, *The Japan That Can Say No: Why Japan Will Be First Among Equals*, New York: Simon & Schuster, 1991.

Johnson, Chris, "Chinese Forces Invited to Observe Valiant Shield Exercise in Pacific," *Inside the Navy*, May 22, 2006.

Johnson, David T., *The Japanese Way of Justice: Prosecuting Crime in Japan*, New York: Oxford University Press, 2002.

Kahn, Herman, *The Emerging Japanese Superstate: Challenge and Response*, Englewood Cliffs, NJ: Prentice Hall, 1970.

Kaplan, Robert D., *Eastward to Tartary: Travels in the Balkans, the Middle East, and the Caucasus*, New York: Vintage, 2001.

"Kato Vows to Speak Out Despite Arson Linked to His Yasukuni Criticism," *Mainichi Daily News*, September 8, 2006.

Kim, Sejin, *The Politics of Military Revolution in Korea*, Durham, NC: University of North Carolina Press, 1971.

Kim, Sung-han, "Peace Regime on the Korean Peninsula and the ROK-US Alliance: Peace and Non-Proliferation on the Korean Peninsula," *IFANS Review*, Vol. 13, No. 2, December 2005.

Klebnikov, Paul, *Grandfather of the Kremlin: The Decline of Russia in the Age of Gangster Capitalism*, New York: Harcourt, 2000.

Kotler, Mindy, "Protecting the Human Rights of Comfort Women," testimony before the Subcommittee on Asia, the Pacific and the Global Environment of the House International Relations Committee, February 15, 2007.

Kreisler, Harry, "Through the Realist Lens: Conversation with John Mearsheimer," April 8, 2002. Online at: http://globetrotter.berkeley.edu/people2/Mearsheimer/mearsheimer-con6.html

Lal, Rollie, "India and South Asia," Santa Monica, CA: RAND Corporation, unpublished, 2005.

————, "South Asia and Strategic Shifts in Asia," Santa Monica, CA: RAND Corporation, unpublished, 2004.

Lee, In-Ho, "The Present Conditions and Prospects for Multilateral Security Cooperation in Northeast Asia," *East Asian Review*, Vol. 17, No. 4, Winter 2005.

Levin, Norman D., and Yong-Sup Han, *The Shape of Korea's Future: South Korean Attitudes Toward Unification and Long-Term Security Issues*, Santa Monica, CA: RAND Corporation, MR-1092-CAPP, 1999. Online at: http://www.rand.org/pubs/monograph_reports/MR1092/

Mahbubani, Kishore, "Will India Emerge as an Eastern or Western Power?" Annual Lecture, Center for the Advanced Study of India, University of Pennsylvania, Philadelphia, PA, November 9, 2006, published as Occasional Paper Number 27, January 2007. Online at: http://casi.ssc.upenn.edu/research/papers/Mahbubani_2007.pdf

————, "The Impending Demise of the Postwar System," *Survival*, Vol. 47, No. 4, Winter 2005–06, p. 7.

Mann, James, *The China Fantasy: How Our Leaders Explain Away Chinese Repression*, New York: Penguin, 2007.

———, "A Shining Model of Wealth Without Liberty," *The Washington Post*, May 20, 2007.

———, *The Rise of the Vulcans*, New York: Viking Penguin, 2004.

McNeill, David, "Japan's History War," *The Chronicle of Higher Education*, April 27, 2007.

Mearsheimer, John J., *The Tragedy of Great Power Politics*, New York: W. W. Norton, 2001.

Moore, Barrington, *The Social Origins of Dictatorship and Democracy: Lord and Peasant in the Making of the Modern World*, Boston, MA: Beacon Press, 1966.

"New Framework for the U.S.-India Defense Relationship, Signed on June 28, 2005 in Washington DC by Minister of Defense of India, Pranab Mukherjee & Secretary of Defense of the United States, Donald Rumsfeld." Online at: http://newdelhi.usembassy.gov/ipr062805.html

Newhouse, John, "Tweaking the Dragon's Tail," *The New Yorker*, March 1993, pp. 89ff.

Oh, Sang-sik, *ODA Policies of Advanced Nations and Related Tasks for Korea*, Institute of Foreign Affairs and National Security, South Korea, Policy Brief No. 2005-7, November 2005.

Okazaki, Hisahiko, "Telling the Truth at Yasukuni," *Japan Times*, February 24, 2007.

Okazaki, Tetsuji, and Masahiro Okuno-Fujiwara (eds.), *The Japanese Economic System and Its Historical Origins*, translated by Susan Herbert, New York: Oxford University Press, 1993.

Organisation for Economic Co-operation and Development, *OECD in Figures, 2006–2007*, Paris: OECD Publications, 2006. Online at http://www.oecd.org/infigures

Onishi, Norimitsu, and Howard W. French, "Chinese Warships Remind Japanese of Challenge on High Seas," *International Herald Tribune* (Asian edition), September 12, 2005, p. 3.

Overholt, William H., "The Chinese Economic Magnet," Santa Monica, CA: RAND Corporation, forthcoming.

———, "A Decade Later: Hong Kong's Economy Since 1997," *Hong Kong Journal*, Vol. 3, July 2007. As of July 27, 2007: http://www.hkjournal.org/archive/2007_fall/4.htm

———, "Hong Kong or Shanghai?" *China Business Review*, Spring 2004.

———, "Japan's Economy: At War with Itself," *Foreign Affairs*, January/February 2002.

———, *Thailand: Reform at a Stately Pace*, Hong Kong: Nomura Securities, July 8, 1999.

———, *The Rise of China*, New York: W. W. Norton, 1993.

———, "The Pacific Basin Model: The Moderation of Politics," in James Morley (ed.), *The Pacific Basin*, Washington, DC: Academy of Political Science, 1986, pp. 35–45.

———, "Progress and Politics in Pacific Asia," *International Security*, Spring 1983.

———, "The Rise of the Pacific Basin," *Pacific Community*, July 1974.

———, "Martial Law, Revolution and Democracy in the Philippines," *Southeast Asia Quarterly*, Vol. 2, No. 2, 1973.

———, "President Nixon's Trip to China and Its Consequences," *Asian Survey*, Vol. 13, No. 7, July 1973.

Overholt, William H., and Marylin Chou, "Foreign Policy Doctrines," *Policy Studies Journal*, Vol. 3, No. 2, Winter 1974.

"Peace Regime on the Korean Peninsula and the ROK-US Alliance: Peace and Non-Proliferation on the Korean Peninsula," *IFANS Review*, Vol. 13, No. 2, December 2005, p. 63.

"Peacefully Rising to Great Power Status," *Foreign Affairs*, September/October 2005, pp. 18–24.

Pei, Minxin, and Michael Swaine, *Simmering Fire in Asia: Averting Sino-Japanese Strategic Conflict*, Washington, DC: Carnegie Endowment for International Peace, Policy Brief No. 44, November 2005.

Pempel, T. J., *Regime Shift: Comparative Dynamics of the Japanese Political Economy*, Ithaca, NY: Cornell University Press, 1998.

Pilling, David, and Richard McGregor, "Japan Says to End Development Aid to China," *Financial Times*, March 17, 2005.

Plate, Thomas, "Thoughts That Deserve to Be Disguised," *Pacific Perspectives*, February 22, 2006.

President of the United States, *The National Security Strategy of the United States of America*, Washington, DC, September 2002.

Pyle, Kenneth B., *Japan Rising: The Resurgence of Japanese Power and Purpose*, New York: Public Affairs, 2007.

Qiao, Helen, "Will China Grow Old Before Getting Rich?" Goldman Sachs, Global Economics Paper 138, February 14, 2006. Online at: https://portal.gs.com

Remnick, David, *Lenin's Tomb: The Last Days of the Soviet Empire*, New York: Random House, 1993.

"Roh Tells U.S. to Stay Out of Regional Affairs," *Washington Times*, March 11, 2005, p. 16.

Romberg, Alan D., *Rein In at the Brink of the Precipice: American Policy Toward Taiwan and U.S.-PRC Relations*, Washington, DC: The Henry L. Stimson Center, 2003.

Saunders, Philip C., "Long-Term Trends in China-Taiwan Relations: Implications for U.S. Policy," *Asian Survey*, Vol. 45, No. 6, November/December 2005.

Schumer, Charles, "China's One-Way Street on Foreign Direct Investment and Market Access," August 18, 2005. Online at: http://www.senate.gov/~schumer/SchumerWebsite/pressroom/record_print.cfm?id=260470

Seagraves, Sterling, *The Soong Dynasty*, New York: Harper & Row, 1985.

Segal, Adam, *Chinese Military Power*, Washington, DC: Council on Foreign Relations, 2003.

Seong, Somi, Steven W. Popper, and Kungang Zheng, *Strategic Choices in Science and Technology: Korea in the Era of a Rising China*, Santa Monica, CA: RAND Corporation, MG-320-KISTEP, 2005. Online at: http://www.rand.org/pubs/monographs/MG320/

Shambaugh, David, *Power Shift: China and Asia's New Dynamics*, Berkeley, CA: University of California Press, 2005.

Shanghai Cooperation Organization website. Online at: http://www.sectsco.org

Shinoda, Tomohito, *Koizumi Diplomacy: Japan's Kantei Approach to Foreign and Defense Affairs*, Seattle, WA: University of Washington Press, 2006.

Siegle, Joseph T., Michael M. Weinstein, and Morton H. Halperin, "Why Democracies Excel," *Foreign Affairs*, September/October 2004, pp. 57ff.

Stiglitz, Joseph E., "The East Asia Crisis," *Globalization and Its Discontents*, chap. 4, New York: W. W. Norton, 2002.

Tamamoto, Masaru, "How Japan Imagines China and Sees Itself," Japan Institute for International Affairs Commentary Number 3, May 31, 2006. As of May 7, 2007: www.worldpolicy.org/journal/articles/wpj06-1/Tamamoto.pdf

Taniguchi, Tomohiko, "A Cold Peace: The Changing Security Equation in Northeast Asia," *Orbis*, Summer 2005, p. 456.

Thomson, James, "US Interests and the Fate of the Alliance," *Survival*, Vol. 54, No. 4, Winter 2003–04, pp. 207–208.

Tillich, Paul, *The Courage to Be*, New Haven, CT: Yale University Press, 1952.

Tkacik, John J., Jr., *Rethinking "One China,"* Washington, DC: The Heritage Foundation, 2004.

Trenin, Dmitri, *The End of Eurasia: Russia on the Border Between Geopolitics and Globalization*, Washington, DC: Carnegie Endowment for International Peace, 2002.

Tung, Chen-yuan, *China Economic Analysis Monthly*, August 2003, p. 3.

The U.S. and Japan: Advancing Toward a Mature Partnership, Institute of National Strategic Studies Special Report, 2001.

U.S. Department of Defense, *Military Power of the People's Republic of China 2007: A Report to Congress Pursuant to the National Defense Authorization Act*, Washington, DC: Office of the Secretary of Defense, 2007. Online at: www.defenselink.mil/pubs/pdfs/070523-China-Military-Power-final.pdf

————, *Quadrennial Defense Review Report*, Washington, DC, February 6, 2006.

van Wolferen, Karel, *The Enigma of Japanese Power: People and Politics in a Stateless Nation*, London: Papermac, 1990.

Vogel, Ezra F., *Is Japan Still Number One?* Malaysia: Pelanduk Publications, 2001.

————, *Japan as Number One: Lessons for America*, Lincoln, NE: iUniverse, 1999.

————, *The Four Little Dragons: The Spread of Industrialization in East Asia (The Edwin O. Reischauer Lectures)*, Cambridge, MA: Harvard University Press, 1992.

Wolf, Charles, "A Test to Determine Who's an Ally," *International Herald Tribune*, July 7, 2004. Online at: http://www.iht.com/articles/2004/07/08/edwolf_ed3__0.php

Xinbo, Wu, "The End of the Silver Lining: A Chinese View of the U.S.-Japanese Alliance," *The Washington Quarterly*, Vol. 29, No. 1, Winter 2005–2006, pp. 119–120.

Yoshisuke, Iinuma, "After Koizumi," *Oriental Economist*, Vol. 74, No. 1, January 2006, p. 11.

Zakaria, Fareed, "Mishandling the China Challenge," *South China Morning Post*, August 9, 2005.

————, "Bush's PR Problem," *Washington Post*, December 2, 2003, p. A27.

Zheng, Bijian, "'Peacefully Rising' to Great Power Status," *Foreign Affairs*, Vol. 84, No. 5, September/October 2005.

Index